The Emerging School Library
Media Program

The
Emerging School Library
Media Program

Readings

Compiled by
FRANCES BECK McDONALD

1988
Libraries Unlimited, Inc.
Englewood, Colorado

LIBRARIES UNLIMITED, INC.
P.O. Box 3988
Englewood, CO 80155-3988

Library of Congress Cataloging-in-Publication Data

The Emerging school library media program.

   Includes index.
   1. School libraries.   2. Media programs (Education)
I. McDonald, Frances Beck, 1934-   .
Z675.S3E38   1988   027.8   88-6784
ISBN 0-87287-660-8

Libraries Unlimited books are bound with Type II nonwoven material that meets and exceeds National Association of State Textbook Administrators' Type II nonwoven material specifications Class A through E.

To Marie Knudson, former public librarian in International Falls, Minnesota, who recognized a librarian in a high school sophomore and hired her, taught her, inspired her, and helped to form the philosophy of librarianship that guides her today.

TABLE OF CONTENTS

Part 6
SCHOOL LIBRARY MEDIA PROFESSIONALS:
LEADERS AND CHANGE AGENTS

INTRODUCTION

An air of productivity permeates the center. Young people move confidently around the room. Their manner illustrates the seriousness of their purpose. They possess the sureness of skilled individuals familiar with their surroundings. Their tasks reveal a planned approach to learning in a rich resource environment.

One person views microfilm looking for a recent article from the newspaper. Another checks the CD-ROM catalog for a source located in another school in the district. Another confers with an adult designing the search strategy to be used to gather information for a science report. Three students position the video cameras for the morning newscast that begins the school day. Another helps a younger child reach a book on the top shelf. Someone returns the 35mm camera used last night to take slides needed to illustrate next week's poetry report. Two young women glance through the newspaper at last night's volleyball scores before moving on to the file of recent fiction reviews written by their friends. A group of young people are huddled around a computer solving another math puzzle. Other students look at their teacher's comments written on their interactive electronic journals. Books are dropped off, books are checked out. Magazines are located, articles copied. Microfilm and portable readers come back, video tapes leave, and video cameras are rolled down the hallway. The computer printers push out the last draft of a class paper due in twenty minutes.

A teacher confers with the computer lab assistant in preparation for his class later today. The media specialist and a teacher discuss a list of resources needed for an upcoming unit. A health teacher picks up the media specialist's evaluations of her students' online searching projects. In one corner, an aide has arranged maps and globes for the class arriving later in the day. The challenge kits are ready for the young people who will use them in their spare time, the learning packages are ready for students, and the writing/research packets prepared by the teacher and media specialist are ready for individual use. A volunteer who will read to young children during the day has selected his picture books. The schedule is set, the resources prepared. All day, individuals and groups, young people and adults will use the media center actively for planned, purposeful learning activities.

Events in this media center do not happen by chance. Evidence of planned learning strategies incorporating readily accessible resources is everywhere. Around the school student productions appear during the day. Classroom activities show planning for the use of a variety of resources. Individuals illustrate information utilization skills. In this school library media program, self-reliant learners accomplish two things: they complete their immediate tasks and they acquire skills needed for a lifetime of information use. The task at hand meets today's need, while the information skills will meet needs into the twenty-first century.

School library media specialists and teachers plan together to identify curriculum areas to integrate information skills with content. Using the day-to-day activities of every classroom, teachers and school library media specialists provide opportunities for students to use and practice recently acquired skills. Information skills are introduced, reinforced, and practiced many times during a student's school years, eventually leading to mastery. Using multimedia resources provides skill in utilizing and evaluating information in written, audio, and graphic format. Critical viewing and listening produce enlightened consumers of information. Using a variety of viewing and listening resources also adapts to individual learning styles. From kindergarten through high school, students learn skills which build upon and reinforce one another.

School library media specialists and teachers recognize that a video production about the art deco movement requires searching, locating, organizing, synthesizing, and evaluating information, as well as an understanding of the television medium. These skills will transfer to television viewing at home and will eventually be used to complete an upcoming assignment in another class. In several decades, the organizing and synthesizing skills will be used to prepare an annual report. The teachers know that generating graphics on the computer for the video production helps teach skills that will be used for future productions and someday could be used to illustrate the brochure for a volunteer organization. The thinking, scripting, and writing skills, and the searching strategies, will be used well into adult life. Both school library media specialists and teachers dedicated to helping students function in an information society know that today's product or answer is important, but the process used in reaching that answer assumes long lasting value.

School library media programs provide the resources, spaces, equipment, services, planning, and skills needed for teaching and learning, individually or in groups. Today school library media specialists consult with teachers to plan learning strategies, teach information skills, design and prepare individual and group learning activity packages, provide resources, arrange spaces, and manage a learning environment to meet the needs of young people and adults. Accessible resources provide an environment rich in information in which young people search electronic retrieval systems, locate information in a variety of formats, read, view, listen, write, think and analyze, produce, critique, manipulate, and transfer skills from one area to another.

The roots of the school library media program described here extend back to the days when libraries housed the printed word and librarians provided reading guidance. The organization and acquisition patterns once used to catalog books now extend to all formats. The shelves once holding books now give space to realia, microcomputer programs, videotapes, kits, and electronic sources of information. The card catalog has been computerized, as have many of the routine functions of the media center, freeing school library media specialists to work with students and teachers. No longer does the media specialist sit waiting for business after the books have been processed and arranged on the shelves. Rather, the media specialist reaches out, identifies curriculum areas where information skills might best be taught and reinforced, and then actively seeks out teachers to plan and design learning strategies together to accomplish their goals. Objectives have changed, the role and function have expanded: today's media center serves an information society. The role of the school library media specialist has evolved from manager of resources to manager of learning, from resource provider to partner in the teaching/learning process.

While libraries changed to media centers, librarians acquired audiovisual skills, audiovisual directors acquired library skills, and both became information specialists. Concerns about utilization of intellectual content replaced concern with container. The growth has been steady. Librarians and audiovisual directors responded to the tenets in the 1960 and 1969 professional standards and incorporated media resources into a media center. Education reacted to Sputnik and to demands for individualization. Media programs responded to education. During the 1970s, James W. Liesener described the consultation and instruction functions of the media professional. The professional organizations formalized consulting and design in the publication of *Media Programs: District and School.* In the 1980s David V. Loertscher provided a taxonomy illustrating the media professional's expanded involvement in the teaching/learning process.

For this transition from library to media center, from passive to active media specialist, a new look at what had always been done was required. Some called it instructional design, others described it as instructional development. Previously librarians taught library skills. Now they recognize they were teaching information skills. The library skills were taught alone to one group at a time. Learning information skills on the other hand requires integrating skill strategies with other educational activities and involving the teacher in the planning process. The research process librarians have always taught parallels the hierarchy of thinking skills. Critical reading has become critical reading, viewing, and listening. Reference services using print resources have expanded to include electronic resources. Today a new focus on excellence in education has library media specialists in the position of leading rather than reacting. In thirty years school librarians have progressed from the marginal role of working in a quiet place and frequently also serving as a study hall monitor, to an integrated role. Today, school library media specialists work with teachers designing integrated learning strategies to assure that each student has an opportunity to learn, practice, and master information skills. But, the biggest change is in the perception of the role of the school library media specialist. Rather than working in isolation, today's school library media specialist is viewed as a leader in the teaching/learning process.

Experienced school library media specialists will recognize that the role described here contrasts dramatically with the quiet, uneventful days of the early school libraries. Then the librarian processed a few books, checked in some periodicals, looked at selection sources and wrote a few cards for the consideration file, read some stories and taught card catalog skills and reference skills to the scheduled twenty-minute classes. Perhaps, additionally, the librarian located some materials for students, did a little reading guidance, answered a few reference questions, maybe even made a few transparencies. Even at that level, the school librarian had a busy day and probably left school with a professional journal or two to examine at home. An examination of this list of activities shows that two factors discriminate between the opening scenario and the school library: staff and schedule. A number of the tasks formerly done by school librarians are now performed by clerks or paraprofessional staff members. Next, planning and designing instructional activities with teachers necessitates a flexible schedule in the media center. While scheduling is perhaps a greater problem in elementary media centers, some secondary school media specialists also suffer from a scheduled center. These centers might still serve as study halls and the media specialist may still act as a substitute when a teacher is absent.

Unfortunately, inadequate staffing patterns and inflexible schedules rather than inclination of the school library media specialists, frequently spell the difference between a media professional actively involved in teaching and learning and a media specialist struggling to keep up with routines. School library media specialists often say that they would become more involved in curriculum and design of instruction if they had time or if there was someone to take over the clerical tasks. No time leads to no evidence of involvement with the instructional program and no evidence of a need for additional staff or a flexible schedule. These media specialists must accept the fact that only a demonstration of benefits is likely to convince administrators and teachers that the instructional program could be improved. Only with this evidence will administrators and teachers support a media specialist's request for support staff and a flexible schedule for the media center.

The purpose of this collection of articles is to illustrate the instructional and consulting roles of library media specialists and the contributions these professionals make to the educational process. The readings provide the rationale and philosophy of a multimedia, integrated approach to learning. Written by thinkers and doers, these articles describe the changing school library media program in a period of educational excellence in an information society. Written during the 1980s, these articles detail the emerging reality of school library media practice into the 1990s. The articles illustrate a profession which is coming of age, recognizing and defining its role, and assuming a position of leadership in the school.

This collection is intended to be a partner to the typical school library media administration textbook. The articles provide concrete evidence of what all the routines described in the administration text allow the school library media specialist to do—help students learn. For the media professional in preparation, these readings illustrate the philosophy of a profession and show the translation of theory into media practice. The authors describe the attitudes, the role, the excitement, and the contribution of a media professional involved in the educational process.

For the practicing media professional, the articles provide a retreat of sorts, a chance to reexamine one's role in an information society. The authors inspire the already overworked school library media specialist to approach the expanded role of a leader in the instructional program. Over and over the authors of these articles advise the media specialist to start small and think big. The path to involvement is just a series of steps from working with one teacher, to a department, to the whole school curriculum. Do the authors ask for a juggling act? Absolutely. But, the rewards of instructional involvement are also described by those who have chosen the emerging role. For the administrator and teacher, these readings may create expectations of their media programs.

No attempt was made to collect "the best," although certainly some of these articles could be called "the best." Rather, from the many available articles those which answer why, what, where, when, and who were selected. Other than the authors providing some examples, no attempt was made to provide a "how to" book. The assumption was that by reading the rationale, professionals will be stimulated to use their own information skills and creativity to create "how to" for their unique educational institutions. Collection development activities and the collection are not addressed here. Resources about the collection development process abound and library media professionals already are familiar with them and use them effectively.

This collection of readings illustrates MEDIA:

Media specialists providing

Excellence in education through

Designing and

Integrating learning

Activities throughout the curriculum.

LIST OF CONTRIBUTORS

Shirley L. Aaron
Professor
School of Library and Information
    Studies
Florida State University
Tallahassee, Florida

Bev Anderson (deceased)
Coordinator, Program Resource Center
Calgary Board of Education
Calgary, Alberta

Melvin M. Bowie
Department of Instructional Resources
University of Arkansas
Fayetteville, Arkansas

Kathleen W. Craver
Head Librarian
National Cathedral School
Washington, D.C.

Elaine K. Didier
Director, Kresge Business
    Administration Library
University of Michigan Business School
Ann Arbor, Michigan

Janice K. Doan
Library Media Specialist
Ruth Moyer Elementary School
Fort Thomas, Kentucky

Michael Eisenberg
Assistant Professor; Coordinator
    for School Media
School of Information Studies
Syracuse University
Syracuse, New York

Barry Eshpeter
Teacher-Librarian
Calgary Board of Education
Calgary, Alberta

Elyse Evans Fiebert
Head Librarian
Radnor High School
Radnor, Pennsylvania

Lee Vae Hakes
Media Specialist
Jefferson School
New Ulm, Minnesota

Carol-Ann Haycock
President
The Human Resources Development
    Group
Vancouver, British Columbia, and
    Seattle, Washington
Editor, *The Emergency Librarian*

Ken Haycock
Director of Program Services
Vancouver School Board
Vancouver, British Columbia
Publisher, *The Emergency Librarian*

David Henschke
Media Specialist
Brainerd Senior High School
Brainerd, Minnesota

May Lein Ho
Director of Learning Resources
University of Arkansas
Fayetteville, Arkansas

Theo M. Holtan
Resource Center Director
Oak Grove Elementary School
Bloomington, Minnesota

Elsie Husom
Media/Technology Coordinator
Brainerd Public Schools
Brainerd, Minnesota

Kay Iseke
Teacher-Librarian
St. Albert Protestant School District
St. Albert, Alberta

M. Ellen Jay
Media Specialist
W. T. Page Elementary School
Montgomery County Public Schools
Silver Spring, Maryland

Carol Collier Kuhlthau
Assistant Professor
School of Communications,
    Information and Library Studies
Rutgers University
New Brunswick, New Jersey

Eleanor R. Kulleseid
Director of Library Services
Bank Street College of Education
New York, New York

James W. Liesener
Professor
College of Library and Information
    Studies
University of Maryland
College Park, Maryland

David V. Loertscher
Senior Acquisitions Editor
Libraries Unlimited
Englewood, Colorado

Roy Lundin
Coordinator of Continuing Education
Brisbane College of Advanced
    Education
Calvin Grove, Queensland, Australia

Jacqueline C. Mancall
Associate Professor
Library and Information Science
Drexel University
Philadelphia, Pennsylvania

Rosalind Miller
Professor
Library Media Education
Georgia State University
Atlanta, Georgia

Janet Noll Naumer
Director, Library/Media Center
Porterville College
Porterville, California

Antoinette A. Oberg
Associate Professor, Faculty of
    Education
University of Victoria
Victoria, British Columbia

Dianne Oberg
Assistant Professor
Faculty of Education
University of Alberta
Edmonton, Alberta

Retta Patrick
School Library Media Consultant
Little Rock, Arkansas

Sheila Pritchard
Consultant, Learning Resources
    Services
Edmonton Public Schools
Edmonton, Alberta

Patricia L. Riggs
School Library Media Specialist
Briar Glen Elementary School
Glen Ellyn, Illinois

Allan Spanjer
Professor, Curriculum and Instruction
Georgia State University
Atlanta, Georgia

Barbara K. Stripling
Library Media Specialist
Fayetteville High School
Fayetteville, Arkansas

Janet G. Stroud
Former Assistant Professor
Purdue University
West Lafayette, Indiana

Philip Turner
Dean, Graduate School of Library
    Science
The University of Alabama
University, Alabama

Sue A. Walker
Program Coordinator for Library
    Media Services
School District of Lancaster
Lancaster, Pennsylvania

Wilma Wolner
Media Specialist
Washington Elementary School
New Ulm, Minnesota

Part 1
The Setting: Education

The school library media program functions in an educational setting — a setting that is currently criticized for failing to meet the needs of students, therefore creating an expectation of failing to prepare the students to become fully functioning members of society. James W. Liesener sets the stage for the readings to come with his response to *A Nation at Risk*. He defines the role of the library media program in lifelong learning in terms of the "higher order cognitive and problem solving skills" needed in an information society. The school library media center is described as an "information learning laboratory" and the library media specialist as an intermediary between the information world and the client. Providing an overview of this role of information intermediary, Liesener advocates intellectual and physical access to ideas and information in the process of developing information skills.

Providing further background, Elaine K. Didier reviews the literature related to student achievement and library media programs. Her examination identifies two factors that influence the impact of library media programs on achievement: the education of library media personnel and the expectations held by educators about the curricular role of media professionals. Didier found that both are positively related to student achievement.

As the title of this collection of readings indicates, the role of the school library media program has been one of change and growth. Using professional literature, professional association documents, educational philosophy, and national standards, Kathleen W. Craver provides a historical look at the changing instructional role from 1950 to 1984. The changes are traced from the establishment of media centers during the 1950s, through the beginnings of an instructional role, to the entrance of technology and its impact on the school library media program during the 1980s. David V. Loertscher further describes the evolution of school libraries into school library media centers and asks library media specialists to assess their past and assume today's essential role in the educational process.

Finally, Loertscher, May Lein Ho, and Melvin M. Bowie provide a profile of the school library media program in exemplary elementary schools. They studied the status of library media programs in 109 of the 270 elementary schools identified as exemplary by the U.S. Department of Education in 1986. Their results show that providing instructional services is directly related to staff. Full-time professionals and full-time clerical staff are the single most important variable in programs providing instructional services. Flexible schedules and reading guidance activities further define the library media programs in these exemplary elementary schools.

LEARNING AT RISK
School Library Media Programs
in an Information World*

James W. Liesener

American education has been described as severely problem stricken in *A Nation at Risk* as well as numerous other studies. The various studies approach the problems from different perspectives and use a wide variety of indicators as evidence of serious problems. As a result, the solutions that are recommended are also varied. However, the consensus appears to be clear that for this country to continue to progress and maintain a competitive position in the global village, significant improvements must be achieved in the educational enterprise.

America has historically expected a great deal of its educational institutions. Every new societal problem becomes a new challenge to at least be partially solved by some addition to the educational mission. In spite of these great and ever growing expectations, the level of resource allocations and the priority and status given to education in this society do not by any means parallel the expectations. It is very interesting in this light to see that the 1982 Gallup Poll referred to in *A Nation at Risk* suggests that people currently view education as the major foundation for the future. This national opinion poll indicated that education is considered "more important than developing the best industrial system or the strongest military force," that "public education should be the top priority for additional federal funds" and that education took first place of the twelve funding categories covered in the survey.[1]

A Nation at Risk very appropriately urges the creation of a "Learning Society" as an effective approach to producing individuals who will be able to function and compete effectively in an information age. For this to occur, the concentration cannot be restricted only to the basic skills but must focus on higher order intellectual skills, for example: analytical, evaluative, inferential, interpretive and problem solving skills, which are necessary to achieve at the levels of sophistication required in the present and future societies.

It is a disappointment to see that in spite of the emphasis on learning and the development of the higher order skills necessary to function and achieve in an information society, so little attention is devoted in *A Nation at Risk* to the units and organizations that specifically deal with information resources and the facilitation of the learning of the information seeking and utilization skills alluded to throughout the report. It is discouraging that, though a behavior pattern of life-long learning is demanded in the report, one of the institutions most associated

*From James W. Liesener, "Learning at Risk: School Library Media Programs in an Information World," *School Library Media Quarterly* 13 (Fall 1985): 11-20. Reprinted by permission.

with and inherently dedicated to nourishing independent and life-long learning, namely libraries, is hardly mentioned in the report. This omission represents one of the major problems faced by school and all kinds of libraries in attempting to perform their educational function. The role of library media programs and their potential for significantly contributing to the solution of information problems must be perceived clearly by clients or their potential will not be realized and others will have to perform the critical information intermediary function.

The objective in this paper is to look at the problems and prospects of school library media programs in contributing to the fostering of life-long learning and the development of the information seeking and utilization skills critical for succeeding in this complex and rapidly changing world. The particular focus in this paper, in contrast to the other papers, is the role of library media programs in the schools and their potential for contributing to the significant improvement being demanded of the schools and all educational institutions in this society.

INFORMATION AND EDUCATION

The Office of Technology Assessment of the U.S. Congress (1982) in its study of the impact of information technology on American education described the information revolution as follows:

> Modern society is undergoing profound technological and social changes brought about by what has been called the information revolution. This revolution is characterized by explosive developments in electronic technologies and by their integration into complex information systems that span the globe. The impacts of this revolution affect individuals, institutions and governments—altering what they do, how they do it, and how they relate to one another. If individuals are to thrive economically and socially in a world that will be shaped, to a large degree, by these technological developments, they must adapt through education and training.[2]

This report also presents two important basic conclusions regarding education:

1. The so-called *information revolution*, driven by rapid advances in communication and computer technology, is profoundly affecting American education. It is changing the nature of what needs to be learned, who needs to learn it, who will provide it, and how it will be provided and paid for.

2. Information technology can potentially improve and enrich the educational services that traditional educational institutions provide, distribute education and training into new environments such as the home and office, reach new clients such as handicapped or homebound persons, and teach job-related skills in the use of technology.[3]

This same study also concluded that the impact of the information revolution is affecting all institutions but "particularly those such as public schools and libraries that traditionally have borne the major responsibility for providing education and other public information services."[4]

The knowledge and skills required to survive and succeed in the technologically and stress-oriented society and world we presently live in are quite different from those required in less complex times. The development of higher level thinking skills is clearly not achieved by concentrating on a rather limited view of basic skills and on drill and practice. Both teaching and testing have to concentrate on higher level skills as well as on the more basic skills.

Sorry to say, this is currently not the case in many situations. As with the learning of the writing process, the learning of information seeking and utilization skills and the fostering of higher level intellectual skills is only accomplished through the repeated use and evaluation of these skills in an adequate information laboratory. These kinds of skills are not developed and nourished in a passive lecture/recitation mode. The active and constant opportunity for the application and practice of these skills in an information rich environment with knowledgeable and accessible assistance is a necessity for success. Learners must have full and unencumbered intellectual and physical access to a wide range of quality materials and information services to attain this level of achievement. In addition, we need to nourish the development of an attitude of excitement regarding ideas and an attitude of ease and competence in interacting with the information sources and services that provide access to these ideas.

REALISM AND INFORMATION USE AND USERS

The challenge to teach higher order cognitive and problem-solving skills more effectively cannot be responded to successfully with a naive view of information use and users. An overly simplistic view of the information world and information use has dictated our past approaches to the provision of library and information services and the teaching of information seeking skills. The advent of computerized data bases and online searching has forced us to evaluate our understanding of information seeking behavior and some of what we have learned challenges our previous perspectives. At this point, a more realistic and knowledgeable approach to the provision of information services to children and youth is mandated.

Simply "preaching" the wonders and benefits of using libraries in the traditional manner and exhorting users to reform when nothing in the last twenty-five years gives us any encouragement that they can or will seems to be a futile and nonproductive exercise. From our limited understanding gained relatively recently of adult information use behavior, serious consideration should be given to a number of actors which appear to be fundamental principles regarding information use. It cannot be asserted at this time that these principles, described in the following paragraphs, have been clearly documented in terms of their applicability to children and youth. Many would feel however that these ideas have at least face validity and there seems to be at least some empirical support in the research literature for some of these ideas.[5]

Proximity

As common sense would tend to indicate, there is a very solid relationship between proximity and use. This probably explains why home libraries play a more important role than was originally assumed. Evidently, the greater the distance either physically or psychologically, the less likely it is that a resource will be used whether it is a library or any other kind of resource.

Considerations of Time and Energy

The time and energy required to find and use information is a serious consideration for most people and it appears that less pertinent or adequate information is frequently preferable to the expenditure of more time and effort to get more and/or better information to satisfy a need. Obviously this consideration is relative to a given individual and a particular situation. In terms of expenditure of time and effort, there does seem to be a serious discrepancy between what library media specialists and most library and information professionals feel is reasonable and what clients feel is reasonable.

Amount of Information Needed

Users evidently have a considerably different perception of how much information is "reasonable" to satisfy a particular need than information professionals. It appears that individuals have a certain sense of what is reasonable and that is difficult for information professionals to change. One of the most insightful analyses of these particular issues was done by Patrick Wilson, which he refers to as the "limits of information gathering."[6] In doing an analysis of an individual's available time, it is apparent according to Wilson that the time for information gathering and use is limited and that there are a number of competing factors. The consideration of time needs to be considered from the standpoint of being a valuable commodity and not "free" as we seem to consider it particularly when it comes to children and youth.

Preference for Personal Intermediary

Numerous studies indicate that when confronted with an information problem, many individuals' first preference is to consult another person who they know and perceive to be knowledgeable and who will assist them (1) in refining the question; (2) in screening or presifting the information alternatives; and (3) in some cases, in providing the answer. This strong preference for personal assistance at least in the early stages of an information inquiry needs to be taken into account when planning and developing library and information services.

It would seem that a more productive approach to planning and developing library media programs that have greater prospects of being successful in meeting the needs of students and teachers would be based on a realistic understanding of user behavior. We need to test the validity of a number of these ideas that have come out of the analysis of adult information seeking behavior in terms of their applicability to children and youth. It is strongly suspected that many of the behavior patterns presently recognized in adult information seeking behavior might very well also apply to students at different levels.

In addition to trying to understand the information behavior of youth, it is also critical to recognize the information needs of teachers in a realistic manner. Teachers probably have a greater diversity of information needs than most other categories of users but yet have fewer serious and sophisticated efforts being made to provide them with realistic and effective assistance. This is true at the school level in spite of the valiant efforts of some library media specialists but generally also in terms of district services and commercially available services.

How many sophisticated current awareness services exist for teachers in the various subject areas and grade levels? What proportion of teachers have available to them, in convenient and realistic ways, online searching of appropriate data bases and information intermediaries prepared and willing to provide searching and synthesizing services? What kind of awareness and skills do teachers have in accessing the information world? From all available evidence, the assessment points to an incredibly low level of both awareness and skills. It is true that there are noteworthy exceptions in terms of both the level of service provided teachers in some districts and the level of awareness and skill exhibited by some teachers. However, these cases are definitely in the minority.

Is it possible that (1) our failure to reach a larger proportion of our potential client population and (2) the apparent ineffectiveness of our public relations and instruction in the past could be largely due to the unrealistic expectations of users or at least due to the lack of understanding of information seeking behavior? Can we afford to ignore the possibilities here?

WHAT ROLE FOR SCHOOL LIBRARY MEDIA PROGRAMS?

It doesn't take much of a perusal of the literature to discover a diverse and rather confused panoply of perceptions of the roles and functions of school library media programs. This confusion and total lack of consensus creates a serious problem in attempting to develop programs. The question at this point is what role is necessary and what functions need to be performed by library media programs considering the view of the information world and the requisite learning needs described previously. The particular problems and issues that arise in trying to develop and sustain what is needed will be dealt with in the next section of the paper.

The older concepts of passive culture repositories or centers for the development of an enjoyment and appreciation for reading good books while identifying very important functions, do not appear to be actively responsive to the entire range of needs identified as crucial for survival and achievement in an extremely complex, information abundant and rapidly changing world.

The level of expectation that is satisfied with a nice and genteel but fairly superfluous resource is no longer relevant or appropriate. The value and utility of information of all kinds has become much more visible and appreciated and it appears that an expectation of a more active and a broader approach to providing information services is developing. It would seem that if we are serious about the learning needs of children in our society, a quantum leap is not only required of what we expect of educational agencies generally but also in terms of what we expect of the sophistication and contribution of such a key ingredient as the information intermediary and information laboratory. The development of higher level intellectual and problem solving skills can only be developed in an environment where they can be repeatedly applied and tested throughout the learner's school experience. The cumulative effect of many of these kinds of experiences is what leads to the development of a self-directed learner able and motivated for lifelong learning. This kind of information learning laboratory requires a level of sophistication and responsiveness far beyond the current service level of "materials availability" combined with the possibility of some limited assistance.

A great deal of progress has been made in the past decade in providing organized and carefully selected collections. The various federal programs that followed the launching of Sputnik in 1957 provided some of the funds and the stimulation that led to the rapid growth in the sixties and seventies. However, this did not result in a well-stocked library media center in every school or the kind of staffing that could provide the services required to serve the needs even as they were defined during those times. Of course the eighties have seen a decline in staff and collection budgets as well as buying power due to declining enrollments, inflation and Proposition 13-like tax limitations. As a result, we have been losing ground at a time when we need to expand and refine the kinds of services we provide to meet the new and expanding learning needs of an information society.

What then is the role of school library media programs in fostering the development of young people who are capable, uninhibited, willing and yearning to deal with the ideas, aspirations and problems of humankind? Our philosophy has always included the goal of nurturing a lifelong inquisitiveness and a comfortableness both with ideas and the variety of media that present these ideas. We believe that knowledge, understanding, appreciation and skills in the critical and discerning use of information in its different forms are fundamental to a democratic society as well as to effective functioning in an information world. A much greater emphasis however needs to be placed on developing an analytical posture toward ideas and the capability of critically evaluating information from different perspectives. It is also important for students to develop an interest and positive attitude toward the vehicles that express ideas if a lifelong positive relationship with ideas and information is to be achieved. The independence of mind that comes with a personal, free and independent interaction with ideas also kindles the kinds of appreciations and understandings that permit the enjoyment of the subtleties of life and the aesthetic aspects of our world.

It is critical at this time to have a clear and comprehensive concept of how school library media programs blend into this scene. The abstract and ambiguous conceptions of the past will not be sufficient. The conception of the function and services of a school library media program that will be used in this discussion was developed by the writer over a period of years as a critical part of the development of a systematic planning and evaluation process for school library media programs.[7] It was discovered early in this work that the conceptualizations and definitions of school library media programs were very inadequate when it came to trying to apply more systematic and rigorous approaches to the planning and evaluation of programs. In order to be able to analyze programs more carefully it was necessary to develop a more comprehensive and cohesive definition. This approach attempts to define from a user's perspective the function and services of school library media programs as comprehensively as possible. This definition is used to illustrate the role of the school library media program in developing the kinds of learners required in our striving for excellence.

The primary function performed by the school library media specialist or program can be viewed as a mediation function. From this perspective, the specialist plays the role of an intermediary between the incredibly complex and rapidly expanding information world and the client. In this sense, the library media specialist is no different than a librarian or information specialist in any other environment. It is the particular environment and the particular needs of the clients served that provides the special focus. Obviously, the environment in this case is the school and the clients are the students, teachers, school staff and, at times, parents.

The concept of intermediary implies that some assistance is frequently required for clients or users to effectively and efficiently interact with the information world. The term information is used here in its broadest sense to include all representations of ideas, including the arts and in any media format. Assistance is used to indicate anything from a little help to higher level services such as formal instruction, assessing and interpreting information needs, stimulating interest, and actually providing the information in some cases.

The information revolution has provided us with an almost unbelievable array of information options. This information world is incredibly large and complex and in spite of the advances in information technology and the much greater potential access this provides us, the need for an intermediary to assist in achieving effective access to this information world has become more apparent. Even though the microcomputer technology particularly has made direct access possible to considerable quantities of information for many users, the need for an intermediary is still vital for most users and at times probably for all users.

The school library media specialist performs this intermediary function for the purpose of facilitating the achievement of learning and instructional objectives. This intermediary function is performed in quite a number of different ways. In order to be able to grasp and deal with the whole range of services provided by school library media programs, these services were clustered into five major service categories (Access, Reference, Production, Instruction and Consulting) which are described below.

Access

The provision of *access* to materials, equipment (for example, audiovisual equipment), and space is the traditional area of strength and most clearly perceived group of services provided by school library media programs and libraries in general. It involves providing intellectual and physical access to the whole range of print and nonprint media. This also involves providing access to equipment as well as the procedures and facilities for the use of both materials and equipment. The provision of access to materials that are not in the particular collection of a specific school library media center but are provided through various interlibrary loan or networking arrangements is also included. The provision of access would also include such considerations as copying facilities, making arrangements for special collections either in the media center or in the classroom, etc. Currently the greatest areas of expansion are in the area of provision of access to computers and computer software and services for learners with special needs. In a number of cases computer facilities are being added to school library media programs and the library media specialists are becoming the computer coordinators for the school.

These services not only provide the basic information laboratory for both teacher and library media specialist initiated instructional activities but also, and possibly more importantly, provide an encouragement and hospitality for learner initiated and directed activities which extend well beyond curricular interests and needs. Considerable strides have been made for some adult populations in providing much greater intellectual access as well as physical access in many areas through computerized searching and resource sharing via networking. However, in the majority of cases these advances have as yet to reach young learners. The problems related to providing the level of service needed here, as well as in the other service categories, will be treated in the next section of the paper.

Reference or Information Services

This service category involves two types of service, the provision of a collection of reference materials for self use and the provision of various kinds of personal assistance to the client in identifying, seeking or interpreting information. This assistance could include: simply helping and identifying where something is in the collection of the school library media center; identifying materials not in the collection but possibly available elsewhere; providing various alerting or current awareness services regarding information on materials or information that clients may not be aware of but which may be of value once they are conscious of them; providing various kinds of bibliographies and pathfinders to assist users in becoming aware of and locating various kinds of sources; as well as the actual answering of questions which could vary from simple to extremely complex kinds of questions.

Very typically the emphasis has been on the lower level services of providing a reference collection and some identification and location assistance. More emphasis has typically been placed on reference services at the secondary level with a heavier emphasis placed on instructions at the elementary level.

The provision of online searching of appropriate data bases for staff, and in rare instances for students, is available in some districts and this will certainly increase. The provision of various computerized services, the development of more data bases appropriate for and accessible to children, and the production of various helping tools to assist clients in analyzing questions and designing search strategies are the activities in this service area that demand immediate attention. Any advance in the development of sophisticated problem solving and information utilization skills will require significant improvement in the level of services in this area. The issue of information services for children and youth needs to receive the level of attention given to these services in the health field, for example, which has been a leader in the development of high level information services. The current approaches to providing reference and information services have not generally been designed on the basis of the understanding of user behavior discussed earlier. Therefore, a significant improvement in this area will require some attitudinal changes as well as technical changes.

Production

Production services involve providing materials, equipment and assistance to teachers, students and staff for producing or adapting various kinds of print but particularly nonprint media. In some cases the production is actually performed for the client but this is normally done only for teachers or school staff and in areas where special equipment or expertise is required. Production can involve anything from making a transparency to producing a television program. These services are provided not only to help make instruction more effective but also to stimulate and facilitate the creative abilities and basic skills of students in effectively communicating their ideas. It will be interesting to see if this function extends in the future into the area of production and adaptation of computer software.

Instruction

Services in this category involve both formal and informal instructional activities as well as reading, viewing and listening guidance activities. Activities can vary from providing various specifically designed self-instructional materials to assist clients in finding and using information, to providing formal instruction programs for both teachers and students in the use of various information resources and information access tools, as well as to providing access and instruction in the use of the newer information technology such as microcomputers. This area also normally involves a great deal of informal instruction for both teachers and students specifically related to particular problems or questions and also involves a variety of guidance activities aimed at stimulating or motivating interest in reading, viewing, and listening. Greatest emphasis has been placed in many cases on the lower level information locating skills; significant improvement is needed in order to develop the strategies and processes necessary to focus more attention on the higher level intellectual skills. A continuing serious problem is the difficulty of integrating the instruction and application of information seeking and utilization skills into the various instructional areas.

Consulting

This group of services involves the library media specialist consulting with teachers regarding the use of various services and the design of instruction with appropriate attention to information utilization skills. This also includes contributing to the curricular and instructional planning efforts at various levels including the district level. Consulting with students would be considered under either reference or instruction depending on the type of activity.

Consulting services focus on the activities of the school library media specialist with individuals as well as groups of teachers. This area includes the work of the school library media specialist in providing suggestions and information for instructional planning to individual teachers as well as the cooperative planning of various instructional kinds of activities, some of which are conducted by the teacher and some by the media specialist. The level of service may vary from the simple suggestion of a few resources to be used in a particular unit to the actual participation in the design and evaluation of various instructional strategies. This category may also involve assisting and performing the function of a clearinghouse in terms of providing information about and sample copies of various instructional materials which are being considered for use in an instructional area. In some cases, the coordination of the selection and evaluation of all instructional materials is also a function of the school library media program in addition to performing the same selection and evaluation function for the library media center collection.

BARRIERS OR CHALLENGES?

There should be no doubt regarding the need for active and expanded library media programs in schools to provide the kind of intellectual and physical access to ideas and information so necessary for the development of the kinds of higher level skills being demanded. The term program here refers to a library media program capable of performing the important intermediary function as well as providing information services and an information learning laboratory at a very high level of sophistication. To presume that excellence, or for that matter even minimal survival, can be achieved in an increasingly complex and competitive information world with horse and buggy information systems and services is absurd. If we are really serious about developing highly capable and competitive adults we must begin by developing the requisite skills and application opportunities at the elementary level and continue facilitating the maturation of these skills. Lifelong learning is not simply a catchword but a concept referring to a constantly evolving set of skills and understandings necessary for effective participation in society and the achievement of a full life. This challenge demands serious attention and a significant and continued commitment of resources if we are to succeed in substantially improving our educational effectiveness.

If we are going to make any substantial progress toward our goal we must take a realistic view of the obstacles in the road ahead. The literature includes an assortment of perspectives on the problems faced in this field. The particular barriers and challenges identified here simply represent one view of some of the most critical issues that must be dealt with if we are to provide the kinds of learning opportunities now being demanded. These problems can be perceived as barriers or challenges and hopefully we will confront these barriers as challenges to be analyzed, confronted and solved.

Attitude Problems

A number of serious problems exist in the area of attitudes toward school library media programs and library media specialists. Considerable confusion exists regarding the roles library media specialists do or do not perform and the roles they are capable of performing. Roles cannot be performed and services cannot be used effectively if they are not perceived accurately by potential clients or if there is a lack of acceptance of these roles by either the individuals receiving the benefits of them or the individuals attempting to perform them. Role conflicts of this sort almost inevitably lead to job dissatisfaction and ineffective performance. This condition ultimately affects the ability of a field to retain talent as well as to recruit talent.

What field am I in anyhow? Who am I? What am I? Am I a teacher like one of my client groups or am I something unique and different? These questions and our inability to answer them satisfactorily present a major problem in developing the kind of role described in this paper. The literature is overloaded with studies which analyze the perceptions of school library media specialists and programs by various individuals including principals, students, teachers, parents and library media specialists themselves. It is not difficult to summarize the conclusions reached in the overwhelming majority of these studies:

> Many of the findings of these studies have negative connotations. In the numerous studies carried out in the past twenty years, a number of conclusions are common: that the school librarian's perception of that role (school librarian's) differs significantly from that of others in the educational system, that the school library seems to play only a marginal role in the total educational program, and that the low regard for the school librarian militates against a direct involvement in the instructional program of the school.[8]

The uniqueness and particular role or function of library media programs desperately needs to be established at this time. It is tragic that the behavior we commonly see is the desperate maneuvering to also be perceived as a "teacher" and to possess a curricular territory in order to increase the odds of preserving one's job. This behavior, while understandable, is serving to further obfuscate the issue rather than contribute to any clarification. The decline in leadership positions at the district and state levels and the organizational and professional isolation of building level library media specialists not only has contributed to the problem but also has created a condition where the likelihood of constructive and effective counter efforts is significantly decreased.

Attitude problems also exist regarding the products of library media programs. Considerable progress has been made in the scope of material formats which we now include in collections but the preoccupation is still too much with the idea containers rather than with the active manipulation of information to facilitate the transfer of ideas to the minds of learners.

The term information itself is a problem in the schools. "Information," as it is used in the schools, seems only to include nonfiction or "fact books" and does not include every form of expression of ideas including fiction. The all-inclusive definition which includes all forms of expression of ideas is the way the term is used here and this appears to be the customary use of the term now in library and information science. The "really desirable" use of information according to some library media specialists seems to refer only to the reading of "good books" which typically refers only to literature of acceptable merit. The development of understanding and appreciation of great literature and literary expression is certainly desirable but it is far from being the whole information ball game. All judgment aside, the rest of the information world is going to play a larger and more important role in the lives of the majority of individuals and therefore needs much more adequate attention.

An attitude that is more understanding of clients' information seeking behavior will be necessary if more clients are to be served and if students and teachers are to develop the higher level problem solving skills which require more sophisticated information skills and knowledge. We have basically designed services in the past on the basis of the philosophy "here we are, come and get it."

The objective is to provide a carefully selected collection of materials and equipment and to provide instruction in how to use them. The rest is up to the client with the library media specialist supplying a little assistance and support if necessary. This concept presumes that it is possible to make clients self-sufficient in their use of information and other services and that this knowledge and the skills learned will provide the basis for lifelong learning. We have implemented organized instruction programs to develop these skills beginning at the elementary level and continuing through the secondary schools but most of the evidence to date suggests that other than a hard core group of "readers," users are neither becoming self-sufficient nor expanding their use of libraries as they mature.

It is time that we take a serious and hard look at this view of providing information services and instruction. Twenty years ago Leonard Freiser suggested that we quit this nonsense and instead of forcing kids to spend the majority of their time searching for information with usually poor results, we should give them the information under certain circumstances so that they do have a foundation of good information to work with and as a result, develop the skills and knowledge necessary to understand, use and appreciate ideas and information sources.[9] The belief is that these skills and knowledge are not only more important but must precede the attempt to develop information seeking skills if such efforts are to be effective. This idea would appear to suggest a very heavy emphasis on information provision and reference services at the elementary level with much of the instruction at upper levels, especially the middle and secondary schools. This, of course, is just the opposite of the current pattern and may explain some of our ineffectiveness in the development of higher level or even lower level locational skills.

The question of the effectiveness of this instruction is very troubling since many of the studies seem to show that the end result of all of this instruction produces college students unable and disinclined to use college and university libraries effectively. There are many studies in this area and most show that if the instruction is isolated from what is going on in the classroom and is not integrated into the classroom instructional activities, the results are dismal.[10] The really discouraging thing however is the fact we have known this for a long time yet our efforts to integrate instruction have, in most cases, been frustrated.

Concern also needs to focus on the content of instruction in information seeking and information use. Ineffectiveness may also result from inadequate or invalid content and a number of factors suggest that this may be the case. Our understanding of information search behavior is still very primitive but considerable insight and new knowledge have resulted from our recent experience with online searching. A detailed discussion of this is not pertinent here, but it is certainly critical at this time to analyze what we have learned and introduce this content into instruction programs wherever appropriate. It is very apparent that the "front end" or question formulation and analysis stage of any search or query needs a great deal more attention. Concerns such as the following must be introduced and applied: how to ask or frame questions, how to proceed to narrow or broaden a topic, how to translate questions into a search strategy, and how to match the strategy with the information system (including traditional manual ones and not only computerized systems). These kinds of considerations are not only important for the development of higher level intellectual skills and knowledge but also intimately relate to many of the curricular content areas, for example, set theory in mathematics and classification concepts in science. It is high time that this profession confront these issues and redesign library media instruction and services in the light of our primitive but growing understanding of information seeking behavior as well as the impact of more sophisticated technology and services. It is also clear that we need to reconsider the concept of self sufficiency in information seeking activities and consider the strong possibility that at least for some activities and groups of individuals, an information intermediary may not only be a luxury but a necessity.

Personnel and Economic Issues

It would seem that if we recognize the need for the development of basic and higher level intellectual skills and that we are not satisfied with our current performance, the logical response would be to improve and expand the programs necessary to accomplish what is desirable. The current scene however does not represent that kind of picture, undoubtedly at least partially because of declining enrollments, inflation and tax limitation restrictions. Accurate data is hard to find here but some things appear fairly clear. Miller and Moran did a very interesting study of expenditures for resources in school library media centers in 1982-83 which reflects a disturbing picture:

> LIBGIS I (1974) reported an average per-pupil expenditure of $4.22 for books and LIBGIS II (1978) an average expenditure of $4.25 per pupil for books. That LMCs are seriously continuing to lose ground in the purchasing of resources can be verified by comparing those amounts with the 1982-83 mean expenditures of $4.58 (median, $3.71)—a modest average increase of $0.33 over a five-year period during which juvenile book prices rose 30 percent. Media specialists purchasing adult nonfiction and reference books face even greater increases.[11]

It is also apparent that in the area of audiovisual materials the picture is even worse.

The very existence of a library media program is not universal. Mahar using U.S. Department of Education statistics for 1981 concluded:

> In that year (1981), three million pupils (7 percent of the total) attended schools without a library/media center. The figure included a decrease in media centers of secondary schools.[12]

Of course the existence of a center and the existence of a program are two different things with the difference being professional as well as support staff. Here the picture also shows a decline.

The writer conducted an informal survey of enrollments and placements in training programs and also queried some library media supervisors to get some idea of the degree of decline in positions as well as in the supply of new school library media specialists. The results of this informal survey revealed a decline in the number of positions from between 5 and 10 percent with district and elementary positions being most heavily affected. The supply side of the picture however revealed a serious decline in enrollments of students planning to be school library media specialists. A number of the preparation programs have folded entirely and the percent of decline in numerous programs is approaching 90 percent. Several parts of the country which have not been as severely affected economically as others or have shown increases in population are already faced with shortages. Other parts of the nation will very likely also face shortages before long, particularly as we move into a period of increasing enrollments, the so-called "shadow baby boom" which is to begin in 1985 and which is already apparent in some primary school enrollments.

This economic and supply/demand situation obviously creates a whole series of problems for program development and improvement. It is exceedingly difficult to be committed to achieving excellence in a "management of decline" climate. It is also especially disturbing to see the loss of positions in the leadership ranks and at the elementary level which is so crucial to the early development of the attitudes and problem solving skills so in need of improvement and support.

Discussions with educators involved in preparing school library media specialists pointed out another disturbing element. It appears that we are having difficulty attracting the level of talent that we once did. This has been pointed out as a problem of the field of education generally but it also appears to be occurring in the school library media field. This very likely is the inevitable result of an employment situation which provides comparatively low financial incentives and low status but still attempts to maintain extremely high performance expectations. An environment which does not respect or treat individuals as professionals may well be the most serious problem we face.

A principal who was interviewed in preparation for this paper suggested that a climate of infantilism pervades relationships of all kinds in the schools. The feeling that one is not being treated as an adult and certainly not provided with the supporting systems and arrangements typically provided professionals appears to be widespread. This is obviously demeaning and not conducive to attracting or retaining capable people and certainly is not an environment which stimulates effectiveness no less excellence. A similar idea was expressed to the writer by a former student who was fired from her school library media specialist position after ten years due to cuts resulting from a tax limitation provision being passed in her district. She was the kind of person who had always wanted to work with children and was very effective in her role but when asked if she would ultimately return to a school library media position, she said very definitely not. Her rationale for this decision reflected an awareness which was made apparent to her when she secured another job as a librarian in a government agency. She commented that, "For the first time in my professional career I was respected and treated as a professional" and as a result she would not consider being reemployed in the schools. If we are really serious about trying to improve the education of children, we have to face the serious issue of the status, treatment and financial remuneration of educational personnel. It should be readily apparent that without a substantial psychological and economic improvement in this work environment, no significant improvement in the learning environment can or will occur.

Planning and Evaluating Programs

Progress in the planning and evaluating of school library media programs has been extremely slow; it also has been slow in other kinds of library and information environments. Some progress has been made in terms of developing improved approaches, but the frame of mind in the field is still centered around the traditional standards approach of measuring one's goodness by comparing what one "has" rather than what one "does" to what is recommended in some arbitrarily derived set of standards. Inadequate progress has been made toward defining the goals and objectives of school library media programs in terms of services provided to clients and contributions made toward achieving instructional and learning goals. As a result, much of the evaluation of library media specialists which is currently performed is based on strictly subjective judgments of the degree to which library media specialists compare to some list of characteristics or attributes that may have nothing to do with the development and delivery of an effective program of services to users.

Another problem resulting from this approach to planning and developing library media programs is the kind of reporting and communicating that results. The focus is not on the goals and achievements of library media programs but rather simply on the means of these programs. The result of this kind of reporting and communicating behavior is the reenforcement of an already exceedingly confused picture of what the library media program is and does. A more rapid movement toward more output and outcome oriented program management and program communication is desperately desired and needed.

Research must also focus on identifying measurable indicators of program quality that are related to learners and the achievement of instructional objectives. This is an extraordinarily complex problem but without something considerably better than what we currently have available, we will continue to evaluate using tests that frequently focus on simple and often irrelevant facts or extremely subjective judgments of people and programs which can be, and are, extremely unfair and unrelated to program effectiveness.

School library media programs need to be brought into the mainstream of library and information activity. In spite of decades of idealistic and involved discussions of cooperation and participation in networking, etc., we have too few examples of active participation. It is time to look more realistically and critically at what is possible and what is really desirable! We presently have several examples of extensive participation of school library media programs in networking, such as New York and Maryland. These experiences as well as other emerging cooperative activities need to be carefully evaluated to identify what works and why. It would be merciful however to the profession also to face the realities of cooperative and networking efforts and move ahead with what seems feasible and reduce the rhetorical abuse directed at those who raise serious questions.

Education of Library Media Specialists

The training pattern for school library media specialists has been essentially different from that of most other library and information professionals. Many individuals have entered the field via undergraduate programs following the training pattern in most of the other teaching fields. Some say that this is one of the reasons why school library media specialists frequently feel like second-class citizens since their initial professional training is less than in other areas of library and information services. Another result may be a primary acculturation into the field of application (Education) rather than the specific professional field one is applying (Library and Information Service). This only serves to reenforce the identity problem.

A number of recent analyses of education have suggested a revamping of the structure of teacher training. It has frequently been suggested that a prime requirement of all educators is a "good basic education" and attempts to combine professional education with this objective at the undergraduate level have only resulted in seriously hampering the achievement of both a basic and a professional education.

This writer is very much in sympathy with the suggestion of moving professional education to the graduate level so that both undergraduate and professional programs can be strengthened. A good basic education must be fundamental to the preparation of all information professionals and even though there are theoretically many ways to accomplish this, the time is ripe for a definite move in the direction of graduate level professional training.

Another crossroad which should be faced at this juncture is the responsibility for the preparation of school library media specialists. There has been some confusion regarding who is responsible for the education of school library media specialists and even who or what group has responsibility for accrediting these programs. Some confusion in this regard exists in many disciplines, particularly in the preparation of secondary teachers since there is a split of responsibility frequently with Colleges of Education being responsible for the instructional aspects of the role and the various academic departments being responsible for the subject matter training preparation of teachers. Both of these concerns or perspectives are important and should be respected and the particular organizational handling of the problem left to the higher education institutions.

This writer believes that it is absolutely crucial for the responsibility for the substantive or subject matter content of the programs to be with the various disciplines if the quality of these programs is to be raised and maintained. Faculty who are at the cutting edge of their field should be providing the substantive input here and that inevitably means they are in departments devoted to their discipline. How one conceives of the function and role of school library media specialists will also influence how one answers the question of what should be responsible for what in the educational preparation of school library media personnel. If one conceives of this person as a teacher who dabbles with media on the side, that is one kind of perspective, but if the information intermediary function is paramount which is the perspective in this paper, then one also must think differently about the discipline of the school library media specialist. The point of view being expressed here suggests that the discipline of the library media specialist is the discipline of any library and information specialist except that the particular application of the discipline or specialization in this case is in the school. Even from the standpoint of instruction, the discipline or instructional specialization of the library media specialist is library and information science and not something else. This is not an attempt to diminish the importance of the application environment but simply to clarify the role and as a result the educational preparation implications. An understanding of the application environment, in this case education, is obviously required but in the case of the school library media specialist a thorough knowledge and skill in the design of instruction is particularly crucial because instruction and participation in the design and planning of curriculum and instruction is an important part of the role of a library media specialist. It is interesting to note that in many other environments the user education function is also being given much more prominence and attention.

The issue of educational responsibility also relates to the identity problem in that it is time for us to come to terms with how we perceive ourselves and our role. We have had innumerable studies relating to the role and it is time we "take the bull by the horns." It is time that we accept and develop the information intermediary function that we perform and not worry about whether we are a teacher or not. Of course we perform a teaching function, but it should be based on our own discipline and related to the essential intermediary role we are playing and need to expand and improve.

Another current danger in relation to educational preparation programs is the diminished scale of the school library media component because of incredibly reduced enrollments. Many of these programs were never very strong but we are now losing relevant faculty positions and our future capacity to continue these programs. The danger of relegating these programs for token attention to colleges of education or maintaining them at a token level in schools of library and information science should be a major concern. At this time we need the highest level of competence by professionals who have been thoroughly trained in their discipline and not some minimal level of performance by individuals who have only had the benefit of some superficial kind of preparation.

A number of related issues should at least be mentioned. The growing power of state departments of education in accrediting or approving the training programs for school library media specialists as well as certifying these personnel has in some cases intruded on the capacity of higher education institutions to design effective programs. When specific credit and course requirements are specified at the state level for every new concern that comes along, it becomes utterly impossible for a university program to design a cohesive and integrated curriculum. It is important at this time that substantive and technological developments as well as significant changes in function be paramount in a major rethinking of the competencies and educational preparation programs for school library media specialists as well as all information professionals. Obviously, the focus of this attention must also include an analysis of the content and effective delivery of continuing education opportunities. Although there has been significant improvement in inservice and continuing education opportunities for school personnel, there is considerable room for improvement particularly in the content of these programs if they are to be a major vehicle for acquainting professionals with the major substantive developments in the field.

Information Systems for Youth

Considering how much research and development activity is currently underway in the information field, it is discouraging to see how little is being done to develop and make available better and more extensive information systems for children and youth. Data bases seem to be multiplying like rabbits but none seem to be addressed to the learning and information needs of children and youth. Some data bases like the New York Times *Information Bank* could be rich resources for children but they are obviously aimed at other audiences and the organizations marketing them are not sensitive or interested in making any special accommodations for students. It would seem that, considering the number of schools and students in this country, it would be commercially feasible to develop and market data bases designed to support instruction and learning in some of the most common curricular areas. The development of data bases that will facilitate children's access to ideas by allowing them to interact with relevant information and ideas in a more free and efficient manner should be seriously encouraged. School library media specialists are in a position to identify particularly opportune areas for this kind of development and should be encouraged either to pass on the suggestion or to cultivate an entrepreneurial bent if such is the inclination.

Subject access to information for children is currently extremely weak and in a number of ways is getting worse. Very likely something around 80 percent of the searching for information in any school library media center is searching by subject. Subject access for books and nonprint items usually consists of three subject headings per item in the card catalog which would seem to be a logical approach for a large library but an inadequate approach for a small library that needs to mine its collection in much greater depth to satisfy the needs of its clients. The indexing of periodicals frequently offers the opposite kind of situation where more in-depth indexing may be done but the collection may only have a small proportion of what is indexed leading to a different kind of frustration. Students are also frequently new to a topic so they need assistance in identifying aspects of a subject or in some cases broader terms that would include their term. They also need to have a little information about the items they identify as potentially useful so that they can reduce their actual physical search to items that have a high probability of satisfying their need. What is described here is a small example of an intelligent search strategy and the kind of approach we should be teaching students. A major problem however is that the subject access we provide in school library media programs makes the application of that kind of search strategy or any kind for that matter very difficult and time consuming. As a result, most users don't follow such a strategy and accept what can be found in more efficient but less effective ways.

The critical need here is for a better and very likely computerized indexing system designed to meet the needs of students at different school levels. What is needed is certainly conceivable and feasible but the intellectual work necessary to develop such a system is not underway, undoubtedly because the incentives for such effort are being directed into other areas. It is even difficult to find individuals in the school field who are interested in this area no less prepared and committed to making a contribution. More and more school processing operations are being discontinued in favor of commercial processing and as a result we are moving more and more to the use of the national schemes devised for adults and large libraries and in many cases inappropriate for small libraries and children. This situation cannot be allowed to continue and substantive efforts directed at devising improved systems for children and youth must be initiated.

CONCLUSIONS

The report of the National Commission on Excellence in Education has identified a number of critical problem areas which must be addressed if we are to achieve our aspirations for excellence and if we are to equip our youth with the skills, knowledge and inspiration necessary to compete successfully in a learning society and an information world. The critical and central role of school library media programs in this venture has been the topic of this paper and the problems that have been identified will have to be solved in concrete and realistic terms if even a modicum of success is to be achieved. It should be clear that library and information programs and personnel of all types and at all levels must be intimately involved if we are to produce the self-directed problem solvers who are not only information literate but who have developed the higher order intellectual skills and attitudes regarding learning that we all seem to feel have become the "new basics."

Our focus must be the intellectual health and productivity of America and it is obvious that there is a serious discrepancy between our current level of performance and our aspirations. This society has the resources and the capability to achieve educational excellence but does it have the will? The educational community has been the whipping boy for all kinds of social issues for too long. It is time that the first class expectations of education be supported with something significantly more than the third class support of the past and simply more rhetoric is not the answer. Possibly even more important, an attitude of respect and regard for the fostering of learning and intellectual health must be developed in this society that compares to the respect and stature given the fostering of physical health.

This shift in national priorities must be combined with a direct attack on the problem areas identified in this paper. In addition, national information policy discussions cannot continue to ignore children and youth. Teachers must be information literate if kids are to be information literate and they must be able to capitalize on the information resources and services available to them. We must be able to recruit and keep a high level of talent. The implications here for teacher training as well as the preparation of library media specialists are readily apparent.

It is inevitable that this kind of analysis raises more questions than answers but this particular field has as many questions or probably more than most particularly as a result of the information revolution. Consequently, research and development must receive a high priority in the multitude of efforts that should be initiated. The highest priority however should be the improvement of the economic and psychological environment for educational personnel including library and information personnel of all kinds so that the talent and commitment that we already have can be retained and actively nourished as well as replenished with a high level of competence. Hopefully, these papers and seminars will contribute to the raising of the national consciousness and the mobilization of the national will that will be necessary to achieve the educational excellence we see as a national and individual necessity and challenge.

NOTES

[1]National Commission on Excellence in Education, U.S. Department of Health, Education and Welfare, *A Nation at Risk: The Imperative for Educational Reform* (Washington, D.C.: U.S. Government Printing Office, 1983), 16-17.

[2]Office of Technology Assessment, U.S. Congress, *Informational Technology and Its Impact on American Education* (Washington, D.C.: U.S. Government Printing Office, 1982).

[3]Ibid.

[4]Ibid.

[5]J. C. Mancall and M. C. Drott, "Materials Used by High School Students in Preparing Independent Study Projects: A Bibliometric Approach," *Library Research* 1 (1979): 223-36. This is a landmark study and an example of the research indicated.

[6]P. Wilson, *Public Knowledge, Private Ignorance: Toward a Library and Information Policy* (Westport, Conn.: Greenwood Press, 1977).

[7]J. W. Liesener, *A Systematic Process for Planning Media Programs* (Chicago: American Library Association, 1976). For the most recent version of this definition of services, see J. W. Liesener, *Instruments for Planning and Evaluating Library Media Programs* (College Park, Md.: College of Library and Information Services, University of Maryland, 1980).

[8]A. Hambleton, "Static in the Education Intercom: Conflict and the School Librarian," *Emergency Librarian* 9, no. 5 (May-June 1982): 18-20.

[9]L. H. Freiser, "Information Retrieval for Students," *Library Journal* 88 (March 15, 1963): 1121-23.

[10]R. Blazek, *Influencing Students toward Media Center Use* (Chicago: American Library Association, 1975). This represents one of the best examples of these studies.

[11]M. L. Miller and B. B. Moran, "Expenditures for Resources in School Library Media Centers," *School Library Journal* 30 (October 1983): 113.

[12]M. H. Mahar, "Office of Education Support of School Media Programs," *Journal of Research and Development in Education* 16, no. 1 (1982): 24.

RESEARCH ON THE IMPACT OF SCHOOL LIBRARY MEDIA PROGRAMS ON STUDENT ACHIEVEMENT

Implications for School Library Media Professionals*

Elaine K. Didier

INTRODUCTION

Over the past two decades, school library literature has frequently specified the need to substantiate the operational efficiency and overall effectiveness of school library media programs. Numerous publications reflect the evolution of quantitative and qualitative standards that attempt to provide a means by which practitioners can measure their programs and thus make a rational case for additional financial and/or other support. Despite the existence and use of such documents, school media programs and personnel are facing increasing pressure to prove their worth. At the same time, school systems are confronted with rising salaries, property tax ceilings, and general inflation, combined with declining state and federal financial support for education.

School media professionals have continually expressed the belief that good media programs contribute to quality education. *Media Programs: District and School*, which sets the current national standards for school media programs, asserts, "Through the use of media, a student acquires and strengthens skills in reading, observing, listening, and communicating ideas."[1] Further recognition of the importance of library media programs and personnel is found in the standards of regional and state accrediting agencies.

Despite this official acknowledgment of the value and contribution of the library media program to the school's total instructional program, some educators remain only partially convinced. In a number of districts, the library media program, particularly at the elementary level, has never been adequately developed and/or is frequently the first to be reduced or eliminated when budget cuts must be made.

In view of current national interest in the improvement of student achievement, particularly reading scores, it is especially critical that empirical evidence be identified to support the belief that library media resources and personnel are

---

*From Elaine K. Didier, "Research on the Impact of School Library Media Programs on Student Achievement—Implications for School Media Professionals," in *School Library Media Annual 1984*, ed. S. L. Aaron and P. R. Scales (Littleton, Colo.: Libraries Unlimited, 1984), 343-61. Reprinted by permission.

not only useful but essential components of the total school program, integral parts of the learning process. With this thought in mind, a survey of literature related to the topic was undertaken by manual and computerized searches of *Library Literature, Education Index, Dissertation Abstracts International* and the database of the Educational Resources Information Center (ERIC). In addition, reviews of research in school librarianship by Aaron,[2,3,4] Lowrie,[5] Barron,[6] and Marchant et al.[7] were examined.

The literature search revealed a number of investigations of library media program impact on student achievement, 38 of which will be discussed in this review. Achievement has been variously defined in terms of performance on tests, grade-point average or problem-solving ability. Subject areas most frequently linked with library media services include reading, writing, language development and library/research skills. Relationships to achievement in mathematics, social studies, and the natural sciences have been reported as well.

Specific aspects of library media programs which have been analyzed include student access to materials, the number and preparation of professional personnel, the instructional and curricular roles of personnel, and the impact of socioeconomic factors on media programs and student achievement. Since individual studies frequently examine achievement in several subject areas and/or the impact of various aspects of the library media program, the research reviewed here is grouped according to school level (elementary, secondary, and post-secondary) followed by research about the education and curricular roles of library media personnel as they relate to the quality of the media program and, hence, to student achievement.

ELEMENTARY LIBRARY MEDIA PROGRAMS

When reviewing research on elementary school libraries, the work of Gaver is especially significant. In 1959-60, she examined the extent and impact of elementary library programs on sixth graders at six schools with varying provisions for school library service: classroom collections only, centralized collections not staffed by a qualified librarian, or real school libraries staffed by a qualified librarian.[8] Factors examined included provision of library-related materials and activities, accessibility of resources, mastery of library skills, and amount and kind of reading done by children. Further, the research sought to measure educational achievement as represented by differences in scores in five basic curricular areas as derived from scores on a standardized test (*Iowa Tests of Basic Skills*) administered in the fourth and sixth grades.

Two of the findings are particularly significant. First, educational gain, based on the difference between fourth and sixth grade test scores, indicated that "higher educational gain is associated with schools which have school libraries."[9] Second, provision of a school library does not depend on the socioeconomic level of the school, although "the ranking for the total community may play a larger part in determining resources and attitudes related to the presence or absence of a school library."[10]

In a similar study conducted five years later, Wilson matched six Detroit elementary schools having centralized libraries staffed by professionals with six schools of comparable educational aptitude and socioeconomic characteristics without libraries.[11] Students with access to libraries scored higher overall on a standardized test for sixth graders, particularly in the areas of reading ability and library skills.

Similar results were reported from a study conducted by DeBlauw, who investigated the effects of a three-year multi-media program on student achievement and attitude.[12] As a part of the program, instructional materials centers were developed in three schools spanning kindergarten through the twelfth grade. Significant gains in achievement were found in the areas of vocabulary and word study skills in the first and second grades, and in word study skills and arithmetic in grades three through eight. Academic performance of the high school students was unchanged by the program.

Becker sought to determine whether social studies achievement of pupils in schools with libraries differed from that of pupils in schools without libraries. For purposes of the investigation, he confined the scope of social studies to information-gathering skills, reading of charts and graphs, map and globe skills, and selected social studies content material. Based on analysis of data gathered from experimental and control groups of fifth grade students in schools with and without libraries, Becker found that "the presence of a librarian and the guidance function of a librarian appeared to exert significant influence on pupil achievement in information-gathering skills and in the reading of charts and graphs."[13] The influence of the library on map- and globe-reading skills and on the acquisition of social studies content was not apparent.

McMillen studied selected elementary schools in Ohio to determine if a correlation exists between the quality of the media program and student achievement.[14] Although there was no significant difference in the area of vocabulary development, students' reading comprehension and knowledge and use of reference materials was superior in schools with good libraries and full-time librarians as compared with those having lesser levels of library service.

An inquiry conducted by the U.S. Office of Education a few years later had a somewhat different outcome. As part of a survey of the impact of Title II of the Elementary and Secondary Education Act, covering the years 1966-1968, nine elementary schools in three inner cities were evaluated to determine whether "the introduction of media services and materials in elementary schools previously without them had a significant impact on the instructional programs of the schools since 1965 with the aid of federal, as well as state and local funds."[15] Although findings showed that students and teachers felt very positive about use of the media center and the new materials, no significant differences in pupils' reading scores emerged. The report did not view this evidence as conclusive, however, because the nine library media centers were still in early stages of development.

As a part of the evaluation of the Knapp School Libraries Project at Allisonville School, Indianapolis, Indiana, Yarling tested fourth and sixth grade students' use of library-related skills, comparing performance by those with and those without access to a central library.[16] Outlining and note-taking skills, as well as general library skills, were significantly improved in the experimental group, as was the students' ability to express ideas effectively.

Similar improvement in library skills was reported by Ainsworth in a study of fifth and sixth grade students receiving extensive library usage instruction as compared with a control group at another school.[17] Students in the control group showed significantly greater proficiency in library skills as a result of instruction and access to a full-service library media program.

Charles Gengler's study of sixth grade students taught by teachers alone as compared with students taught by both teachers and librarians revealed that instruction by librarians contributed substantially to student problem-solving abilities. Both oral and written examinations were administered to test students' ability to locate or acquire information, and to organize, summarize, and evaluate information. "Elementary schools operating library instructional classes obtained a significantly higher mean than the schools not operating such a program."[18]

Another investigation linking library instruction with student performance was conducted by Harmer, who tested whether a library training program might influence the amount of recreational reading done by elementary children in the summer and, hence, offset the traditional summertime decline in reading ability.[19] He established experimental and control groups among fourth grade classes, testing reading ability prior to the end of school in the spring. All pupils in the experimental group then participated in a ten-day training session which included several visits to their local public library branch. Based on posttests administered in the fall, Harmer found that the experimental group was superior both in reading to retain information and in reading for appreciation, leading him to conclude that more rigorous training is needed in the use of the library.

In an earlier study examining the role of the school library in the overall reading program of the elementary school, Masterton discovered that "the activity of a library program as opposed to mere book exposure can be a strong factor in a reading program."[20] Further, students scored higher on reading tests in schools with centralized school libraries and professional librarians.

In research comparing student reading skills and patterns in elementary schools with and without central libraries, Monahan found that children with access to a centralized school library read more books of high quality and greater variety than did students with access to classroom collections only.[21]

The impact of the school library media program on language development was explored by Bailey, who concluded that the psycholinguistic abilities of disadvantaged first grade students were significantly improved as a result of participation in an active library media program.[22] In addition, overall language ability and verbal expression were significantly greater following the twelve-week story-telling program.

Finally, in 1982, this author investigated the relationship between elementary school students' achievement in reading and study skills and several aspects of the library media program: ratio of professional personnel per building, education of personnel, the curricular role of library media personnel, and student access to the library media center.[23] Financial data regarding school district instructional expenditures and State Equalized Valuation were also correlated to assess their relationship to student achievement and library media programs and personnel. Achievement was measured by using district summaries of fourth and seventh grade students' scores on the reading section of the *Michigan Educational Assessment Program* (*MEAP*), a state-wide objective-referenced test. Data on library media programs were based on responses from 94 school districts drawn from a state-wide survey.

My research indicated that the impact of the library media program (staffed by a full-time professional) on student achievement was more clearly visible at the seventh grade level than at the fourth grade level. Specifically, student achievement in reading, study skills and use of newspapers was significantly greater at the seventh grade level in schools with library media personnel as compared to schools without professional personnel. Student access to the library media center was significantly greater at both grade levels in schools with professional library media personnel than in schools without such personnel; however, student access was found to be inversely related to the education of the professional media personnel. Further, the study showed that districts with higher State Equalized Valuation and total instructional expenditures per pupil were more likely to have professional media personnel at the elementary level.

Findings regarding the inter-relationships between education of professional personnel, their curricular role and student achievement were mixed. The education of the library media specialist was inversely related to curricular role and overall student achievement in reading at the fourth grade level, but the curricular role itself was positively related to fourth graders' achievement in reading. Although these findings differ from those of studies discussed in the subsequent sections on education and curricular role, this may be due to differences in research design and focus. It may also indicate gaps between theory and practice, which will be discussed later, as well as a need for further research in this area.

SECONDARY LIBRARY MEDIA PROGRAMS

At the secondary level, a major study was conducted by Greve, who investigated the relationship between the accessibility of library services and the academic achievement of high school seniors.[24] Greve administered the *Iowa Tests of Educational Development* to 232 Iowa high school seniors to determine their overall educational development. Levels of library service available were measured by an index based on the number of volumes per pupil/per capita in the school and public libraries respectively, and on per pupil/per capita expenditures in each type of library.

Greve found that there was a direct, positive correlation between academic achievement and the level of library services available, that as city and/or high school population increased there were significantly greater library services available to students, and, that the number of volumes in the high school library was the best predictor of high achievement on the Iowa tests. Next in order of influence were public library expenditures, the number of volumes in the public library, and finally, school library expenditures.

Another investigation of significance dealt with the effect of textbook versus library resources instruction on student performance in science. Barrilleaux served as teacher for both the experimental and control groups of eighth and ninth grade science classes. Using a variety of measures, he found that growth in science achievement was approximately the same for both the control and experimental groups, but the experimental (library/nontext) group scored significantly higher mean ratings than did the control (textbook) group in critical thinking, science attitudes, writing in science, elective science reading, and library utilization.[25]

In a similar study examining language acquisition, Hastings and Tanner found that regular use of the high school library for planned information-gathering experiences resulted in significantly higher scores in spelling and total language skills.[26] Two pair of experimental and control groups, matched for ability, received a variety of classroom instruction and library experiences. Highest scores were in the group receiving no formal classroom instruction in spelling or grammar, but actively using the library reference collection one day per week.

Three other studies of the impact of library services on achievement at the secondary level should be noted. McConnaha examined the effect of an elementary school library instructional program on ninth grade students' performance on a test of library skills. Significantly higher scores occurred among students who had attended an elementary school with a library and a librarian who had provided library instruction.[27]

Hale sought to determine the impact of library services on the academic performance of twelfth graders in a Virginia high school. Students were assigned to experimental and control groups matched for general achievement test scores and library skills. Students were then instructed with either normal or intensive interaction with library resources and the librarian. Hale concluded that academic achievement increased through exposure to library services.[28] Specifically, she reported measurably improved learning by those students experiencing library instruction and services.

Finally, Thorne conducted a longitudinal study of two groups of junior high school students, one group exposed to the augmented services of a Knapp project demonstration school in Provo, Utah, and the other group subject to the normal library services of another school in the district.[29] The investigation found that the experimental group attending the Knapp project school showed significant gains in reading comprehension and library skills over the two-year span of the study.

POST-SECONDARY EDUCATION

Three studies conducted at the post-secondary level have investigated the impact of high school library service upon students' academic performance in college. In the first, Harkin studied freshmen and sophomores at Ball State University to test the basic assumption that "the availability and use of media will aid students in formal educational pursuits."[30] He found no significant difference in academic achievement or attitude among students who graduated from schools with high ratios of media to students as compared with those from schools with lower ratios.

In a second investigation, Walker tested whether the availability of high school and public library service makes a significant contribution to the formal education of students as measured by college grade-point average.[31] Operating on the assumption that availability is the prerequisite to use, Walker made no attempt to measure either the amount or level of students' prior library use or the efficacy of the utilization. Walker developed an index value for public and high school library services available, and controlled for individual differences in student aptitude and ability. He found no significant difference in achievement as measured by grade-point average for those students from communities with a high level of library services available as compared with those from communities with a low level of library service available.

A final study at the post-secondary level is Snider's investigation of the relationship between students' success in college (as measured by grade-point average) and their knowledge of library skills.[32] He calculated relationships between pairs in the categories of grade-point average, library ability, high school class ranking, and score on achievement tests taken as high school seniors. In his sample of freshmen over a three-year period, Snider found a strong positive correlation between library skills and academic success.

SELECTED FACTORS AFFECTING
PROGRAM QUALITY

Education of Library Media Personnel

In pursuing the question of the impact of the library media program on student achievement, it is both appropriate and necessary to examine concomitant factors which affect the overall quality of the media program. Among the factors which have been identified as contributing to the scope and services of the media program are the number and preparation of professional library media personnel and their curricular role. Five studies have been selected as particularly relevant to a discussion of the relationship between the education of library personnel and the quality of the media program.

Gaver analyzed the development of elementary school libraries and media centers, based on an investigation of the programs of the 46 school districts chosen as finalists in the *Encyclopaedia Britannica* School Library Awards contest, 1963-1968. She reported that schools employing school librarians, whether part-time or full-time, were above the average for all schools and in all areas of a library services checklist. It appeared that elementary schools with librarians provided a greater variety and number of library-related activities and services. Furthermore, Gaver reported a correlation between "the number of activities and library personnel, with little, if any, difference existing in the number of activities between schools with classroom collections but no employed personnel."[33] In other words, the personnel made the difference in creating a library program.

The importance of personnel to staff a library media program is further supported by the research of Loertscher and Land. In a study of teacher and administrator perceptions of media programs and services, they found that "full-time media specialists give a significantly greater number of services than do either part-time professionals or full-time clericals."[34] Further, teachers in schools staffed by full-time professionals were the best informed about the range of services offered by the media program. Next in order of awareness of services were teachers in schools staffed by full-time clericals, followed by those in schools staffed by part-time professionals.

Wert used a causal-comparative method of research to determine whether the amount of formal education of a high school librarian affects performance on the job as defined in terms of readers' services.[35] She studied eight high school library programs, four operated by persons holding master's degrees in library science, and four operated by persons holding an undergraduate minor in library science or less. She found that, as a group, librarians with more education offered more extensive programs of reader services, spent more time providing such services, and that teachers and students used the libraries in which these librarians worked more extensively than they used the libraries staffed by the less educated group.

Hodowanec carried this type of investigation one step further by examining the academic preparation of library media personnel in relation to job performance in selection, acquisition, organization of materials, and user services.[36] He found that library media specialists' academic preparation was directly related to their performance of tasks in each of the four areas. Lack of formal preparation consistently diminished the frequency with which certain tasks were reported as part of job content. The most serious deficiencies in performance were in the areas of curriculum planning and the identification of resources for use in specific courses. Hodowanec did not pursue the relationship of academic preparation and job performance to student achievement.

Natarella used a sample of Michigan elementary schools to examine the activities and services of media personnel with various levels of education in relation to students and trade books.[37] Media personnel were classified as (1) certified librarians, (2) noncertified but having a degree, or (3) noncertified without a degree. Natarella found that the noncertified personnel with degrees (category 2) spent significantly greater time using books with students than did the other two categories of personnel. Both categories of personnel with degrees developed a significantly greater number of activities using books than did the personnel without a college degree. Interestingly, there was no significant increase in the amount of time spent with students or in the number of activities performed when clerical or volunteer help was provided. Although per pupil expenditures for media did correlate significantly with the socioeconomic class of the community, daily use of the library was greater by students from lower socioeconomic communities than from higher ranking communities.

Curricular Role of the Library Media Specialist

The curricular and instructional roles of the library media specialist have been enthusiastically described by Vandergrift[38] and Wehmeyer,[39] and scientifically researched by many others. A recent article by Hodges reviewed a number of studies related to these roles, identifying consistent patterns of research findings in several areas.[40] Among the factors affecting the curricular role of the library media specialist were the size of the media staff and competencies in curriculum planning, evaluation, analysis of materials and instructional design. Hodges also noted that many Delphi studies have stressed the importance of the instructional role of future library media specialists; however, the studies also indicated that changes would have to occur in perceptions of and expectations for media specialists if this role is to be realized.

Literature reviews by both Aaron[41] and Mohajerin and Smith[42] support this last finding in particular. The traditional role expectations can be illustrated by Johnson's finding that "teachers did not consider the librarian's membership on faculty committees or direct involvement in team planning as significant or needed contributions to instructional development."[43] Further, only 20 percent of the librarians felt such membership had any bearing on teacher use.

The generally traditional approach to and expectations of the library media program and library media specialists by teachers and administrators have serious implications for practitioners. Specifically, the influence of the library media program and library media specialist on student achievement can be greatly affected/limited by teacher and administrator expectations of the "proper" role of media programs and personnel.

Another aspect of the curricular role of library media programs and personnel involves the question of teachers' use of the library media center and of media in general, and the impact of such use on student use of the media program. The results of studies examining this question must be considered, because the relationship of school media programs to student achievement would logically be affected by the variables of student and teacher attitude toward and use of media.

Blazek's experimental investigation of teacher influence on student use of the library dealt with this question by examining use of nonrequired materials in mathematics. In 1969-70, the investigator set up control and experimental groups of subfreshman (junior high) students at the University of Illinois Laboratory High School to test the hypothesis that "the greater the teacher utilization of media center resources in his teaching, the greater the use of the center by pupils."[44]

The experimental treatment consisted of a six-item bibliography of books and other media distributed to students each week. Library circulation records were then tallied daily to chart differences between the control and experimental groups.

A dramatic increase in the use of mathematics and other library materials by members of the experimental group occurred, although this increase held during the test period only; after the treatment was completed, usage returned to pretest levels. Blazek also found that the relative inaccessibility of the school library media center (due to scheduling conflicts) did not deter use by students in the experimental group, i.e., students who were motivated through the influence of their teacher.

Two other studies conducted prior to Blazek's support his findings about teacher influence on student use of the media center, but they approached the issue from the perspective of student attitudes toward and use of libraries. Both Ducat[45] and Hsu[46] found that the contribution of the school library to the school's educational program was "conditioned to a great extent by the importance teachers assigned to materials in achieving the teaching objectives of their courses."[47]

Four additional studies conducted more recently have approached the question of the curricular role of the library media specialist and the media program from the perspective of teacher attitude toward and awareness of the role of the library media specialist and the library media center. Newman, Klausmeier, and Bullard,[48] Rogers[49] and Griffin[50] found that use of media and the media center was directly related to teacher attitude toward and competency in using media, raising once again the question of expectations as determinants of or deterrents to use of the library media center.

Newman et al. discovered a great need for in-service training among Iowa teachers and principals in the areas of equipment use and selection and utilization of media. Stroud identified similar in-service needs among Indiana teachers following development and application of the *Purdue Self-Evaluation System (PSES) for School Media Centers*.[51] She found that sex, years of experience, and subject area taught contributed to differences in teachers' use of the library media center: male teachers visited the media center more frequently, but women teachers used a greater variety of services; teachers with over fifteen years of experience utilized a greater variety of media services. Years of experience (over fifteen years) also contributed to the range and number of services offered by library media specialists.

Similarly, Griffin's examination of library instructional support services to elementary schools found that age, education, and familiarity with media were major factors affecting teachers' use of library media services: younger teachers and those holding bachelor's degrees were more likely to use media services and rely upon curriculum planning assistance than were older teachers or those with master's degrees; teachers with some library science or audiovisual training were more likely to use sophisticated media services.[52]

Collectively, the studies identified in this section indicate that the curricular role of the library media specialist, however highly valued by the profession, can be determined or limited by the perceptions, expectations and knowledge of teachers and administrators. Since teachers appear to have significant influence on students' attitudes toward and use of the library media center, the interrelated issues of curricular role and teacher perceptions are critical variables in any examination of the impact of the library media program on student achievement.

SUMMARY OF RELATED LITERATURE

Numerous studies have been identified which investigate various aspects of the relationship between library media programs/skills and student achievement at all levels of education. The findings may be summarized as follows:

1. Research supports the finding that the *presence* of library media programs can be related to

    a. the inculcation of library skills (McConnaha, McMillen, Wilson, Yarling)
    b. overall achievement (DeBlauw, Gaver, McMillen, Madden, Wilson)
    c. achievement in specific subject areas or of specific types of skills (Becker, DeBlauw, Didier, Monahan, Wilson)

2. Research shows that *knowledge of library skills* can be related to the improvement of

    a. student achievement (Gengler, Greve, Hale, Harmer, McMillen, Yarling)
    b. performance on standardized tests (Gaver)
    c. grade-point average (Snider)

3. Research shows that the *level of library media service*, as determined by the quality and size of the collection, number and education of personnel, or amount of library instruction/program activity, can be related to the improvement of elementary and secondary students'

    a. knowledge of library skills (Ainsworth, McConnaha, McMillen, Thorne, Wilson, Yarling)
    b. overall educational achievement (Greve)
    c. achievement in specific subject areas or of specific types of skills (Bailey, Barrilleaux, Didier, Gengler, Hale, Harmer, Hastings and Tanner, McMillen, Masterton, Thorne)

4. Research shows that the *level of high school library service* available, as defined by the size of the collection alone, cannot be related to subsequent overall academic performance of college students (Harkin, Walker).

5. Research shows that *socioeconomic factors* are not necessarily related to library media programs (Gaver, Wilson) although they may influence the amount of funding and utilization by various groups (Natarella).

6. Research shows that the *nature and extent of the education* of the library media specialist can be related to

    a. the number and quality of library media program services provided (Gaver, Hodowanec, Loertscher and Land, Natarella, Wert)
    b. the amount and quality of curricular and instructional involvement (Hodges)

7. Research shows that the *curricular and instructional roles* of the library media specialist and library media center can be related to

    a. teacher and administrator expectations (Hodges, Johnson, Mohajerin and Smith)
    b. teacher and administrator competency with media, and their attitudes toward and use of library media services (Blazek, Ducat, Griffin, Hsu, Newman, Klausmeier and Bullard, Rogers)
    c. students' academic ability in general and their reading ability in particular (Ducat)
    d. teachers' education (nature and extent), sex and years of experience (Griffin, Stroud)
    e. library media specialists' years of experience (Stroud)
    f. the size of the media staff (Hodges)

In summary, these studies identify many factors which can relate to student achievement. With this evidence in mind, the next two sections of this review will discuss the implications of these findings for practitioners, and identify areas in need of further research.

IMPLICATIONS

A number of implications for present practice and future study can be drawn from the studies reviewed here. A few have been discussed in the previous sections; others, pertaining to school districts, library media specialists, and library education, are discussed in this section.

School Districts

First among the implications of these studies for local school districts are the findings that overall student achievement, knowledge of library and information retrieval skills, and achievement in specific subject areas can be significantly greater in school districts where there are library media programs staffed by professional personnel. These findings directly address the questions of superintendents and principals alike regarding the value of library media programs in general and elementary programs in particular. Studies reporting that knowledge of library skills can contribute to student achievement, even beyond K-12, lend further support to the case for developing strong school library media programs.

The finding that student access to the library media center can be significantly greater in districts with professional library media personnel should help clarify the difference between a library media program and a facility. Districts considering reduction of the number of library media personnel should be made aware that in all likelihood there will be a concomitant reduction in student access to media resources.

Once media programs are in place, continued support for acquisitions and staffing and an active, full-service instructional program is essential to ensure maximum impact on student achievement. The specific finding that there was a positive correlation between student achievement and instructional expenditures per pupil in districts with library media personnel serves to underscore the importance of taxpayer support for education and the contribution of library media programs and personnel to student learning.

Findings regarding the strong impact of teacher and administrator expectations and competencies upon the curricular role of the library media specialist indicate that there is great need to educate the educators regarding the multifaceted role of today's library media professionals. Both pre-service and in-service educators must be reached if library media specialists are to be able to offer and exercise the full range of their skills and talents.

The fact that one study showed no relationship between the presence of the library media specialist and performance of fourth grade students raises several questions about the impact of library media programs on students at the lower elementary level. Is it possible that the library media program has little or no influence on early elementary students' literacy as measured by tests of basic skills or minimum competencies? Although influence on students' values, attitudes, interests and general retrieval skills may well be present, these may not be measured by certain instruments. Further, it may be premature to expect a high correlation between the presence of a library media specialist and student achievement when students are just learning to read in the early elementary years. Even in schools with good media programs, use of the library media center may be viewed as peripheral to the acquisition of basic reading skills; activities are frequently classroom and teacher-focused during that period. Although the current literature stresses the role of the school library media specialist in the teaching of reading, it may be that teacher and administrator expectations, once again, inhibit this role.

It is also possible that the impact of the library media program is progressive and thus only measurable after more years of schooling and contact with media resources and activities. One could also hypothesize that the library media center is only usable and helpful after a certain degree of literacy (visual and otherwise) is attained.

Finally, school districts should seek to maximize the contributions of library media personnel to the instructional program of the school. Findings regarding the relationship between the education of the library media specialist and the number and quality of library services/activities offered indicate that school districts would be wise to select the best qualified professional media personnel available. Economics achieved through the hiring of less educated media personnel have been shown to be very expensive in the long run. Library media programs and personnel represent a valuable resource which can contribute to student achievement; districts should work to maximize rather than limit the potential of this resource.

Library Media Specialists

The implications of these studies for library media specialists are several, and there is a need to publicize the results of this body of research. There have been a sufficient number of studies at varying grade levels and subjects to indicate that there can be a positive relationship between the library media program and the following: development of reading skill, overall academic achievement, library skills, vocabulary and word study skills, verbal expression, problem-solving ability, and breadth and quality of general reading.

These findings can be shared through informal discussions with colleagues and neighbors, formal presentations to school and community groups, and newsletters and journals of professional associations and education-minded civic groups. As emphasized in the winter 1982 issue of *School Library Media Quarterly*, the conducting, application, and dissemination of research are the responsibility of everyone in the school media field.

In addition to publicizing positive findings regarding library media programs, practicing specialists should examine their own roles and take steps to strengthen and expand elements of the media program which are thought to have greatest impact on student achievement. Specifically, media specialists should work to strengthen curricular involvement with teachers and students and ensure student acquisition of study skills. Use of the Liesener model[53] may be helpful to analyze allocation of staff time to various functions which are less important for attainment of major instructional goals.

Further, media specialists should actively seek to overcome the deterrents of teacher and administrator expectations and media familiarity/competency by conducting an active program which, by example, educates colleagues about the media specialist's role in curriculum and instruction. Studies showing that teacher attitudes toward and utilization of media have a direct impact upon student attitudes and use must not be ignored. There is tremendous need for in-service and pre-service instruction of teachers regarding the availability and use of media resources.

Finally, both individual library media specialists and the profession at large must consider what can reasonably be accomplished by a single library media professional in a building, as is often the case. The professional literature abounds with articles and books about the role of the library media specialist in teaching basic skills, serving the special child (both gifted and handicapped), writing the curriculum, managing microcomputers and creating multi-media productions. Many of these new roles have developed in response to trends and concerns in education, not the least of which is the desire to survive by showing the library media program to be indispensable to the instructional process.

Consideration should be given to the possibility that the library media specialist cannot be all things to all people. Media specialists need to evaluate their strengths, assess their needs for continuing professional education, and seriously apply their knowledge to achieving the educational goals and objectives of their local school. The impact of the school library media specialist on student achievement can be maximized by focusing activities on instructional goals.

Library Education

The findings of these studies have implications for library education at both the pre-service and in-service level. Pre-service instruction should continue to stress the importance of curricular involvement with both students and teachers, and in-service programs should assist practitioners with developing this role. Additional strategies may need to be developed to help students and practitioners learn how to combat limiting expectations, and alternative styles for consulting with teachers regarding curriculum planning.

It is also important that library educators help students and practitioners balance the seemingly competing demands of media center administration versus direct client contact, stressing the point that greater educational attainment makes media specialists more important than ever to students and teachers.

The larger question of the realistic scope of the library media specialist's role should be studied and discussed by library educators. Some of the commonly held assumptions of those in the field may need to be tested in order that the specific contributions of library media specialists to teaching and learning can be identified and developed. It would be appropriate for library educators to lead the examination process to determine at what levels and in what ways the library media specialist can best influence student achievement.

RECOMMENDATIONS FOR FURTHER RESEARCH

The findings of these studies examining the relationship between student achievement and selected aspects of library media programs have served to identify new questions and to emphasize the need for additional research in this area. Based on the findings and implications of these studies, the following are recommendations for further research:

1. It would be useful to replicate many of these studies in order to identify more precisely the nature of the relationship between library media programs and student achievement.

2. Detailed case studies of selected school districts included in some of these studies would be most useful to illustrate differences in library media programs and personnel and their differential impact on student performance.

3. Alternative tests and measures should be used to investigate the impact of the library media program on student achievement, particularly as pertaining to lower elementary students, and gifted and talented students at all levels.

4. Another way of approaching this question would be to identify schools or districts with professional library media personnel where test scores are extremely high or low. One could then investigate the differences in the media programs of the schools or districts in order to determine the factors with greatest influence on the differential test scores.

5. A longitudinal analysis of test scores for schools identified as being without library media programs staffed by professionals at a given time, and which subsequently develop library media programs, should be conducted. It would be very interesting to investigate the rate at which student performance changes in relation to systematically expanding library media resources and services.

6. Conversely, it would be valuable to conduct a follow-up study of the status of media programs and test scores in districts which did have library media programs staffed by professionals at a given time, but which no longer have them as a result of budget reductions. As in the previous case, it would be interesting to investigate the rate at which student performance changes as library media resources and services decline.

7. Differences in student learning styles and cognitive/affective development should be investigated as related to use of and benefit from library media programs and personnel.

8. The relationships between student access to the library media center, the educational attainment of library media personnel and student achievement should be examined in more detail so as to isolate the major factors and their influence.

9. There should be additional studies examining the relationship between library media programs and student achievement at all levels of the K-12 educational system so as to identify areas and periods of major importance and impact.

10. Additional studies should be conducted regarding the curricular and instructional role of the library media specialist, investigating which strategies are most effective in modifying teacher and administrator perceptions and expectations.

11. In the same vein, strategies for increasing teachers' utilization of media should be examined with the goal of influencing student utilization as well.

12. The impact of the new technologies on schools in general and library media programs in particular should be charted in order to develop new instructional strategies and assess resultant changes in student learning styles and achievement.

13. Finally, research on the effectiveness of library education programs should be continued to ensure that the emerging generation of school library media specialists truly understand and are able to implement a multi-faceted instructional media program.

It is obvious that there is great need for additional investigation of many aspects of school library media programs. The studies reviewed in this paper were performed to evaluate the effectiveness of school library media programs in a variety of settings. Rising to the challenge that "no instructional program should be undertaken or continued in the absence of evidence of its effectiveness in producing learning,"[54] these studies have shown that school library media programs and personnel appear to be positively related to student achievement.

NOTES

[1]American Association of School Librarians and Association for Educational Communications and Technology, *Media Programs: District and School* (Chicago: American Library Association, 1975), 4.

[2]S. L. Aaron, "A Review of Selected Research Studies in School Librarianship, 1967-1971: Part I," *School Libraries* 21 (Summer 1972): 29-46.

[3]S. L. Aaron, "A Review of Selected Research Studies in School Librarianship, 1967-1971: Part II," *School Media Quarterly* 1 (Fall 1972): 41-48.

[4]S. L. Aaron, "A Review of Selected Doctoral Dissertations about School Library Media Programs and Resources, January 1972-December 1980," *School Library Media Quarterly* 10 (Spring 1982): 210-45.

[5]J. E. Lowrie, "A Review of Research in School Librarianship," in *Research Methods in Librarianship: Measurement and Evaluation*, ed. Herbert Goldhor (Champaign-Urbana, Ill.: University of Illinois Graduate School of Library Science, 1968), 51-69.

[6]D. D. Barron, "A Review of Selected Research in School Librarianship: 1972-1976," *School Media Quarterly* 5 (Summer 1977): 271-89.

[7]M. P. Marchant, et al., "Research into Learning Resulting from Quality School Library Media Service," Brigham Young University, Provo, Utah, December, 1982.

[8]M. V. Gaver, *Effectiveness of Centralized Library Service in Elementary Schools*, 2d ed. (New Brunswick, N.J.: Rutgers University Press, 1963), xxiii.

[9]Ibid., 124.

[10]Ibid., 123.

[11]E. J. Wilson, "Evaluating Urban Centralized Elementary School Libraries" (Ph.D. dissertation, Wayne State University, 1965).

[12]R. A. DeBlauw, "Effect of a Multi-Media Program on Achievement and Attitudes of Elementary and Secondary Students" (Ph.D. dissertation, Iowa State University, 1973).

[13]D. E. Becker, "Social Studies Achievement of Pupils in Schools with Libraries and Schools without Libraries" (Ed.D. dissertation, University of Pennsylvania, 1970).

[14]R. D. McMillen, "An Analysis of Library Programs and a Determination of the Educational Justification of These Programs in Selected Elementary Schools of Ohio" (Ed.D. dissertation, Western Reserve University, 1965).

[15]*Descriptive Case Studies of Nine Elementary School Media Centers in Three Inner Cities. Title II, Elementary and Secondary Education Act of 1965* (Washington, D.C.: U.S. Department of Health, Education and Welfare, Office of Education, 1969), cited in Aaron, "A Review of Selected Research Studies ... Part II," 42.

[16]J. R. Yarling, "Children's Understandings and Use of Selected Library-Related Skills in Two Elementary Schools, One with and One without a Centralized Library" (Ed.D. dissertation, Ball State University, 1968).

[17]L. Ainsworth, "An Objective Measure of the Impact of a Library Learning Center," *School Libraries* 18 (Winter 1969): 33-35.

[18]C. R. Gengler, "A Study of Selected Problem Solving Skills Comparing Teacher Instructed Students with Librarian-Teacher Instructed Students" (Ed.D. dissertation, University of Oregon, 1965).

[19]W. R. Harmer, "The Effect of a Library Training Program on Summer Loss or Gain in Reading Abilities" (Ph.D. dissertation, University of Minnesota, 1959).

[20]E. Masterton, "An Evaluation of the School Library in the Reading Program of the School" (Master's thesis, University of Chicago, 1963).

[21]M. Monahan, "A Comparison of Student Reading in Elementary Schools with and without a Central Library" (Master's thesis, University of Chicago, 1956).

[22]G. Bailey, "The Use of a Library Resource Program for the Improvement of Language Abilities of Disadvantaged First Grade Pupils of an Urban Community" (Ed.D. dissertation, Boston College, 1970).

[23]E. K. M. Didier, "Relationships between Student Achievement in Reading and Library Media Programs and Personnel" (Ph.D. dissertation, University of Michigan, 1982).

[24]C. L. Greve, "The Relationship of the Availability of Libraries to the Academic Achievement of Iowa High School Seniors" (Ph.D. dissertation, University of Denver, 1974).

[25]L. E. Barrilleaux, "An Experimental Investigation of the Effects of Multiple Library Sources as Compared to the Use of a Basic Textbook on Student Achievement and Learning Activity in Junior High School Science" (Ph.D. dissertation, University of Iowa, 1965).

[26]D. Hastings and D. Tanner, "The Influence of Library Work in Improving English Language Skills at the High School Level," *Journal of Experimental Education* 31 (Summer 1963): 401-5.

[27]V. McConnaha, "The Effect of an Elementary School Library at High School Level," *California School Libraries* 43 (Summer 1972): 24-25.

[28]I. W. Hale, "October Inspiration: School Libraries Work!" *Wilson Library Bulletin* 45 (October 1970): 127.

[29]L. M. Thorne, "The Influence of the Knapp School Libraries Project on the Reading Comprehension and on the Knowledge of Library Skills of the Pupils at the Farrar Junior High School, Provo, Utah" (Ed.D. dissertation, Brigham Young University, 1967).

[30]W. D. Harkin, "Analysis of Secondary School Library Media Programs in Relation to Academic Success of Ball State University Students in Their Freshman and Sophomore Years" (Ph.D. dissertation, Ball State University, 1971).

[31]R. D. Walker, "The Influence of Antecedent Library Service upon Academic Achievement of University of Illinois Freshmen" (Ph.D. dissertation, University of Illinois, 1963).

[32]F. E. Snider, "The Relationship of Library Ability to Performance in College" (Ph.D. dissertation, University of Illinois, 1965).

[33]M. V. Gaver, *Patterns of Development in Elementary School Libraries Today*, 3d ed. (Chicago: Britannica, 1969), cited in Aaron, "A Review of Selected Research Studies ... Part II," 45.

[34]D. V. Loertscher and P. Land, "An Empirical Study of Media Services in Indiana Elementary Schools," *School Media Quarterly* 4 (Fall 1975): 16.

[35]L. M. Wert, *Library Education and High School Library Services* (Washington, D.C.: U.S. Department of Health, Education and Welfare, Office of Education, 1969).

[36]G. V. Hodowanec, "Comparison of Academic Training with Selected Job Responsibilities of Media Specialists" (Ed.D. dissertation, Temple University, 1973).

[37]M. D. Natarella, "A Survey of Media Center Personnel and School Policies That Relate to Students and Trade Books in Selected Michigan Elementary Schools" (Ph.D. dissertation, Michigan State University, 1972).

[38]K. E. Vandergrift, *The Teaching Role of the School Media Specialist* (Chicago: American Association of School Librarians, 1979).

[39]L. B. Wehmeyer, *The School Librarian as Educator* (Littleton, Colo.: Libraries Unlimited, 1976).

[40]G. C. Hodges, "The Instructional Role of the School Library Media Specialist: What Research Says to Us," *School Media Quarterly* 9 (Summer 1981): 281-82.

[41]Aaron, "A Review of Selected Research Studies ... Part I," 29-46; "A Review of Selected Research Studies ... Part II," 41-48.

[42]K. S. Mohajerin and E. P. Smith, "Perceptions of the Role of the School Media Specialist," *School Media Quarterly* 9 (Spring 1981): 152-63.

[43]H. Johnson, "Teacher Utilization of Librarians in the Secondary Schools of Tucson District No. 1" (Ed.D. dissertation, University of Arizona, 1975).

[44]R. Blazek, *Influencing Students toward Media Center Use: An Experimental Investigation in Mathematics* (Chicago: American Library Association, 1975), 47.

[45]Sister M. P. C. Ducat, O.P., "Student and Faculty Use of the Library in Three Secondary Schools" (D.L.S. dissertation, Columbia University, 1960).

[46]O. B. Hsu, "The Image of the School Library as Reflected in the Opinions and Student Use of the Library in Selected Secondary Schools" (Ed.D. dissertation, University of Michigan, 1970).

[47]Ducat, 246.

[48]J. A. Newman, R. D. Klausmeier, and J. Bullard, "Iowa Survey Shows: Teachers Need More Training in Media" (Iowa City: University of Iowa, 1974), ERIC Document 105895.

[49]J. V. Rogers, "Teachers and Media Resources in Selected Appalachian Secondary Schools: A Study of Attitudes, Usage and Knowledge of Media Center Fundamentals" (Ph.D. dissertation, University of Pittsburgh, 1977).

[50]E. M. Griffin, "Library Instructional Support Services in Elementary Schools in the District of Columbia Public School System" (Ed.D. dissertation, The American University, 1980).

[51]J. G. Stroud, "Evaluation of Media Center Services by Media Staff, Teachers and Students in Indiana Middle and Junior High Schools" (Ph.D. dissertation, Purdue University, 1976).

[52]Griffin.

[53]J. W. Liesener, *A Systematic Process for Planning Media Programs* (Chicago: American Library Association, 1976).

[54]R. L. Ebel, "Three Radical Proposals for Strengthening Education," presented at the Michigan School Testing Conference, Ann Arbor, Mich., 24 February 1981, 2.

THE CHANGING INSTRUCTIONAL ROLE OF THE HIGH SCHOOL LIBRARY MEDIA SPECIALIST
1950-84*

Kathleen W. Craver

INTRODUCTION

The instructional role of the library media specialist in school library media centers has been described in the literature for almost half a century. School library media specialists have been characterized as "instructional leaders, curriculum developers and resource consultants par excellence."[1] Their part in the instructional program of the school has been defined in several sets of national standards and in textbooks published as early as the 1930s and 1940s. The numerous appellations that have been applied to school library media specialists within this relatively short period of time might logically provoke a series of questions regarding such rapid change. Have the different occupational titles been employed to define the legitimate activity of the school library media specialist, or have they been utilized as organization fictions that the profession uses to "overcome an unfavorable stereotype or to provide a more comforting self-image?"[2]

OBJECTIVES

This article will review and examine the relevant literature pertaining to the changing instructional role of the school library media specialist from 1950 to 1984 in order to determine whether the instructional role has changed during this period. Particular attention will be paid to representative literature published during this time span by library/media educators, practitioners, leaders of state and national professional associations, and advisory agencies in order to determine what conditions prevailed during the various time periods. The educational philosophy and practices of each decade will be discussed to demonstrate, where appropriate, their influence on the growth and development of the librarian's instructional role. Standards published by the American Association of School Librarians in 1960, 1969, and 1975 will be analyzed for official

*From Kathleen W. Craver, "The Changing Instructional Role of the High School Library Media Specialist: 1950-84," *School Library Media Quarterly* 14 (Summer 1986): 183-91. Reprinted by permission.

sanctions of changes. Research studies that attempted to document the instructional status of the librarian during various time periods will be reviewed for the purpose of verifying any changes.

THE FIFTIES

The decade between the close of World War II and the mid-fifties was termed by many educators as a decade of American complacency. Americans had emerged victorious from a world war and were exulting in their acknowledged super-power status. School librarians floundered in a wave of anti-intellectualism and the conformity that was precipitated by technological democracy and the cold war. Reactionary citizens groups argued against the need for increased taxes to construct schools, employ additional teachers, and purchase new materials. As a result of this poor financial support, only 37% of U.S. secondary schools reported receiving the services of a centralized library by 1953-54. Teaching, despite the noticeable increase in audiovisual services offered by school libraries, was still dominated by the textbook.

The launching of Sputnik in 1957 was the catalyst that halted America's complacency and expedited the educational process. Sputnik led the way for Americans' receptivity to such reports as *The Pursuit of Excellence*[3] and *The American High School Today*,[4] which demanded excellence in all aspects of the educational endeavor. At this point federal funds were made available for the purchase of instructional materials that helped contribute to the concept of the school library as a resource center, and not merely a depository. By the late 1950s, schools began to focus on learning rather than teaching, and on curriculum methods that permitted a broader instructional role for the school librarian.

Although the previous programs and events greatly influenced the growth and development of the school librarian's instructional role, a survey of the literature demonstrated that practitioners and library educators were already preparing the way for substantial change. In *School Libraries: 1949-1950, A Summary*, Krentzman noted that the librarian is in a "particularly strategic position to participate effectively and to provide some leadership in curriculum development."[5] Her denouncement of the use of the library as a study hall and her promotion of its use as an activity center were prescient. Within the same year, Hunt advocated that the librarian should be a "reader's adviser, a coordinator of instruction and an expert in diagnostic and remedial procedures in reading and should play a key role in the development of the school program."[6] The publication of these two articles should probably be considered more prophetic than descriptive of the period.

A further examination of the literature provides a more realistic set of activities. The majority of librarians in the early fifties had their role officially defined by Fargo in her classic textbook, *The Library in the School*.[7] In it she defined the aims of the school library as being the provision of reading guidance and cooperation with the faculty on curriculum committees. Henne, in *A Planning Guide for the High School Library Program*,[8] relied upon the 1945 purposes set forth by AASL (American Association of School Librarians) as defining the instructional role. These goals similarly encouraged "participation with other teachers and administrators in programs for the continuing professional and cultural growth of the school staff and stimulating and guiding pupils in all phases of reading."[9]

In 1953, Lohrer introduced an issue of *Library Trends* devoted to school librarianship with a statement that indicated that "library service was beginning to be expressed in terms of social, reading and vocational guidance and as part of the teaching functions of the school library."[10] In that same issue, James indicated that the "modern concept of library work included: (1) provision of books and audiovisual materials to the students and faculty; (2) assistance with curriculum development; (3) class visitations; (4) consultation with departmental groups; and (5) preparation of bibliographies for course units."[11] The James article essentially reflected the educational philosophy for school librarians during the early fifties. Although the instructional role of the librarian was delineated, it still remained one of advising, supplying, and guiding students and faculty. Its passivity can be readily detected in such statements as three and four above.

It remained for a professor of education, W. L. Davis, to recommend a more active instructional role for the school librarian. Davis envisioned a librarian who provided course-integrated instruction for students in the use of materials centers. His perceptions were ahead of his contemporaries' and do provide testimony to the fact that progress was being made.[12]

Another prevailing debate of the early fifties that definitely affected the instructional role of the school librarian concerned the study hall concept of the library. A review of the literature reveals the contradictory views regarding this idea and indicates the extent to which libraries were being used in this manner. Goudeau provides a detailed list of the advantages and disadvantages of the concept, while simultaneously asserting that librarians should be regarded as teachers and their departments totally integrated into the curriculum.[13]

By the midfifties, the debate concerning these two issues abated, and the instructional role of the school librarian began to reflect the changes that were occurring in the basic philosophy of education. The most important of these changes in relation to school libraries were (1) emphasis upon the child as an individual; (2) recognition of individual differences and the concept of a developmental rather than a selective-elimination approach; (3) use of many sources of information; and (4) use of small-group as well as individual and class learning activity.

In 1958, Ahlers published an article that precisely defined the instructional role of the school librarian in relation to the faculty and administration. In an attempt to permanently banish the idea that course-integrated instruction was to be the "special province of the librarian alone or of the librarian working with the English teacher," Ahlers advocated that principals, teachers, and librarians coordinate their efforts and incorporate library instruction skills into every subject area.[14]

While a cursory interpretation of these educational positions might lead to a conclusion that there had been no change in the instructional role of the school librarian from the early to late fifties, this assumption would prove specious. From 1950 to 1959, the literature indicated that changes were occurring to the extent that school librarians were perceived as being less passive and were responsible for initiating library instruction that was integrated with class work.

Fain, however, in reviewing the literature on this subject discerned what she termed an "undercurrent of disappointment between the idea of the school librarian as being at the hub of a creative instructional program, and the actuality — the school librarian has frequently had only a marginal role."[15] Although proof of this perception is extremely difficult because of lack of concrete support, an examination of research studies may provide further evidence to illuminate the dichotomy that Fain and others perceived in the literature. During the 1950s, several studies concentrated on the instructional role of the school librarian. Romine, in a 1950 study of reports from 340 North Central Association high schools in twenty states, found that the multitude of services performed by a librarian could be classified in eighteen areas.[16] Of these, three were instructional in nature: (1) assisting pupils in use of the library; (2) assisting teachers in using the library; and (3) instructing pupils in library science. Using a rating scale of zero to three, librarians indicated that they gave little attention to activities two and three and some attention and time to activity one. A second aspect of the study concerned the finding that in schools of less than five hundred pupils, librarians had less than a fifty-fifty chance of operating a study hall library. These findings, while disappointing with respect to the instructional role of the librarian, do corroborate several of the articles that were published during the early fifties.

About the same time, Mahar studied fifty New York state school libraries to determine their contribution to curriculum improvement.[17] Her findings indicated that activities relating to traditional concepts of the school library were performed generally by the school librarians, whereas activities implied by recently developed concepts were not performed to any great extent. Librarians served primarily as providers of materials.

In 1955, Voisard studied high schools with an enrollment of more than one thousand and found that while librarians were frequently included in committees for special curriculum projects, they were rarely full participants.[18] These findings seem to verify the climate of the times. Education was just beginning to acknowledge individual learning styles, to provide other sources of materials, and to permit a more active instructional role for the school librarian. A study by Bianchi involved a survey of five thousand teachers in urban secondary schools to identify teacher attitudes toward the school library and the use they made of it.[19] Although some of the results could be termed disappointing in light of the new concepts proposed in the literature for that time, it seems evident from an analysis of the findings that progress had been made. The library was cited by 88.8 percent of the respondents as playing an important role in the total instructional program of the school.

A third source of material that furnishes information about the degree of change includes the pronouncements and standards of state and national library associations and education departments regarding new concepts.

With the introduction of audiovisual materials into the curriculum, the adoption of less traditional subjects, and the abolishment of the library as a study hall, the road was being paved for the concept of the school library as an instructional media center and for a changing instructional role for the school librarian. As early as 1956, the American Association of School Librarians acknowledged this new concept by issuing a statement that defined the role of the school library as a center for print and nonprint instructional materials and that of school librarians as "coordinators, consultants and supervisors of instructional materials on each level of school administration."[20] This official statement by a national organization representing school librarians invested the changes that were slowly taking place in the literature and in libraries with a degree of certainty. They endowed the literature and even future research studies with a framework of acknowledged reality.

THE SIXTIES

In school library development and education in general, the 1960s can be described as a decade of ferment. "Rhetoric and ideas abounded as to what education would do to solve a number of pressing social issues — from integrating the schools racially to promoting a love of reading among the disadvantaged or disinterested."[21] The curriculum became subject to broad interpretation as students evidenced a growing need for all kinds of education and aspired to greater educational achievement. Learning was no longer viewed as a transitory state, but was instead seen as a continuing and lifelong process. Schools introduced a variety of curricular and instructional changes involving such diverse areas as communication arts, citizenship education, vocational education, fine arts, and the humanities. Innovations in methods of instruction included independent study, advanced placement, greater interrelation of subjects, team teaching, special attention to the socially and economically deprived, track system or ability sectioning, selective instruction to curtail dropouts, and expanded block periods for both large- and small-group instruction.

A larger number of children and youths attended school for longer periods of time. Centralization of school districts occurred, which resulted in gained efficiency and versatility. During this period federal funds became available to schools and libraries with the passage of the National Defense Education Act in 1958, the Library Services and Construction Act in 1964, and the Elementary and Secondary Education Act in 1965. Monies became available for the increased purchase of materials other than textbooks.

The changes that occurred in education in the sixties had a definitive impact on the instructional role of the school librarian. The school's new emphasis on "diversified learning materials — both printed and nonprinted — for all subjects and levels of ability" finally brought to school librarians the opportunity for the greater instructional role that had been described by Berger, Davis, Hunt, Henne, and Mahar in the 1950s.[22] The status of the librarian in Davies' glorified words changed from study hall monitor and book curator to "team teacher, learning expediter and media programming educator."[23]

An examination of the library literature published during this period presents a similar picture built upon the sense of optimistic expectation that characterized the times. One of the first library educators to express such assurance in the changing instructional role of the librarian was Grazier. In a futuristic article, she perceived and defined the librarian's instructional role as that of a provider of "expert assistance in the use of materials based on an understanding of the methods, concepts and data in a given field."[24] Although this role was well established in the 1950s, Grazier developed it a step further by advocating the structured use of book talks, which amounted to an integrated schoolwide reading guidance program cooperatively planned by teachers and librarians. The librarian's role in library instruction was solidly based upon course-integrated instruction.

In 1963, Ellsworth and Wagener published a book that graphically depicted the concept of the school library as a teaching laboratory.[25] Organized within the concept of team teaching, they recommended that librarians serve as members of teams and meet with teachers to evaluate instructional programs. Ellsworth and Wagener drew a parallel to a pattern evident in the development of college librarianship, indicating that there appeared to be a ten-year lag between the introduction of a concept and its actualization in the profession. This observation, while somewhat consistent with a comparison of related literature vis-à-vis research studies, is still difficult to prove. Introduction and acceptance of change in the school library seem more dependent upon the speed with which changes occur in society and education.

A further examination of the literature describing the instructional activities during this period indicated that the librarian's instructional role evolved more rapidly than it did in the 1950s. A series of articles published in the *ALA Bulletin* in 1963 illustrated the more active role librarians were taking in the curriculum. The first in the section described a school librarian's opportunity to demonstrate the values of planning assignments for effective use of library resources.[26] The second article featured a demonstration of a library teaching unit in action via closed circuit television,[27] and the last article discussed the library functioning as a "workshop-laboratory" and the librarian serving in a dual capacity of teacher and materials expert.[28]

Although the previous articles furnished definite clues that the instructional role of the librarian was changing from passive to active, there were still several issues of the early sixties that impeded the progress of change. Also prevalent in the literature were articles that weighed the pros and cons of classroom libraries versus central libraries. While this debate might seem irrelevant in light of today's situation, it was a critical factor in the evolution of the instructional role. Librarians experienced great difficulty in coordinating teaching units with faculty who were ensconced in their classrooms with a sufficient collection to continue their own instruction. A second issue pertained to nonlibrarians who accepted the new concept of an instructional materials center, but who could not conceive of a different instructional role for the librarian in that setting. As late as the mid-sixties, publications continued to describe the instructional role of the librarian as one of sophisticated supplier of print and nonprint items rather than an active participant in the educational process.

In that same year, however, a position paper prepared for the Department of Audiovisual Instruction of the National Education Association described the role of the media professional in education in such new terms that its descriptive standard continued to be employed in the seventies and eighties. DAVI perceived the "role of the media professional as changing from that of a keeper and dispenser of teaching aids to that of an analyst and designer of instructional systems who must be centrally involved in the planning of learning environments, and in providing for related support functions and evaluative procedures."[29] It was proposed that the media professional prepare teaching materials, provide in-service education for teachers and administrators in the selection and use of instructional materials and techniques, and assist with the evaluation of the results of the use of instructional materials and technological resources for teaching.

A content analysis of this proposal reveals a significant synapse in the instructional role described in the library activities of the early- to midsixties and the role described by the DAVI definition. Library educators had not yet employed the terms *analyst, designer,* and *preparer* with respect to materials. Articles continued to depict the instructional role of the librarian as a materials specialist who actively served as a "liaison between knowledge about, interest in, and optimum use of materials."[30]

Although the previous analysis of selected literature helps one to understand part of the changing instructional role of the librarian in the 1960s, a survey of research studies performed coincidently reveals a more realistic aspect. Five studies performed in the sixties attempted to clarify or categorize the instructional role of the school media specialist. In 1961, Lohrer received a grant to conduct a nationwide status survey to determine the role of school libraries that functioned as instructional materials centers. In a progress report, Lohrer reported that the integration of the library program into the overall teaching program appeared to be greater in schools where the library served as the center providing all materials.[31] This finding coincided with the development of the media center concept in the early 1960s.

Lane's findings regarding the instructional role of the school librarian in 265 schools in Oregon were somewhat disheartening.[32] Only 53.9 percent of the librarians reported working with teachers in the selection of materials, 22.9 percent helped in planning units of instruction, 42.8 percent provided professional materials, and 37.5 percent introduced new materials through book talks, demonstrations, or displays.

Another research study performed by Gaver in 1969 attempted to identify the variety of services high school media staffs offered their patrons through a survey using a checklist of approximately 280 items. Although the survey represented the opinions of library media specialists and not the faculty or student body, more than 60 percent of those surveyed identified fifteen instructional services offered in their libraries. Among the instructional activities were (1) orientation given to new students; (2) individual and group instruction in the use of the media center; (3) instruction in the use of the center integrated with English classes; and (4) class visits scheduled for supervised reference work in the media center.[33] A study of these services discloses the extent to which the literature published in the sixties mirrored actual library practice. The results of Gaver's research helped to demonstrate that the instructional role of the librarian was still somewhat static. It can be viewed, however, as a positive change from the passive instructional role that typified the school librarian of the 1950s.

The last research effort that illustrated the instructional role of the librarian was the publication of *Occupational Definitions for School Library Media Personnel*, which described the instructional role of the librarian in terms of the following abilities: (1) contributing to collection development; (2) working cooperatively and effectively with the SLMC head, other SLMC staff, and teachers; and (3) teaching students how to use materials and equipment critically and independently. These three competencies may be considered descriptive of the current practice in the leading school libraries during the late sixties. Their perceptions of the nature and scope of the position depicted "an active teaching role in the instructional program of the school through instruction in the effective use of media and equipment."[34]

A third influence that contributed to the changing instructional role for the school librarian was the issuance by the American Association of School Librarians of two sets of standards, another set published by the National Education Association, and several reports and criteria disseminated by national educational groups. All of these recommended the concept of the school library as a media center and espoused a changed role for the librarian.

The first report, published by the National Study of Secondary School Evaluation, expanded the 1960 edition of *The Manual for Evaluative Criteria* to include a means for evaluating the school library as an instructional materials center.[35] In the same year, the American Association of School Librarians issued a set of standards that recommended an overall plan of instruction in which use of materials is fully integrated with classroom work.[36] By 1963, the National Committee of the National Association Project on Instruction entitled *Schools for the Sixties* declared that "in each school system there should be one or more well-planned instructional materials and resource centers ... staffed by persons who are adequately prepared in curriculum and instruction, and in library service, and in audio-visual education."[37]

All of these reports and proclamations indicated that a change in the educational role for the school librarian was being advocated, and, in 1969, the American Association of School Librarians and the Department of Audiovisual Instruction recognized it by issuing a new set of standards. While similar in many ways to the 1960 standards, the new ones described a more unified media concept. References were made to media specialists, and their instructional role involved: "(1) Acting as resource persons in the classroom when requested by teachers; (2) serving on teaching teams; (3) working with teachers to design instructional experiences; (4) working with teachers in curriculum planning; (5) assuming responsibility for providing instruction in the use of the media center; and (6) assisting teachers ... to produce materials which supplement those available through other channels."[38]

The instructional changes mirrored in the 1969 standards and in literature of the sixties were unfortunately not reflected in the actual practice of school librarianship. But change did appear to occur more rapidly, for the reasons previously noted, than during the 1950s. There was a discernible pattern of progress. More school librarians—now called school library media specialists— when not preparing instructional programs, were consulting and cooperatively working with faculty members to supply them with additional materials. The instructional media center concept, if not the media specialist's more integrated role, had been accepted by administrators, faculty, and students.

THE SEVENTIES

If the sixties were described as a time of ferment in education, the seventies were termed a time of action. Crises precipitated by an economic recession and energy shortages emotionally enhanced the criticism of education that had begun as early as 1956 as a reaction to the level of student achievement. Momentous legislation and the social upheaval of the late sixties reduced the autonomy of schools and culminated in a significantly altered educational philosophy. This period witnessed an actual, rather than merely a proposed, change from passive learning on the part of students to an environment in which students and teachers actively participated together in projects and activities that served to convey information previously provided by a textbook or a teacher. The form of change that occurred in approximately one-fourth of the school districts involved the establishment of some type of alternative school.

The diversity associated with the introduction of these programs produced a climate in which the school became increasingly regarded as an agent of change. A watchword for the curriculum was the term "relevancy." The school that had long been viewed in the community as a self-contained and wholly autonomous structure began to be considered more an extension of the community and an institution whose instruction extended beyond the boundaries of school. The democratization of education emerged as part of the search for greater equality and social justice and was apparent in the priority given to education by minority groups and students residing in rural areas.

By the late seventies, however, educational institutions began to encounter opposition to some of their aims and objectives, and pleas were heard for a return to the basics. Accusations were made that schools in search of a philosophy of education were producing a generation of "idea hoppers."[39] The schools responded with a reexamination of their goals and began formulating standards for minimal competencies. As national test scores plummeted, changes were again made in curricula, and schools began to focus on such areas as (1) adaptation to change; (2) development of competencies; (3) problem-solving skills; and (4) use of research skills.

Within this environment of change, the school library finally received assurance that its educational goals and objectives, which in many cases were ahead of the times, were now appropriate. Some of the literature, however, authored by librarians as well as educators, accused school librarians of laboring under several instructional delusions and cast doubt on the ability of librarians to achieve their goals. In 1970, for example, Brickwell persuasively argued that the school was such a "complex system" that librarians could not successfully accomplish the deep intervention associated with the establishment of an instructional role for themselves that involved consultant services and direct instruction.[40] Hannigan informed librarians in 1973 that they were mired in a world of print and that they lacked sufficient knowledge of nonprint materials.[41] A year later, Miller described the instructional goals of media specialists as "curriculum delusions."[42] These criticisms seemed to reflect an evolutionary pattern as librarians reacted to the permanent addition of nonprint materials, their need to instruct, and their desire to participate in the curriculum process. They had to learn how to incorporate audiovisual materials into learning situations at a time when little research guidance was being provided in the literature. They had to devise methods to wean faculty from their classrooms. They had to become fully informed about the total curriculum, rather than just a particular department's wish to create a new teaching unit.

By the midseventies, books such as *Instructional Design and the Media Program* by Hug,[43] *The School Librarian as Educator* by Wehmeyer,[44] *The Learning Center* by Peterson,[45] and *School Library Media Center* by Prostano[46] defined the accepted role of the librarian in education and even provided a series of course-related suggestions for performing that role. As the decade progressed, the literature was characterized by a plethora of scholarly articles that no longer recommended that the instructional role of the media specialist be active. They instead discussed various factors that affected the further development of the educational role.

Grazier, for example, provided the main characteristics of the old and new instructional roles by contrasting the instructional role under which the librarian operated in the sixties with the new role being recommended in the seventies. Grazier defined a "traditional" media specialist as one who offered "story telling, book talks, recreational reading, viewing or listening."[47] Librarians taught library skills, supervised classes when teachers needed planning periods, and provided resources for students pursuing independent study. In the seventies, the media specialist was an integral part of the teaching and learning function and used a variety of strategies to teach students to locate and evaluate resources. They assisted in the design of instructional strategies and offered in-service programs to help teachers produce and use materials.

By the late seventies, most articles and books focused upon the concept of instructional design and the librarian's role in it. In 1979, Chisholm and Ely published a primer on the subject.[48] In it they described the role of the media specialist with regard to instructional design, and they provided a context for considering ID (instructional design) in relation to the school media program.

The publication of this book precipitated a controversy over the definition of the instructional role of the school media specialist. Some members of the profession placed the instructional responsibility of the librarian solely in the realm of ID, while others subsumed the teaching function in a list of general responsibilities. That same year Vandergrift explored the issue in a book entitled *The Teaching Role of the School-Media Specialist*.[49] She defined the school media specialist as a teacher, and she differentiated between the terms *teaching* and *instruction*.

The research studies conducted during this period did not indicate that such a dichotomy between the terms *teaching* and *instruction* was occurring. They did occasionally indicate that a disparity existed between the perceived instructional role of the librarian and the actual role. Several studies also revealed that the perceptions of media specialists were quite different from those held by teachers and administrators. The first nationwide study, conducted by Lacock, found that both teachers and librarians agreed that the media specialist's role should include involvement in instructional design, development, and consultation, and teachers acknowledged their acceptance of such functions.[50] Laresen's study of secondary school principals and media specialists in Utah, however, concluded that each group often disagreed about the appropriate role for the media specialist.[51] Separate studies conducted by Loertscher[52] and Daniel[53] found that the roles of the library and librarian were marginal in the schools. Kerr's study took a different approach and attempted to determine the psychological and sociological characteristics necessary for an acceptance of the changing instructional role of the librarian.[54] Using an exchange resource theory as the study's framework, Kerr surveyed 450 teachers, administrators, and learning resource specialists to determine which characteristics and roles were valued. He found that the most accepted role concerned the provision of informational services.

From 1977 through 1979, several studies conducted by Jones (1977),[55] Rosenberg (1977),[56] Burnell (1978),[57] Teagarden (1978),[58] and Corr (1979),[59] continued to reinforce the fact that librarians were not practicing the new instructional role prescribed for them in the literature. Almost all of the research studies and literature published during this period, however, indicated "an almost obsessive concern by school librarians to prove their instructional worth as teachers."[60] They had a desire to succeed at achieving educational ideas. Nonetheless, a question remains whether the majority of them succeeded in assuming an active, instructional role in the curriculum. Although some of the studies did discern a more active role with respect to providing materials and satisfying the informational needs of students and teachers, the majority found that practitioners were still only marginally involved in the programs of the school and were practicing an instructional role more characteristic of the midsixties. While many school librarians were clearly ahead of teachers and administrators with regard to their expanded role expectations, their achievements generally trailed their instructional aspirations. All of the studies acknowledged an expanded role for the librarian, but only as reflected in the library literature.

Two other types of publications influenced the evolving instrumental role of the librarian during this period. The first type consisted of guidelines and reports issued by state or national agencies. The second type concerned an AASL set of standards published in 1975.

In 1971, *Schools for the Seventies* emphasized the movement toward the "flexible classroom."[61] The published recommendations of the seminar indicated that curriculum was the single most important part of the instructional program and that new applications of existing curricular methods were needed. Accompanying this pronouncement were descriptions of team teaching, differentiated staffing, individually prescribed and programmed instruction, plus modular or flexible scheduling. As chaotic and disorganized as these approaches sometimes were, they helped to break the bonds formed by the single textbook classroom-approach that dominated education during the early fifties and sixties. The changed methods of instruction recommended in this seminar stimulated the appropriate instructional response from many librarians, as was evidenced by a review of the literature. Many, however, possibly because of the problems associated with the perceptions of teachers, students, and administrators, did not change their instructional role, as was evidenced by the numerous research findings.

Two years later, phase 2 of the *School Library Manpower Project* was completed and the results published as *Behavioral Requirements Analysis Checklist*. BRAC identified approximately seven hundred tasks to be performed by the school library media specialist. This list of functions represented the "first attempt to anticipate, and in some instances conceptualize, the functions and tasks of school media specialists...."[62] They provided a sanctioned definition of the instructional role of the school librarian.

In addition to the recommendations and definitions stated in agency reports, quantitative data were still useful for furnishing evidence regarding the need for change. In 1974, the National Center for Educational Statistics surveyed a nationally representative sample of public school media centers.[63] The findings revealed shortages in collections, acquisitions, professional and support staff, and operating expenditures. The negative aspects of the study were subsequently used to stimulate a response from state and local departments of education and helped to focus attention on the need for a new instructional role for the school media specialist. As guidelines, reports, and recommendations were published concerning the instructional role of the school librarian it became apparent to AASL that the 1969 *Standards for School Media Programs* did not discuss it sufficiently.

The American Association of School Libraries responded to the problem by publishing a new set of standards entitled *Media Programs: District and School.*[64] Two functions directly pertained to the instructional role of the school media specialists. The first function, design, advised media specialists to "initiate and participate in curriculum development." The second function, consultation, encouraged media specialists to recommend media applications to accomplish specific instructional purposes. The new set of standards served to elevate the instructional role of the media specialist, and it delineated the requirements for that role. By the midseventies, librarians were provided with an official interpretation of the instructional role they were to play within the educational framework of the school.

By the end of the seventies, the school media specialist's instructional role had evolved in the literature to one of prominence. The research studies, however, demonstrated a fairly consistent pattern indicating that the evolution had not totally occurred. The controversy over the terms *teaching* and *instructional design* were rendered moot by the empirical evidence documenting the fact that librarians were still confronting the more basic questions surrounding the structuring of an educational role in a setting that, in many instances, had not evolved from the methods and curriculum practiced in the 1950s.

THE EIGHTIES

Although the changes that took place from 1980 to 1984 in education cannot be placed in a decade framework, a set of new issues, which were products of the earlier decades, typified the period. During the latter half of the seventies it was expected that more education for more people would solve a multitude of socio-economic problems. By the beginning of the 1980s, however, many people doubted the school's capacity to contribute to these democratic ideals. In 1974, for example, 18 percent of those asked in a Gallup poll to grade their schools gave them an *A*, while 6 percent gave them a *D*. Eight years later only 8 percent were willing to give the schools an *A*, while those believing the schools deserved a *D* had more than doubled to 14 percent.[65] Accompanying the public loss of confidence in the schools was a decline in the "coalition of legislators, educators, parents and others that held the system together and expanded it."[66] The educating functions that were traditionally performed by the home, school, and church changed.

From 1960 until the mideighties, the number of children affected by divorces doubled. Nearly one out of five families is currently maintained by a woman who is either divorced, separated, widowed, or never married. Two-thirds of these mothers work. Although declining enrollment had been a factor in the late seventies, it became a fiscal reality by 1980. Tax revolts began reflecting parents' growing disillusionment with schools and the feelings of people whose children no longer attended school. As education attempted to respond to these major socioeconomic changes, it was confronted with major technological advances. The rapid development of computer technology had a tremendous impact.

While schools valiantly endeavored to maintain themselves within this mercurial environment, educational issues evolved around themes such as "racial equality, the use and abuse of educational technologies, methods used to deal with individual differences in a society becoming increasingly pluralistic, and religion or moral values in education."[67] The approach adopted by many schools to deal with these challenges reflected a swing from the permissive, open, child-centered education to a return to basics and teacher-centered learning. Efforts were undertaken to tighten standards and inform high school students of what was expected of them. A resulting agenda began to form for a reconstruction of schools based upon the gap created by parents' expectations and perceptions.

Within this milieu, school library media specialists continued to forge ahead by publishing a host of books and articles that further defined their instructional role. Monographs such as *The Library Specialist in Curriculum Development*,[68] *The Library Media Program and the School*,[69] and *The School Librarian as Educator*[70] provided practitioners with a philosophical base for their instructional role and pragmatic examples for implementing it.

In 1980, Biggs wrote a proposal for course-related library instruction that entailed the use of undergraduate reference materials at the high school level.[71] A year later, a sophisticated model was published by Johnson, focusing on the librarian's role in instructional design.[72] In 1982, *Wilson Library Bulletin* dedicated an issue to examining the "school library media center's revolutionary past and future."[73] Termed the second revolution, instructional development was defined as a systematic process of designing teaching units for students by a team of professionals that included a teacher and a librarian knowledgeable in instructional technology. Although the terms and process were not new to the 1980s, this article advanced instructional development by producing a well formulated taxonomy.

Although it is evident that instructional design as a new educational role was based on a firm instructional footing, proselytizing articles — especially those by media educators — continued to appear during this period. In 1983, Turner and Naumer provided a guide to instructional design consultation that possessed four levels. Each level represented a graduated level of involvement in recognition of the facts that the ideal was considered "unrealistic" for many library media specialists to achieve immediately.[74] Cleaver also noted a dichotomy between the actual role of the school library media specialists and the one proposed by the profession in publications. Citing research findings from the sixties and seventies that supported her observation, Cleaver recommended that the instructional role of the library media specialist be expanded more slowly in a planned series of steps.[75]

While the instructional role of the school library media specialist from 1980 to 1984 could be characterized as a period of adjustment concerning the implementation of instructional design activities, the introduction of computers presented library media specialists with a new set of problems. By 1983, librarians were attempting to define their instructional role with respect to this new technology in the literature. As was the case with the introduction of audiovisual materials in the 1950s, most of the recommendations at first placed the library media specialist in the role of supplier and passive resource consultant. Finally, in 1984, Troutner devoted a substantial portion of her book to the instructional uses of the computer. From her perspective, the library media specialist was expected to perform an active role to help design teaching units that integrated the computer into the curriculum.[76]

An analysis of the books and articles published during this short period depicts library media specialists who realized that they must retain an active instructional role with teachers and students while simultaneously adding yet another educational dimension to their role. There is evidence that more systematic approaches were being followed for instruction and that library media specialists were being urged to consider their educational role within the framework of the total program.

A review of research studies conducted during the early 1980s netted three major studies relating to the library media specialist's instructional role. In 1981, Staples published the results of a statewide Texas survey of 224 practitioners concerning their skills and attitudes toward instructional design. Her findings confirmed some of the results discovered in studies undertaken during the 1970s, which had indicated that librarians were not as interested in the instructional function as much as administrative management.[77]

Turner's survey of all U.S. accredited library school programs investigated the extent to which students in the master's level school library media program were provided with instructional design competencies. His findings indicated that schools tended to adopt instructional design as a unitary innovation. A substantial number of programs were discovered to require none.[78]

In 1983, a study by Royal used the survey method to question 235 library practitioners in several midwestern states to ascertain whether school library media specialists were really changing their competency in instructional design.[79] Of the twenty competencies tested in the survey, the only ones performed to a significant degree by library media specialists involved the selection of appropriate media for learning activities and the establishment of efficient schedules to ensure the distribution of resources. Respondents did not indicate to a substantial degree that they performed any instructional design competencies.

The conclusions drawn from the previous studies implied that instructional design, while introduced as an officially sanctioned activity by the 1975 standards, was far from a practiced reality as late as 1984. The gap that persisted between the initiation and acceptance of an idea continued to exist.

The guides and reports issued during this period served to alert educators and the public to the plight of education in general, but none referred to the school library media center specifically. In April 1983 a devastating report entitled *A Nation at Risk* was issued that attempted to warn Americans that "our once unchallenged preeminence was being overtaken by competitors throughout our world."[80] Charging that educators had lost sight of their basic purpose, the report cited evidence such as the decline in test scores and science achievement, lower achievement scores in comparison with other countries, and a possible 40 percent functional illiteracy rate. The report recommended that schools establish a foundation of required courses in English, mathematics, science, social studies, and computer science. Although this report did not specifically refer to libraries, the severity of the noted problems brought numerous responses from practitioners, library educators, and related ALA organizations, all of which served to renew the idea that change should occur. The following year the Carnegie Foundation for the Advancement of Teaching issued a similar report on American high schools.[81] While both reports neglected to cite the library per se, there was no doubt that their publication instigated a more thorough examination of the role of the library media program within the overall school framework.

CONCLUSION

It is evident from an analysis of two data sources that an evolution in the instructional role of the library media specialist did occur from 1950 to 1984. A clear pattern of progressive development of the instructional role has persisted in the standards and the literature. The changes in the library media specialist's role from study hall monitor to curriculum designer can certainly be termed substantive. An analysis of research studies, however, indicates a possible time lag between the practiced instructional role of the library media specialist and the one espoused in the literature. In a profession that has undergone such a tremendous amount of change in such a short period of time, this gap is not surprising. Library media specialists should be congratulated that their professional organizations and publications have responded so quickly and positively to the need for change and that they have continued to successfully expand their instructional role within the school of the 1980s.

NOTES

[1] D. P. Ely, "The Role of the School Media Specialist: Some Directions and Choices," *Journal of Research and Development in Education* 16 (November 1, 1982): 35.

[2] P. Wilson, "Librarians as Teachers," *Library Quarterly* 49 (April 1979): 147.

[3] *The Pursuit of Excellence: Education and the Future of America* (Garden City, N.Y.: Doubleday, 1958).

[4] J. B. Conant, *The American High School Today: A First Report to Interested Citizens* (New York: McGraw-Hill, 1959).

[5] S. M. Krentzman, "School Libraries: 1949-1950: A Summary," *Library Journal* 75 (June 15, 1950): 1023.

[6] H. Hunt, "As the Educator Views the Library," *School Activities and the Library* (February 1950): 2.

[7] L. Fargo, *The Library in the School* (Chicago: American Library Association, 1947), 22.

[8] F. Henne et al., *A Planning Guide for the High School Library* (Chicago: American Library Association, 1951).

[9] Ibid., 3.

[10] A. Lohrer, "Introduction," *Library Trends* 1 (January 1953): 261-62.

[11] V. James, "Service at the Secondary Level," *Library Trends* 1 (January 1953): 318-20.

[12] W. L. Davis, "A New Look at School Library Service," *School Activities and the Library* (February 1953): 1-2.

[13] J. M. Goudeau, "Should We Have a Study Hall-School Library Combination?" *Wilson Library Bulletin* 29 (November 1954): 242-43.

[14] E. E. Ahlers, "Developing Library Skills—Whose Responsibility?" *School Activities and the Library* (1958): 1-2.

[15] E. Fain, "The Library and American Education: Education through Secondary School," *Library Trends* 78 (Winter 1978): 344.

[16] S. Romine, "The Job of the High School Librarian," *Wilson Library Bulletin* 24 (May 1950): 676-79.

[17]H. M. Mahar, "Activities and Services of the School Library as Related to Modern Concepts of Its Educational Function" (Master's thesis, Columbia University, 1950), 22, 49-50.

[18]B. W. Voisard, "Library Participation in High School Programs of Curriculum Improvement" (Ph.D. dissertation, University of Southern California, 1955), 116.

[19]E. S. Bianchi, "The School Library—Room for Improvement?" *School Activities and the Library* (1959), 1-2.

[20]J. K. Gates, *Introduction to Librarianship* (New York: McGraw-Hill, 1968), 235.

[21]D. P. Baker, *The Library Media Program and the School* (Littleton, Colo.: Libraries Unlimited, 1984), 21.

[22]Gates, 255.

[23]R. A. Davies, *The School Library: A Force for Educational Excellence* (New York: Bowker, 1969), 24.

[24]M. H. Grazier, "Implications of the New Educational Goals for School Libraries on the Secondary Level," *Library Quarterly* 30 (January 1960): 38.

[25]R. E. Ellsworth and H. D. Wagener, *The School Library Facilities for Independent Study in the Secondary School* (New York: Educational Facilities Laboratory, 1963).

[26]M. H. Grazier, "Beginning with Assignments," *ALA Bulletin* 57 (February 1963): 154-55.

[27]H. H. Bennett, "Demonstrating Library Use to Teachers and Administrators," *ALA Bulletin* 57 (February 1963): 161-62.

[28]R. A. Davies, "Planning Together in the Instructional Materials Center," *ALA Bulletin* 57 (February 1963): 158.

[29]K. Norbert et al., "The Role of the Media Professional in Education," *Audiovisual Instruction* 12 (December 1967): 1027.

[30]American Association of School Librarians, *Realization: The Final Report of the Knapp School Libraries Project* (Chicago: American Library Association, 1968), 3.

[31]A. Lohrer, "School Libraries as Instructional Materials Centers with Implications for Training: A Progress Report of This Study under Title VII, National

Defense Education Act," in *The School Library as a Materials Center*, ed. M. H. Mahar (Washington, D.C.: U.S. Department of Health, Education and Welfare, 1961), 14.

[32]M. B. Lane, "A Study of School Library Resources in Oregon as Compared to State and National Standards" (Ph.D. dissertation, University of Washington, 1966), 211.

[33]M. V. Gaver, *Services of Secondary School Media Centers Evaluation and Development* (Chicago: American Library Association, 1971), 55-56.

[34]School Library Manpower Project, *Occupational Definitions for School Library Media Personnel* (Chicago: American Library Association, 1971), 10.

[35]*Manual for Evaluative Criteria* (Washington, D.C.: National Study of Secondary School Evaluation, 1960), 257.

[36]American Association of School Librarians, *Standards for School Library Programs* (Chicago: American Library Association, 1960), 14, 18.

[37]National Education Association Project on Instruction, *Schools for the Sixties* (New York: McGraw-Hill, 1963), 98.

[38]American Association of School Librarians and the Department of Audiovisual Instruction of the National Education Association, *Standards for School Media Programs* (Chicago: American Library Association, 1969), 8.

[39]M. Sullivan, "The Media Specialist and the Disciplined Curriculum," *Journal of Education for Librarianship* 10 (Spring 1970): 286.

[40]H. M. Brickell, "Implementing Educational Change," *School Libraries* 19 (Summer 1970): 17-18.

[41]D. R. Bender, *Issues in Media Management* (Baltimore, Md.: Maryland State Department of Education Division of Library Development and Services, School Media Services Section, 1973), 11-12.

[42]N. W. Thomason, *The Library Specialist in Curriculum Development* (Metuchen, N.J.: Scarecrow, 1981), 102-6.

[43]W. E. Hug, *Instructional Design and the Media Program* (Chicago: American Library Association, 1975).

[44]L. B. Wehmeyer, *The School Librarian as Educator* (Littleton, Colo.: Libraries Unlimited, 1976).

[45]G. T. Peterson, *The Learning Center* (Hamden, Conn.: Shoe String Press, 1975).

[46]E. T. Prostano and J. S. Prostano, *The School Library Media Center* (Littleton, Colo.: Libraries Unlimited, 1977).

[47]M. H. Grazier, "A Role for Media Specialists in the Curriculum Development Process," *School Media Quarterly* 4 (Spring 1976): 201.

[48]M. E. Chisholm and D. P. Ely, *Instructional Design and the Library Media Specialist* (Chicago: American Library Association, 1979), vi, 3.

[49]K. E. Vandergrift, *The Teaching Role of the School Media Specialist* (Chicago: American Library Association, 1979), 10.

[50]D. W. Lacock, "The Media Specialist and Tasks Related to the Design, Production and Utilization of Instructional Materials" (Ed.D. dissertation, University of Nebraska, 1971) in M. H. Grazier, "The Curriculum Consultant Role of the School Library Media Specialist," *Library Trends* 28 (Fall 1979): 269.

[51]J. A. Larsen, "The Role of the Media Specialist as Perceived by Himself and His Administrator in the Secondary Schools of Utah" (Ed.D. dissertation, University of Utah, 1971) in "The Curriculum Consultant Role of the School Media Specialist," *Library Trends* 28 (Fall 1979): 271.

[52]D. V. Loertscher, "Media Center Services to Teachers in Indiana Senior High Schools, 1972-1973" (Ph.D. dissertation, Indiana University, 1973), 29, 100-10.

[53]E. H. Daniel, "The Organizational Position of School Media Centers: An Analysis of the Role of the School Library and School Librarian" (Ph.D. dissertation, University of Maryland, 1974), 126, 129.

[54]S. T. Kerr, "Are There Instructional Developers in the Schools?" *AV Communication Review* 25 (Fall 1977): 243-67.

[55]C. A. Jones, "The Georgia Public School Library Media Program, 1965-1975" (Ed.D. dissertation, University of Georgia, 1977) in *School Library Media Annual 1983*, ed. S. L. Aaron (Littleton, Colo.: Libraries Unlimited, 1983).

[56]M. J. Rosenberg, "A Study of the Belief System Structure of Principals and Media Specialists as Related to Their Role Expectations for the Media Specialist" (Ph.D. dissertation, Kent State University, 1977) in *School Library Media Annual 1983*, ed. S. L. Aaron (Littleton, Colo.: Libraries Unlimited, 1983).

[57]S. Burnell, "Principals' Perceptions of Actual and Ideal Roles of the School Media Specialist" (Bethesda, Md.: ERIC Document Reproduction Service, 1978), ERIC Document 171321.

[58]M. B. Teagarden, "The Involvement of Library Media Specialists in the Curriculum Development Process in the Public Schools of Alabama" (Ed.D. dissertation, University of Colorado, 1978) in *School Library Media Annual 1983*, ed. S. L. Aaron (Littleton, Colo.: Libraries Unlimited, 1983).

[59]G. P. Corr, "Factors That Affect the School Media Specialist's Involvement in Curriculum Planning and Implementation in Small High Schools in Oregon" (Ph.D. dissertation, University of Oregon, 1979) in S. L. Aaron, "A Review of Selected Doctoral Dissertations about School Library Media Programs and Resources, January 1972-December 1980," *School Media Quarterly* 10 (Spring 1982): 210-45.

[60]D. P. Baker, "The Media Center: A Review Article," *Library Quarterly* 49 (October 1979): 456.

[61]W. T. Greenleaf and G. A. Griffith, *Schools for the 70's and Beyond: A Call to Action* (Washington, D.C.: National Education Association Center for the Study of Instruction, 1971), 54-56.

[62]R. N. Case and A. M. Lowrey, *Behavioral Requirements Analysis Checklist* (Chicago: American Library Association, 1973), ix.

[63]B. Ladd, *National Inventory of Library Needs, 1975: Resources Needed for Public and Academic Libraries and Public School Library Media Centers* (Washington, D.C.: National Commission on Libraries and Information Science, 1977), 107-50.

[64]American Association of School Librarians, American Library Association and Association for Educational Communications and Technology, *Media Programs: District and School* (Chicago: American Library Association and Association for Educational Communications and Technology, 1975), 6-7.

[65]E. L. Boyer, *High School: A Report of the Carnegie Foundation for the Advancement of Teaching* (New York: Harper, 1983), 22.

[66]J. I. Goodlad, *A Place Called School* (New York: McGraw-Hill, 1984), 34.

[67]H. Ehlers, *Crucial Issues in Education* (New York: Holt, 1981), vi.

[68]Thomason.

[69]Baker.

[70]L. B. Wehmeyer, *The School Librarian as Educator* (Littleton, Colo.: Libraries Unlimited, 1984).

[71]M. Biggs, "A Proposal for Course-Related Library Instruction," *School Media Quarterly* 26 (January 1980): 34-37.

[72]K. A. Johnson, "Instructional Development in Schools: A Proposed Model," *School Media Quarterly* 9 (Summer 1981): 256-71.

[73]D. Loertscher, "School Library Media Centers: The Revolutionary Past," *Wilson Library Bulletin* 56 (February 1982): 415.

[74]P. M. Turner and J. N. Naumer, "Mapping the Way toward Instructional Design Consultation by the School Library Media Specialist," *School Library Media Quarterly* 12 (Fall 1983): 36.

[75]B. P. Cleaver and W. D. Taylor, *Involving the School Library Media Specialist in Curriculum Development* (Chicago: American Library Association, 1983), 13.

[76]J. A. Troutner, *The Media Specialist, the Microcomputer, and the Curriculum* (Littleton, Colo.: Libraries Unlimited, 1983), 82.

[77]E. S. Staples, "60 Competency Ratings for School Media Specialists," *Instructional Innovator* 26 (November 1981): 19.

[78]P. M. Turner, "Instructional Design Competencies Taught at Library Schools," *Journal of Education for Librarianship* 22 (Spring 1982): 276-82.

[79]S. Royal, "Instructional Design: Are School Library Media Specialists Really Changing? (Part I)," *Arkansas Libraries* 40 (September 1983): 8-18.

[80]United States Department of Education, *A Nation at Risk: The Imperative for Educational Reform* (Washington, D.C.: National Commission on Excellence in Education, 1983), 5.

[81]Boyer, 302-3.

SCHOOL LIBRARY MEDIA CENTERS
The Revolutionary Past*

David Loertscher

For all the criticism heaped upon American education for adopting this trend or that and seeming to fail in the attempt, one program advance has been notable for its educational riches—the school library media center.

The school library media center, or LMC, is a new concept. If you were alive during World War II, you have lived almost all of the history of the school library media center. True, classroom book collections existed in most schools, and a few book-oriented school libraries did exist in high schools at the turn of the century, but most of these were very limited in their development. Only since 1960 has a new interest in libraries and their role in modern education fostered the concept of the school lilbrary media center.

What is this new concept? Even a simple definition needs to be understood in a historical context to be appreciated fully. Two revolutions in thought should be reviewed. This article and the one on pages 98 through 103 examine the school library media center's revolutionary past and future.

THE FIRST REVOLUTION

The idea of a school library as a repository for books serving as a supplement to children's education was challenged in the years that followed the Second World War. This challenge came from some great revolutionaries in the library and audiovisual fields, who had a vision of what audiovisual materials, equipment, and printed media could do for American education. They saw that all these media could have a center stage in the educational process rather than a supplementary role, and they agreed that the child would be richer educationally for this new experience.

It is interesting to trace the actions of these revolutionaries as they schemed, individually and in groups, to convince educators, parents, the government, and students that the potential of educational media in all its forms was too great to neglect. These great individuals came to their battle stations armed to the hilt with dreams, theories, research findings, persuasive arguments, and a little political know-how.

*From David Loertscher, "School Library Media Centers: The Revolutionary Past," *Wilson Library Bulletin* 56 (February 1982): 415-16. Reprinted by permission of *Wilson Library Bulletin*.

There was Bob Brown, who worked for Encyclopaedia Britannica and who gave hundreds of demonstrations with groups of school children to show how audiovisual media could be utilized to teach concepts that would never be forgotten. There was Frances Henne of Columbia University and Mary Gaver of Rutgers University, who plotted the 1960 *Standards for School Libraries.* There was Margaret Rufsvold at Indiana University, who argued that audiovisual media had a place in school libraries (a concept that was heretical in 1949). There was Carolyn Whitenack of Purdue University, who bridged the gap between librarians and audiovisualists to forge cooperative standards in 1969 and again in 1975. There was James Finn from UCLA, who preached about the impact that instructional technology could have on education. There was Harvey Frye at Indiana University, who taught us that simple and inexpensive local production of audiovisual materials could have a great effect on teaching. All these and more fought, convinced, trained disciples, and forged the concept of the modern school library media center. Most are still living and have seen many of their dreams come to fruition in thousands of schools all over the world.

Like many revolutions, this battle did not produce victories everywhere at once. In the thirty-year war, some schools developed the multimedia philosophy rapidly, others started late and developed over time, and some pockets of resistance still remain today. Recessions have also had an impact on the development of school library media centers, as the intense fight for funds sometimes crushed both plans and LMCs already in existence.

What did these fighters succeed in doing? The list is long. Classroom collections were merged to form centralized collections, and audiovisual media and equipment were purchased. Print collections were improved and made more appealing. Facilities were constructed and remodeled, and professional and clerical staff were employed. New ways of improving the use of these wide-ranging collections were developed. Public relations programs were fostered.

At first, in many schools, efforts to improve the library of books were paralleled with the development of a separate audiovisual center. Some of the most influential revolutionaries, however, saw this split between media as a disaster and advocated that all media should be merged into a single collection administered by a professional who would be known as the library media specialist. Local economics (when a school could only afford to hire a single specialist) and the multimedia concept teamed to make the merged library and audiovisual departments a single entity as a common organizational pattern.

Today there is still a long way to go to establish the library media center idea—a place with a rich collection of media and a full staff of professional, technical, and clerical personnel in every school. The first revolution is not over. It will not be over until the target is reached. Revolutionaries of the first order will be needed for some time to come.

ROLE PROBLEMS

Where do we stand after thirty years of experimentation in school library media centers? While there isn't a single answer to this question, one principle has emerged. We have discovered (as have principals, parents, and students) that collections, staff, and facilities by themselves contribute very little to the educational process. They are resources, not products. An under-utilized library media center is worth very little to anyone and can be a drain on precious tax revenues.

Like all tools, the school library media center can be properly used or it can be misused; it can add or detract from the educational process in a school. As we look into the 1980s, we need to scrutinize our roles carefully—learning from our mistakes and capitalizing on our strengths. What problems need our critical attention?

We have often promoted materials and equipment for their flashiness rather than as the real workhorses of education. We have remained silent while teachers and students have used educational technology only as an entertainment medium rather than as an instructional medium. We have considered ourselves as "enrichment" for the basics rather than as the fodder on which learning can thrive; enrichment, like butter on bread, can be scraped off or done without when times get tough. We have developed curricula of library skills that children neither enjoy nor need when taught in isolation from classroom curricular units; parading children through the library once or twice a week for forty minutes and teaching them a curriculum of our own design that has little relationship to classroom activities is of doubtful worth. We have encouraged the term paper syndrome—an assumption that the library media center exists primarily for research to support only one expression of literary development.

We have developed organizational and clerical chores that take a great deal of time to accomplish; being busy all day can substitute very easily for challenging activities that could contribute to instruction. We have organized rigid schedules, created restrictive rules, and clamped tight disciplinary rules on patrons to the point that our library media centers are empty and we complain about unwilling teachers, disinterested students, and non-supportive administrators. Finally, we have created national standards that are so poorly understood by our colleagues that they are dismissed and ridiculed: for example, what school could even spend the full ten percent of the per-pupil operating cost on media each year?

Perhaps this picture is painted so dismally that the wonderful things we have accomplished are lost in criticism. We have done great things, and a visit to almost any center convinces us of worth. But we also seem to be on a plateau. We should pause to assess our past and paint a new picture so intertwined in the vision of sound educational principles that we become the essential piece of the puzzle we have convinced ourselves we ought to be.

"EXEMPLARY ELEMENTARY SCHOOLS" AND THEIR LIBRARY MEDIA CENTERS

A Research Report*

David V. Loertscher, May Lein Ho, and Melvin M. Bowie

INTRODUCTION AND PURPOSE OF THE STUDY

During the summer of 1986 the U.S. Department of Education published a list of 270 exemplary public and private elementary schools in 49 states.[1] The selection process began the previous year when the department invited all elementary schools in the country to take part in the "Elementary Recognition Program." The competition required schools to nominate themselves by completing a lengthy application form. The competing schools were then visited and screened by state and national teams of educators.

This report examines the status of library media services in the 209 public schools that appeared on the final list. In looking at them, the researchers had a number of questions to pose. Are library media centers in "exemplary" elementary schools exemplary? What "cutting-edge" services and programs do these library media centers provide? What is exemplary about the library media programs in these schools? What services would the library media specialists in these schools like to add or improve? Answers to these questions could suggest workable guidelines for those elementary schools that did not make the 1986 list.

ANTECEDENTS OF THE STUDY

The current study has been preceded by a number of research projects spanning thirteen years. The first, conducted by David Loertscher in 1973, examined the services of high school library media programs in Indiana senior high schools. He found that most school media specialists had yet to assume a partnership with teachers in improving their schools' instructional programs.[2]

A second related study, conducted by Loertscher and P. Land in Indiana elementary schools in 1976, found that full-time media specialists provided significantly more services than did either part-time professionals or full-time clericals.[3] In addition, the researchers learned that traditional rather than innovative services were being offered in the schools examined.

J. Stroud replicated the Loertscher/Land research and found that in middle schools only one-third of the media specialists took an active role in instructional planning.[4] In a 1985 published review of research, Gerald C. Hodges concluded that "the frequency with which the school library media specialist assumes an active role in curriculum and instruction is directly related to the size of the media staff."[5]

S. Aaron's annual reviews of research have pointed out the importance of media services and professional staff to the overall quality of school programs.[6] Further efforts by one of the authors of this report have also shown that both size and quality of library media staff have been major factors in the variety and frequency of library media center services.

METHODOLOGY

This study's population comprised the 209 public schools of the 270 elementary schools recognized as exemplary by the U.S. Department of Education in 1986. Forty-nine of the fifty states were represented (Arkansas was not). The researchers designed nineteen statements on library media services using PSES, Loertscher's LMC Taxonomy,[7] the current literature, and the researchers' own knowledge and experiences in the field.[8] The items on the questionnaire covered four categories of services: (a) instructional development services to teachers, (b) other important services to teachers, (c) services to students, and (d) collections. Three open-ended questions were also asked:

1. What do you think is the best part of your LMC program?

2. If you had your wish, what would you add or emphasize in your program?

3. What do you need most to implement your wish?

The questionnaire was pretested by school library media specialists and a panel of experts in the field. The questionnaire was then revised, printed, and mailed to the schools the last week of August 1986.

Of the 209 questionnaires mailed, 147 were returned. Of those returned, only one was rated unusable for a net response rate of 70%. Two more questionnaires were returned after the response deadline and were not included in the analysis.

ANALYSIS OF THE DATA

Figure 1 (pages 70-71) summarizes the important demographic data on the participating schools.

Student Enrollment

The smallest school had only 173 students, while the largest school had 1,300 students. About half (48%) of the schools had student bodies of less than 500. Almost one-third (29%) of the schools reported minority enrollments of less than 5%, and only 11% of the respondents said that minorities comprised more than 50% of their student bodies. Almost half (46%) of the respondents reported that most of the students in their schools came from affluent or above-average-income homes. Only 4% of them considered that most of their students were from poor homes. These data strongly suggest that the enrollment of the schools in the study could be primarily classified as mostly white students from middle- to upper-middle-class homes.

Spending

According to figure 1, money spent on library media materials in almost half (43%) of the schools has remained steady over the past five years. However, 44% of the schools experienced spending increases during that same period, and 13% reported moderate to major decreases. It appears that the exemplary schools, to a large extent, have been faring somewhat better than most other schools with regard to maintaining and improving expenditures for library media programs. This conclusion is also supported by the fact that 47% of the respondents reported that their schools could be considered above average in "affluence" or money available for school programs.

Category	Average	Std. Dev.
Students and Faculty		
Number of students	549	225
Number of faculty	29	12
Percent of minority students	22	27
Staff of the Library Media Center		
FTE library media professionals	.78	.39
Average number of years experience (professional)	7	5
FTE clerical staff	.59	.61
FTE adult volunteers	.33	.45
Total FTE staff	1.71	.80

Spending
Spending for library media materials over the past five years:
13% — major increase (more than 10% per year)
31% — moderate increase (5-10% per year)
43% — steady
8% — moderate decrease (5-10% per year)
5% — major decrease (more than 10% per year)

Affluence
The school could be considered:
7% — affluent
40% — above average
40% — average
12% — below average
1% — poor

Family Income
Family income for these schools:
14% — affluent
32% — above average
36% — average
14% — below average
4% — poor

Fig. 1. Profile of exemplary schools.

Staffing

Figure 2 shows that of the 146 schools in the present study, less than half (43%) had a full-time professional and at least one clerk. It was disappointing to see that a fifth of the schools had only part-time professional help and another 12% were totally without the services of a professional staff. One school in the study had no library media center and reported that it relied on classroom collections supplemented by materials from the local public library.

Category	Number	Percentage
Schools with full-time professionals and clerks	63	43
Schools with full-time professionals and no clerks	38	26
Schools with part-time professionals and clerks	23	16
Schools with part-time professionals and no clerks	4	3
Schools with no professionals	17	12
Schools with no library media center	1	
Total	146	100

Fig. 2. Personnel distribution.

The overall staffing patterns in the exemplary schools are somewhat disappointing. Because research has shown that professional staffing is critical to the overall excellence of library media programs, one would have expected that in schools designated as excellent there would have been more with full-time library media professionals.

Services

A school library media center exists to support and carry out the school's curriculum. In order to accomplish this, a number of important services must be rendered. These include more than just the traditional "warehousing" activities. A library media specialist must be a visible and forceful agent to meet the demands of a particular curriculum, a teaching staff, and a unique group of students. How often, then, are the exemplary schools providing those services deemed critical to an effective school program?

The major part of the questionnaire dealt with nineteen "cutting-edge" or critical services. The frequency with which each service is currently offered was rated by the library media specialist as either regularly, occasionally, or rarely or never performed. Figure 3 provides the percentages of schools offering each of these nineteen services.

Item	Regularly	Occasionally	Rarely or Never
A. Instructional Development			
The library media staff assists teachers in unit planning by:			
1. gathering materials	90%	7%	3%
2. helping formulate lesson objectives	61%	27%	12%
3. consulting in advance of unit presentation	47%	43%	10%
4. teaching a library/information or production skill connected with the unit	46%	38%	16%
5. carrying out an instructional activity connected with the unit	31%	49%	20%
6. consulting with curriculum/textbook selection committees	29%	25%	46%
7. helping evaluate the success of the unit	10%	32%	58%
B. Other Services to Teachers			
8. Teachers check out materials for temporary classroom collections	90%	9%	1%
9. In-service training is given to teachers in materials, equipment, computers or other methods of using the LMC	37%	43%	21%
C. Services to Students			
10. Reading and telling stories to students are provided	89%	6%	5%
11. Literature promotion activities (book tales, reading contests, special reading activities, reading guidance) are offered	85%	14%	1%
12. Special programming events take place (book fairs, celebration of National Library Week, author visits, local celebrations, etc.)	73%	25%	1%
13. Students pursue individualized activities in addition to classroom group activities in the LMC	62%	28%	10%
14. Information or materials are provided to students from sources outside the LMC	36%	41%	23%
15. Students produce audiovisual media in the LMC	10%	29%	61%
E. Collections			
The library media collection provides:			
16. a variety of print and AV media for instruction	94%	3%	3%
17. quality materials	92%	7%	1%
18. up-to-date materials	88%	12%	0%
19. enough materials for the number of users	77%	22%	1%

Fig. 3. Services provided by the Library Media Specialists.

Instructional Development. The analysis of the data concerning instructional development is good news indeed. According to the current data, the ten-year effort to encourage library media specialists to become more heavily involved in curricular matters is now beginning to pay off. Although most studies have shown little interest on the part of library media specialists in engaging in instructional development, and many have been quite negative about the role, these data suggest that, while much progress is still needed, inroads are being made toward changing the role of the library media specialist in the schools.

Forty-seven percent of the respondents in this study indicated that they regularly consult with teachers in advance of unit presentations, and 10% conduct exit evaluations with the teachers. These two factors are keys to progress in enlarging the instructional role of media specialists in the schools. Library educators in schools of library science and colleges of education need to concentrate on teaching practical methods for instructional involvement until these skills become second nature to prospective school library media specialists.

Other Services to Teachers. Classroom collections have been praised on a number of occasions. However, these have been replaced in the U.S. largely by centralized collections. The question then arose, "Do teachers still have access to classroom collections?" Happily, the data show that all of the library media specialists, to some extent, still provide temporary classroom collections in addition to maintaining centralized collections. Ninety percent of the respondents reported that they do this on a regular basis. Indications are that many teachers in the exemplary schools enjoy flexibility in using media center materials for instruction. Perhaps materials exist in these schools in sufficient number and variety to satisfy changing curricular needs.

The data also indicate that elementary school library media specialists are very much aware of the need for in-service training for teachers in effective use of the materials and services that are being offered. More than a third of the respondents regularly provide in-service training in the use of materials and equipment (including computers) for teachers. Another 43% do so occasionally.

Services to Students. Interaction with literature appears to be a popular service to children in the exemplary schools, and rightly so. Storytelling, reading activities, and special programming were reported to be regular service features by 89% of the respondents. The researchers also wondered to what extent library media centers provided opportunities for students to interact individually with materials other than those needed for class assignments. Only 62% claim this as a regular feature of programming, which seems low. The researchers suspect that the dogmatic emphasis on teaching library skills has had an undesirable effect on this critical service, although evidence for this was not specifically examined. If such is the case, then library media specialists in exemplary schools, along with their counterparts in other schools, must be convinced of the value of individualized student use of media centers and libraries so that we may produce lifelong learners. More research in this critical area of library media services in "good" schools is suggested.

It was a surprising disappointment that only 10% of the media specialists allow students to produce audiovisual media in the library media center on a regular basis. Progress toward the multimedia concept has certainly been made, but direct student involvement in the process still has a long way to go before it reaches the desired level. Perhaps the often-cited use of student-produced media to motivate students to participate in their own learning is still one of the best-kept secrets of the library media program. Again, there appears to be a critical need in the field to convince library media specialists of the long-term benefits of this vital service.

Collection as a Service. The questionnaire contained four items concerning the library media specialists' overall perceptions of the quality of their collections. The ratings for variety, general quality, currency, and quantity of materials showed a progressive decline, from 94% to 77%, among respondents who could regularly boast about the materials being offered to clients. However, on examining the data from the three open-ended questions (figure 4, pages 76-77), there appeared to be some discrepancy between the ratings on service items and the open-ended comments. In case after case, library media specialists would mark 3 (regular) for each of the four collection items but complain that their collections were out-of-date and lacking in quantity. In this case, the researchers decided that the open-ended comments more nearly reflected the truth of the matter and not the data from the four questions concerning collections. This view has some support, however weak, from the data on the collection items. The researchers are now collecting more extensive data concerning collections from these and other schools, and these data should provide a basis for more extensive analysis.

Predicting Service in Library Media Centers

A total score for the frequency of services was computed for each school (respondents indicated frequency on a scale from 3 to 1, regularly to rarely or never). This score (a minimum of 19 and a maximum of 57) was entered into a regression model to be compared to

- Size of faculty
- Size of library media staff (FTE professionals, FTE clericals, and FTE adult volunteers)
- Number of students in the school
- Spending for library media materials
- Affluence of the school
- Family income
- Experience of the library media specialist

The following were significant at the .05 level:

- Affluence of the school
- Family income
- Number of professional library media specialists
- Total size of the library media staff

This means that a greater variety of library media services can be predicted in the more affluent communities and in schools with larger library media staffs. Such a finding replicates earlier studies in the field. It is simply a matter of parents in more affluent communities demanding and paying for more educational services for their children.

Open-Ended Questions

The library media specialists were asked to respond to three questions:

1. What do you think is the best part of your LMC program?
2. If you have your wish, what would you add or emphasize in your program?
3. What do you need to implement your wish?

A content analysis of the comments was made utilizing the Appleworks spreadsheet. As the researchers read each comment, categories of responses were set up as a row on the spreadsheet, and the number of times those comments were made was recorded in columns corresponding to the type of staffing pattern of the library media center. Figure 4 shows the spreadsheet, which includes the researchers' comments for each category.

Possibly the responses made by library media specialists in the open-ended section were influenced by the nineteen items they had just answered. This point of view can be interpreted both positively and negatively—either the previous answers reminded the respondents of their best and their worst program features or the items unduly influenced their responses. Nevertheless, there were sufficient independent answers to convince the researchers of the value of these data.

The open-ended comments revealed that there was a significant difference between the comments of full-time library media specialists who had full-time clericals and those who worked part-time and/or had no clerical help. This led the researchers to conclude that there is a threshold in library media staffing below which the effectiveness of programs cannot be maintained. It was reasoned that because all library media centers have a very heavy burden of warehousing functions, the full-service program cannot emerge until the staffing threshold of a full-time professional and a full-time clerical is met or exceeded.

This conclusion was influenced by both the tone and the substance of comments. A careful reading of the open-ended comments reveals that library media specialists with a full-time clerical were more enthusiastic, more positive, and more confident than their counterparts with less staff. This was further supported when the researchers did a content analysis of the open-ended comments. The topics discussed as strengths and weaknesses by those with full staffs and those without differed significantly.

Full-time library media specialists with full-time clericals reported the following as their best program features:

1. Support of administration and teachers—42%
2. Literature-based activities—38%
3. Instructional development—31%
4. Individualized help for students—22%
5. Support of the curriculum—25%

Library Media Specialists Are Most Proud Of:

	(N=32) Full-time Prof. + Full-time Clerk	(N=31) Full-time Prof. + Part-time Clerk	(N=38) Full-time Prof. + No Clerk	(N=27) Part-time Prof. with/without Clerk	(N=18) No Prof.: Full/Part-time Clerk	Comments on the Data by the Researchers
Support						
1. Support of administration and teachers	41%	10%	13%	12%	17%	Notice the difference when the LMC has a full staff
2. Support of parents	2%	3%	11%	15%		Support of parents is erratic across schools
Services to Students						
1. Literature-based activities	38%	42%	50%	27%	33%	Important component for all schools
2. Individualized help given students	22%	6%	5%	8%	22%	Note the rapid decline as staff decreases
3. A conducive atmosphere for students	16%	13%	18%	23%	11%	Consistent efforts are made
4. Library skills (isolated)	16%	32%	21%	19%	6%	Much too high in all schools
5. Library skills (integrated)	6%	16%	5%	8%		Too low, considering the encouragement in the literature
Services to Teachers						
1. Instructional development	31%	16%	13%	8%		Note how this vital service fades as staff does
2. Support of curriculum	25%	16%	11%	12%		Fades out of existence as staff does
3. Flexible scheduling	12%	29%	21%	8%		Those who have it, like it
4. Regularly scheduled classes	6%	6%	11%	8%		These persons feel that they reach all students
Other Services						
1. A carefully selected collection	19%	10%	16%	8%	17%	The materials they do have are quality items
2. A multimedia catalog	6%		3%			Shows the effort toward a multimedia center
3. The amount of items circulated	3%		5%			Circ. is not a revealing eval. measure
4. Educational television service	3%				6%	Several noted their great service in this area
5. AV production services			3%			Not nearly as high as one would suppose
6. Computers for students		3%	3%	4%		A number had become centers for inst. computing
7. Learning centers			11%			The service is popular with some LMS
8. Networking with other libraries					6%	Not nearly as high as it should be
9. Special events			24%	4%		Those pressed for time tend to try this approach
Administrative Components						
1. The contribution of automation	6%	3%	3%		6%	Those who have automated laud its contribution
2. The difference clerical help makes	6%	6%	6%	6%		Grateful people
3. Enough staff to differentiate tasks	6%		3%			Understand that full staffing gives possibilities
4. An adequate facility						A surprise even with declining enrollments

Library Media Specialists Feel That the Following Would Be the Most Important Additions to Their Program:

						Comments
Services to Students						
1. More literature activities	12%	13%	11%	4%	11%	Much more could be done
2. Add student AV production	3%	16%	3%	4%		This highly motivating learning strategy would help
3. More independent help for students		10%	3%			LMS give up as staff declines
Services to Teachers						
1. More instructional development	9%	6%	18%	8%	11%	LMS realize that this is a primary goal
2. Implement a flexible schedule	9%	10%	16%	12%	17%	Those who don't have it dream of having it
3. Provide more inservice	6%	3%	3%			Teachers need more training to use media
Other Services						
1. Provide computer services	6%	3%	3%	4%		Some would like to be leaders in this technology
2. Increase AV services	3%	3%	3%	4%		Some haven't made it into the multimedia center
3. Collection renewal	3%	26%	23%	15%	22%	An important factor for national attention
4. Provide summer hours	3%	3%	3%			These people hate to see gains lost
5. Teach more library skills		3%	6%	8%	11%	Some realize they don't have time to teach skills
6. Set up learning centers			3%			
Administrative Components						
1. More time to act as a professional	19%		26%	77%	56%	A dramatic plea for help to become excellent
2. Money	12%	35%	21%	62%	28%	They know what they would spend it on
3. A larger staff (usually clerical)	6%	32%	21%	27%	17%	Clericals are in short supply
4. More space	6%	19%	16%	23%	6%	Program suffers when space is limited
5. More equipment	3%		11%	12%		Requests came from poorer schools
6. Just more time!	3%	23%	3%	4%		A never-ending battle
7. Need a district LMC coord.				4%		Frustration with the administration
8. Automate to provide more professional time	9%	19%	16%		16%	The hope of those lacking help
9. Add more volunteers	6%	3%	5%		6%	Even fully staffed LMCs wanted more
10. Move AV materials to library						

Fig. 4. Open-ended questions.

In contrast, library media specialists without full staffs rated the same five services as follows:

1. Support of administration and teachers — 13%

2. Literature-based activities — 38%

3. Instructional development — 7%

4. Individualized help for students — 5%

5. Support of the curriculum — 9%

Note that literature activities are equal in the two groups but that instructional involvement and help for individual students drop off significantly when staff is reduced.

The second and third questions in the open-ended section of the questionnaire asked what improvements the library media specialists wanted to make. Full-time library media specialists spread their comments across many concerns, the highest being simply more money (19%). Those without full staffs wanted collection renewal, more time to act as a professional, money, larger clerical staffs, more time, more space, and more automation. Such a pattern of responses shows one group almost searching for things to want and the other seeking to keep their heads above water. They realize that most of their problems stem from too many things to do and not enough people to do them.

MAJOR FINDINGS

Staffing

There seems to be a threshold at which the library media program begins to pay the kinds of dividends expected from the investment made in it. This threshold is a staff consisting of a *full-time professional and a full-time clerical person*. This finding was not only statistically significant but was the single most important variable in an excellent library media program. Having a fine facility stocked with ample materials and equipment is essential, but without the critical staffing component, services suffer and the impact on education is drastically lowered. A library media center has such a heavy warehousing function that a professional without full-time assistance gets bogged down in the clerical burdens of the center. A sound analogy seems to be that a library media center without a full staff component suffers the same way a school would without a full-time principal who has full-time clerical assistance.

Evidence is as follows:

- The FTE number of professional library media specialists predicts the frequency of "cutting-edge" services. (Multiple regression comparison $P < 0.0001$)

- The FTE number of total staff (professional, clerical, plus adult volunteers) predicts the frequency of library media services. (Multiple regression comparison $P < 0.0002$)

Services to Students

1. Activities designed to increase enjoyment of literature and to promote reading are the bedrock of the elementary school library media program. These activities range from storytelling and reading guidance to major special events involving the entire school and community. This function is consistent across all schools with all types of staffing patterns.

2. Library media specialists make a great effort to provide a conducive atmosphere for children to interact with literature and a wide range of reference and audiovisual materials.

3. In the best library media programs, children receive individualized attention as they interact with literature and find and use materials to help them in their studies.

4. Library skills are taught regularly but are not always integrated into the curriculum of the school.

Services to Teachers

1. Working with teachers to deliver more effective instruction using the resources of the media center is a strong component of fully staffed centers. This component, known as instructional development, declines as personnel are reduced. Library media specialists in understaffed programs recognize that they should be offering this service regularly.

2. Integrating the materials of the media center into the curriculum is a strong feature of fully staffed programs, but this service fades as staffing is reduced.

3. The meshing of instruction with library media materials occurs where flexible schedules allow for daylong access by individuals, small groups, and large groups to the center. In schools where library media specialists are locked into heavily scheduled days or do not have adequate staff, flexibility and more staffing to make it work are major dreams.

Resources and Operations

1. While many library media specialists are proud of their collections of materials, the majority realize that it is time for a massive effort to *renew the collections* of the school libraries of the nation. The major spending of the 1960s, coupled with the inflation and declining budgets of the 1970s, has created a problem in supplying materials for budding readers and researchers.

2. Support of administrators, teachers, and parents is recognized as an outstanding requisite of excellence in fully staffed library media programs.

3. Full-time library media specialists who lack sufficient clerical assistance hope that automation will provide them with more professional time to interact with students and teachers.

4. Most library media specialists agree that money is desperately needed to improve their programs, and they have very specific plans for those funds, should they be forthcoming.

5. Many library media specialists recognize that their programs suffer because of a lack of space. Crowding is the damper on simultaneous literary activities, student research, and private individual reading or enjoyment. This is true particularly in centers where the bulk of the library day is scheduled with class groups.

Excellent Schools,
Excellent Library Media Programs

The study shows that while not all the "excellent" schools had excellent library media programs, there was a definite overlap of the two concepts.

In schools with mediocre to poor library media programs, the question must be asked: How could a school having inadequate library media service pass through the process of self-nomination and screening at state and national levels and still be considered excellent? Informal feedback from a number of sources indicates that the process may have been somewhat flawed. Nevertheless, the schools in this group have provided a fascinating look into the programs of library media centers.

RECOMMENDATIONS

Based on the findings of this study, the following recommendations are made to administrators, boards of education, parents, and governments seeking to have library media center programs make a significant impact on education.

Inputs

1. While a spacious and attractive center stocked with well-chosen materials is essential, a full-time library media specialist with full-time clerical assistance is necessary if the investment is to pay maximum dividends.

2. It is possible to blunt the impact of the library media center if massive rigid scheduling and time-consuming "courses of library skills" are taught. As one person recently noted, "The children in my school are forced to spend more time learning library skills than I spent getting a master's degree in library science!"

3. Since the U.S. school library media collections are in desperate need of a massive collection-renewal effort, a good rule for spending would be

a. Budget an amount equivalent to *two* books per student. This amount, if spent on all materials, should be sufficient to keep collections current.

b. Require that the materials purchased be focused on supporting specific curricular goals and on providing a flood of good literature of interest to the students in the schools.

Expectations for Impact

To maximize the impact on elementary education, the best advice is to hire a full-time library media staff, provide a flexible schedule, and install a program emphasizing the following prioritized program services:

1. A rich, literature-related program that promotes the enjoyment of reading.

2. A partnership with teachers in a program of instructional development.

3. An emphasis on individual assistance to learners who are using materials.

4. A creative use of new materials, technology, and methods for making the resources of the library media center the core of instruction—not an appendage to it.

5. Library skills programs as a supporting corollary to the above program features rather than the main focus of activity.

NOTES

[1]"They Made the Grade," *USA Today*, July 1, 1986, sec. D.

[2]D. Loertscher, "Media Center Services to Teachers in Indiana Senior High Schools, 1972-1973" (Ph.D. dissertation, Indiana University, 1973).

[3]D. Loertscher and P. Land, "An Empirical Study of Media Services in Indiana Elementary Schools," *School Media Quarterly* 4, no. 1 (1975): 8-18.

[4]J. Stroud, "Evaluation of Media Center Services by Media Staff, Teachers, and Students in Indiana Middle and Junior High Schools" (Ph.D. dissertation, Purdue University, 1976).

[5]G. Hodges, "School Libraries and the Media Program," in *ALA Yearbook*, v. 10 (Chicago: American Library Association, 1986), 254-55.

[6]S. L. Aaron and P. Scales, *School Library Media Annual*, v. 1 (Littleton, Colo.: Libraries Unlimited, 1981).

[7]D. Loertscher and J. Stroud, *PSES: Purdue Self Evaluation for School Media Centers* (West Lafayette, Ind.: Purdue Research Foundation, 1976).

[8]D. Loertscher, "The Second Revolution: A Taxonomy for the 1980s," *Wilson Library Bulletin* 56 (1982): 417-21.

ADDITIONAL READINGS

Callison, Daniel. "School Library Media Programs and Free Inquiry Learning." *School Library Journal* 32 (February 1986): 20-24.

Considine, David. "Media, Technology, and Teaching: What's Wrong and Why?" *School Library Media Quarterly* 13 (Summer 1985): 173-82.

Kuhlthau, Carol Collier. "Student Learning Styles: Implications for the School Library Media Specialist." In *School Library Media Annual*, v. 5. Shirley Aaron and Pat Scales, eds. Littleton, Colo.: Libraries Unlimited, 1987.

Vandergrift, Kay E., and Jane Anne Hannigan. "Elementary School Library Media Centers as Essential Components in the Schooling Process." *School Library Media Quarterly* 14 (Summer 1986): 171-73.

Part 2
School Library
Media Programs: Rationale

While the instructional development role of the library media specialist was extensively written about during the 1970s, the translation of instructional development to models that actually describe the process in school library media centers didn't occur until the 1980s.

This section begins with a look back at James Liesener's description of a user services model of the role of the school library media program. Liesener's focus on services shifted the view of the function of the media center away from the traditional one of providing resources. He categorizes services in terms of access, reference, production, instruction, and consulting. This classification provides the foundation for the instructional role of the school library media specialist.

In their articles, David V. Loertscher, and Philip M. Turner and Janet N. Naumer explain further the consulting and instructional role of the school library media professional by describing levels of service. Loertscher provides a developmental taxonomy as a guide to media specialist's involvement in instruction. His description of involvement moves from no involvement at level one, through informal and formal interactions with teachers, to instructional design and participating in evaluating students at levels nine and ten, culminating in curriculum development. Level eleven describes the role of the media specialist in the planning and structure of what actually will be taught. While acknowledging that the media professional functions at every level at some point with every teacher, Loertscher builds a rationale for media specialists moving to more complete instructional involvement at higher levels.

Using a traditional instructional design model, Turner and Naumer describe four levels of performance for school library media specialists ranging from no involvement (as in Loertscher) through passive, reactive, to active participation. In contrast to the integration emphasized by Loertscher, the examples in this article place a heavy emphasis on staff development and in-service. This emphasis is of value to individuals just beginning to implement a partnership in instructional design with teachers. The examples show how school library media specialists participate in the ID (instructional development) process through the active and passive interactions that occur in virtually every media center every day. The article also includes an instructional design assessment chart (IDAC) for media specialists to use to chart their levels of involvement.

Ken Haycock's position paper describes the role of the "teacher-librarian" in curriculum planning and integration of learning resources into the curriculum. He sees information skills as a developmental process and provides the psychological principles underlying a developmental skills program. Using practices in her media center, Carol-Ann Haycock outlines a three-phase implementation plan. Starting by assessing the current situation, the media specialist then defines roles and establishes guidelines, finally becoming high profile through communication and by being accountable. Her practical approach recognizes that instructional development begins slowly with one teacher, one grade level, finally leading to total school curriculum planning.

This section ends with a philosophical statement. Set in the context of quality education and prepared by the Learning Resources Council of the Alberta (Canada) Teachers' Association, the statement describes the need for information utilization skills now and in the future. This philosophical statement provides a model for media specialists to use to chart their own courses.

A USER SERVICES MODEL OF THE ROLES OF SCHOOL LIBRARY MEDIA PROGRAMS*

James Liesener

It doesn't take much of a perusal of the literature to discover a diverse and rather confused panoply of perceptions of the roles and functions of school library media programs. This confusion and total lack of consensus creates a serious problem in attempting to develop programs. The question at this point is what role is necessary and what functions need to be performed by library media programs considering the view of the information world and the requisite learning needs described previously.

The older concepts of passive culture repositories or centers for the development of an enjoyment and appreciation for reading good books while identifying very important functions, do not appear to be actively responsive to the entire range of needs identified as crucial for survival and achievement in an extremely complex, information abundant and rapidly changing world.

The level of expectation that is satisfied with a nice and genteel but fairly superfluous resource is no longer relevant or appropriate. The value and utility of information of all kinds has become much more visible and appreciated and it appears that an expectation of a more active and a broader approach to providing information services is developing. It would seem that if we are serious about the learning needs of children in our society, a quantum leap is not only required of what we expect of educational agencies generally but also in terms of what we expect of the sophistication and contribution of such a key ingredient as the information intermediary and information laboratory. The development of higher level intellectual and problem solving skills can only be developed in an environment where they can be repeatedly applied and tested throughout the learner's school experience. The cumulative effect of many of these kinds of experiences is what leads to the development of a self-directed learner able and motivated for lifelong learning. This kind of information learning laboratory requires a level of sophistication and responsiveness far beyond the current service level of "materials availability" combined with the possibility of some limited assistance.

A great deal of progress has been made in the past decade in providing organized and carefully selected collections. The various federal programs that

*Reprinted with permission from James Liesener, "A User Services Model of the Roles of School Library Media Programs," *School Learning Resources* 5 (Spring/Summer 1986): 24-27. Copyright © 1986 by the Association for Educational Communications and Technology, 1126 16th Street N.W., Washington, DC 20036.

followed the launching of Sputnik in 1957 provided some of the funds and the stimulation that led to the rapid growth in the 60's and 70's. However, this did not result in a well-stocked library media center in every school or the kind of staffing that could provide the services required to serve the needs even as they were defined during those times. Of course the 80's have seen a decline in staff and collection budgets as well as buying power due to declining enrollments, inflation and Proposition 13-like tax limitations. As a result, we have been losing ground at a time when we need to expand and refine the kinds of services we provide to meet the new and expanding learning needs of an information society.

What then is the role of school library media programs in fostering the development of young people who are capable, uninhibited, willing and yearning to deal with the ideas, aspirations and problems of humankind? Our philosophy has always included the goal of nurturing a lifelong inquisitiveness and a comfortableness both with ideas and the variety of media that present these ideas. We believe that knowledge, understanding, appreciation and skills in the critical and discerning use of information in its different forms are fundamental to a democratic society as well as to effective functioning in an information world. A much greater emphasis however needs to be placed on developing an analytical posture toward ideas and the capability of critically evaluating information from different perspectives. It is also important for students to develop an interest and positive attitude toward the vehicles that express ideas if a lifelong positive relationship with ideas and information is to be achieved. The independence of mind that comes with a personal and free interaction with ideas also kindles the kinds of appreciations and understandings that permit the enjoyment of the subtleties of life and the aesthetic aspects of our world.

THE PRIMARY ROLE — MEDIATION

The primary role performed by the school library media specialist or program can be viewed as a mediation role or function. From this perspective, the specialist plays the role of an intermediary between the incredibly complex and rapidly expanding information world and the client. In this sense, the library media specialist is no different than a librarian or information specialist in any other environment. It is the particular environment and the particular needs of the clients served that provides the special focus. Obviously, the environment in this case is the school and the clients are the students, teachers, school staff and, at times, parents.

The concept of intermediary implies that some assistance is frequently required for clients or users to effectively and efficiently interact with the information world. The term information is used here in its broadest sense to include all representations of ideas, including the arts, and in any media format. Assistance is used to indicate anything from a little help to higher level services such as formal instruction, assessing and interpreting information needs, stimulating interest, and actually providing the information in some cases.

The information revolution has provided us with an almost unbelievable array of information options. This information world is incredibly large and complex and in spite of the advances in information technology and the much greater potential access this provides us, the need for an intermediary to assist in achieving effective access to this information world has become more apparent. Even though the microcomputer technology particularly has made direct access possible to considerable quantities of information for many users, the need for an intermediary is still vital for most users and at times probably for all users.

The school library media specialist performs this intermediary function for the purpose of facilitating the achievement of learning and instructional objectives. This intermediary function is performed in quite a number of different ways which need to be clearly articulated if users are to understand and use these services effectively.

USER SERVICES MODEL OF ROLES

It is critical at this time to have a clear and comprehensive concept of how school library media programs are adapting to the new information technology but even more important how they are refining their roles in relation to the changing needs of the education community. The abstract and ambiguous conceptions of the past are not sufficient.

The conception of the roles or functions of a school library media program used in this discussion was developed by the writer over a period of years as a critical part of the development of a systematic planning and evaluation process for school library media programs.* It was discovered early in this work that the conceptualizations and definitions of school library media programs were very inadequate when it came to trying to apply more systematic and rigorous approaches to the planning and evaluation of programs. Most definitions of library media program services or outputs do not adequately express (1) total range and level of potential services, (2) the roles or functions performed from the user's standpoint, or (3) include the detail and conceptual coherence necessary to identify and relate the specific resources and operational requirements for the delivery of specified services. As a result, efforts to communicate and evaluate programs are severely hampered.

In order to be able to analyze programs more carefully it was necessary to develop a better definition. The approach used attempts to define from a user's perspective the roles or functions (referred to as services) of school library media programs as clearly and comprehensively as possible. The basic model for facilitating these distinctions is shown in figure 1 (page 92). User services — program outputs or ends — must be defined as clearly and elaborately as possible. This is necessary to differentiate ends, or user services, as distinctly as possible from means, resources, and operations, but also so that the specific resource and operational requirements of each specific user service can be made explicit.

The relative value of the alternative service outputs and the requisite resources and operations in effecting these service outputs must be assessed, ultimately, from the perspective of their contribution to instruction and the achievement of learning outcomes. This relationship is depicted in figure 2 (page 92), which also indicates that this contribution occurs both indirectly (by the provision of

*The model is an application of basic systems analysis. The model is partially based on the work of Dr. Richard H. Orr at the Institute for the Advancement of Medical Communications and the pioneering work of Dr. Mary V. Gaver regarding school library services. See the following for more detailed descriptions of this model and the user services: James W. Liesener, *Instruments for Planning and Evaluating Library Media Programs* (College Park, Md.: College of Library and Information Services, University of Maryland, 1980); James W. Liesener, *A Systematic Process for Planning Media Programs* (Chicago: American Library Association, 1976).

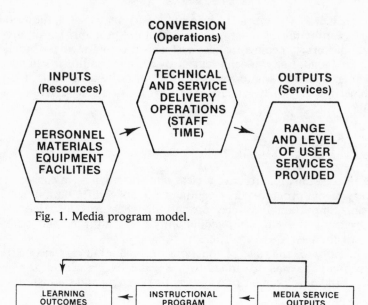

Fig. 1. Media program model.

Fig. 2. Media program accountability model.

services to teachers in support of their instructional activities) and directly (by the provision of services to students).

ELABORATION OF USER SERVICES

The services (outputs) aspect of the user services model is obviously the most pertinent in relation to the discussion of roles. From the viewpoint of the user services model, the school library media program is an aggregation of services (or roles or functions) provided to facilitate the accomplishment of clients' learning and instructional goals and objectives. The number and variety of potential services is large, and as a result, the organization and presentation of these services had to be done carefully if this definition was to effectively communicate the intended discriminations.

The elaboration of these services was clustered into five major categories of services, each with a number of subcategories. The objective was to define each category and each service in such a way as to be as discrete as possible and not overlap or duplicate any other—recognizing, of course, that all of these services are closely related.

Within each of the five discrete kinds of categories of service the subarrangement attempts to be hierarchical, moving from "least" to "most" service in user terms or from the least complex or difficult to the most complex services. An example of this continuum, illustrated in figure 3, would be the simple provision of reference materials for self-help, at one extreme, and the complete performance of the service, in terms of providing answers to questions, at the other end. It is obvious that the more one approaches staff performance of a service for users or the more complex services, the greater the resources needed to support the library media program. This approach therefore provides a clear reflection of levels of service, but in terms that have distinct resource and operational implications.

| SELF-HELP | STAFF | STAFF PERFORMS |
| COLLECTION | ASSISTANCE | SERVICE (ANSWERS) |

Fig. 3. Service continuum.

The services are expressed as much as possible, in terms of what is actually done for or provided to the user rather than in terms of the ultimate intent of providing the service. The intent and value of each service can therefore be judged locally and the services can be expressed much more explicitly. This definition is intended for elementary, middle or junior, and secondary programs and has been tested at these levels.

Access

This service area includes the following subcategories:

1. Provision of Materials

2. Provision of Equipment (eg. AV Equipment, Microcomputers, Television, and emergent technologies)

3. Provision of Space

4. Provision of Circulation Services

5. Provision of Materials Not In The Collection

6. Provision of Special Collections (temporarily to classes, reserves, professional collections)

7. Provision of Copying Facilities (copying pages etc. from items in the collection)

The provision of **access** to materials, equipment (for example, audiovisual equipment), and space is the traditional area of strength and most clearly perceived group of services provided by school library media programs and libraries in general. It involves providing intellectual and physical access to the whole range of print and non-print media. This also involves providing access to equipment as well as the procedures and facilities for the use of both materials and equipment. The provision of access to materials that are not in the particular collection of a specific school library media center but are provided through various interlibrary loan or networking arrangements is also included. The provision of access would also include such considerations as copying facilities, making arrangements for special collections either in the media center or in the classroom, etc. Currently the greatest areas of expansion are in the area of provision of access to computers and computer software and services for learners with special needs. In a number of cases computer facilities are being added to school library media programs and the library media specialists are becoming the computer coordinators for the school.

These services not only provide the basic information laboratory for both teacher and library media specialist initiated and directed activities which extend well beyond curricular interests and needs. Considerable strides have been made for some adult populations in providing much greater intellectual access as well as physical access in many areas through computerized searching and resource sharing via networking. However, in the majority of cases these advances have as yet to reach young learners. The problems related to providing the level of service needed here, as well as in the other service categories, will be treated in the next section of the paper.

Reference Or Information Services

This service area includes the following subcategories:

1. Provision of Reference Materials for Self-Help

2. Provision of Assistance in Identifying and Locating Materials in the Center

3. Provision of Assistance in Identifying and Locating Materials Not in the Center (including computerized searching)

4. Alerting the User and Current Awareness Services

5. Assistance in Compiling Bibliographies (including computerized searching of sources)

6. Answer Services (including the searching of data bases)

This service category involves two types of service, the provision of a collection of reference materials for self use and the provision of various kinds of personal assistance to the client in identifying, seeking or interpreting information. This assistance could include: simply helping and identifying where something is in the collection of the school library media center; identifying materials not in the collection but possibly available elsewhere; providing various alerting or current awareness services regarding information on materials or information that clients may not be aware of but which may be of value once they are conscious of them; providing various kinds of bibliographies and pathfinders to assist users in becoming aware of and locating various kinds of sources; as well as the actual answering of questions which could vary from simple to extremely complex kinds of questions.

Very typically the emphasis has been on the lower level services of providing a reference collection and some identification and location assistance. More emphasis has typically been placed on reference services at the secondary level with a heavier emphasis placed on instruction at the elementary level.

The provision of on-line searching of appropriate data bases for staff, and in rare instances for students, is available in some districts and this will certainly increase. The provision of various computerized services, the development of more data bases appropriate for and accessible to children, and the production of various helping tools to assist clients in analyzing questions and designing search strategies are the activities in this service area that demand immediate attention. Any advance in the development of sophisticated problem solving and information utilization skills will require significant improvement in the level of services in this area. The issue of information services for children and youth needs to receive the level of attention given to these services in the health field, for example, which has been a leader in the development of high level information services. The current approaches to providing reference and information services have not generally been designed on the basis of the understanding of user behavior discussed earlier. Therefore, a significant improvement in this area will require some attitudinal changes as well as technical changes.

Production

This service area includes the following subcategories:

1. Provision of Materials for Production

2. Provision of Assistance in Production

3. Production of Materials by Library Media Staff for Users

Production services involve providing materials, equipment and assistance to teachers, students and staff for producing or adapting various kinds of print but particularly non-print media. In some cases the production is actually performed for the client but this is normally done only for teachers or school staff and in areas where special equipment or expertise is required. Production can involve anything from making a transparency to producing a television program. These services are provided not only to help make instruction more effective but also to stimulate and facilitate the creative abilities and basic skills of students in effectively communicating their ideas. It will be interesting to see if this function extends in the future into the area of production and adaptation of computer software.

Instruction

This service area includes the following subcategories:

1. Directional Services (Materials etc. describing services and resources)

2. Formal Instruction and Orientation Programs

3. In-Service Training for School Staff

4. Informal Instruction

5. Guidance in Reading, Viewing and Listening

Services in this category involved both formal and informal instructional activities as well as reading, viewing and listening guidance activities. Activities can vary from providing various specifically designed self-instructional materials to assist clients in finding and using information, to providing formal instruction programs for both teachers and students in the use of various information resources and information access tools, as well as to providing access and instruction in the use of the newer information technology such as microcomputers. This area also normally involves a great deal of informal instruction for both teachers and students specifically related to particular problems or questions and also involves a variety of guidance activities aimed at stimulating or motivating interest in reading, viewing, and listening. Greatest emphasis has been placed in many cases on the lower level information locating skills; significant improvement is needed in order to develop the strategies and processes necessary to focus more attention on the higher level intellectual skills. A continuing serious problem is the difficulty of integrating the instruction and application of information seeking and utilization skills into the various instructional areas.

Consulting

This service area includes the following subcategories:

1. Advising Individual Teachers

2. Advising Teaching Teams and Department or Grade Level Groups

3. Participation in Overall Curriculum Planning (School Level or District Level)

4. Clearing House Services (Providing sample copies and evaluative information supporting instructional planning of school staff)

This group of services involves the library media specialist consulting with teachers regarding the use of various services and the design of instruction with appropriate attention to information utilization skills. This also includes contributing to the curricular and instructional planning efforts at various levels including the district level. Consulting with students would be considered under either reference or instruction depending on the type of activity.

Consulting services focus on the activities of the school library media specialist with individuals as well as groups of teachers. This area includes the work of the school library media specialist in providing suggestions and information for instructional planning to individual teachers as well as the cooperative planning of various instructional kinds of activities, some of which are conducted by the teacher and some by the media specialist. The level of service may vary from the simple suggestion of a few resources to be used in a particular unit to the actual participation in the design and evaluation of various instructional strategies. This category may also involve assisting and performing the function of a clearinghouse in terms of providing information about and sample copies of various instructional materials which are being considered for use in an instructional area. In some cases, the coordination of the selection and evaluation of all instructional materials is also a function of the school library media program in addition to performing the same selection and evaluation function for the library media center collection.

A clear vision of the roles of school library media programs is essential for both clients and professionals. Library media professionals need a comprehensive and coherent conception of their roles if they are to develop and manage effective programs. Clients must have clear perceptions of what can be expected if they are to make effective use of the programs provided. Hopefully, this effort to systematically define the roles or functions of school library media programs will contribute to the cause of better role understanding on the part of both clients and professionals.

THE SECOND REVOLUTION
A Taxonomy for the 1980s*

David Loertscher

A new concept has emerged in the last ten years from the fields of educational psychology and instructional technology: instructional development. This is a systematic process of creating sound instructional modules or units for learners by a team of professionals that includes the teacher and a person knowledgeable in instructional technology. This new, process-oriented role is a natural extension of the role of the library media specialist. The person who knows materials in all the modern formats and who understands in depth the function of these materials in teaching concepts is a logical partner to the teacher who is a subject matter specialist.

Together, these two persons, assisted by technical, clerical, and volunteer staff, can create exciting units of instruction that will take into account the individual needs of the students in a particular school.

This "second revolution" is led by a small group of revolutionaries who are developing, creating, and carving out a new mission for the school library media center to fulfill. There is Don Ely of Syracuse University, who, together with Margaret Chisholm from the University of Washington, has written about this concept. Robert Gagne and Leslie Briggs of Florida State have developed the concept out of educational psychology.

One of the problems of the new revolution is that it is described in such esoteric and jargon-laden language that some speculate that practitioners neither understand the role nor accept it. New attempts are constantly being made to explain instructional development to library media specialists and to train new persons entering the field in its components.

Some of those who have accepted the philosophical concept of the second revolution seem to be going through an identity crisis. These are the people who have learned the rudiments of instructional development but have not been able to practice it. They feel that their present program of services is already so pressing that there is little time to think about doing instructional development, let alone do it. So they feel guilty. They feel a gap between what they think they should be doing and what they are able to do.

*From David Loertscher, "The Second Revolution: A Taxonomy for the 1980s," *Wilson Library Bulletin* 56 (February 1982): 417-21. Reprinted by permission of *Wilson Library Bulletin*.

THE TAXONOMY—A NEW VIEW

When one considers the best components of traditional library services, audiovisual services, and the new concept of instructional development, is there any way that all these elements can be combined to create a holistic view of this new role? Is there a way that we can offer various levels of service to suit individual needs in a school at a given time without feeling guilty? Such is the goal of the following taxonomy of the role of the library media specialist in instruction.

A taxonomy (do you remember Bloom's?) is defined as an orderly classification of concepts or activities. This means that each level of the taxonomy is a legitimate concern for a given type of situation and that a library media specialist may be operating at various levels of the taxonomy during a typical day and need not apologize for doing so. Each level has its merits. Each level can be abused either by the library media specialist or the teacher. And every level can be practiced by every library media specialist in every single school at least once a year.

Let us explore the taxonomy, which consists of eleven successive levels of involvement:

- *Level One—No involvement: the library media center is bypassed entirely.* Here the library media specialist, for a logical reason, makes no attempt to be involved in a particular sequence in instruction. Not every unit can be plugged into the center at maximum usage at all times during the school day. Teachers who are experienced often collect their own specialized materials that serve very specific needs in an instructional segment and so require nothing from the LMC. A problem occurs, however, if non-use is a habitual pattern for either teachers or students.

- *Level Two—Self-help warehouse: facilities and materials are available for the self-starter.* Level two is basic to the complete program of library media services. At this level, the library media specialist has worked hard to organize materials and equipment for the browser. The center is inviting and attractive. Patrons can find the materials or equipment they need, know how to use them, and can check them out for use at home or in the classroom. This level involves the selection, acquisition, presentation, and maintenance of the collection. Services at this level are the kind that no one notices when they are running smoothly, but everyone complains when things go wrong.

- *Level Three—Individual reference assistance: students or teachers get requested information or materials for specific needs.* Here the library media specialist assumes the magician role—the ability to know where to locate important and trivial information and materials from a vast array of sources, whether these be in the LMC's collection, in a neighboring LMC, from the district LMC, from the public library, from an academic library, or from a national network. It also involves reading, viewing, and listening guidance for students and teachers.

- *Level Four—Spontaneous interaction and gathering: spur-of-the-moment activities and gathering of materials occur with no advance notice.* During many instructional periods, a teacher and/or student will discover a new direction that is not in the instructional plan yet is too exciting to neglect. The library media specialist might respond at a moment's notice with materials, resource people, production activities, research projects, games, or any other activity that capitalizes on the unique teaching moment. These instant projects might last a few minutes in a single class or might grow to involve the whole school for a semester or even a year. Spontaneous services, however, might become an excuse for a lack of planning by teachers or turn into a babysitting service. For students, this spontaneous need and subsequent interaction can spark life-long interests and even direct vocational choices.

• *Level Five—Cursory planning: informal and brief planning with teachers and students for library media center involvement.* This is usually done in the hall, the teachers' lounge, the lunchroom, etc. (Here's an idea for an activity and new materials to use. Have you seen ... ? Can I get you a film?) When the teacher accepts the library media specialist as an idea person and the specialist blooms in this role, all kinds of great things can occur. The library media specialist collects a bag of tricks—ideas that have worked from teachers, other library media specialists, principals, conventions attended, professional journals, and from his or her own creative mind. The library media specialist knows the sources for help—people, materials, and equipment—and knows where and how to get them. Teachers learn to depend on the library media specialist to generate solutions and end stagnation. Similar services are given to individual students and groups of students.

• *Level Six—Planned gathering: gathering of materials is done in advance of class project upon teacher request.* When there is time to communicate with the teacher concerning the topic of an upcoming unit, the library media specialist can assemble materials from many sources. Materials from the LMC can be gathered before the "eager beaver" students have time to raid the cache; neighboring schools can lend their materials; public libraries can be put on notice of an impending demand; materials from other libraries, rental sources, and free materials from agencies and businesses can be assembled. Given enough lead time, the library media specialist can flood the teacher with materials. Gathering the right things at the right time for the right uses is no small task.

• *Level Seven—Evangelistic outreach: a concerted effort is made to promote the multimedia individualized instruction philosophy.* This might include teaching in-service workshops to promote audiovisual production and/or use of audiovisual materials, showing teachers the various uses of equipment and materials and explaining how a medium can suit various ability and interest levels, promoting the usefulness of high interest/low reading-level books, or encouraging the use of interdisciplinary materials. For students, motivational campaigns are conducted to involve them in media experiences. Here one thinks of a library media specialist who enthusiastically preaches the gospel of media through promotion, cultivation, stimulation, testimonial, recommendation, and selling—all with the concerted purpose of gaining converts among the students, the teaching staff, and the administration. As with other types of evangelistic movements, the inattentive, the antagonistic, and the backsliders have to be contended with.

- *Level Eight — Scheduled planning in the support role: formal planning is done with a teacher or group of students to supply materials or activities in response to a previously planned unit or project.* At this level there is no media specialist involvement in goals or evaluation of the unit or project. With reference to students, the library media specialist may expend a great deal of effort working with individuals or groups of students in gathering materials, interpreting them, or helping to create materials for presentation. When we think of formal planning here, we think of individual or small group planning between the library media specialist and the teacher for at least a twenty-minute segment.

  The same amount of planning can be done with individual students or groups of students. In this case, the library media specialist does not take the leadership role but is able to discern the objectives of the unit that the teacher or student has in mind and then suggests, integrates, and promotes LMC services that would fill the need. Detailed plans for LMC activities are drawn up, responsibilities assigned, materials selected, and materials produced or purchased. This level of involvement works particularly well in a team teaching approach, where the library media specialist is considered a participating and contributing member of the team. With students, the library media specialist is a facilitator, letting the student take as much responsibility as possible. We are looking at a servant/master role here, which of course can be very satisfying at its best but can also create situations where the library media staff can be exploited.

- *Level Nine — Instructional design, level I: the library media specialist participates in every step of the development, execution, and evaluation of an instructional unit, but there is still some detachment from the unit.* At this level of the taxonomy, formal planning for the unit begins far in advance and will require a number of preparatory planning sessions, planning while the unit is underway, and a formal evaluation at the end. Here the library media specialist assumes a leadership role, particularly if an interdisciplinary unit is anticipated. The teachers view the library media specialist, if not as a leader, at least as an equal partner — a partner with specialized types of skills to contribute to the unit. The library media specialist works with teachers to create the objectives of the unit, assembles materials, understands unit content, and participates in the instructional process. Projects and activities with students range from simple to complex but are designed for maximum learning and growth. Here we think of a team approach with neither partner of the team exploiting the other.

- *Level Ten — Instructional design, level II: the library media center staff participates in grading students and feels an equal responsibility with the teacher for their achievement.* The difference between levels nine and ten is subtle. Here, the students realize that the library media specialist is a coequal teacher not only as a resource person but also as an evaluator of student progress. The students know that the library media specialist's opinions will have an impact on the grade assigned to any test, project, or activity carried out as a part of the unit.

• *Level Eleven—Curriculum development: along with other educators, the library media specialist contributes to the planning and structure of what will actually be taught in the school or district.* Curriculum development is more than just an invitation to attend curriculum meetings—it means that the library media specialist is recognized as a colleague and contributes meaningfully to planning. The knowledge of materials, sources, media attributes, present collections, and teaching/learning strategies makes the library media specialist a valuable asset as curricular changes are considered and implemented.

WORKING WITH THE TAXONOMY

This taxonomic concept of the school library media center has two essential components: first, the development of a place in each school where a rich collection of multimedia materials and equipment is available and easily used by teachers and students, and second, a library media staff that has a direct involvement in the educational process.

As this concept has emerged since the 1940s, there have been many elements that are similar to public, academic, and special library programs, but the differences are significant. These differences are the result not only of visionary dreams but also of the demands of the general public on the public schools. School library media centers are being asked to make a measurable difference in public education or else face extinction. This demand legislates against the passive role of a self-help warehouse as an end in itself and requires active outreach into every classroom and into every student's life, as exemplified in the upper levels of the taxonomy.

As the new role of the school LMC has emerged, a number of our school library media specialists have become guilt-ridden. They have often seen the new role as an addition to an already overcrowded role. Some don't even know a new role exists; others have rejected it. But many are experimenting and succeeding with the curriculum in ways that are giving them a most exciting and satisfying experience.

The first step in putting the taxonomy into practice is to accept the entire taxonomy as legitimate roles of instructional involvement. This means that each level is accepted as "good"—each is necessary to achieve a comprehensive impact on instruction.

Next, the taxonomy will require sound and consistent planning on the part of the library media specialist. We must realize that any level can become a rut and a dead end if it is so overworked that it crowds out services on other levels. Beware! Each level can also be used improperly and can contribute to poor instruction. The planning necessary to implement a total program needs time to develop, needs the support of an administrator who has been involved in the planning, and needs administrators who fully understand the concept and the potential of each level and who are willing to facilitate its fulfillment.

Teachers need time to think through the concept—to discuss it formally in order to understand the differences between traditional program services and services at levels that have been untried. Teachers need to understand clearly the advantages and the pitfalls of each of the levels and to help the library media staff achieve the best of each level.

There are many schools in which schedules, long-standing expectations, and traditional approaches lock the LMC staff into a narrow range of services to the exclusion of others. The taxonomy is just one way of re-examining our role and focusing on the very purpose for our existence. If library media specialists can take the best programming ideas they have now and integrate them into the instructional program rather than concentrating on enriching the curriculum or supplementing it, they will be demonstrating their worth instead of just talking about it.

MAPPING THE WAY TOWARD INSTRUCTIONAL DESIGN CONSULTATION BY THE SCHOOL LIBRARY MEDIA SPECIALIST*

Philip M. Turner and Janet N. Naumer

A little over a decade ago, the role of the school library media specialist (SLMS) appeared to be on the threshold of expanding in a new and exciting direction, that of instructional design consultation. While this expanded role has continued to be discussed in the literature (Margaret Grazier lists more than fifty articles dealing with this topic in her 1979 article[1]), the SLMS who has accomplished the transition to this role is in a distinct minority. Most school library media specialists seem either never to have chosen to pursue this expanded role or to have soon become frustrated in the attempt.[2,3]

Various studies have enumerated reasons why instructional design consultation has remained beyond the reach of so many. A very important factor is the attitude of the SLMS.[4,5]

Perhaps a reason that school library media specialists have a negative attitude toward this role, or if positive, despair of ever realizing it, can be discovered by an investigation of the route through which the innovation arrived at the doorstep of the SLMS. Instructional design has traveled from the military through industry and higher education to arrive at the K-12 level virtually intact. A perusal of the instructional design models presented for use by the SLMS reveals few differences from their more ambitious predecessors. The average SLMS consequently perceives little, if any, connection between the recommended role of instructional design consultant and "real life" in the media center.

Given that instruction that has been systematically designed is more effective than instruction that is not, and given that the SLMS should be involved as a consultant in the systematic design and implementation of instruction, what can be done to promote a greater fulfillment of this role by the SLMS?

The first task is to recognize that instructional design consultation by the SLMS at the K-12 level has far more logistical constraints than that found in the military, industry, and higher education. The second task is to recognize that the instructional design process, nevertheless, is not something external to the average school library media center program, but has as its basis many of the less

---

glamorous activities performed every day. Accomplishment of these tasks should result in the viewing of an increased involvement in instructional design consultation as an obtainable goal.

The first task is easily facilitated by considering the differences between scale of projects, size of staff, amount of funding, time allocation, and many other factors found in the military, industry, and higher education versus K-12 media programs. Such instructional development programs and the school library media program may be distant cousins; they are certainly not twins.

Accomplishing the second task begins with choosing an instructional design model that delineates the steps typically found in a systematic approach to instruction (see figure 1). The performance of *every* step on the model with *every* teacher is regarded as the ideal goal that an SLMS should keep in mind.

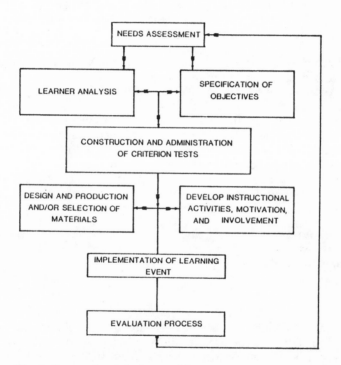

Fig. 1. Instructional design model.

Within each step, four levels of activity are proposed. It is also proposed that *all levels, except the very lowest, be considered involvement in the instructional design consultation process*. The four levels are:

1. *Action Education.* This is formal, full-scale instructional design consultation. The interaction at this level serves to educate the faculty, increasing their design skills. SLMS/faculty interaction might include membership on an instructional design team or implementation of in-service workshops.

2. *Reaction*. This level involves a more informal contact between the SLMS and the faculty, usually instigated at the request of the faculty member. In fulfilling the request, there is little attempt to improve the design skills of the faculty member.

3. *Passive Participation*. At this level, there is no contact between SLMS and teachers involving the instructional program. The SLMS selects and maintains materials, equipment, and facilities for use by faculty and students in the design, implementation, and evaluation of instruction.

4. *No Involvement*. The SLMS is not involved at the particular step of the design process.

Each step in the instructional design model can be viewed as consisting of these four levels of involvement (see figure 2). The vast majority of everyday activities of the SLMS should fit on one of the levels within one of the steps of the model.

As an example, the SLMS who arranges to have a 16mm projector delivered to a teacher *is involved in the instructional design consultation process* (step 7, reaction). An SLMS who builds a collection of works on test design for use by the teachers *is involved in the instructional design consultation process* (step 4, passive participation). See figure 2 for further examples.

The realization that many commonly performed activities can be considered instructional design consultation should help dissipate the view of instructional design consultation as an unobtainable ideal. Of course, if the only result of accepting such levels as legitimate components of instructional design consultation is in self-congratulation, the redefinition is not efficacious. The proper employment of the levels lies in their use in mapping a realistic path toward higher involvement.

INSTRUCTIONAL DESIGN ASSESSMENT CHART

The Instructional Design Assessment Chart (IDAC) (see figure 3, page 111) serves as a map, enabling the SLMS to locate areas of the process that can be improved. The IDAC can be used to illustrate involvement with a single teacher over a short period of time or with the entire faculty over a year or more. To use the IDAC, the SLMS:

1. Identifies the teachers who are the subjects of the instructional design consultation to be graphed.

2. Selects the time span in which the activities are to be considered.

3. Marks the level for each step that represents the highest level of activity in the chosen time span.

STEP 1:   Determines Goals and Needs Through a Formal Needs Assessment Procedure

LEVEL	SAMPLE ACTIVITY
Action/Education Participates as an active member in the goal-setting process at all stages	Conducted in-service for English teachers on the process of set-ting unit goals
Reaction Upon request, helps to acquire and to establish in priority order goals and needs	Mrs. Jones, the second grade teacher said, over coffee,; "I'm supposed to teach a unit on plants, but I am not sure what to include. The SMS responded by providing from the files a unit developed at another elementary school.
Passive Participation Maintains a collection of works on needs assessment. Maintains sources of potential goals.	Purchased copy of *Needs Assessment* for the professional collec-tion in the Media Center
No Involvement Not Involved at this step.	

STEP 2:   Derives Terminal and Enabling Objectives from Goal Statements, Identifies as to Type
            of Learning and Arranges in a Learning Hierarchy

LEVEL	SAMPLE ACTIVITY
Action/Education Acquaints teachers through workshops and consultations with the writing of objectives and their use.	Made regular visits to the Social Studies faculty meetings to assist with the writing of objectives
Reaction Upon request, assists in any aspect of creating and using objectives	After being informed by the Principal that her objective, "The students will *really* understand the value of good citizenship", was not adequate, the new social studies teacher asked for help. The SMS helped her re-write the objective.
Passive Participation Maintains a collection of works on objectives and previously formulated objectives.	Purchased a copy of *Writing Objectives* and placed in the Media Center
No Involvement Not Involved at this step.	

(Figure 2 continues on page 108.)

Fig. 2—Continued

STEP 3: Analyzes Learner to Determine Characteristics that will Influence Methodology and Message Design

LEVEL	SAMPLE ACTIVITY
Action/Education Acquaints teachers through workshops and consultations with learner analysis processes and uses	Conducted an inservice workshop for Math teachers on learning styles
Reaction Upon request, assists teachers in selecting appropriate learner analysis methods and categorizes student(s) in terms of learner characteristics	When returning a filmstrip after school, the Science teacher said: "A few of my students can't seem to locate important information in a visual. What is wrong with them?" The SMS discussed the characteristic of field dependence.
Passive Participation Maintains a collection of works on learner analysis. Maintains hardware/software necessary for learner analysis	Obtained a learner analysis diagnosis kit and put in the professional collection
No Involvement Not involved at this step	

STEP 4: Constructs and Administers Appropriate Criterion Tests

LEVEL	SAMPLE ACTIVITY
Action/Education Acquaints teachers through workshops and consultations with the design and implementation of criterion tests	Conducted a workshop for the History Department on deriving test items from objectives
Reaction Upon request, assists in any aspect of test design and implementation	Over Coffee, Mr. Jones asked whether the SMS thought that multiple choice vs essay questions were best for a history unit. The SMS responded by presenting pros and cons of each type.
Passive Participation Maintains a collection of works on test construction and administration. Maintains pool of test items and hardware/software for analysis.	Maintained files in Media Center on performance measures other than tests
No Involvement Not involved at this step	

STEP 5:	Designs/Produces/Selects Instructional Materials Based Upon Objectives and Learner Characteristics
LEVEL	*SAMPLE ACTIVITY*
Action Education Conducts workshops on the materials selection process and production techniques. Regularly designs/produces/selects instructional materials based upon consultation.	Implemented a program to train new teachers in design and production of slide presentations
Reaction Acts as a clearinghouse for preview requests. Produce/obtain instructional materials upon request.	The third grade teacher mentioned that she was teaching a unit on planets. The SMS sent her an instructional kit on the Solar System that had just arrived.
Passive Participation Maintains a collection of instructional materials. Maintains a production area. Maintains a collection of works and facilities required to produce/select/preview materials.	Unilaterally selects, orders, and catalogs a filmstrip for the general collection.
No Involvement Not involved at this step	

STEP 6:	Develops Activities in Support of Sequenced Objectives
LEVEL	*SAMPLE ACTIVITY*
Action Education Acquaints teachers through workshops and consultation with the process of matching learning activities with objectives and learners	Devised instrument for matching activities with type of objective and distributed to faculty
Reaction Upon request, discusses methodologies and options to meet a given objective for a specific learner type	During a faculty meeting, the Social Studies teacher mentioned that he was having difficulty thinking of an activity to use in teaching the concept of economy. The SMS helped him design a simulation exercise.
Passive Participation Maintains a collection of materials on activity design	Started a vertical file of descriptions of activities for teaching the Kindergarten units
No Involvement Not involved at this step	

(Figure 2 continues on page 110.)

Fig. 2 – Continued

STEP 7: Implements Learning Event	
LEVEL	*SAMPLE ACTIVITY*
Action/Education Acquaints teachers with effective utilization of materials, equipment, and facilities through workshops and consultation	Implemented a series of "hands-on" workshops on equipment operation and utilization for the third and fourth grade teachers
Reaction Upon request, demonstrates operation of and delivers items of equipment. Upon request, assists with assigning of tasks and scheduling of facilities	Arranged to have a 16mm projector delivered to the third period art class
Passive Participation Maintains a collection of works on equipment operation and usage and on communication theory. Maintains a collection of equipment. Maintains Media Center for group and individual usage.	Set up Media Center for use by the Social Studies classes
No Involvement Not involved at this step	

STEP 8: Expedites and Interprets Evaluation	
LEVEL	*SAMPLE ACTIVITY*
Action/Education Acquaints teachers through workshops and consultation with evaluation techniques and utilization	Served as a member of a building-level evaluation team
Reaction Upon request, advises on the design of evaluation strategies, implementation of evaluation, or interpretation of results	During hall patrol, the Science teacher said: "I just finished my taxonomy unit, but I am not really sure whether it was successful or not." The SMS provided assistance in setting up an evaluation strategy for the next implementation.
Passive Participation Maintains a collection of works on evaluation and hardware/software necessary for evaluations.	Purchased a statistical program for the microcomputer for use by the faculty.
No Involvement Not involved at this step	

Fig. 2. Levels of instructional design consultation.

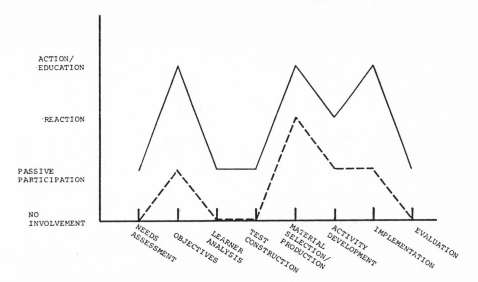

Fig. 3. Instructional design assessment chart.

IMPROVING THE LEVELS
OF INSTRUCTIONAL
DESIGN CONSULTATION

In figure 3, the broken line represents the instructional design consultation activities with an entire faculty by an SLMS during the past academic year. If this particular SLMS decides to raise the levels on instructional design consultations performed, the chart points to the following activities:

1. Developing the professional collection to include works on needs assessment, learner analysis, test construction, and evaluation.

2. Publicizing willingness and ability to work with teachers upon request in the areas of objectives, activity development, and implementation of instruction. This might take the form of items in the library media center newsletter, notices on the faculty-lounge bulletin board, or announcements at faculty meetings.

3. Formulating and offering a workshop on some aspect of material selection/production or becoming a member of a materials selection team.

The SLMS represented by the solid line in figure 3 evidently has operated during the past year at a much higher level of instructional design consultation. While little additional effort in the area of collection development seems to be required, willingness and ability to assist in problems with needs assessment, learner analysis, test construction, and evaluation should be publicized. The highest level can be reached under the instructional activity development step by holding a workshop(s) and through continued publicity resulting in widespread consultation at this step.

OTHER USES OF THE IDAC

Obtaining Administrative Support

The principal may have specific ideas about the role of the SLMS. Use of the IDAC allows the SLMS to determine these limits in terms of instructional design consultation and to obtain needed administrative support as well as to expand the principal's perceptions.

Allocation of Resources

Once areas of improvement are located and chosen, other benefits of the use of the IDAC become apparent. By setting certain activities as goals, required resources such as time, materials, and staff become apparent. The SLMS may request funds for purchase of several works on needs assessment in order to reach the passive participation level and may request the principal to remove the study hall group from the media center at the end of the day so that a workshop on evaluating instructional materials can be developed.

Identifying Areas for Continued Education

The possession of competencies in an area of instructional design consultation prior to upgrading a level is necessary. Since many school media preparation programs do not provide training in the entire range of these competencies,[6] further preparation might be required. The IDAC, in conjunction with a school library media specialist's knowledge of competencies possessed, can serve as a basis for continuing education decisions.

Accountability

Clearly, the benefits of an SLMS delineating the extent of involvement in the instructional process are manifold. The most important use, in this era of accountability, might be to illustrate activities and progress made. How impressive it would be to show graphically the progress that has been made in a given time period and how involved the media center is in the instructional program of the school!

CONCLUSION

This article has proposed the inclusion of collection development and the informal giving of advice as part of the K-12 instructional design consultation role. It questions previous paradigms, imposed from more affluent contexts, as being intimidating, even self-defeating when applied without modification to the school library media center.

While some may consider the proposed inclusion as heretical, the key to improvement of education at the K-12 level remains the involvement of the SLMS throughout the entire instructional process. Continued presentation of an unrealistic role will not lead the SLMS into a more meaningful involvement with the entire instructional process, and this should now be recognized. Graduated levels of involvement, on the other hand, create a series of reachable steps toward the ideal. The levels also provide the SLMS with a powerful tool to locate current position, plan and justify activities, and publicize progress. If the average SLMS can come to view instructional design consultation as a possible as well as desirable goal, the next decade might find the SLMS, as predicted more than ten years ago, in the center of the instructional program.

NOTES

[1]M. H. Grazier, "The Curriculum Consultant Role of the School Library Media Specialist," *Library Trends* 28 (1979): 263-79.

[2]Ibid.

[3]G. P. Corr, "Factors That Affect the School Library Media Specialist's Involvement in Curriculum Planning and Implementation in Small High Schools in Oregon" (Ph.D. dissertation, University of Oregon, 1979); C. G. Hodges, "The Instructional Role of the School Library Media Specialist: What Research Says to Us Now," *School Media Quarterly* 9 (1981): 281-84; S. T. Kerr, "Are There Instructional Developers in the Schools? A Sociological Look at the Development of a Profession," *A V Communications Review* 25 (1977): 243-68.

[4]Ibid.

[5]J. A. Larsen, "The Role of the Media Specialist as Perceived by Himself and His Administrator in the Secondary Schools of Utah" (Ph.D. dissertation, University of Utah, 1971); P. M. Turner and N. N. Martin, *Environmental and Personal Factors Affecting Instructional Development by Media Professionals at the K-12 Level* (Bethesda, Md.: ERIC Document Reproduction Service, 1979), ERIC Document 172796.

[6]P. M. Turner and S. K. Stone, "Instructional Design and the Curricula of Southeastern Library Schools," *Southeastern Librarian* 30 (1980): 200-201; P. M. Turner, "Instructional Design Competencies Taught at Library Schools," *Journal of Education for Librarianship* 22 (1982): 275-82.

THE ROLE OF THE SCHOOL LIBRARIAN AS A PROFESSIONAL TEACHER

A Position Paper*

Ken Haycock

INTRODUCTION

In the last fifteen years changes in education have been rapid and decisive. The traditional lock-step methods of teaching in small enclosed classrooms using limited instructional resources, mainly textbooks, have developed into more innovative approaches based on research related to children, teaching and learning. Due to changing environments and the information explosion, instruction now centres more on the process of learning itself than on subject content. It is becoming far more important that the student understands factors which contribute to a given situation than to memorize data describing it. The method of the subject specialist is of concern but specific knowledge of the field is less necessary. Discovery and inquiry methods of teaching are becoming increasingly common and contribute to the development of independent, disciplined learners who can recognize problems, formulate hypotheses, ask important questions, locate, analyze and evaluate information and reach valid conclusions.

Students are treated on a more individual basis as it is finally accepted that everyone does not learn in the same way or at the same rate. Each child is not necessarily following an individual program but efforts are made to correlate expected performance with individual ability levels to ensure realistic goals. Grouping of students is used to an increasing extent to match what is to be taught to those who need to learn it, whether it is a large group lecture to introduce facts or a small group work session to reinforce skills. These trends have also led to more independent study programs at all levels of education. The three R's (reading, writing, arithmetic) are still among the basic skills of schooling but the three I's (inquiry, individualization, independent study) represent an improved approach to teaching and learning.

School resource centres have been a vital part of these changes in education. Indeed, many innovations would not be possible without the services of a resource centre. As a reflection of these changes, emphasis has shifted from the traditional library base of selecting, organizing and circulating books to the more pronounced educational and teaching services of planning for the effective use of book and nonbook media through program planning and cooperative teaching. If the resource centre has any validity whatever in the school it must be on this

*From Ken Haycock, "The Role of the School Librarian as a Professional Teacher: A Position Paper," *Emergency Librarian* 8 (May/June 1981): 4-11. Copyright © 1981 Dyad Services. Reprinted with permission from *Emergency Librarian* (ISSN 0315-8888).

firm theoretical and educational foundation. Libraries per se are not seen as particularly significant in a formal education context; the planned use of learning resources is, however. The development of the school library to a resource centre then represents more of a change in function than a change in name. The implications of educational research and the implementation of new programs have led to a need for a vital integral resource centre. With a strong movement towards more effective team work, professionals in schools need a common base of concern and understanding to exploit the full potential of instructional methods.

TEACHER-LIBRARIANS

Traditionally, the person in charge of the school library has been called the school librarian; today, however, since all roles in education are being redefined in light of new trends and priorities and, since the term "librarian" should include professional library qualifications, school "librarian" is less acceptable to many. The school librarian is usually not a professional librarian in education, training or outlook; indeed, perhaps it was a mistake to ever use the terms school library and school librarian. The school librarian is, or should be, an outstanding or master teacher with specialized advanced education in the selection, organization, management and use of learning resources, and the school library, a resource centre inseparable from the instructional program. For the sake of clarity and simplicity the terms "teacher-librarian" and "resource centre" are used here. Teacher-librarian clearly denotes a teaching role with a library-related specialization. A teacher-librarian is not an unqualified or "under-qualified" librarian but a professional learning resources teacher who may also be a professional librarian. The term refers to a single unified teaching/librarianship role and not to the amount of time spent in the classroom or the resource centre.

Teacher-librarians are increasingly involved in curriculum development and in cooperative teaching situations where each teacher — classroom and resource centre — prepares for instructional responsibilities based on areas of expertise. Teachers accept teacher-librarians as equal partners in the school when they witness competence in the planning and implementation of curricula. With increased attention to the needs of individual students communication must be particularly effective between the classroom teacher and the teacher-librarian; the same professional language and education as well as the same core of experience — classroom teaching — go a long way toward reaching this goal.

PROGRAM PLANNING

In the development of any specific unit of study in a school certain factors predominate. Societal needs and influences determine the direction mandated by a provincial government, the curriculum followed by a local board of education and the program implemented by a school within its community. The curriculum designer brings to the task a theoretical knowledge of teaching and learning supplemented by subject content, tested with practical classroom experience. The foundations of society and of education in conjunction with the implications of individual differences, group relations, growth, motivation, teaching methods, learning processes and evaluation are examined and considered. Although it is far too narrow to categorize youngsters by specific characteristics at definite ages it is recognized that mental and physical development generally proceeds on a continuum. The characteristics of varying levels of this development can be identified and do have significant implications for appropriate teaching methods and the resulting use of the resource centre.

In order for learning resources to have validity in the instructional program, their use must be carefully planned through integration with this curriculum. As a specialist in the selection, organization, management and, most important, the utilization of all manner of book and nonbook media, the teacher-librarian is most concerned with the quality of use of reference and research tools and learning materials. The subject specialist has an intimate knowledge of an academic discipline or content whereas the teacher-librarian's "subject" is learning itself. There is no teaching content to a library or resource centre, only the process of unlocking knowledge and critical thinking, the process of learning. As a learning resources teacher, the teacher-librarian is concerned with those skills which are necessary to the development of motivated independent learners who can locate, analyze and evaluate information in all media formats.

The following psychological principles have been identified by the National (U.S.) Council for the Social Studies as essential for undergirding a developmental skills program:[1]

1. The skill should be taught functionally, in the context of a topic of study, rather than as a separate exercise

2. The learner must understand the meaning and purpose of the skill, and have motivation for developing it

3. The learner must be carefully supervised in his first attempts to apply the skill, so that he will form correct habits from the beginning

4. The learner needs repeated opportunities to practice the skill, with immediate evaluation so that he knows where he has succeeded or failed in his performance

5. The learner needs individual help, through diagnostic measures and follow-up exercises, since not all members of any group learn at exactly the same rate or retain equal amounts of what they have learned

6. Skill instruction should be presented at increasing levels of difficulty, moving from the simple to the more complex; the resulting growth in skills should be cumulative as the learner moves through school, with each level of instruction building on and reinforcing what has been taught previously

7. Students should be helped, at each stage, to generalize the skills, by applying them in many and varied situations; in this way, maximum transfer of learning can be achieved

8. The program of instruction should be sufficiently flexible to allow skills to be taught as they are needed by the learner; many skills should be developed concurrently.

In planning for the implementation of a program based on these principles the teacher-librarian joins with the classroom teacher to form a horizontal team of two equals working toward established objectives. This dyad cooperatively plans what is to be done and the most effective way to accomplish the task. The classroom teacher and the teacher-librarian each bring different backgrounds and strengths in teaching but they do understand the potential of various approaches to learning and recognize common goals. Through planning with other teachers the teacher-librarian is also a source of ideas for program development.

If the use of learning resources is intended, the teacher-librarian is involved in preplanning before a unit of study begins. In this way the teacher can at least ensure that appropriate materials are available. Since the teacher-librarian will be working with a class, group or individuals, it is important to know what the preliminary objectives of the teacher are. The teacher decides on a unit of work and outlines its scope. General teaching strategies which may be conducive to resource centre use are considered. The teacher meets with the teacher-librarian to select and plan the use of materials and services. The teacher and teacher-librarian determine the sequence of content on the basis of the availability of materials and necessary personnel.

The dyad or teaching team redefines objectives and determines the skills to be stressed in relationship to local curricula, student needs and available learning resources. These may be subject skills, study and critical thinking skills, reference and research skills or listening and viewing skills. The teacher and teacher-librarian then set up a series of learning experiences involving individual students, small and large groups or whole classes. Selected materials may be kept in the resource centre or moved elsewhere, whichever is most appropriate. At this point the unit is introduced by a team member. The students work on the unit in the resource centre and the classroom with the classroom teacher and teacher-librarian stressing skills related especially to the program unit. The teacher-librarian may teach a short integrated skill lesson, develop a series of related lessons, offer an enrichment lesson or give a book talk on the theme.

When planning with one teacher, a group or committee of teachers, or a teaching team, the teacher-librarian *cooperatively*[2]

determines the contribution that the resource centre is to make to the overall teaching plan

determines specific teaching objectives to be accomplished through the use of learning resources and guidance

identifies basic concepts and skills to be introduced, reinforced, or extended

structures learning guides; reading, viewing, listening checklists; summary forms; reaction charts; critical evaluation cards

determines appropriateness of proposed assignments and the availability of suitable materials sets target dates for each phase of the resource centre role in the program

designs specific teaching strategies requiring resource centre support

designs specific learning experiences and activities requiring learning resources

designs specific unit and support activities

designs strategies for meeting student needs, interests, goals, abilities, progress rate, concerns, and potential

identifies specific media uniquely appropriate for each of the teaching and learning designs

programs for the most logical use of media in progressive, sequential order

designs appropriate culminating teaching and learning activities

designs appropriate evaluating activities to determine the effectiveness of the resource centre role

COOPERATIVE TEACHING

In this cooperative teaching situation the teacher-librarian may work with a group of students over an extended period of time while the classroom teacher works with another group in the classroom. The contribution of the teacher-librarian extends to the specific needs of the student. This means that the teacher-librarian may be offering remedial teaching, leading novel study, managing behaviour or teaching in other ways suitable to the particular level, subject, unit and objectives related to resource centre use as determined cooperatively by the team. Throughout the project, the teacher and teacher-librarian evaluate the growth made by students in planned skills, the effectiveness of the materials as well as the effectiveness of the unit itself.

With the movement from an insular school library to an integrated resource centre the skills for using libraries effectively have been better integrated with the curriculum. Scheduled library science classes are inappropriate and no longer offered where effective programs predominate. These classes were not based on the principles of learning and psychology outlined. They were taught out of context, were not seen as relevant by the learner, were not necessarily given when needed and were generally ineffective. Scheduled classes on a regular timetable persist only where the principal has little notion of the educational foundation of the resource centre, where the classes provide spare periods for teachers—an expensive and dubious practice—or where the teacher-librarian is not prepared to become actively involved in program development and curriculum implementation.

COLLECTION OF MATERIALS

Although a professional librarian, given a knowledge of curriculum content, can obviously select materials to support units of study from appropriate reviewing tools, the criteria for previewing and reviewing learning resources involve additional factors often not included in selection for a general or public library audience. The teacher-librarian needs to know not only the community and users, the nature of the existing collection, general and specific criteria for different types of subject material and sources of bibliographic and review information but also needs to have a professional knowledge of other teachers, of instructional strategies used for specific units of study, of the instructional design of products examined, of the intended audience in grade and ability levels, of curriculum relationships and of the principal and potential uses of the material. Learning resources must have a planned purpose or at least the possibility of such and this means a more complete integration with teaching/learning processes.

The balanced collection found in many public libraries is a mistake in the school resource centre. To select material on all topics, a financial impossibility at best, is to neglect the context of the service. If one country is studied using Socratic approaches and the textbook and another is studied using inquiry approaches and learning resources then little should be purchased on the former since the teaching method does not necessitate material and a great deal more purchased on the latter since the strategy here means that support will be necessary for a specific number, usually at least class size, of users. Similarly, when organizing resource centre information the nature of the users and elements of the school curricula are taken into account. The subjectivity of the selection and organization of materials can become more precisely defined in the school setting.

INTERAGENCY COOPERATION

With increasing demands on learning resources, coupled with decreasing tax dollars, there should be improved cooperation among schools and among schools and other libraries. Such cooperation is based on a clear understanding of the role of each agency and a commitment to sharing materials and services where mutually beneficial. Each agency serves a quite different purpose with specific criteria for attempts at combining services.[3] Librarians must recognize the unique expertise of the teacher-librarian and be knowledgeable about the role of the resource centre. The development of the resource centre as an integrated learning centre to provide the skills for self-realization means that public library use will increase tremendously; if the public library is relatively untapped by students as a community resource, this can be overcome through cooperation. The school must also be aware of the services of the public library and actively promote its use with both staff and students.

DESIGN AND PRODUCTION OF MATERIALS

Should suitable material not be available in the resource centre, not available on loan from another school or agency, and not available from commercial sources the teacher-librarian has the ability as a media specialist to determine the instructional need and design a product based on theories of learning and educational technology. The appropriate medium is matched to the instructional purpose and message to be conveyed. The teacher-librarian then produces or supervises the local production of needed learning resources. Too often the production of materials is seen as a purely technical matter but in the resource centre the instructional design function is an important factor in the development of media. The unique characteristics of a filmstrip, for example, with its fixed sequence and visual qualities might be much more justifiable for the intended purpose and audience than a sound recording which can require a higher level of motivation and improved listening skills.

PROMOTION OF READING

Reading continues to be of prime importance to the teacher-librarian and numerous methods of motivating voluntary reading are common in resource centres. In conjunction with fellow teachers, the teacher-librarian works toward broadening horizons, increasing language proficiency and resolving student problems through storytelling and book talks as well as improved reading guidance (which can approach bibliotherapy), creative dramatics, puppetry and related programs.

INFORMATION SERVICES

Information services are offered to students and teachers with the reference interview becoming a professional teaching situation in many cases. Since the teacher-librarian is familiar with individual units through advance planning the student may receive precise information immediately or have skills introduced or reinforced depending on defined individual objectives. Teachers gain the ability to ask questions at a variety of levels, from the recall of information to the evaluation of abstract concepts, through professional education and classroom experience. These techniques are necessary in the resource centre to gauge the precise information needs of the student and the level of specific skill attainment at that time. Reference and research skills are taught as an integrated part of the instructional program in each subject on a continuing sequential basis. Where desirable and valid, however, some skills may also be reinforced and extended as a short unit themselves. For example, a cooperative unit may be planned for a senior commercial class where the student will need to know a variety of specific skills such as how to use a dictionary as an aid in typing, how to locate quotations for speeches, the correct form of address to be used in given circumstances and how to file information for easy retrieval in order to function effectively and efficiently in a business office. Evaluation of learning always takes place in the context of classroom teaching and its extensions.

MEDIA SKILLS

The teacher-librarian is also actively engaged in teaching students the effective use of nonbook media and equipment; this includes the skills necessary to report research in many and varied ways other than the traditional essay format. The student of today must be knowledgeable about the electronic environment outside the school. We know that by the time a student completes secondary school more time has been spent watching television than has been spent in school—it would be gross negligence to overlook the skills necessary to evaluate this and other nonbook sources of information or to relegate these learning skills to a single separate course in screen education. Graphic analysis and visual and aural literacy are necessary components of a student's education; as a media specialist, the teacher-librarian works with other teachers to integrate these learning skills with appropriate areas of the curriculum.

PROFESSIONAL DEVELOPMENT SERVICES

Two of the most important areas of competence in school librarianship are professional development services to teacher and strategies for change, both of which necessitate teacher education for maximum effect. Educational information services for staff members are necessary and useful if the teacher-librarian considers the specific interest, time and energy of the user. An even more fundamental professional development service is in-service education. As a curriculum developer and educational leader the teacher-librarian has a professional obligation and responsibility to lead seminars and workshops on the effective use of the resource centre. Topics range from the operation of audio-visual equipment to the implementation of effective teaching strategies. In-service education is carefully planned and pursued. It demands a critical analysis of need based on relevant educational principles, a real reason for teachers to attend, effective teaching by the teacher-librarian and involvement by participants. Evaluation of the session itself and how well it met the need originally identified provides guidance for future workshops. Only through increased knowledge of resource centre services as necessary components of teaching methodology will the potential of teacher-librarians and resource centres be realized.

A parallel consideration is the area of strategies for change in which in-service education programs are one part. Through perspective as a teacher plus an intimate knowledge and understanding of the institutional framework within which the resource centre operates, the teacher-librarian can identify areas of potential support and hindrance more easily. By exploiting political realities and building on aspirations of administrators and the goals of teachers the teacher-librarian can not only integrate services better but also develop a well-supported program.

The debate over faculty status for community college and university librarians has raged for years but is not a concern in schools. The teacher-librarian has full faculty status and is recognized as an equal partner in education in terms of salary, working conditions and vacation leave. This status was gained by the most obvious means possible—the same basic qualification to be in the school in the first place followed by a similar role through specialization within the field. Indeed, most school districts have defined the role and expectations of the teacher-librarian as a master teacher and have granted additional responsibility allowances for department headships and educational leadership.

Collegiality is a characteristic of the teaching profession that cannot be ignored; just as the professional with a Master of Arts or Master of Science degree has a teaching certificate so too does the professional with a Master of Library Science degree. Professional roles in a school, other than peripheral or support positions, begin with teacher education and classroom experience followed by additional qualification for specialization. Whether one agrees or not, it is a fact of life in a school that teachers do not extend their privileges, rights and status to non-certified personnel, regardless of position or qualification. Familiarity with curriculum design and particularly successful experience in the classroom provide a respectability that cannot be achieved by academic qualifications alone.

STANDARDS

Comparison of libraries is often done by examining quantitative data but in a school the number of personnel, book and nonbook materials, equipment and square feet per student are relatively meaningless for determining the level of development and value of resource centre services. Numbers are significant only when establishing new resource centres to equalize tangible products and potential. Much more useful but more difficult to measure are qualitative considerations. The resource centre can be distinguished from a library by its specialized curriculum implementation (program development and cooperative teaching) services; the teacher-librarian and resource centre represent a variety of teaching strategies found to be educationally effective. The school which practices inquiry-centred approaches to learning requires much more personnel, resources and space for the same number of students than a school which stresses textbook-oriented Socratic methods. The resource centre must be essential to the instructional process if it is to have significance or even to survive. With budgetary restraints the resource centre is using money that could mean smaller classes, more counselors or more remedial assistance. Unlike an integrated resource centre, a children's or young adult library added to the school could not and would not outlast financial cutbacks and the setting of priorities. Perhaps a more reasonable method of informal evaluation would be to close the resource centre for a month to see if teaching and learning continue as before. If a teacher can teach and if the student can learn without the resource centre and the teacher-librarian, the service as it exists in that situation is merely a beauty spot on the body politic, an expensive and doomed educational frill. The following problems have traditionally prevented the full implementation of a planned program for facilitating independent learning using the resource centre:[4]

1. lack of a school district K through 12 developmental study skills program that mandates the integration of independent learning skills with all aspects of the program

2. limitation of instruction in the use of the resource centre to a brief orientation session

3. failure to include in provincially or locally developed courses of study, specific learning experiences requiring resource centre support and specific reference to the necessity of integrating instruction in the use of the resource centre within the framework of the teaching-learning program

4. isolation of the teacher-librarian from curriculum study and revision activities

5. failure of teacher education institutions to include in basic programs an adequate understanding of the function of the resource centre as a learning laboratory and the role of the teacher-librarian as a fellow teacher

6. failure of the teacher to expand class knowledge beyond textbook content and classroom confines

7. reluctance of the teacher to preplan with the teacher-librarian for the effective use of the resource centre media, facilities, and services before a unit is introduced to the class (or, unfortunately, the reluctance of the teacher-librarian)

8. lack of sufficient staff — both professional and para-professional — to support adequately a comprehensive, diversified instructional program in the use of the resource centre — methods which effectively utilize resource centre personnel and services.

The resource centre will never be really necessary until students are unable to do satisfactory work without access to the professional teaching and library media services which it provides.

EDUCATION FOR TEACHER-LIBRARIANS

Although it is possible to define the role of the teacher-librarian as a teacher and as a librarian it is most unwise to do so. Indeed, this is a common mistake made by educators of teacher-librarians. There are essential competencies necessary from teacher education, classroom experience, library and media education but it is the fusion of these that leads to excellence, not dual qualifications in themselves. Until programs which educate teacher-librarians, whether Faculties of Education or Library Science, recognize, require and develop these areas of competence, there will continue to be a chronic shortage of teacher-librarians who understand this specialized teaching role and have the necessary skills to implement it. The time is long overdue for instructors in school librarianship to examine the basic research and get on with the job of developing the necessary course components.[5] A specialized Master of Education degree in school librarianship would provide sufficient scope at the appropriate level to build on a teacher's background and experience. It would also provide a suitable framework for the components which are too often missing: instructional design, program planning, cooperative teaching, human relations, selection of learning resources in all formats, the institutional setting, design and production of media, developmental reading. For too long we have paid lip service to a specialized teaching role and translated it into courses in administration, cataloguing and literature.

CONCLUSION

The school must examine its own program in order to determine the type of service that it requires from the resource centre. If the only concern is the circulation of materials, then parent volunteers or a clerical assistant may be sufficient. If selection and organization warrant increased attention as well as children's and young adult services and programs then a library technician or librarian should be employed depending on the scope and quality of service preferred. If the utilization of learning resources through valid, planned experiences leading to independent learning is of prime importance then a master teacher with advanced education and training in school librarianship is required.

Teacher-librarians have progressed from the days when it was all too common for refugees from the classroom to be placed in charge of school libraries to a time when outstanding specialist teachers head vital resource centres. School libraries have moved from their position outside the mainstream of education to resource centres at the physical and philosophical heart of the school. This development is a direct result of changes in education and, more specifically, changes in teaching strategies. Instruction in learning skills is integrated with all aspects of the curriculum and taught together by the classroom teacher and the teacher-librarian. The direction of teaching and learning focuses increasingly on learning how to learn so that students will have the necessary motivation and the skills to examine their own environment, evaluate it and perhaps even reform it.

NOTES

[1] E. Johns and D. M. Fraser, *Skill Development in the Social Studies*, ed. H. M. Carpenter, v. 33 (Washington, D.C.: National Council for the Social Studies, 1963), 311-12.

[2] R. A. Davies, "Education Users in the Senior High School," in *Educating the Library User*, ed. J. Lubans, Jr. (New York: R. R. Bowker Company, 1974), 41.

[3] K. Haycock, *The School Media Centre and The Public Library: Combination or Co-operation* (Toronto: Ontario Library Association School Libraries Division, 1973), 17.

[4] R. A. Davies, *The School Library Media Center; A Force for Education Excellence*, 2d ed. (New York: R. R. Bowker Company, 1974), 46-47.

[5]R. N. Case and A. M. Lowrey, *Behavioral Requirements Analysis Checklist: A Compilation of Competency-based Job Functions and Task Statements for School Library Media Personnel* (Chicago: American Library Association, 1973), xi-60; R. N. Case and A. M. Lowrey, *Curriculum Alternatives, Experiments in School Library Media Education* (Chicago: American Library Association, 1975), xii-241; C. D. Fink and H. Wagner, *Evaluation of Alternative Curricula; Approaches to School Library Media Education* (Chicago: American Library Association, 1975), xi-183.

BIBLIOGRAPHY

Anderson, Robert H. *Teaching in a World of Change.* New York: Harcourt, Brace and World, 1966.

Brown, Ian D. R., and Martha A. Baldwin. "Teachers and Librarians Look at the Elementary School Library and Each Other." *Orbit* 5, no. 5 (December 1974): 6-8.

Case, Robert N., and Anna Mary Lowrey. *Behavioral Requirements Analysis Checklist: A Compilation of Competency-based Job Functions and Task Statements for School Library Media Personnel.* Chicago: American Library Association, 1973.

Chapman, Geoffrey. "Faculty of Education Viewpoint." In *The Canadian School Librarian; Issues for the 70s: Education.* Ottawa: Canadian School Library Association, 1973.

Church, John S. "The Library and the Learner." *Moccasin Telegraph* 13, no. 3 (May 1971): 49-59.

Dale, Edgar. *Building a Learning Environment.* Bloomington, Ind.: Phi Delta Kappan Foundation, 1972.

Darling, Richard. *Teams for Better Education; The Teacher and the Librarian.* Champaign, Ill.: Garard Publishing Company, 1969.

English, Patricia. "Teacher Librarianship—The Challenge." *Alberta School Library Review* 11, no. 2 (Winter 1974-75): 32-34.

Fink, C. Dennis, and Harold Wagner. *Evaluation of Alternative Curricula; Approaches to School Library Media Education.* Chicago: American Library Association, 1975.

Gaver, Mary Virginia. *Services of Secondary School Media Centres; Evaluation and Development.* Chicago: American Library Association, 1971.

Goodlad, John I. *Planning and Organizing for Teaching*. Washington, D.C.: National Education Association, 1963.

Haycock, Ken. "Teacher-Librarian: Education Leader or Technician?" *Ontario Education* 5, no. 6 (November-December 1973): 10-15.

Irvine, L. L. "The Trench of the Ivory Tower?" *The Medium* 15, no. 4 (June 1974): 21-23.

Johns, Eunice, and Dorothy McClure Fraser. "Skill Development in the Social Studies." In *National Council for the Social Studies Thirty-third Annual Yearbook*, edited by Helen McCracken Carpenter, 310-27. Washington, D.C.: National Council for the Social Studies, 1963.

McCordick, Irene. "Is There a Future for Teacher-Librarians?" *Moccasin Telegraph* 15, no. 3 (May 1973): 6-7.

Nordin, Adelaide Louise. "High School Teachers' Attitudes towards the School Library." Master's thesis, University of Alberta, 1968.

Pile, A. R. "The Role of the Professional Teacher-Librarian in the Education Systems." *The N.T.A. Journal* 64, no. 1 (Winter 1972): 42-49.

Reid, Helen Audrey. "An Investigation of the Role of the School Librarian in Alberta." Master's thesis, University of Alberta, 1971.

Sayles, Lois H. "The Role of the School Librarian." *Moccasin Telegraph* 12, no. 2 (February 1970): 47-52.

Wiedrick, Laurence G. "Student Use of School Libraries in Edmonton Open Area Elementary Schools." Ph.D. dissertation, University of Oregon, 1973.

DEVELOPING THE SCHOOL RESOURCE CENTRE PROGRAM
A Systematic Approach*

Carol-Ann Haycock

INTRODUCTION

The need for clearly defined approaches to developing a resource-based program is expressed frequently, but university classes and articles are too often of the "glad tidings" or "how I run my library good" nature. The three-to-five-year plan outlined here refers to a resource centre program based on cooperative program planning with colleagues to develop, teach, and evaluate units of study in a flexibly scheduled resource centre.

This approach necessitates that the "teacher-librarian" clearly understand and be able to articulate this role, and have a strong commitment to it. The major function of the role is to plan, develop, and teach programs cooperatively with classroom teachers as *equal* teaching partners. To suggest that this is but one facet of the role, or one that takes place after the resource centre is made technically perfect, or one that takes place at a different level—once teachers have been "won over"—is to move it from a central focus to a peripheral position.

Two common attitudes tend to characterize teacher-librarians who do not have a clearly defined role that is internalized. First, there are those who, because they presume rejection, continue to function as reactors rather than initiators. Second, there are those who hold the view that they must start "where the teachers are at".

Each of these types operate from positions of servitude or relative powerlessness because they lack not only a clear understanding of this specialized role, but also of the process of change itself.

The very nature of the role of the teacher-librarian is that of initiator and change agent.

*From Carol-Ann Haycock, "Developing the School Resource Centre Program—A Systematic Approach," *Emergency Librarian* 12 (September/October 1984): 9-16. Reprinted by permission of *Emergency Librarian*.

Note: The approaches and processes outlined here have been developed and implemented by the writer in a variety of situations and replicated by several others as a result of in-service programs. The external reviewers believe that this *systematic* and unified approach to the development of an integrated, flexibly scheduled resource centre program constitutes an original contribution to the professional literature.

This includes not only encouraging teacher and student use of the resource centre, but also involvement as an equal partner in planning for research and study skill development and language improvement. A jointly planned and taught program such as this often involves a change in the teaching strategies and learning activities commonly used in the school. The collaborative input and involvement of teachers becomes essential for a successful resource centre program.

It is important for teacher-librarians to be aware of both the formal and informal structure of the school and to be prepared to work at both levels, particularly since the fate of most programs is decided at the informal level. The "informal covenant" or agreement that exists between administrators and teachers regarding the day-to-day operations of the school supports the administrator as spokesperson for the school and grants him or her some decision-making power regarding school policies and programs; the teacher, however, maintains final authority in the classroom and expects (and gets) administrative support for instructional decisions. Any school program then needs a two-level implementation plan—administrators are critical in the adoption phase of a program while teachers are critical in the implementation phase.

THREE PHASES OF DEVELOPMENT

The developmental approach is described in three phases. Throughout these phases, strategies for change and a multi-level plan for implementation are interwoven.

Phase I

1. *Assess The Current Situation*
   Knowledge of the present status, behaviour, and expectations for people and programs in the school is important. Analyze the strengths and weaknesses of the facility, collection, and budget. Also analyze the administration, teaching staff, support staff, student population, and community. Identify key people on staff. On any given staff, ten percent "set the tone" and "run the school". They have a lot of power, whether they recognize it or not. Support from people in these positions is essential for successful change. Identify key programs or subject areas in the school and look for entry points into them. The focus might be on the effective use of existing materials for a new social studies program or an emphasis on inquiry skills in the science program, or the need for a sustained silent reading program. Based on this assessment, identify the discrepancies between the current and the desired resource centre program.

2. *Define The Role*

   One of the major tasks in the development and implementation of any new program is to define the program itself and the roles and responsibilities of those to be involved. This is also an important step when the teacher-librarian is new to the school. Never presume that the role of the resource centre and the teacher-librarian is understood. Similarly, never confuse support for the teacher-librarian as an individual with understanding of, and commitment to, the *role* of the teacher-librarian.

   Roles and responsibilities need to be defined formally, through discussion with the principal, through in-service sessions, and through staff meeting presentations. In all cases, the purpose is to provide information and seek support. (Seeking permission is a dangerous approach! What if the answer is "no"?) Adopting a collaborative approach, assuming a partnership and a trial period, asking for a chance to try out a role or an approach with teacher and administrator support is a much more successful way to gain acceptance and bring about program adoption. For example, you might conclude an orientation for teachers by saying, "My major goal for this term is to plan just one unit with each of you. I hope you will support me in this. I'll get in touch with each of you tomorrow to schedule some planning time."

   Definition of the role of the resource centre and the teacher-librarian should also take place informally, through the school's daily bulletin, a corner in the monthly newsletter, displays of new materials, and over coffee or lunch in the staffroom.

3. *Establish Guidelines*

   Two sets of guidelines can serve the teacher-librarian well: guidelines for flexible scheduling and guidelines for cooperative planning and resource sharing.

   Guidelines for flexible scheduling should specify that:

   (1) cooperatively developed programs take precedence for teacher-librarian time and available space,

   (2) classes are not booked on a regular (every Tuesday at 9:30) basis,

   (3) total class bookings presume cooperative planning between the teacher-librarian and teacher and that the two are functioning as partners in the teaching and supervision of the class,

   (4) small group bookings may involve cooperative planning followed by either the teacher-librarian and students working together, or independent work on the part of the students for which space and materials have been made available, and

   (5) individual students are welcome at any time with a library tag; in this instance, the classroom teacher assumes responsibility and is reasonably confident that the student understands and can carry out the specified task, whether it is to select a book for recreational reading or to find information. The teacher also establishes a specific time limit with the student.

Guidelines for cooperative program planning and resource sharing can be provided through the use of a monthly topics sheet. The topics sheet should be a "two-minute item" for teachers—filling in the topics to be covered in each subject area for the upcoming month and checking off whether or not resources are required and planning time needed. (See figure 1.) Resources are pulled or secured and shared among teachers on the basis of the topics sheets submitted each month. Through this approach, one teacher doesn't end up with all the dinosaur books or all the resources on insects while others go without. The topics sheets are compiled into a monthly program chart which is distributed to the entire staff. The administrator's copy is asterisked to indicate the teacher-librarian's involvement in programs at each grade level. This monthly program chart indicates the curriculum that is being taught throughout the school at a glance. It facilitates the communication and sharing of ideas among staff as well as the sharing of resources.

The rationale for, and benefits of, the topics sheet should be discussed first with the administrator and then outlined, with examples, in a presentation to the staff. Most teachers are very receptive to this approach, and even a partial return of forms means that the teacher-librarian has more information than would have otherwise been the case.

TOPICS	For the month of _____	Teacher _____
		Please return by _____
Language Arts		
Social Studies		
Science		
Math		
Other		
Support Materials Needed	Library	
	School	
Planning Time	Do you wish to arrange PLANNING TIME for cooperative teaching? Yes _____ No _____	

Fig. 1. Monthly topics sheet.

The topics sheet facilitates cooperative planning in both a formal and an informal sense. There is a place provided on the sheet for teachers to indicate whether or not they would like planning time. Entry points into other programs can often be identified and informal approaches to teachers made on this basis. One of the advantages of this system is that it provides specific information for the teacher-librarian and points of discussion with teachers, thus eliminating the "how can I help you?" shopkeeper approach to teacher librarianship.

4. *Communicate Often and Well*
   Regular communication with the administrator, as well as with staff members, is of paramount importance. Effective communication can create an awareness of, and support for, the adoption of the program. Possible strategies for implementing changes, based on assessment of the current situation, should also be discussed. Through such discussion, priorities can be established and both teacher-librarian and administrator can concentrate efforts in specific areas.

   Focus on program strengths and weaknesses, not individuals and personalities. Keep in mind that the most successful approach is to emphasize the positive aspects of the program and the progress being made *before* introducing the problem or issue to be discussed. Remember — all of the problems in the school end up at the principal's door! Seek advice, but don't presume the administrator is going to take action. Be prepared to act on suggested approaches or solutions if they will indeed enhance the program.

5. *Start With One Teacher (Start Small ... Think Big)*
   Based on the initial assessment, identify the teachers who appear to be most receptive to new ideas and programs or with whom you succeed in establishing rapport quickly. Start with them to ensure that you and they meet with success! Never underestimate the "ripple effect" — accept small increments of change and avoid large-scale disappointment. Keep the developmental approach clearly in focus!

   Be sure to write up units of study which are developed with teachers and keep these on file as a basis for sharing with others and to ensure availability for use in subsequent years. This is well worth the extra time and effort in the long run; it provides a foundation for continued development and saves time when redesigning and revising units and programs to use again. The importance of this component cannot be over-emphasized.

6. *Establish A School-Based Skills Continuum*
   It is essential that a continuum of research and study skills be developed and agreed to by staff to ensure that some skills are not being omitted, that a developmental approach is being taken to skills coverage, and that skills instruction is being integrated with, and embedded in, the curriculum. This provides a framework for cooperative planning and a needed structure for resource-based programs.

Teacher involvement in this process is crucial. If teachers work as partners in developing a continuum that is relevant to the teaching and learning situation in a specific school, they will assume some responsibility for skill development. (The term "library skills" is both too narrow in scope and inappropriate to this process; it suggests a regular dose of skills given by the librarian, in the library, in total isolation. The terms "research and study skills" or "information skills" help to overcome this problem.) Appropriate aspects of cultural and literary appreciation might also be included in this type of continuum.

The following five-step process has been initiated and successfully worked through with several staffs in order to develop a school-based, research and study skills continuum:

Step 1: Select or devise a research and study skills list as a starting point for staff to react to. Provincial or state curriculum guides, school district guidelines, or any one of a variety of standard sources of resource and study skills lists might be used. The simpler the list, the easier the task.

Step 2: Don't ask each staff member to react to a long skills list initially. Provide the appropriate sections to groups of staff. For example, ask primary teachers to react to a list of primary skills and intermediate teachers to react to a list of intermediate skills. Work with grade levels or primary/intermediate groups, or subject groups, depending on the size and nature of the staff. Meet with each group, in sequential grade level order, to come to a group/grade level consensus.

Have each grade level provide input/feedback both a grade level below and above the level at which they are presently teaching.

Step 3: Seek ratification from the primary and intermediate/junior sections of staff. Meet with each group and look at the continuum for each grade level within that group.

Step 4: Submit the rough draft to the total staff for reaction. Discuss the "transition" years, such as grades 3-4, 6-7, and 9-10, in particular.

Step 5: Seek final staff ratification of the document as a statement of expectations for which they accept some responsibility.

The teacher-librarian has several important roles to play in this process—initiator, partner, and liaison, among them. Regardless of the particular expertise which the teacher-librarian may bring to this task, it is important to keep these roles in mind, or teachers may be inclined to view the final product as the teacher-librarian's list and, therefore, not a shared responsibility.

7. *Be Accountable*

Establish credibility and support through regular reporting procedures. A monthly written report to the administrator might consist of a listing of planning meetings, cooperative programs, and other professional undertakings, such as committee involvement and in-service presented or attended. Technical or support services which have involved a considerable amount of teacher-librarian time or energy might also be listed in this category; examples might include the preparation of major book and media orders, or reorganization of the audio-visual collection. Written reporting can also provide the basis for oral reporting to both staff and administration.

An annual report is mandatory for teacher-librarians who are operating a flexibly scheduled resource centre based on cooperative program planning, whether or not it is required by the district or administrator. The annual report serves several purposes. It provides an overview of the year, highlights the progress made in program development, and assists the teacher-librarian in feeling some sense of closure at year end. The annual report also serves as the basis for establishing program priorities for the following year.

If cooperative program planning and teaching is the framework for the resource centre program, then the emphasis in the annual report should be placed here. A chart of cooperatively developed programs can be drawn as a major part of the annual reporting procedure. The chart provides an overview of the year and highlights the strengths and weaknesses of the program. It serves as a useful discussion paper with the administrator. It can also be used to facilitate sharing of program ideas among staff. (See figure 2.)

COOPERATIVE PROGRAM PLANNING AND TEACHING - THE YEAR IN REVIEW										
GRADE	SEPT	OCT	NOV	DEC	JAN	FEB	MAR	APR	MAY	JUNE
K	Orientation (Ba,Bu) 3 sessions			Bears theme stories & listening centre (Bu) 4 sessions	Chinese New Year stories (Ba,Bu) 3 sessions	Dragon stories (Ba,Bu) 3 sessions		Farm Animals theme stories and collage (4 sessions)		
1	Orientation (J,H,R) 3 sessions					Gr. 1,2,3 Dennis Lee program at V.P.L. 3 sessions			Research project/Pets (J) 4 groups/5 sessions each	
2	Orientation (Pi,M,Pa) 3 sessions			Jacob Two-Two Day (M,Pa)	Mammals Research (H) 3 groups/4 sessions each Space Research(E) 3 groups/5 sessions each					
3	Orientation (Pi) 3 sessions	Dictionary Skills (Pi) Dictionary (Pi) 3 groups/8 6 sessions sessions each				Reptiles research group (F) 7 sessions	Chocolate Day (Pi)		Dinosaurs Research (Pi) 4 groups/5 sessions each	
4	Orientation (S,R,P) 2-3 sessions		Gr. 4/5 Enr. groups Xmas research (S) 2 sessions		O.A. Jacob- Two-Two Day (R,P)	O.A. Research/Human Body (F,N) 2 total group lessons 3 groups/3 sessions each				
5	Orientation (P,G,W,M) 3 sessions		S.S. unit/Pioneers (W) 20 sessions Novel Study Group (M) 15 sessions			Research on Beavers (N) 4 groups/ 5 sessions		Fur Trade Project (W) 15 sessions Novel Study Ancestry Unit Group (M) (G) 3 sessions 10 sessions		
6	Orientation (W,B,G) 2-3 sessions	Culture Realms Picture Study (G) 12 sessions	Human Body Research (B) 4 sessions notetaking	B.C. Study (G) 2 groups 6 sessions each	Japan research (G) 10 sessions Novel Study Group (G) 9 sessions				Pre-Camp program (G,B) 3 groups/4 sessions each	
7	Orientation (H,C,Mc) 3 sessions Pre-historic Man (C,S) 7 sessions each		Gr. 6/7 (S) f	Enr. Groups s. project /2 sessions		Research Project/Greece (P,P,P) 3 classes/10 sessions each Pre-Camp Program				
OTHER	New Teacher Orientation Student Teacher 4 sessions	Sci. Space Research (D) 5 sessions In-Service	Mothers Program Canadian Lit. Program	Primary Stories I.R.P. Xmas Party & Puppet Show				8 groups/ 1 session E.S.L. group Preschool Alphabet Book Program Activities		Class visits re. Public Library Summer Programs

Fig. 2. A chart of cooperatively developed programs.

The various strategies described for Phase I can be accomplished over a period of a year to eighteen months, provided there is effective, continuing communication with the administrator and no "waffling" on the part of the teacher-librarian. Strategies for Phase II extend and build on those outlined in Phase I.

Phase II

1. *Be High Profile*

   The teacher-librarian must be as visible, accessible and involved as possible in order to be viewed as a professional *teaching* colleague. Continue to initiate and/or provide in-service for staff. Provide an in-service session for new teachers at the beginning of the year and invite all teachers—and be sure that the administrator attends. Provide in-service for student teachers. There are double dividends here. Student teachers provide one more avenue to working with staff. And who knows—one of those student teachers may be a colleague one day!

   Where teacher-librarians are part-time, work in two different schools, or in a situation where there are multiple buildings on site, post and distribute a timetable, indicating "locations" for morning coffee and lunch breaks. Times and locations for planning with teachers should also be established.

   Become a member of the professional development committee, or other key committees in the school. Is there a school budget committee? How are budget decisions made? Is there a school interviewing committee? There is a sound rationale for the teacher-librarian being a member of this committee. If in fact the teacher-librarian is expected to plan and work with all teachers on staff, then it seems only reasonable to have some involvement in the decisions made regarding the hiring of new staff members. This involvement may be in a variety of forms. If a staff interviewing committee exists, the teacher-librarian should be a member. If it is a committee of one—the administrator—then the process of interviewing for new staff members and the criteria by which decisions are made are still worth discussing. Perhaps the administrator would include a question about resource centre use in his or her interview format! (Examples: "Can you tell me how you've made use of the resource centre in your teaching?" "How have you worked with the teacher-librarian?" "How have you ensured coverage of the necessary research and study skills?") Through questions such as these, the administrator will have an idea of the candidate's experience with, and attitude towards, resource centre use. The administrator is essentially saying, "I feel the resource centre is important in this school".

   Establish a profile with the community. Set an objective to attend all parent meetings, or every second one, or select those you feel are important and be there. Arrange to make at least one presentation to the parent group each year. Make every effort to find out what their questions, concerns, and perceived needs are. Communicate through interpreters if necessary in a multi-ethnic community and provide pamphlets and written messages in translation. One of the most effective means of addressing parent groups is through a brief slide presentation. Let parents see their children at work in the resource centre.

Seek out adult volunteers in the community. Be sure to talk to them about the role of the teacher-librarian and resource-based programs in the school. Adults who give their time are often the community members who have a wide sphere of influence.

Establish liaison with the local public library branch. Invite the children's librarian to tell stories, give booktalks, collaborate on a puppet show, and explain the services of the public library. Encourage student and class visits to the public library.

Maintain visibility through report card inserts—a bookmark will do! Send notes home with student library monitors. When assessing student work in cooperatively planned and taught programs, always comment on the work and sign your name. That always gets home!

2. *Change The Approach/Not The Tune*
   Continue to meet with the administrator on a *regular* basis. Be careful not to stop at the "awareness level" and silent support! Place the emphasis in Phase II on the administrator's role regarding expectations of and for teachers. It is unreasonable to expect that the teacher-librarian will succeed in working well with all teachers on a staff without administrative support. If the resource centre program is viewed as a partnership, there will be some expectation that classroom teachers will work with the teacher-librarian to ensure adequate development of research and study skills, and effective resource centre use, on the part of the students for whom they are primarily responsible. The only place this expectation is going to come from is the administration.

   Active, positive, administrative support can increase teacher commitment to a successful resource centre program. Suggest subtle ways that the administrator might commend a staff member for a program that has been planned. Visiting the resource centre while the program is in operation, a note in the teacher's mail box, a word in passing in the hallway, or, better still, in the staffroom where other staff members will overhear, are all effective ways of intrinsically rewarding teachers and reinforcing desired approaches.

3. *Take Bigger Steps/Grade Level Planning*
   Once you have succeeded in planning at least one unit with the majority of teachers, there is another approach to be taken in Phase II. Approach teachers at one grade level and attempt to plan a program together as a team. Base the approach and planning on the research and study skills continuum developed in Phase I. Emphasize the importance of those skills outlined in the continuum that require resource centre use. Again, start at the grade level where there is the greater likelihood of success, and persuade other grade levels by effective example.

   Highlight the benefits of grade level planning. Sharing ideas, materials, and the preparation workload can be stimulating, challenging, and time-saving. When a group plans, develops, and implements a program together, everyone tends to put forth their best effort. The benefits for students lie in what are often better programs. The prerequisite should be that at least one cooperative program exists for each grade level.

Hold grade level meetings to discuss the progress being made with research and study skills commitments. Are all areas being taught? If some are being missed, or need greater emphasis, how can this best be done? Is revision of the continuum necessary? At the same time, review the cooperatively developed programs which are on file for that grade level and attempt to agree on a program, or choice of programs, that will provide for development of a specific skill and a common experience for all students at that grade level. This helps strengthen the developmental aspect of the resource centre program by providing a link from year-to-year, yet it remains a strong, curriculum-integrated approach.

There are other benefits to this type of approach as well. Most importantly, it allows some teachers to become involved at the cooperative teaching or implementation stage, rather than at the planning stage. If it is a positive, successful experience in which educational benefits and student enjoyment are demonstrated, those more reluctant or hard-to-convince teachers may be inclined to get involved at the cooperative planning stage in future programs.

Phase III

By the beginning of Phase III, there is a solid foundation and strong framework for the resource centre program, firmly establishing it as an integral part of the school's curriculum.

The teacher-librarian's initiative and leadership to this point puts him/her in a position to take the development of the resource centre program to its logical conclusion.

Take A Giant Step/Total School Programming

In its simplest form, total school programming is often undertaken in preparation for a theme day, week, or month. The type of total school program referred to here, however, is one which, regardless of the curriculum area(s) included, involves extensive cooperative planning and teaching with all staff members and working with all students in the school. It is one in which the resource centre is truly the central focus, or such an integral part that the total school program could not function without it. It is developmental and it is one which staff have a long-term commitment to.

The key to total school programming is often a staff member with expertise and interest in an area, whether it be environmental education or computer literacy. The "seed" for a total school program can be most successfully planted by first working through a program with that teacher and subsequently developing a proposal to take to the entire staff.

Planning for a school-wide program includes:

(1) the identification of a subject-related scope and sequence continuum of content and skills, to ensure a developmental approach across the grades,

(2) the integration of research and study skills from the school-based continuum at each grade level,

(3) a specific approach to program planning, development, and implementation to determine and facilitate the process staff will work through,

(4) a realistic timeline,

(5) opportunity for evaluation and revision of the program by all teachers, and finally,

(6) provision for the maintenance of grade-wide units developed in Phase II. (See figure 3.)

Essentially, throughout Phase III, this means there will be a minimum of two grade-wide programs in existence, providing a strong basis for further program development of this nature.

GRADE/TEACHER(S)	LANGUAGE ARTS	MATH	SCIENCE	SOCIAL STUDIES	OTHER
Kindergarten					
Gr. 1 (Smith) (Petersen)	Dolch primer, blending consonants, creative writ.	Joining; sets	The Sky (Planetarium Visit)	All About Me! Nutrition	Cooking
	Blending, Alphabet review	Addition to 10, Greater-Less, Shape	Planets/Space/Weather/ Seasons	All About Me! Community Helpers/Nutrition	
Gr. 2 (Johnson) (Taylor)	Dinosaurs Poetry Journals	Sums and Differences to 20 Missing addends	Weather, cont.	Communities - cont.	
Gr. 3 (Scott) (Neeland)	Journals Double Vowels	Math Stations Multiplication	Nutrition	Trains	Hansel & Gretel (Musical)
Gr. 4 (Wesley) (Meyers)	Fairy Tales & Unlikely Comparisons, Flights Backpacks/Nature	Complete Measurement Numbers & Numerals Review Add'n & Subt'n			
Gr. 5 (Anderson)	Basal reader, Cr. Writ. Cinquains & Haiku, News Spelling, Novel,Notetaking	Geometry, Number drills logic, games re place value, & multiplication	Human Skeleton/ Nutrition	Routes to East/Shipbuilding Explorers	
Gr. 5/6 (Bragg)	Novels	Problems, Patterns, Area Volume	Human Skeleton/ Nutrition	Middle East	
Gr. 6/7 (Howell)					
Gr. 7 (Rankin)	Punctuation/History of writing & writing styles	Complete Geometry/ Start Percentage and Average	Tree Study/Mapping Small Places/Completion of Rock Study	Continue Local Area Mapping Study - public service in the area	Pacific Press Visit (Nov. 25th)
ESL (Ferrier) (Diggings)					
LEC (Twaits)	Communication/Time Inventors/Inventions		Dinosaurs		
LAC (Poon)					

Fig. 3.

CONCLUSION

The introduction of any change involves a number of steps. For teacher-librarians, one might identify five stages in the change process:

Awareness ...

An understanding of the roles and responsibilities of teachers, teacher-librarians, and administrators in developing an effective resource centre program is not going to happen by osmosis. While district leadership is important, effective program implementation requires someone at the school level to take responsibility for explaining the program. If not the teacher-librarian, then who?

Understanding ...

A well-articulated rationale and full information can assist administrators and teachers to understand the conceptual framework of a resource centre program. Understanding can streamline communication and planning.

Acceptance ...

Demonstration and practice lead to acceptance. Interaction among the teacher-librarian, administrator, and teachers promotes cooperation.

Commitment ...

Professionalism is determined not only by level of academic achievement, but also by degree of commitment. The professional teacher-librarian will have a strong commitment to a clearly defined role in resource-based learning. Administrative support is critical and is also the most effective means of gaining and/or solidifying teacher commitment to the implementation of a program.

Renewal ...

Review and Revision should be an ongoing part of the change process. If teachers remain active partners in implementation, the continuation of a program is much more assured. And the measure of successful implementation is in program continuation.

New areas of expertise take time to develop. Implementation should be viewed as a process. As a process, it should involve a well thought-out plan covering a three-to-five year period. If this three phase approach cannot be accomplished in a period of five years, it is probably time to decide that it is just not going to happen in this school, or that someone new might be able to do it in this particular situation ... and, in either case, transfer!

The key criteria to success with this approach are a strong commitment to a well-defined role, administrative support, a high profile, and accountability.

The result should be a resource centre program that is embedded in, and essential to, the school curriculum and, as a consequence, is both educationally viable and politically justifiable.

SCHOOL LIBRARIES
A Rationale*

Contributors: Bev Anderson, Barry Eshpeter, Kay Iseke, Sheila Pritchard, and Dianne Oberg

- **Future**

  How should schools prepare students for an increasingly uncertain future? This issue is raised frequently by concerned parents, by educators, and by the media.

- **Technology**

  Our society is an information society—characterized by rapidly advancing technology and overwhelming change. Information available is now doubling every eight to ten years.

- **Changes**

  This creates serious problems for information users. For example, students need to learn how to separate the meaningful and useful from the irrelevant. The skills of "learning how to learn," the skills of lifelong learning, are necessary to prepare them to cope with change.

- **Democracy**

  This preparation for life should be regarded as fundamental. Our commitment to a free and open society is dependent upon having citizens who are able to acquire and analyze information in order to make independent decisions. As the pervasiveness of electronic media increases, the individual's skill for analyzing information becomes more critical.

- **Bias**

  Students must learn to detect bias, to evaluate information sources, to consider both sides of an issue. They must practice these skills throughout their education if they are to participate effectively as adults in our society.

*From "School Libraries—A Rationale," *Emergency Librarian* 11 (March/April 1984): 6-7. Reprinted by permission of *Emergency Librarian*. The Learning Resources Council of the Alberta Teachers' Association was challenged to prepare a brief but clear rationale for school libraries. Their objective was to explain the critical function of school library programs in preparing students to become life-long learners who are able to cope with change, and who are able to fulfill their roles in society, both now and in the future. Contributors to this paper were Bev Anderson and Barry Eshpeter of Calgary, Kay Iseke of St. Albert, and Sheila Pritchard and Dianne Oberg of Edmonton.

- **Learning Styles**

  Students practice these skills when they are taught using a wide variety of materials in a wide variety of ways. As well, the diverse needs and learning styles of individual students are best met when this approach to education is chosen. Not all of us learn best from the printed page; for some of us, other formats provide better ways to learn.

- **Gifted/Special**

  This is true of all students, not only the gifted or special education student. The teacher and the textbook, once considered adequate sources of information, are no longer sufficient.

- **Deficiency**

  Are Alberta students being prepared for an effective role in their society? Unfortunately, many students in this province are denied the opportunity to develop the skills necessary to participate fully in their society.

- **Effective Programs**

  There are vast differences in the levels of school library development in Alberta. In some school districts, school libraries are seen as a priority. In such areas, students can select from a wide range of learning resources. They are instructed in locating and using information by professional educators. Teachers and teacher-librarians co-operatively develop lesson plans, and learning activities for their students.

- **Lack Staff/ No Services**

  In some districts, although facilities and basic resources appear to be in place, the staff or time needed to plan learning activities is not provided. In other districts, no library services or programs exist.

- **Goal of Schooling**

  The third Goal of Schooling, as defined by the Government of Alberta in 1979, states that
  > "programs and activities shall be planned, taught, and evaluated ... in order that students:
  > — develop the learning skills of finding, organizing, analyzing, and applying information in a constructive and objective manner."

- **Libraries Essential**

  School libraries are essential in ensuring that students "learn to learn". Students who have not had access to quality school library programs lack adequate skills to effectively use public and academic libraries and other information sources important for their work and for their personal lives. A viable school library program should be available to every student in Alberta.

- **Crucial Time**

This is a crucial time in the development of school library services in Alberta. There are indications that students are graduating from school now without skills for either post-secondary education or lifelong learning.

- **Action**

Action on this issue must begin now.

- **Elections**

Although provincial leadership is critical, decisions regarding staffing and funding libraries are made at district and school levels. Municipal and school board officials are elected on October 17, 1983. Their positions on this issue will greatly affect the quality of education in our province.

ADDITIONAL READINGS

Haycock, Ken. "Strengthening the Foundations for Teacher-Librarianship." *School Learning Resources* 4 (June 1985): 4-8, 19-20.

Vandergrift, Kay E., and Jane Anne Hannigan. "Elementary School Library Media Centers as Essential Components in the Schooling Process." *School Library Media Quarterly* 14 (Summer 1986): 171-73.

Part 3
School Library Media Specialists: Consultants and Instructional Designers

Since the consultant and instructional design functions represent the emerging role of the school library media specialist, the following articles were chosen because they show a variety of approaches and views about these functions. Retta Patrick illustrates the active role promoted in David V. Loertscher's taxonomy with actual practices of media professionals. She uses vivid examples to show how media specialists perform at various levels of integration in the learning process. Janet Stroud defines the expanded role as a partnership that begins with nurturing the teacher to gain competence. She addresses the lack of confidence of school library media specialists and suggests minimizing this by working first with teachers who share similar views. Stroud advises making instructional activities the top priority in the day's schedule.

Antoinette Oberg takes the mystery out of instructional development (ID). Rather than the traditional textbook approach to instructional development, Oberg offers a simplified model stressing the underlying assumptions and the deliberations of the process.

Finally, Barbara Stripling asks the question which is on the mind of every school library media specialist approaching instructional development. How and why should busy school library media specialists implement a process devised and thrust upon them by ivory-tower academics? Examining the appeals and dangers, Stripling describes the evidence that convinced her of the worth of instructional development—increased media center use, more visibility, and once again experiencing the creativity, innovation, and fun of being involved in what she calls teacher-type activities.

SCHOOL LIBRARY MEDIA PROGRAMS TODAY

The Taxonomy Applied*

Retta Patrick

On a scale of one to eleven, how do you rate your involvement in your school's instructional program? Can you, as a school library media specialist, prove your contribution to teaching and learning? Do you have a step-by-step plan for improvement? These are critical questions that must be addressed by all practitioners if we are to survive the eighties.

Analysis of library media activities in a given school on a given day will, it is hoped, reveal a relatively wide range of taxonomic levels in operation. Each is important, and each succeeding level builds on the foundation laid at the preceding level. The sequential progression may be compared to Bloom's taxonomy: knowledge, comprehension, application, analysis, synthesis, evaluation.

Level one of the taxonomy acknowledges the existence of the library media center and a library media specialist, totally ignored by the faculty. (If you are at this level, be prepared to move up—or out—quickly!) Level two involves the stage of developing, organizing, and maintaining resources, providing access, and creating an inviting school library media center atmosphere. Levels three and four find the library media specialist becoming thoroughly familiar with the center's resources and applying this knowledge by responding to individual student and teacher requests. At level five the library media specialist begins to collect successful, new, and creative ideas and to expand information sources. Through brief, informal planning, he or she suggests ideas and resources to teachers. Level five begins the transition from the traditional passive/reactive role to active instructional involvement.

Movement into the higher levels of the taxonomy can be accelerated as the library media specialist builds credibility. How can credibility be established? One step at a time—assessing strengths and setting goals and objectives that will ensure initial success (for example, by working with a teacher who is receptive). The library media specialist must streamline administrative responsibilities, delegate nonprofessional tasks to support staff, and give top priority to instructional involvement.

Each of the following examples of instructional involvement, levels six through eleven, is preceded by the objective for that level.

*From Retta Patrick, "School Library Media Programs Today: The Taxonomy Applied," *Wilson Library Bulletin* 56 (February 1982): 422-27. Reprinted by permission of *Wilson Library Bulletin*.

LEVEL SIX—PLANNED GATHERING

Objective: Given advance notice by a teacher, the library media specialist will gather resources from a wide variety of sources to fill the request for a class project.

Ruth Tucker, library media specialist at Baker Elementary School, Pulaski County Special School District, utilizes her broad knowledge of resources, curricula, teaching, and learning styles (gained from fifteen years as a classroom teacher and eight years as a library media professional), to give this type of support to teachers. The principal at Baker fully supports the library media center instructional involvement and demonstrates this support by encouraging teachers to prepare advance lesson plans that involve a variety of library media center resources and activities. The teachers plan units well in advance and are committed to meeting individual student needs through a variety of media and strategies. Ruth Tucker is considered a full partner on the teaching team. Teachers have learned through experience that spontaneous requests are filled promptly but that, given time for a thorough search, the library media specialist will literally flood them with resources.

Two sixth-grade teachers developed a social studies unit on the Middle East. They completed a standard request form three weeks in advance, listing the topic to be studied and specifying the types of resources and the dates needed. On receiving the form, Tucker contacted the teachers to clarify the request. She then retrieved books, filmstrips, study prints, maps, and other resources from the school library media center collection. She requested additional materials through interlibrary loan from the Central Arkansas (Public) Library System, the Pulaski County Special School District Media Center, and other schools within the district. In further discussion with the teachers, Tucker offered to contact a retired agronomist who had spent fifteen years in the Middle East with the U.S. Department of State. The teachers were enthusiastic, and the library media specialist made the contact. Dressed in native costume and armed with a host of artifacts, household items, and clothing, the former agronomist brought Middle Eastern culture to life for the students—a learning experience that would not have happened without the library media specialist.

Ruth Tucker readily locates and taps information sources, many of which are free. In gathering resources for a kindergarten career awareness unit, she obtained donations of firefighters' and nurses' uniforms and a basic nurse's kit. After one of the school's students was killed in a hunting accident, Tucker contacted the Arkansas Game and Fish Commission and arranged for hunter safety instruction in the school. This presentation was correlated with an environmental protection unit in science. It's easy to understand why Ruth Tucker's former principal remarked, "She gives curb service to our teachers!"

LEVEL SEVEN—EVANGELISTIC OUTREACH

Objective: The library media specialist will actively promote the multimedia individualized instruction philosophy through workshops for teachers and/or administrators.

Elaine Hamada, over the last seven years, has mounted an extensive campaign to inform the school and community of the involvement of the library media center with the educational program. Through weekly reports submitted to the building principal and all certified and classified staff and monthly reports to district level personnel such as the superintendent and members of the board of education, data on library media center activities is distributed. "This effort," she says, "has reaped dividends in terms of creating positive attitudes toward library media programs."

Developing positive attitudes toward library media programs is the first step in preparing teachers and administrators to be "converted." The library media specialist must respond to teacher needs, and mutual understanding must be developed. The "evangelist" (the library media specialist) can then get on with the "sermon." It may be directed to the individual or a group (such as subject area or grade-level specialists) or toward the entire faculty.

Betty Costa, a Broomfield, Colorado library media specialist, describes her involvement: "Operation at level seven is a very important part of my library program. One activity at this level is my periodic 'Open House.' Each one has a main theme or emphasis such as equipment usage, social studies resources, or math resources. The sessions which emphasize equipment also publicize media as a secondary emphasis, and vice versa. These sessions not only include building level resources but also district and community resources.... Periodic newsletters are written to increase staff awareness, and materials are displayed in the teachers' lounge. The letters and displays usually include topical suggestions related to current events, season, or units being taught in the building.... Personal contacts are made when a new item, workshop, or article is noticed that I feel will particularly appeal to a staff member or members."

Elaine Hamada extends "operation outreach" beyond the scope of the immediate school. She has worked with groups of academically talented students to develop higher level inquiry and logical reasoning skills using manipulatives. She has shared her expertise by conducting in-service workshops for specialists at the district level on the use of manipulatives for mathematics. Beyond the school district, Hamada has shared her instructional involvement with current and future administrators and teachers at a curriculum conference. Her commitment is to "sharing the wealth of our doing to all persons involved in education."

LEVEL EIGHT – SCHEDULED PLANNING

Objective: The library media specialist will participate on the teaching team by responding to a previously planned unit, supplying materials and/or activities to complement the unit.

"Converts" brought into the fold through the various level-seven approaches offer the library media specialist the first real opportunity for jointly planned participation on the teaching team. During formal planning sessions, the library media specialist and the teacher develop a unit that may have once been planned by the teacher alone.

Bob Winn, a library media specialist at North Pulaski High School, worked with an English teacher who was preparing to teach a unit on reference sources found in the tenth-grade English textbook. During the planning conference, Winn and the teacher examined the textbook unit and decided to redesign the content to fit local students' needs and to include the additional sources found in the school's reference collection. (This step moves the unit toward level nine).

Working together they determined which information sources to present and who would be responsible for each phase of the presentation. In preparation for the unit, Winn produced a short slide/tape presentation on the *Readers' Guide* and developed sets of reference questions based on the tools to be introduced. For nine days students alternated between classroom and media center with teaching responsibilities shared equally by the library media specialist and classroom teacher. The teacher administered a test at the end of the unit and assumed responsibility for grading.

LEVEL NINE—INSTRUCTIONAL DESIGN

Objective: The library media specialist will assume a leadership role in developing and implementing instructional units, working as a team with other teachers to create unit objectives, to determine resources and activities, and to participate in the instructional process.

Ann Keck, library media specialist at Otter Creek Elementary in Pulaski County School District, is a typical example of the library media professional who uses her expertise to design instruction geared toward meeting specific needs of learners. She knows the curriculum in her school and continually searches for resources and new or proven techniques for strengthening the teaching and learning processes.

In describing her involvement with instructional design, Keck says, "The teacher wanted a unit on insects for third-year students who were reading on or slightly above level. The unit would cover insects as animals: their body structure, homes, food, reproduction, and the ways in which they help or harm man. The teacher also wanted students to collect specimens to share with the class." In the initial planning meeting, the library media specialist assumed a leadership role by guiding the teacher through the development of clearly stated learning goals and objectives and by determining the evaluation procedure.

Working as a team, the teacher and library media specialist began to research and develop materials to be used for instruction, reinforcement, and enrichment. The library media staff gathered all types of resources relating to insects—books, filmstrips, film loops, study prints, "read alongs"—and prepared a bibliography. The library media staff produced posters for classroom use, prepared detailed instructions for making insect nets and killing jars, and wrote a letter to parents explaining the unit and asking for assistance with student projects.

Using the text and the supplementary resources provided by the school library media center, the teacher began instruction of the unit. The library media specialist visited the classroom to explain her role and to encourage students to seek help when needed. Identification of the collected insects required skill in locating information in the encyclopedia, skills that were introduced to the group by the library media specialist. Individual help was then given as small groups visited the library media center throughout the day to work on identifying their insect specimens.

After successfully using the encyclopedia to identify ten insects, each student selected one specimen to research in depth. After the written report was completed, Keck guided students through the production of a slide/tape presentation entitled "Creepy Critters." Each child prepared one slide using the Visual Maker and a one or two minute audiotape describing the research in his or her study. Student work was evaluated on the basis of successful completion of the collection, correct identification of all insects, and preparation of the report. The teacher graded the students' work. Although the production of the individual slide/tape was required, no grade was given on the quality.

In her evaluation of this unit, Ann Keck states: "In addition to being a fun unit, these students learned much about the insect world, sharpened their reference skills, and became excited about media production. Parents became interested in what was going on in the classroom and the library media center. Although the library media center shared in evaluation of the steps necessary to receive a grade for this unit, we did not share responsibility for grading it. We hope to share this responsibility in future units." She adds, "I'll be a ten yet!"

LEVEL TEN—INSTRUCTIONAL DESIGN

Objective: The library media specialist will team with teachers to create unit objectives, determine resources and activities, share equal responsibility for learning, and participate in grading.

Two enthusiastic library media specialists, Trina Lummus and Sandra Steele, teamed with a creative English teacher, Jan Pratt, to develop an in-depth Shakespearean study at West Orange High School in Winter Garden, Florida. Their desire to find an alternative to research papers for eleventh-grade students prompted the three to initiate this unit. In her description of the unit, Trina Lummus says: "We felt that only the writer of the paper, the teacher, and, sometimes, the library media specialist ever got an opportunity to see the completed project. Our students needed some experiences in group projects and in learning to work together. Also, many had never had the opportunity to actually participate in audio-visual production."

Working together, the library media specialists and the teacher developed objectives based on these purposes. A large amount of time was spent in selecting resources, planning activities, and developing work schedules. Responsibilities capitalized on the knowledge and skills of each member of the teaching team. The teacher selected the research topics, introduced the unit, organized student groups, and monitored their progress throughout the unit; the library media staff introduced information resources, assisted students with their research, and taught the production skills (video, slide/tape). Each member of the team was involved in all areas for consultation and assistance.

For seven weeks the team guided the three English classes through their individual and group projects. Teaching and learning alternated between classroom and library media center. On the final day, a Shakespearean festival in the library media center produced a full day of "what students enjoy best—food, music, TV, and live entertainment." Live scenes from six Shakespearean plays were interspersed with videotaped reports (shown on six TV monitors) of the research completed on various aspects of Elizabethan life: food, games and entertainment, manners and etiquette, education, music, clothing, furniture, actors, and the Globe Theater. Dressed in Shakespearean costume, students served lunch, Elizabethan-style. Selected performances were given for many of the school's 1,700 students. Local newspapers came to take pictures and interview students, and many parents came also. This provided excellent public relations for the school and the library media program.

In evaluating the unit, the two library media specialists note that they shared equal responsibility with the teacher by discussing student grades for research, production work, and the ability of students to work together in groups. They conclude that "learning can be entertaining and that a close encounter with Shakespeare was ... worthy of a re-run."

LEVEL ELEVEN—CURRICULUM DEVELOPMENT

Objective: The library media specialist will team with other educators to plan and structure what will actually be taught in the school or district.

Peggy Pfeiffer, a district library media supervisor in the Lafayette (Indiana) Public Schools, describes her involvement in curriculum committees: "We have always had at least one library media specialist on the district-wide curriculum committee. This probably stemmed from the fact that a former assistant superintendent had a library degree, and superintendents since then have known how strongly I felt about the matter."

Sue Duncan, a building-level library media specialist in Lafayette, outlines the role of the curriculum committee and her involvement in it. The curriculum committee is made up of representatives from every school in the district and is charged with approving all curriculum change. This includes approving new courses, deleting courses, and approving changes. In addition, all proposed research and special projects are channeled through the committee.

Asked what contribution the library media specialist brings to the curriculum committee, Sue Duncan notes that two contributions stand out: first, the library media specialist is in a better position to view the entire curriculum than any specific subject or grade-level teacher; second, the library media specialist can offer suggestions on use of technology and resources to be considered in the early formulation of new courses or revised courses.

Peggy Pfeiffer adds that the district administrators and teachers now recognize that library media specialists know curriculum—and they value that knowledge. She also points out that teachers are now looking at course changes and additions with technology in mind. And most important, the library media centers in the district are now able to prepare collections in advance of curriculum changes—a real improvement.

YOU CAN DO IT

The activities described in the first five levels of the taxonomy are representative of the contributions that library media specialists in thousands of school districts make every day. But for the upper six levels, experience indicates that certain essential requirements are needed for success in furthering instructional goals. Each requirement relates to the knowledge, attitude, and commitment of the people involved—the teacher, the library media staff, principals, and the superintendent.

First, the library media staff needs competencies that include a thorough knowledge of resources and their application to teaching and learning, a fundamental understanding of the school's curricula, and a knowledge of students' abilities, interests, and learning styles.

Second, the principal, as the instructional leader of the school, needs to understand the value of a strong school library media program and its role in the teaching and learning process. He or she must promote adequate budgeting to provide professional and support staff and other resources to develop and implement the program. Additionally, principals should encourage teachers to use multimedia materials to promote learning and should provide the time and motivation for instructional planning between library media staff and teachers.

Third, the teachers are a vital part of the library media program. They must come to understand the potential contribution the school library media program can make in meeting individual student needs. Recognizing the valuable role the library media specialist can assume in supporting and extending the curriculum, teachers must take time in their own instructional planning to include communication with the library media staff. They must become committed to meeting individual student needs through the use of a variety of library center resources and strategies.

Finally, the superintendent and district level staff must demonstrate commitment by providing staff development programs designed to prepare, implement, and maintain integrated programs. They must also provide the financial support required to employ qualified professional and support staff as well as the resources and facilities necessary for fully developed library media center programs.

While few school systems or individual schools can boast that all these pieces of the puzzle fit together perfectly, we can no longer justify a school library media program based on a level-one philosophy. Every program in education today must produce dividends directly related to teaching and learning. The taxonomy offers a rational approach to program building if the positive attitude, ability, desire, initiative, and fortitude are there. Some library media specialists are already doing it, and many more can!

LIBRARY MEDIA CENTER TAXONOMY
Future Implications*

Janet Stroud

For many years theoreticians have advocated an expanded role for the library media specialist — a role that requires increased involvement in the instructional design function. Fulfilling this expectation means assuming a partnership role with the classroom teacher in implementing specific instructional units, assuming a policy-making position with regard to curriculum decisions, and accepting increased responsibility for in-service education.

Although this expanded role has long been promoted, practice has lagged far behind. Relatively few library media specialists are actively involved in the instructional design process. The question then arises as to why they aren't involved. Is it because teachers and administrators don't want them in that role, or is it because library media specialists have little inclination to assume that role? There is evidence to suggest that either or both reasons may be the case.

WHO IS AT FAULT?

Certainly there is concern on the part of some classroom teachers that library media specialists may be trying to involve themselves in a role that teachers regard as theirs alone. Many teachers highly value their autonomy and do not want to share their role even though the quality of their teaching is likely to improve if they do.

Some research indicates that it is the classroom teachers who may feel the most reluctance to enter into this partnership. Steven Kerr concludes that at best, some administrators and teachers are indifferent to the involvement of library media specialists in instructional development activities. At worst, they are reluctant to concede any of their "territory" to the library media specialist and therefore view such activities on the part of the library media specialist as encroachment.[1] Evelyn Daniel found that teachers were not accepting of library media specialists who were more active, aggressive, and independent.[2] D. C. Lortie asserts that teachers often find it too costly to accept or solicit this type of assistance from library media specialists, because to do so means to admit a lack of competence.[3]

*From Janet Stroud, "Library Media Center Taxonomy: Future Implications," *Wilson Library Bulletin* 56 (February 1982): 428-33. Reprinted by permission of *Wilson Library Bulletin*.

But reluctance is also present among the library media specialists. Kerr also found in his study that library media specialists showed little interest in assuming an instructional development role and instead identified more closely with the more traditional role of the library media specialist's responsibilities. David Loertscher[4] and Janet Stroud[5] concluded that library media specialists either preferred to perform or were performing the more traditional library media services.

Kerr's report asserts that the library media specialist with better "role-taking ability" may be more successful in working with classroom teachers. Certainly the library media specialist who can understand the problems encountered in the classroom and who can approach solutions in the manner that the classroom teacher does has a better chance for success than the library media specialist who is unfamiliar with the classroom teacher's day-to-day responsibilities and activities. Also, many library media specialists feel reluctant to assume the instructional design role because of feelings of inadequacy. Many, perhaps because they have had little or no actual classroom experience, feel that they know too little about the teaching process. These inadequacies could be corrected to some extent at the pre-service level with a program of study that contained more emphasis on curriculum development and teaching methods combined with student teaching in a subject area as well as in the library.

One factor that cannot be overlooked is that many library media specialists select library work because they don't want or like to teach, and many practicing library media specialists leave teaching to become librarians for the same reasons. It is foolish to expect that the segment of library media specialists who feel this way are going to look upon the instructional design role with positive feelings, especially when the rewards or incentives are not clearly and immediately perceived. Conversely, there are no apparent penalties for the library media specialist who does not assume this role.

There are substantial indications that library media specialists are not a part of the curricular process in their schools and do not want to assume these responsibilities. Although Dorothy Hellene's research was primarily interested in exploring the school principal's support of the library media center program, she also found that library media specialists who were poorly trained or who had little inclination to get involved in curricular activities impeded program development.[6] Dennis Leeper compared library media centers in open-space and closed-space schools and concluded that it was the specialist who was most responsible for determining the quality of a library media center program.[7]

EDUCATING THE EDUCATORS

It should be apparent from studying the taxonomy presented by David Loertscher on pages 99 through 102 that many of our traditional library media center operations must change if the library media specialist is to successfully assume the instructional design role. To operate at the higher levels of the taxonomy requires a change in thinking about the role of the library media specialist and about the media center in the school setting on the part of library media specialists, teachers, and administrators.

If Leeper's and Hellene's findings are valid, it would seem that the responsibility for educating others to the instructional development capacity of the library media specialist must fall to the library media specialist. A familiar fallacy with role studies (i.e., asking teachers and administrators what role they feel the library media specialist should assume) is that the respondents don't perceive an expanded role as being possible or necessary because they haven't experienced it before. Unless users have been educated or exposed to an expanded curricular role on the part of the library media specialist, they're not likely to regard it as a viable option for the future.

The first efforts should be in the area of in-service education for library media specialists: in-service opportunities provided by universities, state departments of education, and professional organizations. Such education must try to correct the deficiencies library media specialists feel they have by offering opportunities for them to gain competencies in working with teachers in planning and developing units of instruction, achieving input in curricular developments, and linking the use of media to these new curricular developments.

As great a need as in-service to library media specialists is in-service to teachers. Although some feel that teachers should bear a substantial amount of the responsibility for seeking out library services, the fact is that teachers know very little about the services already offered by their school libraries, and they know even less about potential services. Therefore, the only logical person to assume the responsibility of educating others is the library media specialist. As teachers become more aware of media center services that can benefit them, they will become more amenable to the library media specialist's efforts to work cooperatively with them on instructional units.

Also mandated for the person who intends to initiate instructional development services is a familiarity with the curriculum being offered, a familiarity best gained through service on the school's curriculum committee. Unfortunately, many schools do not have a standing curriculum committee but instead form such committees as needed — these are essentially textbook adoption committees. In either case, it behooves the library media specialist to participate actively in the curriculum development process. In lieu of curriculum committees, attempts should be made to work closely in the same capacity with department or grade-level representatives.

The library media specialist who is not involved is forever reacting to and trying to cope with the decisions others have made rather than participating in the decision-making process. If, as so often happens, the media specialist is unaware of a curricular need until students begin requesting certain materials, the opportunity to bring teachers, students, and materials together is lost.

THE TEAM TEACHING OPTION

It would seem that the library media specialist, if not the most important determinant of the potential success or failure of the school library media center program, is at least recognized as being one of the most important determinants. What characteristics must a library media specialist possess in order to work effectively with others?

Team teaching and group dynamics are two areas with much to offer those of us who are interested in expanding the instructional design role of the library media specialist. In order for people to work together effectively in the classroom, they must see eye-to-eye on important philosophical issues. This need manifests itself in several areas: agreement on major instructional objectives, on the amount of classroom structure needed, on the methods of instruction, on the types of materials used, on the evaluation procedures employed, etc. Major disagreements on any of these issues can negate all efforts. Unless media specialists can successfully put themselves into the teacher's place, effective interaction can never take place.

Both teacher and library media specialist must have confidence in their own abilities. This has definite implications for the library media specialist who often does not feel this confidence. Lack of confidence is quickly conveyed to others. People working together as a team must be willing to give and receive criticism without personalizing it. Instructional methods and procedures must be constantly evaluated and improved, and this cannot occur if suggestions for improvement are viewed as criticism of oneself.

These attributes are not easily attained. Most teachers and library media specialists have definite views on how instruction and students should be handled, and the chances that one's philosophy toward education is going to change is slim. Therefore, it behooves the library media specialist to work with someone who holds similar views. Compatibility with one's teaching partner is a must.

STAFFING PATTERNS: A NEW VIEW

The implications for the library media center that adopts the taxonomy philosophically are far-reaching but not out of reach. They affect every aspect of the school library media center: staffing, resources, accessibility, production, budgeting, and evaluation.

Library media center staffing patterns vary from school to school and program to program, but there's no question that operating at a mix of the levels of the taxonomy will require different competencies of a library media center staff, necessitating either an effort to hire new staff or to retrain existing staff members. If wise hiring practices have been applied in the past, staff members will have complementary competencies or areas of specialization. If not, this will become a goal to work toward when hiring in the future, especially if the taxonomy is to be effectively implemented.

The size of the staff will vary not only with the size of the school but with the extent to which the library media center is involved in the instructional function. As the success of the school library media program grows, the number of clients should increase, which will in turn increase the need for staff.

The structure of each staff member's day will need to be organized to allow instructional concerns to come first. Library media specialists can do this even now to help move toward increased involvement in the instructional functions of the school. Higher-level activities often fail to get implemented in the library media center because lower-level activities are always present in abundance and are easier to do.

Several things can be done to insure that instructional concerns are given top priority in the day's schedule. One method is to set aside consultation times that coincide with teachers' preparation periods. If teachers do not have specified preparation time, perhaps time before or after school can be set aside for teacher consultation. When teachers know that specific times are being set aside for them, they'll be more apt to use those times for that purpose. Another way is to consciously seek out teachers and the opportunities to work with them. If this is done on a systematic and regular basis, it will become a way of life for both teachers and the library media specialist.

RESOURCES FOR INSTRUCTIONAL SUPPORT

In the past, library media center collections have reflected the "something for everyone" philosophy. A balanced collection was considered a good collection. If one is to accept the taxonomy, the collection must be aligned with curricular needs, an objective that may not be consistent with a balanced collection.

Materials purchased to fulfill the special needs generated by instructional units will be designed for specific purposes and will be maintained at a certain size and quality level to accomplish specific requirements of instructional units. Efforts to create a collection that would meet these special needs will be related to efforts at the higher levels of the taxonomy and should reflect the library media specialist's participation in the structuring, execution, and evaluation of instructional units.

Because the materials needed to meet specific purposes will be more detailed in nature, library media specialists will need to use more specialized selection sources. In addition, there should be conscientious efforts to involve teachers and students in the selection process and increased previewing to assure that instructional objectives are met.

The materials collection will have to pass easily back and forth between classrooms and the library media center. This option will dictate the arrangement of the materials. Teachers have often complained about materials in "their topics" being scattered throughout the collection. Perhaps we should take a closer look at our collections and see if the materials could be arranged in ways that would better meet the instructional needs of our clients. If shelving and storage units are portable, the collection can be arranged and rearranged as necessary. The use of portable shelving can also help delineate areas within the media center for individual, small group, and large group use.

The increased use of computers in the library media center offers unlimited possibilities. Many of the routine, time-consuming tasks library media specialists have been required to perform can be eliminated in the future. With the use of computer-generated lists, teachers can be given a printout listing materials pertinent to a specific topic that could be revised quickly and easily. With the use of microcomputers, students and teachers alike can "pull up" all the library media center's holdings on a specific topic. Indexes can be put into the computer, but only the materials actually held by the library media center will be entered, thus saving many hours of wasted time searching for articles in journals not available at that particular library media center.

The use of microcomputers can also help the library media specialist keep track of collection use, monitoring what percentage of materials is circulating the majority of the time, what materials circulate only at particular times of the year, which subject areas or topics are undergoing the greatest circulation or demand, and how many requests for materials cannot be fulfilled.

Dependence on networks should increase. No library is going to be able to afford the sheer numbers of materials that will be needed in the future. A viable alternative is to use networks to increase the number of materials that can be accessed for use in the local school situation. Coordination among teachers and libraries will enable schools to shift materials on a specific topic as needed, and materials that are no longer needed for specific instructional units can be traded to other schools.

The consideration file, traditionally an alphabetical "want list," will be more functional when it is divided into instructional unit categories, with items for the file selected with the instructional unit needs in mind. As a unit is completed, gaps in the collection can be identified and tagged for future consideration.

MAKING INSTRUCTIONAL MATERIALS AVAILABLE

In order to provide services at the upper levels of the taxonomy, the library media center will need to be physically located to allow for free movement of materials and people between classrooms and library media center. Transferring equipment and materials up and down several flights of stairs is a deterrent to even the most dedicated user.

The library media center facility needs to be able to simultaneously accommodate individuals, small groups, and large groups. In many elementary schools, the library media specialist and the library media center are used to provide preparation time for teachers, or library media specialists are expected to tell stories and teach library skills once a week to each class. In some cases, the library media specialist is scheduled for as many as sixty classes a week, and during these periods the library media center is virtually inaccessible to students who want to come to the library media center individually or in small groups; a similar situation is often found in secondary schools when the library media center is so clogged with study halls that it cannot accommodate those who wish to use the library. A physical facility used in this manner will never be able to accommodate the different levels of the taxonomy.

Increased accessibility to materials will require flexible and variable loan policies. Materials that ordinarily circulate may need to be put on reserve, and materials and equipment that normally would not circulate must be allowed to do so. Loan periods and policies will vary depending on the size of the class, disposition of the activities, and the formats used.

Accessibility to the library media center can be enhanced or impeded by attitudes held by either the teacher or the administrator. If the administrator cannot see the use of the library media center for anything other than teaching library skills, it's unlikely that the teachers will feel very differently. If the administrator encourages teachers to incorporate media into their lesson plans, they will probably do so. Similarly, if the teacher views the library media center only as a place to go for storytelling, the students will hold similar expectations. If using media and the library media center is an integral part of the school day, students will be more likely to view the library media center as a necessary part of their lives.

Production will also require a different approach in the years to come. We have always advocated producing materials locally for instructional units, but we often apply available materials to a unit whether they promote an instructional objective or not. Our production efforts should be geared toward looking first at the objective, then to the medium that will best convey a concept. If services at the upper levels of the taxonomy are implemented, materials that will augment instructional needs should receive the highest priorities.

PROVING YOUR WORTH

Program needs will have to be even more clearly articulated in the future, because the success of the taxonomic approach will depend to a great extent on how well the library media center program is funded. The taxonomic approach should make it much easier for the library media specialist to articulate budgeting requirements to administrators. If the library media center program is seen as an integral part of the curriculum rather than a frill, funds are less likely to be cut. There's no question that the taxonomic approach can require increased funds, but this approach will also make it easier for administrators to support such requests. Administrators are loathe to allocate funds to programs that cannot be justified or that fail to show measurable benefits.

In the past, LMC budgets have been allocated by format: a portion for magazines, a portion for books, a portion for audiovisual materials. Logically, if one is to follow the thinking advocated by the taxonomy, the budgeting process will be more effective if funds are allocated in terms of function. If one implements this collection mapping and evaluation strategy the change in procedure can be easily absorbed. That particular mapping strategy will enable the library media specialist to quickly identify collection needs and priorities.

Evaluation of school library services has always been a difficult task. Because it's been elusive, we've attempted to evaluate what we could evaluate easily—items and numbers. But it soon becomes apparent that, although quantitative aspects are important, the survival of the library media center will depend upon evaluative procedures that can measure the *qualitative* aspects of media center operations.

The library media specialist can streamline some of the more time-consuming evaluation routines. For example, instead of attempting to evaluate the collection as a whole, examine only segments of it. Instead of copiously keeping track of how many materials circulate, why not indicate how often the library media specialist worked cooperatively with teachers on instructional units? How well were these activities supported? What types of activities took place in support of instructional units? Were the needs identified by instructional development projects adequately met?

If the taxonomy is accepted as a viable strategy for the future, it is reasonable to assume that evaluation instruments and techniques based on the taxonomic approach will emerge and will provide library media specialists with more comprehensive and valid evaluation procedures than presently exist.

While there are obstacles that confront the library media specialist who wishes to assume an expanded instructional role, there is evidence to suggest that these obstacles are not insurmountable and that one of the largest obstacles is reluctance on the part of the library media specialist to take on instructional design responsibilities. The ability to teach, a background in curricular design, and self-confidence seem to be the variables that can eliminate this reluctance.

In most cases, adoption of the taxonomy does not mean large outlays of money for bigger collections or an increased number of staff members or substantial remodeling of physical facilities. It does mean a radically different way of looking at things, perhaps by realigning staff responsibilities, questioning routine practices and procedures, and evaluating utilization patterns to find out what they mean and how they can be changed. The library program can grow only if the entire staff works to ensure that all efforts and resource allocations are directed toward and contribute to the goal of participation in activities at the higher levels of the taxonomy.

NOTES

[1]Stephen T. Kerr, "Are There Instructional Developers in the Schools? A Sociological Look at the Development of a Profession," *Audiovisual Communications and Review* 25, no. 8 (1977).

[2]Evelyn H. Daniel, "The Organizational Position of School Media Centers: An Analysis of the Role of the School Library and School Librarian" (Ph.D. dissertation, University of Maryland, 1974).

[3]D. C. Lortie, *Schoolteachers: A Sociological Study* (Chicago: University of Chicago Press, 1975).

[4]David V. Loertscher, "Media Center Services to Teachers in Indiana High Schools, 1972-73" (Ph.D. dissertation, Indiana University, 1973).

[5]Janet G. Stroud, "Evaluation of Media Center Services by Media Staff, Teachers, and Students in Indiana Middle and Junior High Schools" (Ph.D. dissertation, Purdue University, 1976).

[6]Dorothy L. Hellene, "The Relationships of the Behaviors of Principals in the State of Washington to the Development of School Library/Media Programs" (Ed.D. dissertation, University of Washington, 1973).

[7]Dennis P. Leeper, "A Comparative Study of Open Space and Self-Contained Elementary School Library-Media Centers" (Ph.D. dissertation, University of Colorado, 1975).

THE SCHOOL LIBRARIAN AND THE CLASSROOM TEACHER

Partners in Curriculum Planning*

Antoinette Oberg

The role of the teacher-librarian has expanded to include cooperation with classroom teachers in planning the instructional program. This cooperation takes many forms, depending on the skills and inclinations of both teacher-librarians and teachers. When a full planning partnership develops, the teacher-librarian can provide not only a welcome support to the classroom teacher, who usually faces the complex and demanding task of curriculum planning alone, but also an occasion for expanding and improving the curriculum planning process. The extent to which this occurs depends largely on the teacher-librarian's knowledge of curriculum planning.

Curriculum planning is something every teacher does daily. Regardless of how detailed the provincial or state curriculum guides may be, teachers have a great deal of planning to do to tailor guide suggestions or prescriptions to their own and their students' knowledge and interests. Although most teachers plan their programs with apparent ease and efficiency, curriculum planning is actually a very complex process. Proper planning requires not only a thorough grasp of the subject matter of a lesson or unit, but also a sensitive understanding of the learners for whom it is intended, and awareness of the many contextual factors which define and influence the situation, as well as knowledge of the planning process itself.

Ideally, in order to marshall the knowledge and resources necessary, curriculum planning is carried out in groups rather than individually, by people who all have first-hand knowledge of the situation for which they are planning. School department or grade level groups are best suited for this task. However, regardless of how well experienced and proficient their members may be in individual curriculum planning, such groups typically lack knowledge of the subtleties and complexities of joint curriculum planning.

It is in this area that the teacher-librarian can make an important contribution. When department and grade level groups are not active in joint planning projects, the teacher-librarian's role becomes even more important. It is the teacher-librarian who can change the teacher's solitary curriculum planning into a more broadly based and cooperative venture.

*From Antoinette Oberg, "The School Librarian and the Classroom Teacher: Partners in Curriculum Planning," *Emergency Librarian* 14 (September/October 1986): 9-14. Reprinted by permission of *Emergency Librarian*.

The teacher-librarian is ideally positioned for this role as a member of a large or small curriculum planning team. First, as a regular member of the school staff, the teacher-librarian has first-hand, intimate knowledge of the school setting — school curriculum policies; principal expectations; teacher predilections, interests and non-interests; parent sentiments; available facilities and materials. Second, the teacher-librarian has expert knowledge of prescribed curriculum and of available print and non-print resource materials. When knowledge of the curriculum planning process is added to this already substantial body of expertise, the teacher-librarian is in a position not only to respond to teacher requests for help in curriculum planning, but also to go beyond teacher requests and make suggestions that can improve the curriculum planning process.

A TRADITIONAL VIEW OF THE CURRICULUM PLANNING PROCESS

For the better part of this century, teachers and curriculum developers have been taught that the ideal curriculum planning process is a rational series of steps beginning with the definition of goals and objectives (sometimes preceded by identification of student or societal "needs") and ending with a check on the accomplishment of those objectives and subsequent revision of instructional plans.

A typical version of this Tyler planning model, named after the man who first laid out its rationale[1] can be summarized in eight steps:

1. Specify goals and objectives.

2. Assess student status.

3. Determine needs.

4. Rank needs.

5. Plan a program.

6. Implement program.

7. Evaluate program.

8. Continue, modify or abort program based on the evaluation.[2]

This view of curriculum planning has a number of things to commend it as a prescription for the planning process. For one thing, curriculum planners should certainly consider what educational ends they are aiming for, although these need not and often should not be stated in terms of precise student behaviors, as later interpreters of the Tyler rationale (most notably Mager and Popham) have incited.

Another commendable feature of the Tyler model is its emphasis on what happens with students as an important ingredient in subsequent planning. The teacher's sensitive judgement of the nature of the students' experiences in relation to educational aims should be the primary determinant of what is subsequently planned.

Unfortunately, these emphases have tended to be overshadowed by a view of curriculum planning as a technical process initiated and controlled by the precise specification of behavioral objectives. Not only does this view mistake important features of education, as Stenhouse[3] argues, but it fails to capture what little is known about how teachers go about the planning process either individually or in groups.

CURRICULUM PLANNING AND DELIBERATION

A better representation of the curriculum planning process as it actually occurs in groups of experts is the model developed by Walker (see figure 1).[4] The three key elements in this model are the curriculum's platform, its design, and the deliberation associated with it. The platform consists of the curriculum planner's assumptions, and it is the source of educational aims and goals. The platform includes conceptions or beliefs about what exists and about what is possible. For example, "We believe there is a learnable strategy for interpreting historical events," states a conception of what is learnable. The platform also includes theories, or beliefs about what relations hold between existing entities. An example given by Walker, "The teacher imparts attitudes toward a subject, and, indeed, attitudes towards learning itself," states a theory about how attitudes toward learning develop.

Beliefs about what is educationally desirable are also part of the platform. Another of Walker's examples, "We teach a subject not to produce little living libraries on that subject, but rather to get a student to think mathematically for himself, to consider matters as a historian does, to take part in the process of knowledge getting," states a general aim of education. Two other less explicit but nevertheless important platform components are images and procedures. Images are another form in which some educationally desirable condition or state of affairs is thought of, without specifying why or in what way it is desirable. Heroes are cultural images. So are outstanding works of art or admired scientific theories. The image of a home may be a very important source of aims and goals for an elementary teacher.[5]

Images are realized through procedures, which specify courses of action or decisions that are desirable without specifying who or in what way they are desirable. Some people would also call these principles.[6] Examples include, "Be honest," and "Minimize the time necessary to learn," and "Create situations in which learners can share with each other".

The significance of the platform is two-fold. First, every curriculum planner has a platform whether it is made explicit or not. When teacher-librarians plan with a teacher, they work from a platform. When curriculum planners appear to speak at cross purposes or do not see eye to eye, it is often because they are working from different curriculum platforms. Making platforms explicit is a useful way to get beyond misunderstandings and even disagreements about curriculum and curriculum planning. Secondly, the curriculum planning platform

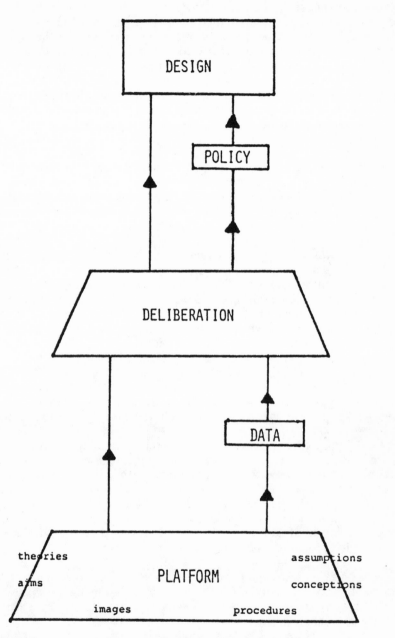

Fig. 1. Walker's naturalistic curriculum planning model.

is the source of justification of all the decisions made during planning. A teacher decides to have students generate their own questions about air pollution rather than answer the ones on the worksheet because he or she believes the development of inquiring citizens is an important educational aim. In order to defend a curriculum or a curriculum decision, one refers to the platform on which it is built.

The key element in Walker's model with which teacher-librarians are likely to be most concerned is the process of deliberation. This is a way of describing the planning process teacher-librarians and their teacher colleagues undertake. According to Walker,

> The main operations in curriculum deliberations are (1) formulating decision points, (2) devising alternative choices at these decision points, (3) considering arguments for and against suggested decision points and decision alternatives, and, finally, choosing the most defensible alternatives subject to acknowledged constraints.[7]

The process is actually more circular than it sounds in this description, with each decision influencing every other one, so that early decisions must always be considered in light of later ones. There are five important bodies of experience which must be considered during deliberation. These are (1) the subject matter, (2) the learners for whom the plan is intended, their abilities, aspirations, anxieties, (3) the milieu in which the learning is to take place; that is the classroom, the school community, biases, expectations, beliefs and values, power relationships, social norms, and so on, (4) the teacher, her approach to learners, to the subject matter, to planning, to teaching, and to colleagues, and (5) curriculum planning.[8] All of these must be considered equally, without overdue emphasis on any one, especially subject matter and the materials which embody it.

As Walker points out, deliberation is a horribly complicated process.

> We should not be surprised to find out that curriculum deliberations are chaotic and confused. But we must not be misled into believing either that such confusion is worthless or that it is the inevitable consequence of deliberation. Deliberation is defined by biological, not sociological, criteria, and it may take many forms. The most common form in current practice is argumentation and debate by a group of people. But it could be done by one person, and no logical barrier stands in the way of its being performed by a computer.[9]

Schwab makes the same point and adds another. He argues that "the process of deliberation is not only difficult and time consuming; it is also often unsatisfying because there is no point at which it is clear that the course has been completed and completed well."[10]

The final component of Walker's model is the design of the curriculum. His conception of design is different from the traditional definition of design as the arrangement of the parts of the curriculum: that is, the relationship among objectives, activities, content, materials, and evaluation. Instead, Walker sees design as the set of relationships embodied in the materials-in-use which can affect students. He explains,

We are accustomed to speaking of curricula as if they were objects produced by curriculum projects. The trouble with this view is that the curriculum's effects must be ascribed to events, not materials. The materials are important because their features condition the events that affect those using the materials. The curriculum design—the set of relationships embodied in the materials-in-use which are capable of affecting students—rather than the materials themselves are the important concerns of the curriculum specialist. The trouble with the concept of design is that the curriculum's design is difficult to specify explicitly and precisely. One way to specify a curriculum's design is by the series of decisions that produce it. A curriculum's design would then be represented by the choices that enter into its creation.[11]

This concept of design reminds us that students may demonstrate accomplishment of objectives in ways not anticipated, depending on how the lesson proceeds. When teachers are oriented to learners and what they are experiencing rather than to subject matter or prescribed outcomes or discipline or the clock, what happens in the classroom is and ought to be unpredictable except in very general terms. The teacher works with the potential inherent in the curriculum materials, in students, and himself or herself to create the best possible opportunities for learning.

Let us return to the core of the curriculum planning model, deliberation. This conception of curriculum planning as deliberation is quite different from the objectives-first, subject matter dominated model on which we have all been brought up. It portrays curriculum planning as circular, indeed circuitous, uncertain, complex, and time consuming rather than as a unidirectional, ends-driven deductive process. Perhaps the most important difference between the deliberative and the Tylerian models is that while the Tylerian model was developed to guide curriculum developers through a tidy planning procedure, the deliberative model was developed to describe what groups of teacher-experts actually did in planning a curriculum. Understanding that it is the inherent nature of the curriculum planning process-in-action to be unstraightforward might alleviate some of the frustration of finding it so.

The aim of this planning process is to clarify what kinds of learning (not behaviors) are desired and why, and what materials, arrangements, and activities are likely to contribute to them. If realizing that planning is as complex as teaching is little comfort for the teacher-librarian attempting to facilitate it, perhaps some general knowledge of how teachers tend to approach curriculum planning will help. Interestingly, this description of deliberative curriculum planning as it occurs in groups is compatible with an entirely different body of literature which describes what we know about individual teachers' planning predilections. Although teacher planning may not always exhibit the ideal characteristics of deliberation as described by Walker and Schwab, it is closer to the deliberative model than to the objectives-first model, into which curricularists so often try to force teachers.

HOW INDIVIDUAL TEACHERS PLAN

One group of teacher planning studies groups teachers into two sorts of planners: comprehensive and incremental. Comprehensive planners build detailed plans of how the lesson content and activities will be worked out, based on expectations of how students will react. Incremental planners, on the other hand, plan only an initial activity and then try it out with students before planning further.[12] Most teachers do not begin their planning with statements of objectives.[13] Some consider objectives later in the planning process, and some do not consider them explicitly at all, though they are implicit in every planning decision, buried subconsciously in the teacher's platform.

There are also some differences depending on subject matter and grade level. Teachers of English and social studies tend to consider broad goals more and more often than do teachers of mathematics, science, and geography, who tend to focus instead on content.[14] It seems that many teachers rely on the teacher's manual or the curriculum guide statement of objectives and see planning as the generation of a set of reminders about how they intend to go about accomplishing what is prescribed in the guide.[15] The emphasis in plans of secondary teachers is typically on content, while the emphasis in plans of elementary teachers is typically on activities.

The biggest influences on the selection of content and activities are the teacher's perception of student interests and anticipated student responses. Teachers plan what they think will grab student interest and keep the lesson flowing smoothly. The second strongest influence on planning decisions is the teacher's own preference, knowledge, and skills. Teachers will select activities and content which they themselves like and feel comfortable handling. The third most important influence on teacher planning decisions is curriculum materials.[16] Here is a particularly potent point of influence for the teacher-librarian. *Teachers tend to plan around materials they have at hand. They avoid topics for which they lack materials.*

Some teachers do not write down many plans at all. For them, planning is primarily a mental activity during which they rehearse the lesson privately.[17] The actual plan comes alive only in interaction with students. Most teachers plan, as they teach, in isolation. They typically do not refer to professional publications, colleagues, consultants, or the principal.[18] Given all these things that teachers tend to consider during planning, one might ask in what order teachers typically make these considerations. The answer is that there is no typical order of consideration. Moreover, there is no correlation between order of consideration and quality of the plan which results. Planning procedures are variable among expert planners as well as regular classroom teachers.[19] The circularity and circuitousness characteristic of deliberation seem to be the order of the day.

IMPLICATIONS FOR TEACHER-LIBRARIANS AS CO-PLANNERS

If we adopt deliberation as our view of the planning process, then successful planning sessions are those in which all five commonplaces (subject matter, learners, milieux, teachers, planning) are thoroughly considered, alternatives have been considered before choices were made, and planners can justify their decisions in terms of their curriculum platform. Achieving success in these terms is a tall order even for expert planners. A group of experienced teacher-librarians with whom these ideas were shared listed some key points for those who undertake curriculum deliberation to keep in mind:

1. Objectives need not be considered first.

2. The platforms of both teacher-librarian and teacher should be clarified.

3. Planning involves risk taking.

4. Some platforms may not mesh.

5. Knowing student interests helps teachers plan.

6. Find out what student responses the teacher expects.

7. Make teachers aware of resources appropriate for their particular students.

8. Be aware of the content of curriculum guides.

9. Focus on process as well as content learning.

10. Build good relationships with teachers and supervisors.

11. Teacher-librarians need many different approaches to curriculum planning.

12. Flexibility in planning approach is essential.

13. Planning is different in each situation.

SOME CONCEPTS IN CURRICULUM PLANNING

Other points useful in curriculum planning can be gleaned from some distinctions among key curriculum concepts: curriculum materials, curriculum content, and learning activities.

Curriculum Materials

Materials are an embodiment of subject matter and although they loom large as an influence on the teacher's planning, Schwab advises that they should not overshadow the importance of the other commonplaces, namely learners, milieux, the teacher, and the curriculum planning process itself. Schwab's admonition is easily taken into account if curriculum materials are used not, as teachers typically use them, to define de facto the curriculum, but in the way teacher-librarians are more likely to see them, as resources which can be used in a variety of ways. Decisions about how to use any given set of curriculum materials are made in light of students' needs, community and school expectations, and teacher preferences. For example, students who are knowledgeable about a particular historical event may be given by a teacher who values critical thinking two sets of source materials from that era, not to learn more about the historical event, which they could do with those materials, but to compare the opposing points of view presented in the materials. Schwab[20] says that any given materials may be used by students in three different ways: (1) to learn what the materials convey, for example, a story, a scientific explanation, an historical event; or (2) to learn how a story, scientific explanation or historical account is constructed; or (3) to learn how to interpret the story, scientific explanation, or historical account. Helping teachers see the potential in curriculum materials in varied ways is a valuable function of the teacher-librarian. It is easier to see the varied potential uses of curriculum materials if one is clear on the distinctions between curriculum content and curriculum goals.

Curriculum Content

Conceptions of curriculum content are often fuzzy. Teacher-librarians who can clarify what is meant by curriculum content in their own minds will be of greater help to teachers than those who cannot. Content is the facts, ideas, concepts, skills, attitudes, and so on which make up the curriculum. Sometimes the content is defined entirely by the goal or objective statement. "Students should know the causes of the revolution" is a goal statement which also defines the curriculum content. The content is the concepts and generalizations which define the causes of the revolution. Sometimes the content is only instrumental to the goal. If the goal is that students should learn skills of critical thinking, any of a wide variety of content areas, likely one from the social sciences or humanities, may be used for this purpose. Typically, content plays an instrumental role when the goal is a cognitive skill. Clarifying the kind of learning intended puts curriculum content and materials in perspective.

In order to determine the appropriate relationship between content and materials then, it is important to know which type of goal is intended. Curriculum goals are of four types: cognitive knowledge, cognitive skills, affect, and psychomotor skills. Teacher-librarians are most often working with teachers concerned with one or more of the first three types. If teachers are not explicit about the goals they intend, then teacher-librarians must uncover those goals in their conversations with them. Note that goals are statements of intentions about what students will learn; that is, what they will know about (cognitive concept knowledge), what they will know how to do (cognitive skill knowledge), what they will be able to do (cognitive skills), what traits they will exhibit (affect). Note also that goals or objectives need not be stated behaviorally, except for psychomotor skills goals. There is usually a variety of observable indicators of what a student has learned, and to restrict the demonstration to one behavior is unnecessarily and harmfully limiting. So, for example, "to build a cedar box" is not a goal because it does not reveal what students are intended to learn. As soon as the teacher explains what she wants the students to understand about West Coast native culture through the activity of building the box, the teacher-librarian as well as the teacher will be in a much better position to suggest appropriate learning materials.

Activities

Knowing what kind of goal is intended is also important for determining appropriate activities. The crucial feature of learning activities (presuming we are intending some kind of cognitive or affective learning) is what kind of mental activity they occasion. Building a cedar box is an appropriate activity if students are to calculate and measure, to attend to the physical and/or aesthetic qualities of the wood, to demonstrate artistic prowess in the decoration of the box, to show care, diligence, and attention to detail in their work, to reflect on the life-style and values of the native people who produced such boxes, or any of a number of other worthwhile goals. Notice that goals, along with other elements of the planner's platform, provide the justification for the learning activities.

CONCLUSION

This article has touched only briefly on a number of complicated curriculum matters. The aim here has not been to present recipes and formulae, but to share some theoretical and practical distinctions and some empirical findings which might be helpful to teacher-librarians in thinking about their role as a help to teachers in their curriculum planning. Because the planning process is inherently complex, unpredictable, and contingent, it cannot be accomplished well with straightforward technical procedures. What is required for successful curriculum planning is broad and deep knowledge of subject matter, learners, teachers, and milieux; sensitivity to the way these elements combine in any given case; and a capacity to revel in the many intricacies and multiple possibilities in any given instance of planning.

NOTES

[1] R. Tyler, *Principles of Curriculum and Instruction* (Chicago: University of Chicago Press, 1949).

[2] G. Tankard, *Curriculum Improvement: An Administrator's Guide* (West Nyack, N.Y.: Parker, 1974).

[3] L. Stenhouse, *An Introduction to Curriculum Research and Development* (New York: Heineman, 1975).

[4] D. Walker, "A Naturalistic Model for Curriculum Development," *School Review* 8, no. 1 (1971): 56-65.

[5] J. Clandinin, "A Conceptualization of Image as a Component of Teacher Personal Practical Knowledge in Primary School Teachers' Reading and Language Program" (Ph.D. dissertation, University of Toronto, 1983).

[6]F. Elbaz, *Teacher Thinking: A Study of Practical Knowledge* (Dover, N.H.: Croom Helm, 1983); A. Oberg, "Using Construction Theory as a Basis for Research and Professional Development," *Journal of Curriculum Studies* (in press); R. S. Peters, *Authority, Responsibility and Education* (Winchester, Mass.: Allen and Unwin, 1959).

[7]Walker, 54.

[8]J. Schwab, "The Practical 3: Translation into Curriculum," *School Review* 81, no. 4 (1973): 501-22.

[9]Walker, 55.

[10]J. Schwab, "The Practical: Arts of Eclectic," in *Science, Curriculum and Liberal Education: Selected Essays of Joseph J. Schwab*, ed. I. Westbury and J. Wilkoff (Chicago: University of Chicago Press, 1978).

[11]Walker, 53.

[12]C. Clark and R. Yinger, *Three Studies of Teacher Planning* (East Lansing, Mich.: Institute for Research on Teaching, Michigan State University, 1979), Research Series No. 55.

[13]J. Zahork, "Teachers' Planning Models," *Educational Leadership* 33 (1973): 134-39.

[14]P. Taylor, *How Teachers Plan Their Courses* (London: National [UK] Foundation for Education Research, 1970).

[15]G. McCutcheon, "How Elementary School Teachers Plan Their Curriculum: Findings and Research Issues," presented at the Annual Meeting of the American Educational Research Association, San Francisco, Calif., 1979.

[16]K. S. Leithwood, S. Ross and D. Montgomery, "An Empirical Investigation of Teachers' Curriculum Decision Making Processes," presented at the Annual Meeting of the Canadian Society for the Study of Education, Fredericton, New Brunswick, 1978.

[17]McCutcheon.

[18]A. Oberg, "Information Referents and Patterns in Curriculum Planning of Classroom Teachers" (Ph.D. dissertation, University of Alberta, 1975).

[19]A. Oberg, "Characteristics of Classroom Teachers' Curriculum Planning Decisions," presented at the Annual Meeting of the Canadian Society for the Study of Education, Fredericton, New Brunswick, 1978.

[20]Schwab, "The Practical 3."

BIBLIOGRAPHY

Clark, C., and P. Peterson. *Teachers' Thought Processes.* (East Lansing, Mich.: Institute for Research on Teaching, Michigan State University, 1984), Occasional Paper No. 72.

Mager, R. *Preparing Instructional Objectives.* (Belmont, Calif.: Fearon, 1962).

Popham, W., and E. Baker. *Systematic Instruction.* (Englewood Cliffs, N.J.: Prentice Hall, 1970).

Schwab, J. "The Practical: A Language for Curriculum." *School Review* 81, no. 4 (1973): 501-22.

_____. "The Practical 4: Something for Curriculum Professors to Do." *Curriculum Inquiry* 13, no. 3 (1983): 239-365.

Shavelson, R., and P. Stern. "Research on Teachers' Pedagogical Thoughts, Judgments, Decisions and Behavior." *Review of Education Research* 15 (1983): 455-98.

WHAT PRICE ID?

A Practical Approach to a Personal Dilemma*

Barbara Stripling

All right, all right, I'm convinced. The role of the school library media specialist (SLMS) today certainly should involve instructional development. I even have a workable definition for instructional development — direct involvement by the SLMS in the curriculum at all stages, from needs assessment to evaluation. I believe. I do. I don't even resent (too much) the fact that this role was semithrust upon us by those who have time in the university environment to devise new models, construct taxonomies, and design evaluation instruments. But no matter how valuable I think instructional development is, I still have to find time in my day to carry it out. And that's my problem — what price will I have to pay to redirect my energies toward instructional development? Is the payoff for students and teachers worth the expense? What can I do to lessen the expense?

In the past few years, especially since the publication of *Media Programs: District and School* in 1975, increasing emphasis has been placed on the direct involvement of the SLMS in all areas of the curriculum. Margaret Hayes Grazier advanced the cause in 1979 by summarizing the evolution of the school library media specialist's role in curriculum development and by reviewing the research that had been done on defining that role.[1] Numerous instructional development models have been proposed, from the Instructional Development Institute (IDI) model (three stages: define, develop, evaluate)[2] and a variation called the School Instructional Development (SID) model (three stages: define, design, evaluate)[3] to the TIE model (three stages: talking, involving, evaluating)[4] and others. All of these models follow essentially the same process — that which teachers follow whenever they create a unit: perform a needs assessment; set up the objectives; gather materials and prepare the activities; teach the unit; and, finally, evaluate the learning.

At each stage of the instructional development process the SLMS can become involved to various degrees. David Loertscher has devised an eleven-stage taxonomy of involvement ranging from "level 1: no involvement" to "level 11: curriculum development."[5] Philip Turner and Janet Naumer have outlined four levels of activity, from "no involvement" to "action education."[6] The point in the instructional development process at which the SLMS becomes involved is also important. We are told that school library media specialists have traditionally been reactive (involved only after the unit has been planned by the teacher) instead of proactive (involved from the inception of the project).[7]

Mixed up with all these models and levels of involvement are studies about the perceptions held by principals, teachers, and library media specialists themselves about the role of the SLMS.[8] We find out that teachers, media specialists, and principals sometimes do not agree about what the role of a SLMS should be; at times all three groups have been somewhat resistant to an expanded instructional development role for the media specialist.[9] In a study conducted by E. Susan Staples published in 1981, school library media specialists ranked competencies associated with consultation, instruction, and utilization (in other words, instructional development) very low in value as compared to organization and management competencies and acquisition and dissemination competencies.[10]

It is interesting to note that essentially all of this researching, theorizing, and model building has been done by those in higher education, not by the practicing school library media specialists. Perhaps therein lies some of the resistance to the "new role" of the SLMS. Rarely has anyone acknowledged the fact that we media specialists are already busy, even without doing instructional development, or that it may *not* be just an excuse if we say, "I don't have time to develop units and teach classes; I have to run the library."

David Loertscher is one who has recognized the demands on a school library media specialist's time and the guilty feelings that arise when a SLMS cannot be deeply involved in instructional development with every teacher. His taxonomy was devised to recognize the many levels of involvement that are possible and acceptable.[11] Philip Turner and Janet Naumer have acknowledged some of the difficulties of the library media specialists in trying to fit instructional development activities into their already full schedules. They, too, have suggested that all levels of involvement between the teacher and the SLMS (even informal advice) are part of instructional development. They emphasize that care should be taken not to expect unrealistic amounts and levels of participation by media specialists when they first begin to incorporate instructional development into their library operations.[12]

Others, however, have tended to blame the slow acceptance of instructional development on the library media specialists themselves, on their lack of awareness of this "new" trend or their lack of understanding of the role of the SLMS in instructional development.[13] Some also have claimed that library media specialists have failed to establish proper priorities to make time for instructional development.[14]

Speaking as a practicing school library media specialist, I refuse to accept the blame for my difficulties in beginning and pursuing instructional development. I have been doing an increasing amount of instructional development every year for the past few years. Certainly I recognize the positive aspects, the appeals, of instructional development. I believe in the value of integrating the media center into the curriculum; consequently, I have been willing to rearrange library operations to accommodate those activities. But I also recognize the negative aspects, the dangers, of instructional development. Often I have been extremely frustrated because I do not have time to do everything to keep my library media center operating smoothly. My frustrations have led me to examine both the appeals and the dangers of instructional development and to devise some methods of reducing the cost of instructional development to myself, my students, my teachers, and library operations.

APPEALS OF INSTRUCTIONAL DEVELOPMENT

The greatest appeal of instructional development to me is the increased opportunity for creativity and innovation. I have the chance to develop units (as I loved to do in the classroom), to devise exciting ways for students to pursue their interests through research, reading, or viewing and to present the results of their research to their teachers or classmates. Through instructional development, I have the opportunity to work in a team situation with the classroom teacher. Our team-planning sessions not only reduce the isolated feeling that I often experience as a media specialist but also leave me thrilled with the creative art of teaching.

Instructional development seems more powerful to me than one-on-one teaching of library skills. Surely it must be more effective and more efficient to teach thirty students at one time. I won't have to answer the question "How do I find a magazine article on my subject?" more than five or six times after I have taught that skill to the whole class. The power of instructional development also stems from the fact that library skills taught in relation to specific assignments are better learned and better retained than those taught in isolation. By working with a classroom teacher in developing a research unit, my fellow librarian and I have devised a research process which is being used by several teachers at our school. It is possible for students to leave our school with a solid background in doing research, because they have encountered aspects of that process through several of their classes.

I find it very appealing that our library media center materials have been circulating at a steadily increasing rate as I have been gradually expanding my instructional development activities. I select and buy heavily for those units which are taught in the library, and the students seem to use and appreciate those materials. The circulation of noncurricular materials has increased as well, perhaps because students have gotten accustomed to checking out materials for their classes.

Rewards often come to those who are most visible; instructional development is certainly more visible than almost any other SLMS activity to teachers, students, and administrators. Administrators generally have no idea about the quality of my book selection or the accuracy of my cataloging, but they are impressed by the amount of teaching that I do. The more visible I am, the greater may be my share of the budget. Teachers rarely ever know when I help their students individually, nor do they realize that I am teaching library skills every time I work with a student. But when I instruct their class, suddenly I become a fellow "teacher," and my input and comments take on a new credibility. A couple of students have innocently commented to me, "Do you have to go to college to be a librarian?" My only defense is that, when I teach skills to them in a class situation, they finally recognize that perhaps I have some useful knowledge and a solid educational background. I become their teacher.

The final appeal of instructional development, and I almost hate to admit it, is that it is definitely more fun than most library detail work – the work that used to define the role of librarian. I know that books have to be processed, cards have to be typed, and materials must be ordered; I realize the hundreds of detail chores that must be done to keep a library media center in condition to operate smoothly. But it is more enjoyable to teach classes. And that leads me directly to the dangers of instructional development.

DANGERS OF INSTRUCTIONAL DEVELOPMENT

Units planned and prepared with the classroom teacher must be taught when they are scheduled. Most of the detail work of the library media center can be put off until another day. Further, detail work cannot be taken home, while instructional unit folders are easily transported. When faced with the choice between carrying home six volumes of *Books in Print* or one manila folder, I choose the folder every time. The net result is that often I do the instructional development work first, and the detail work of the media center — an essential part of media center operations — never gets done or gets done after much delay. For awhile, that does not seem to do much harm to the media center's operations or image. However, at the point that students get frustrated by not being able to find a book because I have not had time to pull discards from the card catalog, then not only my library media center but also the students have suffered.

My involvement with instructional development has had a mixed effect on my working relationship with the students. True, they recognize me as a teacher, but because I am so often teaching classes, or planning classes, or preparing handouts for classes, or pulling books for classes, my availability for individual help has been restricted. Library skills mean much more to the students if they can see immediate results. When I teach a class on the *Readers' Guide* (and I generally teach whole classes rather than small groups of students), some students get lost in the shuffle. For one reason or another, some may be unsuccessful at finding articles for their research, and in a class situation, I often do not have time to work with each one individually. Students do not understand (and probably cannot be expected to understand) the importance of information-gathering skills for lifelong learning. I have to give them those skills now; later they will discover their lifelong usefulness. One-on-one follow-up may be more successful in embedding those skills in the student's psyche. If a media specialist is doing quite a bit of instructional development, time for individual follow-up and reinforcement is severely limited.

I have also encountered a danger in my relationship with teachers when I do a great deal of instructional development. It is frustrating for teachers, who have only a limited amount of planning time, to come to the library media center for help only to discover that I am not available because I am teaching someone else's class. The teacher may only want help in checking out a piece of equipment or in finding an audiovisual kit, but he or she wants help then, not later. Since instructional development can never be done with every teacher in the school, the possibility of jealousy arises when some teachers see other teachers getting special help from the media specialist. The teachers who are jealous may even be those who would never accept a library media specialist's input, but that does not seem to alleviate their irritation.

Another danger for both students and teachers is the lessening of spontaneous use of the library. Because classes must be scheduled far in advance, and often the library media center is fully scheduled, neither students nor teachers have the opportunity to follow up on an idea that might have come up in class. We can almost always accommodate individual students, but groups of students and certainly whole classes that have not been prescheduled have little chance of finding room in our library media center. After awhile, teachers stop asking if there is room; they automatically assume that there is not. The teachable moments may be lost.

Finally, I have discovered two dangers for myself in extensive involvement with instructional development. First, involvement with the curriculum on the library media center level leads to involvement with the curriculum on the whole school level (the final step in Loertscher's taxonomy).[15] I find that I naturally tend to involve myself with curricular matters that do not directly affect the library. That is good, in one way, because it helps to strengthen my credibility as a curriculum developer; however, it leaves me little time for my own library media center. My media center services have suffered as I have become more involved in school curricular matters.

The greatest danger to my own well-being caused by instructional development is that I wear myself down trying to accomplish all of the traditional library tasks, along with instructional development and schoolwide curriculum development. Increased instructional development by the library media specialist should naturally lead to increased aide time for the media center, to relieve the SLMS from some of the clerical duties while he or she assumes more teaching duties. However, in my experience, administrators love the additional involvement by the library media specialist but have no recognition of the absolute necessity for more clerical help. Burnout is a term that has become very real to me.

COUNTING UP THE COST: THE PROBLEM

Despite all the dangers that I have listed, I remain firmly convinced that instructional development through the library media center is the way to accomplish the integration of library materials and information-gathering skills into the curriculum. I am left with the problem of trying to decide how to accomplish instructional development and not sacrifice myself or my media center. How can we library media specialists accomplish every bit of the greatness that has been "thrust upon us"? The answer is, "We *can't* do everything." Then what price shall we pay to allow ourselves the time to pursue instructional development? I have discovered that the cost can be held to a minimum if I set my priorities, organize my operations, practice time management, and increase the visibility of my noninstructional activities (which alerts others to the fact that I am indeed working even if I am not teaching a class). I would recommend that library media specialists try any or all of the following solutions.

COST REDUCTION: THE SOLUTIONS

1. Do a Needs Assessment

Base your job priorities on a needs assessment (obtained through a survey of teachers, administrators, and a sample of students) about the relative importance of various facets of your job. List the areas and have them rate their opinion of the importance of each on a Likert scale (not important, moderately important, very important, extremely important). Not only would the survey let you know what others consider to be the most important services that you offer, but also it would be educational for those who filled it out. What do you do if the results indicate that no one thinks instructional development activities are important?

You start back from ground zero building faculty and student support through successful units. What do you do if students think the most important thing you do is to check out books? You make sure your circulation procedures are streamlined and hassle-free, while you begin to re-educate the students into the modern concept of a school library media specialist. But no matter what the results, deal with them; don't ignore them. If most of the students indicate that book talks are the most important task that you do, then you might need to list book talks as your number one priority.

2. Use Business Techniques to Streamline Your Operations

If things are not running smoothly in your library, it might help to get better organized. Set up a folder for every month in which you can poke relevant handouts, forms, deadlines, business items, etc. If your magazine order is due in March, put the teacher handout you sent out last year in your March folder. If your supply order is due in April, put all your supply needs in that folder as you come across them throughout the year. Set up an accounting system for your funds if you do not already have one in place. You should be able to account for every penny of your budget at any time. With a system set up, the amount of time it takes to maintain the books is minimal.

Compile an operating manual for your library media center. Do not try to sit down and write it; instead, compile all the procedures and policies that you use throughout the year, so that next year you will have a completed manual. The manual should include step-by-step instructions for all clerical chores, as well as professional items like your selection policy. It should also include a copy of every form that you have devised. Use the forms. It does not make business sense to write an individual note to each teacher about procedures for library overdues when a form would do as well. Finally, organize your volunteers or aides. Have regular operating procedures for them so that they feel comfortable enough about their situation that they do not have to ask questions continually.

3. Employ Time-Management Techniques

Time management is the only way to have time to do instructional development without sacrificing other areas of library operation. Some of the techniques are quite obvious, but you need to keep reminding yourself of them as you get busier and busier. First, you probably need to decide your overall priorities, the percentage of your time that you would like to spend on various tasks (e.g., 30 percent instructional development, 5 percent accounting, 10 percent working with equipment, etc.). Figure out the number of hours per day or per week that you would be spending on each category if you were able to follow those priorities.

Using those time allotments, plan out your schedule a week at a time. Make lists daily of those tasks that you hope to accomplish. Put priorities next to each item on those lists, so you will know where to start. To accomplish the big tasks (like compiling large book orders, preparing the budget, or creating a slide/tape program), break them into smaller units that can be accomplished without herculean effort. Through this "Swiss cheese" approach, you will have a sense of accomplishment each day, and the large tasks will be finished before deadlines loom.[16]

The most important time-management technique, and one of the hardest for many people to remember, is "Do it today." Opening the same piece of mail for three straight days, and deciding each day that it is too much trouble to deal with the problem at that point, multiplies by three the amount of time you have spent on that situation. If you cannot finish with the task on the first day, at least make a note on it about what must be done, so you will not have to figure out what to do again.

4. Increase the Visibility of "Invisible" Media Center Operations

Library detail work can never be eliminated, nor can it ever be done entirely by paraprofessionals or clerks. Only you as a professional can decide that, for your media center, the biography of Pete Rose would be more accessible to the students in the 700s than in the 92s. Most library media center tasks are invisible to teachers, students, and administrators, and yet they must be done carefully and with a great deal of thought. The goal should be to increase the visibility of those operations, so that others will recognize that you are performing necessary functions even when you are not teaching classes.

How could you increase the visibility of book orders, for example? Request book titles from teachers; let them know when you are compiling an order. Publicize new books by putting them on display, by arranging special checkout procedures for them, by creating a bulletin board about them. You might even do a bulletin board detailing the steps involved in bringing a book to the patron—from the inception of the book to its display on the shelf.

To increase your visibility to administrators, send them a monthly report about the library media center highlights for the month. It does not have to be dry and full of statistics, but you could let them know the projects that you accomplished, the new books you added, anything that would help them understand what you did with your time and energies. Ideally, of course, they would be in your library media center enough to know what had happened, but administrators are busy, too.

To keep the teachers involved, be sure to route information to appropriate teachers about television specials, materials of particular interest, or community resource people who would come to their class. Devise a form that can be sent out with this information, such as "Thought you'd like to know...." It would take just a moment to fill out the form and the individual teachers would feel that you had given them a special gift. They might remember the special bits of information you sent to them better than they remember a class you taught for them.

Work in plain sight on your "invisible" library chores, so that anyone coming to the media center can see that you are busy. But do not be so busy that you are unapproachable. The biggest advantage to being visible is that both students and teachers feel that you are a hard-working library media specialist who is also accessible and ready to help them.

ACCEPT THE FACT THAT YOU WILL ALWAYS BE SLIGHTLY MISUNDERSTOOD

No one can really understand another's situation unless he has experienced a similar one. Teachers will never understand everything that library media specialists must do. They will be responsive to instructional development if they have positive experiences with it. They will not understand if you are late to teach their class because you were helping another teacher with a film projector, nor will they understand if they want help with a film projector and you are not available because you are teaching a class. But if you approach the whole situation with a sense of humor and do your best to manage your time according to the priorities that you have set, based on the needs assessment filled out by the school, that's all anyone could ask.

You *can* do instructional development without paying too high a price. Instructional development will increase your involvement with the curriculum and will increase the use of the library media center materials by both students and teachers. The dangers associated with instructional development can be lessened by conducting a needs assessment, using good business techniques, employing time-management tricks, and increasing the visibility of other library media center operations. What price ID? Not too much. It's worth it.

NOTES

[1]M. H. Grazier, "The Curriculum Consultant Role of the School Library Media Specialist," *Library Trends* 28 (Fall 1979): 263-79.

[2]M. E. Chisholm and D. P. Ely, *Instructional Design and the Library Media Specialist* (Chicago: American Library Association, 1979), 10.

[3]K. A. Johnson, "Instructional Development in Schools: A Proposed Model," *School Media Quarterly* 9 (Summer 1981): 256-71.

[4]B. P. Cleaver and W. D. Taylor, *Involving the School Library Media Specialist in Curriculum Development* (Chicago: American Library Association, 1983), 27.

[5]D. Loertscher, "Second Revolution: A Taxonomy for the 1980s," *Wilson Library Bulletin* 56 (February 1982): 417-21.

[6]P. M. Turner and J. N. Naumer, "Mapping the Way Toward Instructional Design Consultation by the School Library Media Specialist," *School Library Media Quarterly* 12 (Fall 1983): 29-37.

[7]Cleaver and Taylor, 7.

[8]P. M. Turner, "The Relationship Between the Principal's Attitude and the Amount and Type of Instructional Development Performed by the Media Professional," *International Journal of Instructional Media* 7 (1979-80): 127-38; K. S. Mohajerin and Earl P. Smith, "Perceptions of the Role of the School Media Specialist," *School Media Quarterly* 9 (Spring 1981): 152-63; P. M. Turner, "Levels of Instructional Design Involvement by the School Media Specialist: Perceptions of Selected School Principals," *International Journal of Instructional Media* 11 (1983-84): 11-25.

[9]Grazier; Mohajerin and Smith, 155; J. N. Naumer and G. Thurman, *ID in School Media Centers; Possible or Probable? A Position Paper* (Bethesda, Md.: ERIC Document Reproduction Service, 1981), ERIC Document 222 198; J. Stroud, "Library Media Center Taxonomy: Future Implications," *Wilson Library Bulletin* 56 (February 1982): 428-33.

[10]E. S. Staples, "60 Competency Ratings for School Media Specialists," *Instructional Innovator* 26 (November 1981): 19-23.

[11]Loertscher.

[12]Turner and Naumer.

[13]J. S. Sullivan, "Initiating Instructional Design into School Library Media Programs," *School Media Quarterly* 8 (Summer 1980): 251-58; Naumer and Thurman.

[14]Sullivan, 258; Stroud, 431; Cleaver, 17.

[15]Loertscher, 421.

[16]A. Lakein, *How to Get Control of Your Time and Your Life* (New York: New American Library, 1973), 104-5.

ADDITIONAL READINGS

Ainsley, Lucy E. "The Changing Role of the Library Media Specialist." *School Library Media Annual*. v. 2. Shirley Aaron and Pat Scales, eds. Littleton, Colo.: Libraries Unlimited, 1984.

Hodges, Gerald. "Educating School Media Professionals to Perform Their Instructional Role." *School Library Media Annual*. v. 3. Shirley Aaron and Pat Scales, eds. Littleton, Colo.: Libraries Unlimited, 1985.

Hortin, John A. "The Changing Role of the School Media Specialist." *Tech-Trends* 30 (September 1985): 20-21.

Part 4

School Library Media Services: Library Skills to Information Skills

While instructional design illustrates the consulting function of the school library media specialist, much of what the media specialist does is still directed toward helping students acquire skills to use information effectively. And, much of the change in school media center programming centers on these skills. Formerly called library skills, the media profession now recognizes that in reality what are being taught are information utilization skills, including thinking skills. This, coupled with the current educational emphasis on critical thinking, provides the rationale for school library media programming efforts toward information/thinking skills rather than just library skills. Jacqueline C. Mancall, Shirley L. Aaron, and Sue A. Walker discuss the role of the school library media program in developing thinking skills. Using a research based rationale to establish need, they discuss practical implications and applications of life-long information skills.

Roy Lundin introduces one of the crucial factors in implementing and assuring success of an integrated information skills curriculum—the role of the school principal. He advocates the role of principal in fostering the creation of teacher/media specialist partnerships. Carol Collier Kuhlthau compares the research process with the thinking process and suggests that writing problems are in reality thinking problems.

Michael Eisenberg suggests using curriculum mapping as a method of implementing media skills curriculum into the school curriculum. A content analysis of curriculum documents, as well as state, district, and school guides reveals the topics, time, materials, methods, and evaluation of the actual curriculum. Eisenberg describes a computer-based method that media specialists might use to identify appropriate units in which to integrate media skills.

M. Ellen Jay builds a case for the teaching of inquiry skills and explores whether the library media program is able to accommodate the shift from the traditional methods of teaching focusing on content, to an inquiry approach. She provides practical ideas to bring about the change, including staff development activities, and illustrates changing a typical lesson plan to an inquiry plan teaching thinking skills.

EDUCATING STUDENTS
TO THINK

The Role of the
School Library Media Program*

Jacqueline C. Mancall, Shirley L. Aaron,
and
Sue A. Walker

> All which the school can or need do for pupils, so far as
> their minds are concerned, is to develop the ability to
> think. (John Dewey, *Democracy and Education*, 1916)

INTRODUCTION

On July 6, 1985, the National Commission on Libraries and Information
Science conducted an informal meeting of a small group of invited library media
administrators, educators, concerned citizens and publishers.[1] The group was
convened to discuss ways to define, develop, and promote the role of the library
media program in teaching information-finding/utilization skills to children and
young adults. After considering various alternatives, the participants
recommended development of a document designed to provide a conceptual
framework for examining this area in an organized way. We deal here with three
principal components of such a framework.

- The role of school library media programs in helping students develop
  thinking skills;

- Theoretical implications of current research on how children and
  adolescents process information and ideas;

- Practical implications and applications of the concepts described in the
  first two parts of the paper as a basis for developing an educationally
  sound information skills program in all curricular areas.

*From Jacqueline C. Mancall, Shirley L. Aaron, and Sue A. Walker, "Educating Students to Think:
The Role of the School Library Media Program," *School Library Media Quarterly* 15 (Fall 1986):
18-27. Reprinted by permission.

PART ONE: THE SCHOOL LIBRARY MEDIA PROGRAM'S ROLE IN DEVELOPING THINKING SKILLS

In recent years educators have directed considerable attention to perceived deficiencies in how students are taught to think. Thus, Lockhead has observed that our educational system focuses primarily on teaching youth what to think rather than how to think.[2] Goodlad's study of schooling supports this notion, in that he found that only 1 percent of the classroom time devoted to student-teacher interaction required students to engage in anything more than mere recall of information.[3] Failure to help students develop higher-order thinking skills has seriously limited their ability to cope adequately in an increasingly complex society. Indeed the 1979-80 assessment of reading comprehension conducted by the National Assessment of Education Progress indicates:

> While students learn to read a wide range of materials, they develop very few skills for examining the nature of the ideas that they take away from their reading. Students seemed satisfied with their initial interpretations of what they had read and seemed satisfied with their initial efforts to explain or defend their points of view. Few students could provide more than superficial responses to such tasks, and even the better responses showed little evidence of well-developed problem-solving strategies or critical thinking skills.[4]

It need hardly be stressed that in a society whose political foundation is built on an informed citizenry able to evaluate the merits and determine the consequences of various courses of action, an ability to think effectively is essential. Glaser logically observes that good citizenship requires the attainment of a working understanding of our social, political, and economic arrangements, and the ability to think critically about issues concerning which there may be an honest difference of opinion.[5]

A Rationale for Participating in the Development of Student Thinking Skills

An investigation of the literature on teaching thinking skills demonstrates remarkably few references to the role of the library media program. Further, major initiatives such as the establishment of a "Collaborative on Thinking," which involves twenty-two national educational associations in a joint venture to study how to bring about improvements in student thinking, have failed to include any representation from the library media field. Circumstances such as these suggest the existence of serious problems related to general awareness of the degree and type of potential involvement of library media professionals in the development of student thinking skills. In providing a rationale for involvement of the library media specialist in this vital area, two basic questions will guide our discussion, viz.:

- Under what circumstances is the development of thinking skills a central concern of the library media professional?

- What contributions can the school library media specialist make to the development of thinking skills?

Library media specialists have traditionally described their raison d'etre as one of promoting access to a broad range of information and ideas, in order to assist students in acquiring the knowledge, skills, and attitudes necessary to function effectively in an information society. However, there has been disagreement among professionals in the field, as well as among educators in other areas, as to how this mission should be accomplished. A central issue is one of definition of the term *access*, and determination of how such *access*, however defined, can be translated into a program of library media services for students and teachers. In its narrowest sense access to information and ideas has been interpreted as the provision of services that help the user locate the physical unit containing the information or idea sought. Under a broader interpretation of the concept of access, a program emerges characterized by a wide range of resources and services designed to bring the user into contact with special information, whether in book, magazine, film, database, or other physical unit, and to help him/her evaluate and use the desired information or ideas effectively. Archibald MacLeish clearly distinguishes between these two concepts of service, stressing that the former focuses on the "physical book," while the latter provides entrée to the "intellectual book"; the first thus emphasizes the cover or package (that is, the book), the second emphasizes its content. MacLeish points out that those concerned with content are constantly searching for ways to get young people as well as adults to examine critically the broad range of wares in the "marketplace of ideas"—the library.

Library media specialists who advocate the second, i.e., broader, concept of services realize that a major part of their time must be spent helping students develop the thinking skills that will equip them to not only locate but also evaluate and use information effectively and thereby become information-literate. Primary functions performed by the library media staff that contribute directly to the development of these skills include collection development, organization for retrieval of materials and information, information guidance services, materials production, student instruction, and instructional development services. The following examples of activities in each of these areas will clarify the fundamental role of the library media specialist in promoting positive outcomes in the development of thinking skills in the school.

1. *Collection Development.* Appropriate collection developments efforts should result in a well-equipped information laboratory that can serve as a basic resource for students who require ongoing exposure to a wide range of different ideas. In such a facility students can practice problem-solving strategies and information finding and utilization skills, gain access to information not available elsewhere in the school, compare different points of view, and explore personal interests in an environment that is equipped to serve both individual and group needs. Simultaneously, teachers can secure relevant resources essential to teaching thinking skills.

2. *Organization for Retrieval of Information and Ideas.* Sophisticated organizational efforts are essential for adequate retrieval of information and ideas from any collection. In developing an information laboratory the library media specialist works with and selects information in a variety of formats, including books, magazines, pamphlets, films, filmstrips, audio- and videocassettes, etc., that are physically selected and brought into local collections, as well as providing options to information from remote databases that can be accessed electronically. The massive number of documents of all types that are available can only be successfully located and retrieved if systems are created to describe these resources in meaningful ways to library users. Organization of the materials within the local collection has, and continues to be, an important role of the professional library media specialist. Organizational schemes employed involve classification and cataloging of materials in order to enhance access opportunities, with a primary local tool being the card catalog. Recent technological developments such as the development of online catalogs and electronic networks now allow users to explore and perhaps access the collections of many libraries. In fact, technology is reaching the stage where it is not unrealistic to imagine a quantum leap in the ability to organize information to meet the personalized requirements of students and teachers.

3. *Information Guidance Services.* Information guidance services provided by trained intermediaries offer assistance to students as they attempt to find, interpret, and evaluate materials, information, and/or ideas. Liesener highlights the mediation function of the library media professional in this area.[6] He points out that the increasingly complex array of information options available to students and teachers often requires an intermediary to facilitate effective and efficient interaction with the information world.

4. *Materials Production.* Provision of production opportunities for students promotes the development of thinking skills in a variety of ways. Students develop an understanding of the different languages of communication offered by various media formats, and production experiences provide opportunities to code and decode ideas effectively and efficiently based on the format selected. In addition, the availability of production services to teachers means that they will have more flexibility in choosing and using the most effective format(s) for conveying information to their students. This assists them in providing various learning alternatives and accommodating individual and small-group needs.

5. *Student Instruction.* On both an individual and a group basis library media specialists systematically offer instructional opportunities to help students locate, organize, analyze, evaluate, synthesize, and utilize information as needed to make rational decisions for both formal educational and other more personal settings. These instructional activities are most effective when they are based on pedagogical or personal need as expressed by the individual student and closely integrated into classroom units.

6. *Instructional Development Services.* Vandergrift has reminded library media specialists that they are generalists in the areas of information, media, and materials, while most teachers are more specialized by virtue of curricular content, age level, and grade level.[7] As professionals dedicated to promoting access to information and ideas across curriculuar areas, library media specialists must therefore be responsible to a large extent for incorporation of critical thinking skills (organizing, analyzing, synthesizing, and evaluating information) throughout the curriculum. In addition, possessing specialized technical expertise in the use of media, library media specialists can and should act as process specialists to help teachers plan, implement, and evaluate learning alternatives that effectively communicate meaningful content.

These brief explanations of some of the unique ways library media personnel can support programs dedicated to the development of thinking skills in the school indicate the need to insure their full participation in the planning, implementation, and evaluation of activities related to this important area. However, if library media professionals are to assist other educators effectively in providing sound educational programs, they must become more knowledgeable about the ways in which children and young adults actually process information. We shall therefore next consider the theoretical implications of relevant major research studies in furthering such an understanding of student information-seeking behavior and what these mean for the development of an information skills curriculum that achieves the school library media center's, and the school's, basic purpose: teaching students to think.

PART TWO: THE RESEARCH BASIS FOR THE RECONSIDERATION OF INFORMATION SKILLS INSTRUCTION

Information management skills instruction is essential if students are to exert control over school-related and lifetime information needs. Unfortunately, many existing programs are library-centered rather than information-centered, concentrating on the physical objects collected rather than their intellectual contents (i.e., stressing *cover* over *content* — see above). All too often they regrettably also provide instruction in every conceivable skill, and in every form of information source available. Individual student's fundamental mental processes, including their developmental aspects, are often neglected, and the implications for both teachers and students of helping the young develop the ability to think about *how* they are using information to solve problems are frequently ignored.

Whatever the terminology traditionally used to describe programs over the years, the basis for library skills, or what are currently termed information management or utilization skills, lies in adding substance to John Dewey's belief that "all which the school can or need do for pupils, so far as their minds are concerned is to develop the ability to think." Contemporary library media programs have approached this task through concerted and articulated efforts designed not only to provide children with an appreciation of literature, but also to teach them how to locate, retrieve, and evaluate the worth of information contained in graphic, recorded, and printed records in the belief that such skills are essential for survival in a rapidly changing world. *Survival skills are thinking skills.* The literature that deals with these skills, i.e., those of critical thinking and metacognition, is therefore an essential starting point for consideration of a more effective approach to the education of students in management of their own information needs.[8]

Critical Thinking

Although there is no absolute agreement on a definition of critical thinking, much research addresses the issue of what students should be taught in order to be better observers, appliers, and evaluators of ideas and information, all areas fundamental to the process of thinking in a critical fashion. Norris points out that "students need more than the ability to be better observers; they must know how to apply everything they already know and feel, to evaluate their own thinking, and especially, to change their behavior as a result of thinking critically."[9] Such skill allows students to be more productive, in the sense of selecting alternative meaningful courses of action, and enables them to produce reliable observations, make sound inferences, offer reasonable hypotheses, and be able to think productively and critically about issues.[10]

Beyer has emphasized that critical thinking is not the same as problem solving per se. He sees agreement among specialists that critical thinking is "the ability to assess the authenticity, accuracy and/or worth of knowledge claims and arguments."[11] He perceives this as "a collection of discrete skills or operations, each of which to some degree or other combines analysis and evaluation." In setting up a core group of competencies related to the acquisition of the ability to think critically, Beyer focuses on those areas school library media specialists have consistently identified as central to their instructional programs. The ten skills that represent a consensus of scholarly reflection, as well as learning research and classroom experience, include

distinguishing between verifiable facts and value claims;

determining the reliability of a source;

determining the factural accuracy of a statement;

distinguishing relevant from irrelevant information, claims or reasons;

detecting bias;

identifying unstated assumptions;

identifying ambiguous or equivocal claims or arguments;

recognizing logical inconsistencies or fallacies in a line of reasoning;

distinguishing between warranted or unwarranted claims; and

determining the strength of an argument.[12]

However, critical thinking is sensitive to context, and this list can be and has been expanded for its more specific implications in the various subject disciplines.[13]

Additional insights into this problem are provided from research on the modes of thinking of experts in particular areas compared to those of novices. Examining how experts think in a particular subject or discipline area provides an understanding applicable to educating novices in these or other fields. Two distinctive features of experts are that (1) they possess more information than novices; and (2) they have unconsciously automated many of the sequences in a problem solution.[14] By looking at what experts do in various disciplines it may be possible to derive ideas of how novices can become more critical in their own approaches. Recognition of the student's status as novice rather than experienced professional or scholar is a basic consideration in any instructional setting.

Since the ability to think critically appears to be cross-disciplinary, training approaches for students can and should be incorporated into many curricular areas. Students should be consciously taught to "think about their thinking." This process is referred to as *metacognition*.[15]

Metacognition

Although there is no rigorous definition, metacognition, as noted above, is most simply explained as "thinking about thinking." Paris and Lindauer expand the definition to include "knowledge we have about people's mental states, abilities and processes of behavioral regulation ... including our understanding of task goals and the strategies that are useful for accomplishing different purposes."[16] Consider this now in terms of a student's approach to solving a critical school-related problem, such as preparing a research paper. The interaction of three types of variables must be assessed: person, task, and strategy.[17] *Person variables* include beliefs (assessment of knowledge states) we have about ourselves and others as thinkers and about the amount of knowledge we have about a subject, such as a student's estimate of personal knowledge of a potential subject for a paper. *Task variables* are perceptions of the mental difficulties involved in a cognitive situation, e.g., perceptions of the difficulties in finding the information needed for a research paper. *Strategy variables* refer to knowledge of strategies available to carry out a cognitive activity, such as note-taking as an aid in gathering information for the paper in question.

Synthesizing research findings and their implications, Robinson raises the question of age-related and task-related differences in the amount of conscious processing individuals actually do.[18] In her overview of the findings of Brown and de Loache[19] she examines a critical point for information theorists: the novice-expert dimension, a point already touched upon above. She states: "Novices at any task not only lack the skills needed to perform it efficiently, but are also deficient in self-conscious participation and intelligent self-regulation of their actions." Robinson speculates on the existence of the same patterns both developmentally and within any task by which an individual progresses from being a novice to being an expert. First, there appears to be a little or no intelligent self-regulation. This is followed by a period of deliberate self-regulation as the role and subprocesses become familiar, and eventually culminates in expert behavior as the necessary components are overlearned and become relatively automatic. A critical point in thinking about the education of children lies in the difference between what Robinson calls the "child novice" and the "adult novice," the latter having available and using more general metacognitive skills which can be applied to a wide range of problems.

Unresolved questions focus on age-related and task-related differences in the amount of conscious processing individuals are capable of doing. In terms of information-processing capacity, Robinson calls attention to Shatz' description of age-related differences: "conscious monitoring occurs only when capacity is not fully taken up with actually carrying out the task in hand.... Since adults have more well learned routines, they are more likely to have the space capacity for indulging in metacognitive activity."[20] Here, metacognitive activity refers to the individual's ability to give appropriate reasons for choices, with appropriateness more likely to occur when the task is less of a strain on the individual's cognitive capacity. The implication of this for construction of an information skills curriculum lies in the importance of finding out what students already know about particular tasks. One approach is offered by verbal reports of how students remember, communicate, or solve information-related problems. Asking students "how would you do it better next time?" may help children develop their metacognitive knowledge verbally. (Robinson points out that telling children explicitly when and why their verbal communications were not understood helped them to understand that messages can be ambiguous and that ambiguity can cause communication failures.)

The pioneering work of the Soviet psychologist Vygotsky appears important in considering metacognitive research studies and their implications for targeting information skills instruction in the school setting. Vygotsky draws attention to the fact that young children appear to think without thinking about their own thought processes.[21] It is their response to schooling that moves their thought processes to a reflective level, one in which there is a new awareness of their own activity. But the "when" of this metacognitive development is not yet clearly defined. Vygotsky claims that in order to incorporate school-related concepts, children must become aware of their thought processes as well as products. The key for instruction in various areas appears to be identifying the point at which children develop this awareness. Vygotsky calls this the "Zone of Proximal Development"—a period in which a child is able to carry out a task with the assistance of an adult or a more capable peer which the child could not do alone.[22] This period represents a preview of what the child will eventually attain on his or her own, and is the time when instruction in a developing skill could be the most effective. If such instruction is to be effective, two conditions must be met: first, the student must be developmentally ready to learn the skill; and second, the student must realize that use of the skill will be effective in solving a personal cognitive problem. Isolated or premature approaches to teaching information use may not be effective in advancing the student in a developmental sense.

Bertland's review of metacognitive studies and their relation to information skills instruction stresses the fact that the question of precisely when children develop metacognitive abilities is not yet clearly defined.[23] Studies have measured metacognitive activity either by looking at products produced by children as a result of a cognitive process or by actual analysis by students of what they did and the cognitive processes they followed. Elementary children appear to develop slowly in terms of being able to formulate strategies to test their own comprehension of gaps and inconsistencies in information in materials they read, with "total comprehension monitoring still not developed at the sixth grade level." Information skills programs must consider levels of cognitive development and, as importantly, pay attention to the process skills students need to plan and evaluate all aspects of information utilization and retrieval.

General Suggestions for Educators

In offering suggestions to educators to help students to "think about thinking" Bondy[24] suggests that general awareness of metacognitive activity can be achieved through:

- Student-created learning logs that contain reflections and reactions to academic activities;

- Teacher-demonstrated and shared strategies for tackling the unfamiliar, including estimates of task difficulty, goals, strategies, action steps, and evaluation plans;

- Teacher-provided opportunities for feedback;

- Training of students in self-questioning of their own understanding;

- Teaching students how to summarize material in order to test their own understanding;

- Instructing students in how to monitor their understanding and comprehension of material;

- Developing a systematic approach to learning and problem solving that incorporates assessment of the nature of the material to be learned, the learner's current skills and knowledge, activities necessary, and evaluation criteria.

Sancore extends these observations, suggesting that the focus should be on helping students develop conscious awareness of what is important to study, how to study, and how much studying is needed.[25] Useful strategies include teaching students to:

- generate questions as they read and study expository texts;

- create story-specific questions from schema, i.e., create general questions during reading of complex narrative texts;

- monitor and resolve blocks to comprehension;

- understand the structure of textbook chapters, i.e., guiding them to use strategies that increase comprehension and retrieval of information.

Bertland also calls attention to what metacognitive research indicates is essential for instructional practices.[26] In her review of metacognitive studies as they relate to children's use of the library she emphasizes that researchers believe that those who teach should act as models of metacognitive behavior. As such, they should:

- Think out loud about the processes in which they engage, in terms of planning their approach to a problem, monitoring their comprehension, developing strategies, and performing self-evaluation. Such an approach is easily translated to techniques for teaching students how to approach a research paper.

- Engage students in activities that force them to think about their own thinking. Help them to take a hard and clear look at what they know about a problem they are trying to solve; assist them in clearly spelling out what tasks are essential in solving the problem and in identifying the strategies they will use to perform the tasks.

- Allow students to teach each other by working in small groups. Have them keep records of their goals, the strategies used for reaching them, and evaluations of ongoing efforts. (In many ways this type of thinking copies what has already been proven successful by adult management teams).

- Provide opportunities for training in strategies that will help students monitor their own comprehension and planning activities.

- Help students develop the ability to ask the right question.

- Provide actual hands-on experience.

- Work with teachers on precise explanations of the exact nature of assignments so students are aware of the task parameters involved and the possible difficulties they may encounter along the way.

Metacognitive research thus carries important messages for information skills instructional programs. It is clear that greater attention should be paid to developmental levels of children in setting instructional goals and in helping them develop the ability to think.

The importance of the three basic components of *evaluation, planning,* and *regulation* in this process would be difficult to overestimate. These components are, of course, also the elements of the information search process in general. *Evaluation* may be simply defined as the ability of the individual to assess his/her own knowledge state and understanding of the tasks essential to solve a problem. In searching for information this element of the process includes topic definition or question analysis. The second component, *planning*, refers to the ability to select appropriate strategies to reach a desired goal. The obvious translation to information seeking is the development at this point of appropriate search strategies, including but not limited to strategic use of print and online tools in an appropriate sequence. The third component, *regulation*, implies the development of techniques to monitor the effectiveness of the steps essential to reaching a goal. In the information-seeking process this connotes evaluation of the results of each step in sequence.

Conscious control of knowledge may be the key to success in a rapidly changing world. Such control suggests that individuals are capable of thinking about their thought processes with the implication that those who are able to do this are in command of their ability to predict the consequences of their actions, check their own results, monitor ongoing activity, examine the sense of their actions, and coordinate and control their approaches to problem solving. Although such process skills are basic for lifelong learning, they are not the focus of many current educational efforts that instead place emphasis on what children can do at the moment (i.e., learning *outcomes* may be more highly prized than learning *processes*). The implication for information management skills instruction is that it must be broad and more process oriented. Focus must go beyond locational skills and "correct answers" and more to strategies that will help students to develop insight and facility in structuring successful approaches to solving their information needs. Although there is no commonly agreed upon theoretical base for the teaching of what has been called library or information skills, these studies of the metacognitive process should force us to reexamine what we do.

PART THREE: PRACTICAL IMPLICATIONS AND APPLICATIONS

The concepts identified in this paper have both political and instructional implications for building- and district-level information management skills curricula that have been integrated with other content areas and for the library media programs that translate those curricula. From a *political* perspective, there has never been a more propitious time for school library media specialists to define and articulate the role that information management skills curricula and programs can serve in teaching critical thinking skills. For reasons well known to educators—declining test scores, critical national reports, and improved research on teaching critical thinking—the impetus to teach children to think critically has never been greater. As a result, the attention of administrators and other educational decision makers is easily directed to any vehicle within the educational setting that shows potential for delivery of a critical thinking skills component. Since research indicates that activities for teaching students to think critically should be incorporated into many curricular areas, no better vehicle exists to deliver a thinking skills initiative than an information management skills curriculum that has already successfully demonstrated its ability to function as an integral part of various other curricular areas, such as English and social studies.

From an *instructional* point of view, the time is appropriate to assess critically the information management skills curricula and programs that school library media specialists labored to put in place during the 1970s, even though admittedly many practitioners have only recently completed this process. The information world is one of constant change; the curricula and programs developed to teach management of that world must face continued revision to reflect those changes. School library media professional publications, as well as other current professional publications in other content areas, are beginning to reflect some concerns about how effectively current information management skills address the analysis, evaluation, and synthesis of information. The present critical-thinking skills initiative provides an excellent framework within which an assessment of existing information management curricula and programs may be structured.

The most pressing need and the *first task* in this assessment process is the examination of existing information management skills programs in light of the critical thinking skills impetus, with an eye toward effecting revision to accommodate a critical thinking skills component. That is, one must rethink the curriculum by posing the question Is this what a student must know to make a logical decision? The *second task* is to determine whether or not other library programming components are in place at levels of proficiency high enough to translate successfully the revised information management skills program. The remainder of this paper suggests an approach for such an assessment.

A Six-Step Curriculum Revision Process

In assessing and revising a curricular document, one basically follows the steps used to develop the document initially. Representatives of the groups originally involved in the development should be included in the assessment and revision.

The *first step* in the revision process is the analysis of the overall goal statement with the specific intent of rewording the statement, if necessary, to accommodate a critical thinking skills emphasis and process orientation. To achieve such an accommodation, the goal statement must address analysis, evaluation, and synthesis of information. An example of a goal statement that meets such criteria is *The student will identify, locate, utilize, analyze, and evaluate an information source, regardless of format, to meet a specific need or to create new information.*

The *second step* is to review the conceptual groupings of skills to ascertain that there are groupings that accommodate the higher-level thinking skills. *For example, in addition to identification, location, and utilization skills categories, there should be conceptual groupings to reflect analysis, evaluation, and synthesis skills.* Establishing a conceptual category of production skills is a good method of addressing the synthesis of information. If desirable, some of these groupings can be combined under generalized headings, such as "Comprehension of Information."

The *third step* in the curriculum revision process is the assessment of the information management skills scope and sequence for the purpose of modification, specifically deletion, addition, and leveling changes. Of these three possible actions, deletion is the easiest to address. *Examine the list carefully to identify skills statements that do not contribute directly to information management.* A good indicator of skills that are candidates for deletion is failure to support any of the conceptual groupings determined in the previous step.

The next phase of the modification is the addition of skills where appropriate. Given recent technological developments and resulting enhanced access possibilities, this phase becomes most challenging, especially in the context of critical thinking. *Several areas of skills addition should be carefully considered, with final determination reflecting the local situation.* Specifically, skills categorized as study skills, computer literacy skills, thinking skills and search strategy skills, including online retrieval skills, should be scrutinized to identify those skills that directly affect a student's ability to manage information.

Two recently published lists of skills related to social studies have implications for information skills instruction.[27,28] Two of the three broad conceptual groupings presented relate to acquisition, organization, and use of information. The first of these two is entitled "Skills Related to Acquiring Information," with specific subdivisions dealing with reading skills, study skills, reference and information search skills, and technical skills. Among the actual skills statements are:

- Evaluate sources of information — print, visual, electronic.

- Recognize author bias.

- Use picture clues and picture captions to aid comprehension.

- Use a computer catalog service.

The second relevant conceptual grouping is entitled "Skills Related to Organizing and Using Information," with subheading for intellectual skills and decision-making skills. Some of the specific skills statements include:

- Compare and contrast credibility of differing accounts of the same event.

- Combine critical concepts into a statement of conclusions based on information.

- Propose a new plan of operation, create a new system, or devise a futuristic scheme based on available information.

- Estimate the adequacy of information.

The sequence, which is organized K-12, serves as a useful standard against which to measure a comprehensive information management skills curriculum.

Skills or groups of skills, such as those reported above, that are not presently included in a local scope and sequence should be considered for inclusion in order to create a more process-oriented approach to teaching students how to manage the informational aspects of school-related work. The end result should be students who can evaluate the ideas and facts they retrieve and who can bring an understanding of how to apply what they already know to a new problem. In light of the research reported previously in this paper, it is probable that most expansion will occur at the secondary level and will reflect primarily the refinement and addition of search strategy/research skills. Brainstorming and classification skills, online retrieval skills, and critical viewing skills are examples.

The *fourth step* in the revision process is analysis of the leveling. Research findings imply that changes should specifically reflect developmental readiness of the student. Consideration should be given to emphasizing identification, location, and utilization skills during the elementary school years while evaluation and synthesis skills should be targeted for guided practice during the middle school/junior high years and then practiced independently during the senior high years. The guiding principle for leveling should be the premise that the information-processing capacity of a student comes into play only when the student reaches a developmental stage where the task at hand does not take all of the student's time, energy, and effort. As an example, a third grader may be totally consumed in the attempt to handle the location of a resource using a call number from a catalog entry. Fourth graders work hard to make a conscious choice about author, title, or subject accessing of a resource. Fifth and sixth graders are ready with adult guidance to deal with the card catalog or its electronic equivalent as an index to a total collection of resources. Middle school/junior high school students may be ready to make some value judgments about that total collection. Finally, senior high students are ready to deal with how adequately the total collection meets an information need and to make conscious networking decisions.

Obviously, the above example is a generalization. Educators know there is no such thing as a generic seventh grader! The benefit of a sequential information management skills program based on developmental readiness is that a student can progress in the sequence when developmentally ready rather than remain confined to grade level entry.

The *fifth step* in the revision process is a final examination of the scope and sequence to ensure that skills grouped under a conceptual heading do indeed support that concept. A breakout of the conceptual groupings that deal with analysis, evaluation, and synthesis of information will begin to address process orientation characteristic of critical thinking. Such a breakout also becomes an effective way to communicate to administrators and teachers how, when, and where the information management skills curriculum delivers to students some very vital components of a critical thinking skills initiative.

When the steps above have been completed, and all who were involved in structuring the original information management skills curriculum have reached agreement on suggested changes, the revised scope and sequence should be formalized by submitting it to the curriculum approval agency at the local level. Once the revised skills scope and sequence has been approved, mastery levels and evaluation strategies should be determined for the added skills in accordance with local policy. In assessing mastery, it is crucial to examine the process, including appropriate use of resources, that a student applies to complete an assignment as well as the end product produced. Therefore, it becomes more important than ever for librarians and subject area teachers to work as a team in determining mastery. Such an approach is a direct application of the novice/expert dimension discussed above. In assessing process the librarian will be looking at the student's search pattern as well as examining actual use of resources in terms of observable elements that are or are not congruent with those an expert might consider appropriate in seeking an answer to a similar information related problem.

The *sixth and final step* in the revision process involves the analysis of existing teaching activities, as well as the creation of activities for the added skills, to ensure that skill statements are addressed at the appropriate cognitive levels. The research cited in this paper probably holds more implications for this particular step than for those previously described. In examining the K-6 activities in light of the findings of metacognitive studies one should look for, and build in where necessary, opportunities for groups of students to brainstorm and to classify, with adult direction, while structuring a strategy to address an assignment. Such an approach enables elementary age students to practice these thinking patterns often and in a variety of contexts. Then, as students mature developmentally and are ready to evaluate their own information seeking behavior, they have already practiced patterns of thinking they are now ready to apply consciously in meeting information needs.

The research cited above holds additional implications for developing and revising activities for junior high school and senior high school students. First, junior high school activities should include, wherever possible, opportunities for students to analyze relevant resources in terms of synonyms, key words, identification of people associated with ideas presented, as well as the appropriateness of the currency of the information presented. At the senior high school level activities should provide students with opportunities to access appropriate resources by designing search strategies that reflect knowledge of the use of synonyms, key words, identification of particular people with ideas, and designation of desirable age range for information. Also, at the secondary level, assignment time lines must be expanded so students can reasonably build networking considerations into the design and evaluation of a search. Such networking would include use of appropriate local libraries as well as use of interlibrary loan. At the secondary level, too, and even in the upper elementary grades, assignments should be provided in written form so students have the opportunity to analyze carefully the posed problem before they structure a strategy to find the information to solve it.

The last three implications to be addressed apply to all levels, K-12, and are perhaps the most important in preparing students to think critically about the process followed in accessing information. First, activities should provide frequent opportunities for students to develop questions relevant to an information related problem because the act of posing appropriate questions is basic to finding workable solutions. At the primary level, such opportunities can be built into pre- and postactivities for storytelling while at the senior high level students can be asked to develop a given number of questions that can be used to flesh out a thesis statement for completion of a research paper. Second, students should have opportunities to solve information related problems in groups. Again, at the elementary level, after posing an assignment, the teacher or librarian can solicit suggestions from the entire class on an appropriate approach, while at the junior high level small groups of students can generate a variety of approaches, ultimately to be shared with the entire class, to the same assignment. Even at the senior high level, where students work independently on individual assignments, it is important to structure opportunities for peer reaction to a suggested search strategy.

The final implication has the greatest potential to cause change in student information seeking behavior from a metacognitive perspective. Specifically, at increasing levels of complexity and reflecting developmental readiness, a requirement that students project strategies at the initiation of assignments and critique those same strategies at the completion of assignments, should be written into appropriate activities. Students in grades five or six through twelve should be asked to go through this process in a written form for every problem-solving assignment. The process need not be a burdensome one; it can be effected through development of a form that poses two questions:

1. How do you plan to complete this assignment? Specify the major steps and time you believe each step will take.
   Step One:
       Time Estimate:
   Step Two:
       Time Estimate:
   Step Three:
       Time Estimate:
   Step Four:
       Time Estimate:
   Step Five:
       Time Estimate:

2. Now that you have completed the assignment, what would you do differently?

The end result will be students who are not only able to project strategies that address information related problems, but who are also able to evaluate the success of their strategies in terms of time spent and end product produced. Frequent practice will increase the potential of evaluation, planning, and regulating functions becoming automatic processes for students.

Sternberg reinforces these suggestions as he calls attention to the errors he believes are being made in designing activities to teach critical thinking:

- Educators define problems for students to solve while in the everyday world the first and often most difficult step is recognition that a problem exists;

- Educators pose well-structured problems while life poses ill-structured ones;

- Educators provide in the problem information to solve the problem, while in everyday problem solving it generally is not obvious what information is needed or where it can be found;

- Educators pose problems in isolation while solutions to everyday problems depend on context and interaction;

- Educators endorse a "best" solution while everyday problems generally have no one right solution and no obvious criteria for a best solution;

- Educators pose problems based on formal knowledge while solution of everyday problems requires as much informal as formal knowledge; and

- Educators design problems to be solved on an individual basis while everyday problem solving often occurs in groups.[29]

Sternberg's points should serve as constant reminders to school library media specialists of pertinent current concerns as they design and evaluate activities. It seems clear that it is the process that is important, not the ability to perform isolated exercises correctly.

In summary, students need to know what information is available in their information universe, how to locate it, and most importantly, how to use it effectively. While school library media specialists are designing activities to teach information management skills, attention also must be directed to the teaching and learning strategies implied. Role modeling is essential. Those who teach information management skills must demonstrate and articulate for students appropriate search strategies whenever real or contrived information needs are being addressed. In addition, an information guidance function by the specialist should be part of the activities.

Finally, when the integrated, process-oriented information management skills curriculum is in place, the school library media specialist is ready to address the second assessment task, the reexamination of the total school library media program to see if it adequately corresponds to and supports the revised curriculum in much the same way a good curriculum writer examines a textbook to see if it supports the written curriculum. The alternative is not acceptable in either case; the library media program should not determine the vitality of the skills curriculum any more than the textbook should drive the written curriculum.

Several programming areas that need to be in place, functioning, and adequately developed are:

- Resource collections to implement skills curriculum;

- Technology to utilize resources;

- Staffing to develop program and teach skills as well as administer and maintain facilities;

- Local production capacity to provide synthesis options;

- Flexible scheduling;

- Staff development for school library media personnel in areas of collection development, questioning techniques, and technical skills.

When a process-oriented, integrated information management skills curriculum is in place and based in a physical facility with services that are capable of translating that curriculum into active teaching and learning, library media specialists will be successful in providing to students access to information and ideas in the broadest sense of the word.

The interest of the National Commission in how students are taught to locate, evaluate, and use information is a timely and welcome one. The ability to find and use information effectively is fundamental for success in a rapidly changing, information-oriented society such as ours. Articulating what this means in terms of basic information management skills for students falls directly into the purview of the school library media program and fits well with the instructional role of the school library media specialist.

NOTES

[1]Shirley Aaron, professor, Florida State University; Charles Benton, chair, Public Media Inc., Illinois; Elise Brumback, assistant state superintendent, Education Media and Technology Services, North Carolina Department of Public Instruction; Daniel Callison, assistant professor, School of Library and Information Science, Indiana University; Thomas Downen, associate professor, Department of Educational Media and Librarianship, University of Georgia; Frank Farrell, president, Grolier Electronic Publishing Inc., and vice-president, Reference Group, Grolier Education Corp.; Lillian Gerhardt, editor, *School Library Journal*, R. R. Bowker; Carolyn Kirkendall, Eastern Michigan University Library, LOEX Clearinghouse; Jacqueline C. Mancall, associate professor, College of Information Studies, Drexel University; Joe Shubert, state librarian and assistant commissioner for libraries, New York State Library; and Sue A. Walker, acting curriculum coordinator, J. P. McCaskey High School, Lancaster, Pennsylvania. NCLIS staff: Tony Carbo Bearman, executive director; Diane Yassenoff Rafferty and Christina Carr Young, research associates.

[2]J. McTighe and J. Schollenberger, "Why Teach Thinking: A Statement of Rationale," in *Developing Minds: A Resource Book for Teaching Thinking*, ed. A. L. Costa (Alexandria, Va.: Association for Supervision and Curriculum Development, 1985), 11.

[3]J. Goodlad, "A Study of Schooling: Some Findings and Hypotheses," *Phi Delta Kappan* 65 (March 1983): 465-70.

[4]"Reading, Thinking and Writing," in *The 1979-80 National Assessment of Reading and Literature* (Denver, Colo.: National Assessment of Education Progress, 1981).

[5]McTighe and Schollenberger, 5.

[6]J. W. Liesener, "Learning at Risk: School Library Media Programs in an Information World," in *Libraries and the Learning Society* (Chicago: American Library Association, 1984), 69-75.

[7]K. E. Vandergrift, *The Teaching Role of the School Library Media Specialist* (Chicago: American Library Association, 1979).

[8]M. Scriven, "Critical for Survival," *National Forum* 65, no. 1 (Winter 1985): 9-12.

[9]S. P. Norris, "Synthesis of Research on Critical Thinking," *Educational Leadership* 42, no. 8 (May 1985): 40-46.

[10]Norris, 43.

[11]B. K. Beyer, "Critical Thinking: What Is It?" *Social Education* 49, no. 4 (April 1985): 270-76.

[12]Ibid., 272.

[13]E. S. Quellmalz, "Needed: Better Methods for Testing Higher-Order Thinking Skills," *Educational Leadership* 43, no. 2 (October 1985): 29-35.

[14]Norris, 43.

[15]E. Bondy, "Thinking about Thinking," *Childhood Education* 60, no. 4 (March/April 1984): 234-38.

[16]S. G. Paris and B. L. Lindauer, "The Development of Cognitive Skills During Childhood," in *Handbook of Developmental Psychology*, ed. B. Wolman (Englewood Cliffs, N.J.: Prentice-Hall, 1982), 333-49.

[17]J. H. Flavell, "Metacognitive and Cognitive Monitoring," *American Psychologist* 4, no. 10 (October 1979): 906-11.

[18]E. Robinson, "Metacognitive Development," in *Developing Thinking*, ed. S. Meadows (London: Methuen, 1983), 106-41.

[19]A. L. Brown and J. S. deLoache, "Skills, Plans and Self-regulation," in *Children's Thinking. What Develops?* ed. R. S. Siegler (Hillsdale, N.J.: Lawrence Erlbaum Associates), 13; cited by Robinson, "Metacognitive Development," 1983.

[20]M. Shatz, "The Relationship between Cognitive Processes and the Development of Communication Skills," in *Nebraska Symposium on Motivation*, ed. B. Learey (Lincoln, Nebr.: University of Nebraska Press, 1982).

[21]L. S. Vygotsky, *Thought and Language* (Cambridge, Mass.: MIT Press, 1962), 82-118.

[22]L. S. Vygotsky, *Mind in Society* (Cambridge, Mass.: Harvard University Press, 1978), 86.

[23]L. H. Bertland, "An Overview of Research in Metacognition: Implications for Information Skills Instruction," *School Library Media Quarterly* (in press).

[24]Bondy.

[25]J. Sancore, "Metacognition and the Improvement of Reading: Some Important Links," *Journal of Reading* 27 (May 1984): 706-12.

[26]Bertland.

[27]National Council for the Social Studies, Task Force on Scope and Sequence, "In Search of a Scope and Sequence for Social Studies," *Social Education* 48, no. 4 (April 1984): 260-61.

[28]Beyer, 273.

[29]R. J. Sternberg, "Teaching Critical Thinking, Part 1: Are We Making Critical Mistakes?" *Phi Delta Kappan* 67, no. 3 (November 1985): 194-98.

THE TEACHER-LIBRARIAN AND INFORMATION SKILLS

An across the Curriculum Approach*

Roy Lundin

THE RATIONALE

Four conclusions I have arrived at over the past fifteen years should be kept in mind throughout this paper. They provide a kind of rationale for an integrated approach to skills development across the curriculum.

Conclusion 1:

The flood of information is now unmanageable.

There is little doubt that the flood of information, which is in fact accelerating, is completely unmanageable by any person. For most students — and principals, teachers, and teacher-librarians, for that matter — the enormous bank of information is relatively unknown; they are simply not aware of the magnitude of the universal data base.

Those who have a glimmer of the amount of information available, even in areas of specialization, are absolutely exasperated and even terrified. Libraries and librarians are also finding it impossible to cope; all the skills possessed by reference librarians still seem not enough to manage the growing amount of information, even with the aid of automated storage and retrieval systems.

How much, then, can we expect of school students in their attempts to survive in this deluge?

Conclusion 2:

People do not value information-based decision-making, nor libraries as a source of information.

Perhaps a personal example may be acceptable here. While visiting a brother in Canada some time ago, I was caught up in the idea of mixing up that Hawaiian drink called a "mai-tai". My brother's solution was to search a

*From Roy Lundin, "The Teacher-Librarian and Information Skills — An across the Curriculum Approach," *Emergency Librarian* 11 (September/October 1983): 8-12. Copyright © 1983 Dyad Services. Reprinted with permission from *Emergency Librarian* (ISSN 0315-8888).

bookshop for a book of drink recipes which he could buy. I suggested, to his surprise, the public library where we did find a book with the appropriate recipe and obtained a photocopy of it for ten cents.

Information is everywhere but libraries do not have a monopoly on it. Many people are motivated to use information to meet various needs from time to time, but they obviously tend to go to sources other than the library to get answers. Why?

It may be true that the *need* for selected information will increase with increased competition for *survival*. Perhaps our main hope here is that schools at all levels will continue to work on the development and reinforcement of "information skills" so that new generations will increasingly value information-based decision-making. The importance of this cannot be underestimated. Information is of value to all forms of decision-making from voting and furthering one's education to purchasing a car or hi-fi equipment and getting a job.

Conclusion 3:

The formal teaching of "library skills" in a vacuum to users is not a fruitful exercise.

Much more will be stated about this shortly, but skills are developed through experience and regular practice in constant settings. There are, of course, certain identifiable skills necessary in the location of information, but these skills do not necessarily apply to every search, nor is there automatic transfer of skills from one setting to another, nor has every user a perfect memory.

Autonomy in the *search* for information may be a good objective, but considering Conclusions 1 and 2, it is unlikely that many users will ever become completely autonomous in running the maze.

"Resourcefulness" may be a better objective. It is the knowledge and ability to use alternative support systems. Above all, however, users need the skills of analysis, synthesis, and evaluation so that they can make effective use of the information obtained.

Conclusion 4:

The role of the teacher-librarian is to coordinate and facilitate the organization and use of educational resources.

After fifteen years of significant development in school librarianship in Australia, we are now reaching the point where the role of the teacher-librarian is becoming clear.

The main aim of the teacher-librarian is working towards the improvement of the quality of the experiences which children and teachers have in school. To achieve this, the teacher-librarian must fulfill the role of coordinating and facilitating the organization and use of educational resources.

The role, then, falls into two main parts:

I Resource Management which involves the aspects of administration, selection, acquisition, and organization of the resources collections and systems of use in the school.

II Cooperative Planning and Teaching which may well be a plain way of saying "involvement in curriculum planning and implementation".

These two aspects of the teacher-librarian's role are put very well into priority order by Ken Haycock:[1]

> In times of declining financial support for public institutions and services of all kinds, it is perhaps useful to remind ourselves of the basic principles on which school library services thrive and prosper and the major issues confronting the profession. Too often we deal well with the symptoms but ignore the causes, resulting in an inevitable rematch, as symptoms, like weeds, keep coming up.
>
> The research and the experience of those developing support for teacher-librarians and school resource centres, is quite clear. The single most important role of the teacher-librarian is cooperative program planning and teaching with classroom teachers. This major shift for the teacher-librarian from determining what the student is to do, to cooperatively determining what the student is to learn, has resulted in the teacher becoming the primary focus. Cooperative planning and team teaching not only provide better opportunities for purposeful use of library resources and the integration of media, research, and study skills with classroom instruction but also provide better opportunities for classroom teachers and administrators to learn first hand the role of the teacher-librarian as a teaching partner, something quite different from a teaching adjunct.

*****

> It's time to stand up and be counted as a professional with integrity, confidence, and skill. The management of newer materials and technology, while important, will not save or even necessarily enhance the status of the teacher-librarian if undertaken outside this framework. The future lies in working closely with teachers within the context of a clearly defined role, understood and advocated by teacher-librarians and thus by administrators, teachers, and the community.

*****

It is on the basis of these conclusions that the concept of integration of skills is proposed.

THE CONTEXT

The teacher carefully diagnoses the needs of the learners, then matches the strategies and resources which will meet those needs. There are a whole range of strategies from which the teacher can select, involving children in individual, small group, and large group activities. Unfortunately, the range of strategies used by teachers is often limited to lecturing, worksheets or projects with the odd film or excursion thrown in for good behaviour. Teachers still spend an average of about 70 percent of their time in the classroom talking.[2] With this amount of talk time there is little time left for children to learn and practise a range of information skills.

The "resources" element of the new curriculum paradigm helps to free up education—that is, to open up the educational options available to teachers and children in schools—and this is important to the quality of educational experiences. There is an intrinsic reward for children in the use of resources, and this use allows children choices of what to do and how—i.e., some control over their own learning.[3]

Most school syllabuses now contain outlines of content/knowledge, skills and attitudes, three basic areas. The importance of this is that skills are seen as a part of all curriculum development so that integration of skills with content and attitudes can be ensured. It is the integration of skills which is the main focus here.

WHAT SKILLS?

There is no shortage of lists of skills, but there is some lack of sound organization of these skills.

MacColl[4] provides a clear definition of "skill":

"...the term 'skill' can be applied to the ability to do something with a degree of expertness in repeated performances."

"...implications for skill development which can be drawn out as follows: (i) a skill is an *ability*, which implies learning; (ii) it involves *'expertness'*, which implies mastery; and (iii) it involves *repetition*.

The skills domain includes four major areas:

Receptive: These involve the whole range of location, reading, looking, and listening skills:

- reading skills

- listening skills

- observation skills

- time and space skills

- data gathering (search or location) skills

- quantitative skills

Reflective: These internal, process skills bring the isolated bits of information into meaningful relationships:

- problem identification and solving skills

- critical thinking skills (especially inference, interpretation, association, assumption, analysis, synthesis, and evaluation)

- lateral thinking skills

Expressive: These skills enable the student to organize and pass on (communicate) knowledge gained through the receptive and reflective skills:

- writing skills

- speaking skills

- recording skills

- presentation (including production) skills

Personal/Social: These are forms of expressive skills which tend to have some influence, or tend to "colour" the other processes:

- manipulative skills

- interpersonal skills

- community participation skills

These categories could then be developed into an exhaustive listing of a myriad of skills and subskills and sub-subskills.[5]

APPROACHES

Skills teaching has not only been a neglected area, both in research and in practice, but also has usually occurred in formal, unrelated isolation.

The most common approaches to the teaching of information skills are as follows:

The *structured, formal/unrelated* approach, sometimes referred to as the content approach, usually takes the form of class "library lessons", card kits, activity sheets or specially made up library assignments on such topics as: "How To Use the Encyclopaedia" or "Using The Dictionary Card Catalogue". A number of skill building kits are available commercially and tend to be fairly widely used. Quite frankly, such kits are not really needed. They encourage the skills to be taught in a fancy and expensive vacuum, and this leads to a *waste* of existing resources in a school's collection.

There are two types of *formal/related* approaches. The first is when the teacher-librarian, for one reason or another, runs a series of library lessons parallel to what teachers are doing in their classrooms in an effort to make relevant skills development happen as closely as possible to when they are needed. The hard-working teacher-librarian can make such a program fairly effective. The second type, also called the question approach, usually involves activities, in the library periods, built around needs or questions that students have or are likely to ask. Materials are developed or sessions conducted around questions such as: "How do I find a good book to read?" or "I want some materials on the topic—How do I get them?" Emphasis in this approach is on the learning of skills and processes that are transferable to other life situations.

The *unstructured, incidental* approach is effective as far as it goes in that the teacher and teacher-librarian seize on the teachable moment when a child expresses a need. The weakness is that many needs go either unexpressed or unnoticed.

By far the superior approach is the *integrated* approach. This is when the whole range of skills, knowledge, and attitudes are built into existing or cooperatively planned curriculum activities in the various areas such as science, social studies, language, mathematics, and so on. In this approach the teacher-librarian works with the teacher (a) at the planning stage, incorporating skills and resources into the unit, matching them to needs; (b) in the implementation of the unit, at times team teaching as appropriate; and (c) in the evaluation of the unit, to determine both student performance and the strengths and weaknesses of the program itself. This also allows for incidental, individual attention to ensure all students are able to master the skills.

This approach is based on the following principles of learning and teaching skills first published as an appendix to *Skill Development in Social Studies, Thirty-third Yearbook of the National Council for the Social Studies:*[6]

1. The skill should be taught functionally, in the context of a topic of study, rather than as a separate exercise.

2. The learner must understand the meaning and purpose of the skill, and have motivation for developing it.

3. The learner should be carefully supervised in his first attempts to apply the skill, so that he will form correct habits from the beginning.

4. The learner needs repeated opportunities to practise the skill, with immediate evaluation so that he knows where he has succeeded or failed in his performance.

5. The learner needs individual help, through diagnostic measures and follow-up exercises, since not all members of any group learn at exactly the same rate or retain equal amounts of what they have learned.

6. Skill instruction should be presented at increasing levels of difficulty, moving from the simple to the more complex; the resulting growth in skills should be cumulative as the learner moves through school, with each level of instruction building on and reinforcing what has been taught previously.

7. The student should be helped, at each stage, to generalize the skills, by applying them in many and varied situations; in this way maximum transfer of learning can be achieved.

The key processes are:

- cooperative planning which leads to

- an overall, coordinated program in which skills are

- integrated systematically, sequentially and accumulatively with all other aspects of the curriculum, and

- the teacher and teacher-librarian work cooperatively to ensure all students' needs are met.

There are a number of ways of approaching cooperative planning between teachers and teacher-librarian. Perhaps a simple but effective way is to plan topics or units of study on a form sheet with the following headings:

- Time

- Place

- Content

- Attitudes

- Strategy/ies

- Skills

- Resources

- Assessment

Such a form is easily copied and filed for future reference.

There is, some may say, an element of coercion involved in this process. That is, the students' motivation to learn and use skills comes from the perceived need to meet the requirements set down by the teacher in league with the teacher-librarian. Caution is required here. Coercion as a form of extrinsic motivation can produce stress which, if not relaxed in a healthy way, can lead to fear, guilt, and neurosis rather than the development of positive values. This is well-documented in the literature which differentiates between motivation through the need to achieve and motivation from fear of failure. Such coercion, furthermore, will not necessarily lead students to the library or its services; they will go to each other for support. On the other hand, if there is a warm and supportive climate in the school where students are encouraged to take part in the planning as well, then the motivation comes through participation rather than coercion.

There is a great difference then between simply having a list of skills and having an effective integrated learning program. Sequencing and timing are important considerations here as well.

With regard to sequencing, consideration needs to be given to when a certain part of a skill should be introduced, how and when it should be repeated and added to, to result in skill building in an accumulative manner. Many schools have started with basic lists of research and study skills and then planned similar charts where the teachers and teacher-librarian have worked cooperatively to determine which skills should be where.

Timing is important in the introduction of skills, not only to match students' needs but also to take account of readiness. For example, it would be a mistake to introduce the complex use of subject headings in the card catalogue to primary students. A Canadian study showed that only around the ages of 11 to 15 years, in keeping with Piaget's stages of cognitive development, can children move from a specific to a general heading, e.g., cats to pets to animals.[7]

It is important that schools do not adopt, uncritically, charts, lists, or programs from other sources. To do this is not an easy way out; it simple reduces the relevance of the whole program. Again, cooperative planning by the school staff needs to be emphasized to ensure the development of an effective, relevant curriculum for the school.

SUMMARY GUIDELINES FOR PRINCIPALS, TEACHERS, AND TEACHER-LIBRARIANS

All members of the school staff should share the common goal of helping every student to become an autonomous learner. They should, therefore, share the responsibility of developing policies, setting up structures or systems, developing programs and teaching in such a way as to facilitate a well-rounded learning experience for every student.

Principals can facilitate the integration of skills by:

(a) providing opportunities for teachers and the teacher-librarian to plan cooperatively;

(b) involving teachers and teacher-librarians in the development of school goals and policies governing the curriculum;

(c) scheduling class and teacher times to facilitate resource-based/library-oriented programs;

(d) arranging inservice for teachers and teacher-librarians to help them update or upgrade their abilities;

(e) showing leadership through demonstration or pilot programs within the school, and supporting teacher/teacher-librarian initiatives;

(f) budgeting to allow for adequate provision of resources to support the programs;

(g) maintaining an open school climate where communication is free and where staff and students experience satisfaction;

(h) presenting a positive image of the school to the community.

Teachers can contribute to integrated programs by:

(a) participating in the planning and implementation of the school's total curriculum;

(b) involving the teacher-librarian in all stages of planning, teaching, and evaluating units of work;

(c) accepting prime responsibility for the learning experience of the students assigned to them;

(d) designing relevant activities for students to ensure the integration of content, attitudes, and skills in all subjects;

(e) actively selecting resources in cooperation with the teacher-librarian.

Teacher-librarians can contribute to an integrated program by:

(a) participating in the planning and implementation of the school's total curriculum, particularly by advising on the use of resources;

(b) selecting with the involvement of teachers, acquiring, organizing and operating a collection of resources and services appropriate to meet the needs of the school;

(c) cooperating with teachers in the planning, teaching, and evaluation of units of work;

(d) coordinating with teachers to determine what will be covered for particular groups of students, when and who will accept prime responsibility for the teaching and application of skills;

(e) teaching some of the skills as mutually agreed upon;

(f) giving incidental, follow-up support and reinforcement to individual library users;

(g) extending children's interests and skills beyond the traditional subject areas of the school's curriculum;

(h) assisting students to make transitions from one setting or stage to another—i.e., primary to secondary school, secondary to university, college or work;

(i) provide any service which will help improve the quality of the experience which teachers and children have in schools.

The all too common isolation of the teacher-librarian through the teaching of "library skills" lessons in separate library periods served only to provide a spare period for classroom teachers and to delay unnecessarily the integration of research and study skills and the teacher-librarian into the mainstream of the school's curricular concerns.

The integration of information skills across the curriculum on the other hand offers an exciting challenge for teacher-librarians not only to provide leadership in a critical educational area but also to forge new partnerships with administrators and teaching colleagues.

NOTES

[1] K. Haycock, "Editorial—Hard Times ... Hard Choices," *Emergency Librarian* 9, no. 5 (1982): 5.

[2] M. Marland, *Language across the Curriculum* (London: Heineman, 1977), 77.

[3] B. Bahnisch, "Some Observations on the Role of the Teacher-Librarian," *Journal of the School Library Association of Queensland* 12, no. 2 (1980): 15-16.

[4] P. MacColl, "Skill Development," *Journal of the School Library Association of Queensland* 12, no. 3/4 (1980): 12.

[5] Ibid.

[6] H. M. Carpenter, ed., *Skill Development in Social Studies, Thirty-third Yearbook of the National Council for the Social Studies* (Washington D.C.: National Council for the Social Studies, 1963).

[7] M. Kogon, "Does Age Make a Difference in Ability to Use Subject Headings in a Catalogue?" *Moccasin Telegraph* 17, no. 2 (1974): 36-37.

BIBLIOGRAPHY

Berner, Elsa. *Integrating Library Instruction with Classroom Teaching at Plainview Junior High School.* Chicago: American Library Association, 1958.

Beyond Reading Lists: Academics, Librarians, and Reader Education. Proceedings of the Third Reader Education Seminar sponsored by the Association of Librarians in Colleges of Advanced Education, Queensland Division, held in Brisbane from the 28th-29th August 1978 at the Library of the Queensland Institute of Technology.

Bowers, Norma. "Resource Based Skills Activities." *Journal of the School Library Association of Queensland* 12, no. 3/4 (1980): 5-11.

Davies, Ruth Ann. *School Library Media Program: Instructional Force for Excellence*. 3d ed. New York: Bowker, 1979.

Fraser, Barrie J. *Test of Enquiry Skills: Handbook*. Hawthorn, Victoria: Australian Council for Educational Research, 1979.

Guenther, Elsa. *How to Study Through Your Library*. Melbourne: Australian Library Promotion Council, 1972.

Irving, Ann. "Teach Them to Learn: Educating Library Users in Schools." *Education Libraries Bulletin* 21, no. 3 (1978): 29-39.

Johns, E., and D. M. Fraser. "Social Studies Skills: A Guide to Analysis and Grade Placement." In *Skill Development in Social Studies*, edited by H. M. Carpenter, 310-27. Thirty-third Yearbook of the National Council for the Social Studies. Washington, D.C.: National Council for the Social Studies, 1963.

Lundin, Roy. "The Relevancy of the Library Skills Programme." In *Prospects*, edited by Peter J. Pegg. Brisbane: School Library Association of Queensland, 1973.

MacColl, P. "An Approach to Skill Development." Unpublished. Curriculum Branch, Queensland Department of Education, 1981.

Piper, K. "Evaluation in the Social Sciences for Secondary Schools." In *Teachers' Handbook*, 63-70. Canberra: A.C.E.R. and A.G.P.S.

Reed, Estella. "Building Library Skills at the Secondary School Level." *Education* 88 (1967): 353-56.

Resource Management for Secondary Schools. 3d ed. Queensland: Department of Education, Library and Resource Services, 1981.

"Synopsis of Selected Seminar Papers, 1970. Library Research Skills — The Organizational Framework." Queensland: Department of Education, Circular to schools, 1970.

A PROCESS APPROACH TO
LIBRARY SKILLS INSTRUCTION*

Carol Collier Kuhlthau

For many years elementary and high school librarians have been conscientiously teaching library skills to their students. Academic librarians, however, continue to find that incoming students have difficulty using the library for their research assignments. Biggs notes that "incoming freshmen lack all but the most rudimentary library skills. They have no inkling of what sources are available, when to ask questions or even what to ask for."[1] Dickinson warns that there is "an epidemic in library illiteracy."[2] A study of Bucknell students found that "students failed to use logical progression and systematic approaches to checking sources of information.... The concept of research on the part of many students appears to be limited and unsophisticated."[3]

Biggs suggests that the problem centers around librarians assuming a title orientation to library skills instruction, rather than a process orientation. Students are introduced to various library sources and access points, but they rarely learn the process of developing an understanding of a topic through library research. "To be of maximum use the skills must be more process oriented."[4]

Designing process oriented instruction was the problem which I investigated in my doctoral dissertation. A group of high school seniors were studied while they used the library for two assigned research papers. I sought to learn more about the process which they were experiencing and to design instruction which would assist them in learning the process of library research as well as the sources in the library.

The research process of the students was traced through a number of devices including questionnaires, interviews, journals, timelines and flow charts. I found that students not only needed but wanted guidance in the process which they were working through as they were using the library. One student described the need for more guided instruction in this way.

> I would prefer if teachers were more demanding. I guess it's more grownup to say, "Here you have a research paper. It's due in four weeks, do it." It's all on your own, I guess, research papers are. But they never ask during the four weeks, they never remind you that you're doing a research paper. Just at the end of three and a half weeks they say, "Your research paper is due in three days." The teacher could have done something in between, given us ideas.

*Reprinted with permission of the American Library Association, "A Process Approach to Library Skills Instruction" by Carol Collier Kuhlthau. Taken from *School Library Media Quarterly* 14 (Winter 1985): 35-40; copyright © 1985 by the American Library Association.

Teachers are so nonchalant about giving research papers.... I don't know what teachers expect because it seems they just say you have this research paper due. They don't discuss it with you. I don't know if they think you are really researching for four weeks or if they know that you are procrastinating because they used to do it. In the meantime, the teacher isn't really being there. I don't think teachers should say, "Let me see your note cards." But they should say, "Ok, tomorrow we will talk about what you found and if you have any problems or what point you are at." [They should] not pressure you. "Well, if you haven't started, just forget it." Sometimes you haven't started because you don't know what you are about. It would help to know if everyone else was lost too.[5]

"Being there" involves seeing the research through, from beginning to end. Students need help in recognizing the various stages typical to the research process. They also need guidance in learning useful strategies to apply at the various stages in the process. Once they understand the process and know some useful strategies, they are better equipped to transfer their library skills to other research situations in other libraries.

COGNITIVE PROCESS USED IN LIBRARY RESEARCH

The process of developing an understanding of a topic through library research may be compared to the process of incorporating any new experience into one's existing system of constructs. Swiss psychologist, Jean Piaget described the process as assimilating and accommodating new information into a schema. The study of cognitive processes has become a major thrust in current psychological inquiry. Jerome Brunner called the cognitive revolution the "Big Bang" in psychology.[6] Ulrich Neisser and other cognitive psychologists continue to study the process which encompasses all learning.

Psychologist George A. Kelly described the feelings one might expect to experience in the process of assimilating new experience or information. First, there is a feeling of doubt in both the capacity to understand and the validity of the new idea. Then, as more information is encountered, the person becomes confused and sometimes threatened. At this point, the person chooses to abandon the new idea or to press on by forming a hypothesis. Kelly turns to a scientific analogy for describing the remainder of the process. The person tests the hypothesis and assesses the results, accepting or rejecting the new information accordingly. On the basis of the results, a new construct is formed or an existing one is verified.[7]

The high school students in my study were found to experience a similar succession of feelings to those described by Kelly. When they first were given a research assignment, they were uncertain as to how to proceed and what was expected of them. As they encountered the variety of information in the library, they became confused, discouraged, and even threatened. At this point, they were encouraged to form a focus for their research, much like Kelly's hypothesis. After the focus was established, they were able to move on to gather information and to prepare their presentation.

Studies of the search behavior of information users also shed light on the research process of students. Information scientists have found that people experience different levels of information need. In a study of college students, Taylor identified four levels of information need.[8]

Visceral—An actual but unexpressed need; a vague sort of dissatisfaction.

Conscious—An ill-defined area of indecision expressed in an ambiguous, rambling statement.

Formal—An area of doubt described in concrete terms.

Compromised—A need for information translated into what the files can deliver.

The levels of information need parallel the cognitive psychological stages of assimilating new information. The levels and stages describe a hierarchy which people work through in the library research process. At each level, library sources are used in different ways for different purposes. Students need to learn search strategies which match their level of information need.

The process of assimilating new information is the complex process which students are involved with in library research. They need to understand the research process in order to be able to effectively locate and use information in libraries.

TIMELINE OF THE LIBRARY RESEARCH PROCESS

A model of the library research process was developed from the findings of the study of the high school seniors. Six successive stages were identified which can be used for describing the process to students enabling them to visualize what they can expect to encounter (see figure 1). In addition, some strategies were developed for each stage to help students work through the process.[9]

Stage 1: Initiating a Research Assignment

The task of the first stage is to prepare for the decision of selecting a topic. Students often feel apprehensive and uncertain of what is expected of them. Some students in the study described feeling "depressed and bogged down" and "overwhelmed at the amount of work ahead." It is helpful to acknowledge these feelings and to offer specific directions on how to begin.

At the beginning, students need to visualize the entire process that is ahead of them. The timeline of the research process can be used to demonstrate the stages and the tasks which need to be accomplished within each stage. When students know what to expect, they can learn to plan their research to allow for sufficient time to work through the entire process.

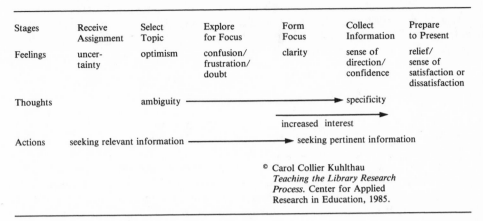

Stages	Receive Assignment	Select Topic	Explore for Focus	Form Focus	Collect Information	Prepare to Present
Feelings	uncertainty	optimism	confusion/ frustration/ doubt	clarity	sense of direction/ confidence	relief/ sense of satisfaction or dissatisfaction
Thoughts		ambiguity ⟶			specificity	
				increased interest ⟶		
Actions	seeking relevant information ⟶		seeking pertinent information			

© Carol Collier Kuhlthau
Teaching the Library Research Process. Center for Applied Research in Education, 1985.

Fig. 1. Timeline of the library research process.

Students should have a genuine need for information which motivates and stimulates interest in their library research. Although this is not easily accomplished, it should be one of the main objectives in designing a research assignment. Broadening the audience of library research is one way of establishing a meaningful purpose for an assignment. For example, the audience might include other class members, a debating club, civic groups, or elected officials. Also, articles in the school newspaper, contests, forums are some devices which can be used to present student library research findings beyond the traditional audience of the teacher.

In this stage, students need to begin to think of possible research topics. Talking and writing helps students to think about their research in preparation for selecting a topic. Brainstorming sessions are useful for generating ideas for research topics. Keeping a journal of their thoughts, feelings and actions is also helpful for students in this stage.

Stage 2: Selecting a Topic

The task of the second stage is to decide on a topic to research. Students need to think of possible topics and to choose the one with the most potential for success. The possible topics may be weighed against the criteria of personal interest, assignment requirements, information available, and time allotted.

During the period when students are uncertain about what topic to choose, they may become somewhat anxious. After they decide on a research topic, they often experience a brief sense of elation followed by apprehension at the task ahead. They usually move through this stage quickly, experiencing the feelings in rapid succession. However, if they are unable to decide on a topic, they may become progressively more anxious.

Although the library is rarely used in this stage, students can learn to make effective use of the library collection to help in their topic selection. They can learn that a preliminary search of library sources may indicate whether a topic is viable for library research. They also can learn that the reference collection, particularly encyclopedias, offers a useful overview of prospective topics.

Talking about possible topics is helpful in this stage and is a strategy some students use on their own. Opportunities for discussion with other students and with the teacher or librarian can be arranged to help students to make good choices in their selection of a topic.

Stage 3: Exploring Information

The task of the third stage is to explore information with the intent of finding a focus. Students need to become informed about the general topic and to identify possible ways to focus the topic.

As they find information about their topic, they frequently become confused by the inconsistencies and incompatibilities which they encounter. The feeling of confusion can become quite threatening and some students want to drop their topics at this point. For many students, this is the most difficult stage of the library research process.

Students need to learn to tolerate their own uncertainties when the information they encounter is confusing. They need to read to learn about the topic. They should be encouraged to slow down to absorb what they are reading. In addition, they need to be alerted to the necessity of intentionally seeking a focus for their research.

Most students start to take detailed notes as soon as they begin to find information about their topic. Extensive note taking should be deferred to a later stage, after a focus has been formed. During the exploring information stage, notes should consist of lists of such information as terms, events, people, and places and brief notations of ideas. However, students should be urged to keep bibliographic citations of all sources which they use in order to locate them later in the research process and also to avoid plagiarism.

Students should be encouraged to explore a wide range of materials in preparation for forming a focus for their research. They need to become familiar with the various collections in a library and to learn the differences in the information presented in each type of source.

Stage 4: Forming a Focus

The task of the fourth stage is to form a focus for the research from the information on the general topic found in library sources. Students need to identify possible ways to focus their topic and choose one around which to center their information gathering.

The four criteria used to select a topic may be again employed to choose a focus. The focus should be of personal interest, meet the requirements of the assignment, be able to be researched in available materials, and be able to be accomplished within the time allotted.

Strategies which help students to form a focus again involve talking and writing. By listing possible ways to focus a research topic, students can begin to see the pitfalls in some of their ideas. Discussing possible choices also helps students to think through their decisions. In these ways, they learn to intelligently form a focus for their library research.

Stage 5: Collecting Information

Once students have formed a focus for their research, they are ready to begin to collect information. The task of this stage is to gather information which defines, extends, and supports their focus.

At this point, students have a sense of direction and are more confident, although they also realize the extent of the work to be done. Their interest in their topic often increases during this stage. In this stage, many students use library sources quite independently. They have reached Taylor's formal level of information need and can express what they are seeking in clear, concrete terms.

Students need to learn to collect only information which is pertinent to their focus. They need to learn to make a comprehensive search of all of the sources in the library, including periodicals and reference materials which might be overlooked. They need to learn to think of the library as a whole information source and to extend their search beyond being satisfied with a few books located through the card catalog. Detailed notes with complete bibliographic citations need to be taken in this stage.

Stage 6: Preparing to Present

The task of the last stage of the library research process is to conclude the search for information and to prepare to present the findings. Students can learn to recognize the signs that they have exhausted the library resources available. The information they are encountering should be decreasing in relevance and increasing in redundancy. They can also learn to identify any need for additional information.

Students usually feel a sense of relief in this stage. When the library research has been successfully completed, they have a sense of satisfaction. However, they may experience disappointment in the way they approached the assignment or in the results of their library search.

Students can learn to make a summary check of library sources to confirm information and to note anything that may have been initially overlooked. Finally, they need some direction in organizing their notes, making an outline, writing a rough draft, and preparing their final copy with footnotes and a bibliography.

Assessing the Process

Evaluation is an important part of learning. Students need constructive feedback on the effectiveness of their library research process. The traditional grade on the research paper rarely tells students much about how to improve their library research.

There are some techniques to help students reflect on their library research. They can draw timelines and flow charts of the process which they have experienced. Opportunities to discuss their process may be offered in individual conferences and group sessions. Also, having students write a summary paragraph on the focus of their paper helps them to determine whether they had a clear, central idea for their research.

Engaging the Intellect of Students

Lindgren recommends that library skills instruction seek a "more active engagement of the intellect of users."[10] What has frequently been diagnosed as a writing problem in student research papers is actually a thinking problem. Students have not sufficiently thought through their topics to write an intelligent research paper. The thoughts to be presented in a research paper need to be developed during the library research process.

One student described difficulty writing a paper which was not researched around a central focus.

> I had a general idea not a specific focus, but an idea. As I was writing, I didn't know what my focus was. When I was finished, I didn't know what my focus was. My teacher says she doesn't know what my focus was. I don't think I ever acquired a focus. It was an impossible paper to write. I would just sit there and say, "I'm stuck." There was no outline because there was no focus and there was nothing to complete. If I learned anything from that paper it is, you have to have a focus. You have to have something to center on. You can't just have a topic. You should have an idea when you start. I had a topic but I didn't know what I wanted to do with it. I figured that when I did my research it would focus in. But I didn't let it. I kept saying, "this is interesting and this is interesting and I'll just smush it altogether." It didn't work out.[11]

The process approach to teaching library research seeks to "Actively engage the intellect of users." Students need to be guided through the levels of thinking while they are researching a topic in the library. Understanding the research process enables students to more intelligently use library sources and to transfer their ability to other situations of information need in other libraries.

NOTES

[1]D. W. Dickinson, "Library Literacy: Who? When? Where?" *Library Journal* (April 15, 1981): 853-55.

[2]M. Biggs, "Forward to Basics in Library Instruction," *School Library Journal* 44 (May 1979).

[3]J. G. Reed, *Information-seeking Behavior of College Students Using the Library to Do Research: A Pilot Study* (ERIC Document Reproduction Service, 1974), ERIC Document 100 306.

[4]Biggs, 44.

[5]C. C. Kuhlthau, "The Library Research Process: Case Studies and Interventions with High School Seniors in Advanced Placement English Classes Using Kelly's Theory of Constructs" (Ed.D. dissertation, Rutgers University, 1983).

[6]J. Nessel, ed., "Understanding Psychological Man," *Psychology Today* (May 1982): 41-59.

[7]G. A. Kelly, *A Theory of Personality: The Psychology of Personal Constructs* (New York: W. W. Norton and Co., 1963).

[8]R. S. Taylor, "Question-negotiation and Information Seeking in Libraries," *College and Research Libraries* (May 1968): 178-94.

[9]C. C. Kuhlthau, *Teaching the Library Research Process: A Step-by-Step Approach for Secondary Students* (Englewood Cliffs, N.J.: The Center for Applied Research in Education, 1985).

[10]J. Lindgren, "Toward Library Literacy," *Reference Quarterly* (Spring 1981): 233-35.

[11]Kuhlthau, "The Library Research Process," 357.

CURRICULUM MAPPING AND IMPLEMENTATION OF AN ELEMENTARY SCHOOL LIBRARY MEDIA SKILLS CURRICULUM*

Michael Eisenberg

Since the late 1960s, numerous states and local school districts have developed articulated library media skills curricula.[1] Among these efforts, the Bureau of School Libraries of the Education Department of the State of New York published in 1980, an elementary (K-6) library media skills curriculum.[2] The entire New York effort rested on the premise that skills instruction is best implemented through integration with the everyday curricular activities of the classroom. While easy to state, the practicality of accomplishing this task is another matter. This paper focuses on the first step in the implementation process, namely the gathering and evaluating of information about the curriculum in a given school. A method is needed to identify those curricular units particularly appropriate for coordination with library media skills instruction. The technique of *curriculum mapping* has been found to be a useful information management tool to meet this need. Furthermore, the application of computer technology to the mapping task results in an easily managed, multifaceted, and flexible data base of curriculum information useful in many educational administrative situations.

CURRICULUM

Curriculum is a central concern in education at all levels. Encompassing the objectives of instruction and the scope and sequence of content, curriculum is the conceptual heart of the education process. Curriculum relates to the specifics of what students do, i.e. how students, teachers, and content interact. Curriculum defines what is taught, in what order, with what methods and materials, and how it is evaluated. Implementation and administration of curriculum and its components (course content, time frame and sequence, teaching methodologies, instructional materials, evaluation methods) are difficult tasks at best.

*Reprinted with permission of the American Library Association, "Curriculum Mapping and Implementation of an Elementary School Library Media Skills Curriculum" by Michael Eisenberg. Taken from *School Library Media Quarterly* 12 (Fall 1984): 411-18; copyright © 1984 by the American Library Association.

Added to this burden for a library media skills curriculum is the increasingly accepted assumption that teaching library media skills in isolation is ineffective. Library media skills are most successfully learned when integrated with the content of subject area curricula. The Walker and Montgomery book, *Teaching Media Skills*[3] championed this view and provided many useful examples of how to creatively intertwine the objectives and activities of subject lessons and units with those of library media skills. As stated previously, the designers of the New York State curriculum recognized this approach as essential. The structure, defined objectives, and model units of the curriculum reflect the central concept of integrating library media skills with the other curricular areas.

Integration of library media skills with classroom content must rest on a knowledge of both the library media curriculum and the school's curriculum by those involved in the process. While this includes teachers and administrators, the library media specialist in particular, must be well-acquainted with the curriculum in a school. "Knowledge of your school's curriculum is essential for determining which of the skills ... should be part of your program, at which grade level they first seem necessary, and within which subject area they can best be taught."[4] The designers of the New York State library media skills curriculum clearly agree stating that "an appropriate first step at the local district level is to review existing local curricula that guide instruction in the academic areas and in library media skills. The purpose of this is to determine if there are any connections, apparent or implied, between library media skills and other content area skills."[5] Frequently, the building-level library media specialist is the only individual in a school in a position to gain an overview of what is being taught. Unfortunately, that person's picture is rarely a complete one. It is more likely that certain subject areas are visible and favored while others are overlooked. In their positions, library media specialists must be able to *systematically* review and document the school's curriculum.

A review of this nature will also provide a way to determine if the curriculum in operation reflects the goals and objectives as stated. While standardized test results may give some insight into overall effectiveness, they do not provide much detail and are not always available in the areas desired. Local test scores indicate how well students are meeting the internal requirements of the curriculum, but not whether or not the curriculum meets the overall intentions of the program. This calls for a method of curriculum analysis.

There have been detailed research studies of curriculum in relation to program objectives. In the library field for example, Daniel and Ely[6] conducted an "evaluation of competencies" study to determine if the objectives, content, and evaluation procedures of designated school media courses at Syracuse University covered the competencies as defined in the school media program. Relying primarily on direct evaluation by instructors, the Daniel and Ely study demonstrated useful strategies for the assessment of competency effectiveness. More recently, White and Calhoun[7] used multidimensional scaling of enrollment data to create a "map" of the curriculum of the library school at Drexel University. An analysis of patterns revealed a de facto core of courses and also that intended specializations (e.g. educational media, applied information science, technical services librarianship) did hang together.

Both these studies offer insights into the analysis of curriculum. They are, however, special research projects covering limited areas and relying on sophisticated methodologies. Although focusing on a different level of analysis, they are related to the more general curriculum mapping technique described below.

EXISTING CURRICULUM INFORMATION SOURCES

What tools presently exist which aid in the examination of curriculum?

One source of readily available information for elementary and secondary education is the curriculum guide: state, district, or building. The most well-known of these are the overview, global guides published by the education departments of all states. For example, the one most appropriate for elementary educators in New York is *The Elementary School Curriculum: An Overview.*[8] These guides provide a valuable overview of what the curriculum "should be", what is considered important state-wide, and serve as a common point of reference for the various districts in a state. Although a general time frame is usually noted, there is little attempt to specify the degree of emphasis or time schedule of particular topics. For library media specialists in individual schools, these guides do not represent the actual district or classroom curriculum and are of limited value in identifying areas for coordination.

District or building-level guides are more detailed in outlining subject areas and sequence within and across grade levels. These documents, often created by a committee of teachers and administrators, reflect the overall emphasis and intent of curriculum. Fenwick W. English, referring to these local curriculum guides, acknowledges that "curriculum guides assist teachers in knowing that a topic or subject came before or will come after another topic in a particular K-12 sequence, but within these parameters, the amount of time, emphasis, pacing, and iteration are the domain of teachers to decide."[9] Even these guides are of limited value to the library media specialist or district media supervisor interested in analyzing existing curriculum. They are vague, lack specificity, and do not represent actual curriculum as applied by individual teachers. English has called curriculum guides, "the fictional curriculum." They state what someone wishes the curriculum to be, not what it really is.[10]

AN ALTERNATIVE: CURRICULUM MAPPING

Rather than general, future-oriented documents, library media specialists need accurate assessments of the current state of affairs in a school. A process for identifying the status quo, for revealing the existing curriculum, has been labeled *curriculum mapping* by Fenwick English. English bases his technique on the descriptive research method of content analysis. Content analysis relies on analyzing written or oral communication by such procedures as counting the number of newspaper pages or column inches dedicated to various issues to determine predominant attitudes, interests, or values. A curriculum map documents the elements of curriculum—topics, time, materials, methods of teaching and evaluation—in much the same way. A curriculum map is a "descriptive portrait of what tasks and how much time were spent on any given set of items, concepts, skills, or attitudes ... A map is not a lesson plan. A map is past oriented; it is a recording of what was taught."[11] Mapping is intended to reveal the bottom line, the actual curriculum being taught to students.

Gathering data for mapping is a relatively simple process. The basic component for analysis, usually the instructional unit or topic, must first be established. Secondly, the elements of interest relating to the unit must be identified, e.g. unit sequence, total time allotted, instructional methods, resources, the organization of instruction, and evaluation procedures. Actual data can be collected through independent observation or having teachers document their classes in response to the designated categories. Figure 1 is a form designed for either approach. In both cases, there must be systematic and consistent compilation of data independent of what others are doing. There must be an earnest attempt to record what is "real" not what "should be". Using outside observers can save valuable teacher time and lead to increased uniformity and reliability of results, however the costs are greater.

DATE _____

GRADE _____ INSTRUCTOR _____ SUBJECT _____

UNIT _____

TOTAL HOURS OF INSTRUCTION _____

WEEK STARTED _____

WEEK ENDED _____

LEVEL OF INSTRUCTION _____

     INTRODUCED
     REINFORCED
     EXPANDED

PRIMARY TEACHING METHOD _____

     DESK WORK   INDEPENDENT STUDY
     LECTURE   PROGRAMMED
               (Includes Learning Station)
     DEMONSTRATION   PROJECT
     DISCUSSION   REPORT

MATERIALS _____

     TEXT
     ONE SOURCE
     MULTIPLE SOURCES

ORGANIZATION OF INSTRUCTION _____

     LARGE GROUP   INDIVIDUAL
     SMALL GROUP   COMBINATION

EVALUATION

     TEST
     OBSERVATION
     PRODUCT
     REPORT

OBJECTIVES (OPTIONAL) _____

_____

_____

Fig. 1. Curriculum mapping worksheet. Adapted from a form used by the East Baton Rouge, Louisiana Parish Schools, see Fenwick W. English, Quality Control in Curriculum Development (Arlington, Va: American Association of School Administrators, 1978) pp. 36-39.

In most instances, the library media specialist interested in studying curriculum in order to coordinate with skills objectives will probably initiate the mapping procedure, collect data, and compile the maps. If the utility of mapping for administrative and educational development purposes can be demonstrated to administrators and teachers, they should enthusiastically support and assist in the effort. Some examples, in addition to library media purposes, where a curriculum map can be valuable include: the identification of repetition or gaps in content; how much of what is taught is assessed; the focus of a given grade level, course or subject area; patterns and variations across grade levels or among instructors teaching the same course; the degree to which curriculum guides, outlines, syllabi are being implemented; and the level or potential for inter-disciplinary cooperation.

Once data has been collected, a compiled articulation of some or all of the elements in a chart or graph is a curriculum map. The completed map can serve to highlight those units in a school's curriculum already dealing with library media skills as well as those most suited for integration with library media skills objectives. For example, a unit organized for small group instruction, which used multiple materials, on an expanded level of instruction, is a more likely candidate for coordination with library media skills than an introductory unit relying on the lecture method and a single textbook. Similarly, a unit which resulted in a project, paper or product indicates more of a need for library media center activity than one which ends in a multiple-choice test.

CURRICULUM MAPPING IN ACTION

In 1981, a pilot study was initiated to test the feasibility and usefulness of curriculum mapping in identifying subject area curricular units with potential for library media skills development. As anticipated, little trouble was encountered in setting up the parameters and gathering data. However, while a simple map consisting of three aspects of curriculum could be generated, it soon became apparent that as the number of aspects of interest increased, the storage and display of information became difficult and unwieldy. A re-examination of the maps generated by English confirmed that none dealt with more than four attributes at a time. While this limitation did not negate the advantages of mapping, a way to easily manage the full range of data was sought. At this point, a computer-based information system was suggested.

The first automated attempt to overcome the problems of manipulating the extensive data collected for mapping was a system called CMAP, based in a main frame computer developed in the APL programming language. Designed as a computerized curriculum information system, CMAP was structured on the curriculum unit as a primary field with other fields reflecting information collected about the unit (see figure 2).

CMAP successfully demonstrated that most of the data management limitations of manual mapping could be eliminated by an automated system. Unfortunately, since it existed in a main frame computer environment, the system was not immediately accessible to a wide range of users. Furthermore, in discussions with library media specialists and others interested in the system, it became apparent that the ability to modify the system for individual needs was highly desirable. For example, a school organized on a team structure might require slightly different information areas (fields) than a self-contained classroom situation.

```
107        (RECORDNUMBER)

1     (GRADE)
15    (MINUTES/WK/SEM)
1ST 2ND 3RD 4TH QUARTER(S)       (CALENDAR)
HOLIDAY PROJECTS        (UNIT)
ART   (SUBJECT)
COMBINATION       (METHOD)
MULTIPLE SOURCES        (MATERIALS)
INTRODUCED        (LEVEL OF INSTRUCTION)
SMALL GROUP       (ORGANIZATION OF INSTRUCTION)
PRODUCT        (EVALUATION)
```

Fig. 2. A record in CMAP.

Thus, the ability to easily adapt the system to local situations became a central concern. Consideration was given to the design of a microcomputer-based CMAP system which would fulfill the dual objectives of automated curriculum mapping and local design of the file structure. However, rather than program a new CMAP for micros, it was decided that many of the existing file/data base management systems for popular microcomputers might be successfully adapted for the curriculum mapping purpose.[12] The particular file system selected was not crucial as the intent was to demonstrate that the tool of automated curriculum mapping was not tied to a specific hardware/software configuration.

Mapping was successfully implemented on both an Apple IIe and a TRS-80 Model III using three different file/data management software packages. The various systems require the user to define the logical record structure thus allowing for the desired flexibility in file definition. Storage capacity, while limited by the mass storage devices present (typically one or two 5¼" floppy disks allowing 200-1000 records), do provide enough space for analysis of major portions of a school's curriculum. As systems do in search, sort, and report capabilities, the creative manipulation of these features is necessary to produce a desired map.

The major objective of providing an alternative to the time-consuming and inefficient task of manually creating a map is accomplished. Manual mapping is static and rigid while computer-based mapping is flexible and allows the user to directly interact with the curriculum information.

CURRICULUM MAPPING AND LIBRARY MEDIA SKILLS

Returning to the original intent in proposing a curriculum mapping effort, the mapping procedure can be used to identify units in a school's curriculum appropriate for integration with library media skills. Figure 3 (page 234) is a reproduction of a portion of an elementary school curriculum map created using a TRS-80 Model III and the Profiles III + file management system. The chart represents only part of the third grade curriculum, but there is still much valuable information. For example, the "weather" unit in the science area can be identified as potentially valuable for media skills integration as it was a major unit (total time allotted is 500 minutes), used a combination of teaching methods and coincides with the second quarter library media skills unit of "location/non-fiction." A more detailed look at the record (figure 4) lends further support to the unit as it calls for multiple sources, a combination of instructional arrangements, and a product for evaluation. A final push for working with this topic is the model unit, "Air, Water, and Weather," included in the New York State curriculum.[13]

UNIT	SUBJECT	CALENDAR	TIME	METHOD	GRADE
Bookmarks	Art	1000	100	combination	3
Desert	Social Studies	0001	360	lecture/discuss	3
Folktales	Language Arts	0100	200	combination	3
Locate-nonfiction	Library Media	0100	150	individualized	3
Mythology	Language Arts	0011	400	lecture/discuss	3
Weather	Science	1100	500	combination/lab	

Fig. 3. Elementary school map.

```
UNIT: Weather                          SUBJECT: Science

GRADE: 3                               TEACHER:

TOTAL TIME (minutes of instruction): 500
CALENDAR QUARTERS (0000): 1100
  (coded 0=no, 1=yes for each quarter)

  MATERIALS: multiple
  LEVEL: introduced
  ORGANIZATION: small group
  EVALUATION: product
```

Fig. 4. Record from an elementary map.

The map also shows a "bookmarks" unit in the art curriculum and "folk tales" and "mythology" units for language arts. Although occurring in different quarters, there may be the possibility of changing the sequence in order to bring one of the language arts units and the art activity together with appropriate library media skills. The library media specialist would probably look at the full record for each unit and review the library media skills curriculum before proposing a cooperative, integrated effort to the teachers.

These brief examples are intended to demonstrate the type of analysis that is possible with a multi-attribute curriculum map. The pilot project has demonstrated that curriculum mapping can be implemented in settings with minimal microcomputer capabilities. Local needs and the particular hardware/software systems employed will dictate the exact nature of the curriculum maps, however the underlying approach remains consistent.

In the effort to integrate library media skills with existing school curriculum, a review of existing subject area curricula has been presented as a necessary first step. In the same way, English originally proposed using mapping for curriculum development by stating that "... it is the first step a school district should take to engage in the process of curriculum development."[14] Curriculum mapping is a technique which can provide the information base necessary for successful coordination of a library media skills curriculum with everyday classroom activities. By applying microcomputer-based file management capabilities to the task of mapping, library media specialists have a powerful tool for analysis, planning, and evaluation.

NOTES

[1]Selected library skills curricula are available through ERIC including recent efforts by the states of Hawaii, New York and Alaska. Persons interested in the efforts of a particular state are encouraged to contact the education department of that state. In addition see: L. Wehmeyer *The School Librarian as Educator* (Littleton, Colo.: Libraries Unlimited, 1976); H. T. Walker and P. K. Montgomery *Teaching Media Skills*, 2d ed. (Littleton, Colo.: Libraries Unlimited, 1983).

[2]*Elementary Library Media Skills Curriculum* (Albany, N.Y.: New York State Education Department, 1980).

[3]Walker and Montgomery.

[4]L. S. Ericson and J. Carmody, "Integrating Library Skills with Instruction," *Wisconsin Library Bulletin* (January-February 1971): 23-26.

[5]*Elementary Library Media Skills Curriculum*, 4.

[6]E. Daniel and D. Ely, *Assessing the Competencies of Media Professionals: A Model for Determining Costs and Effectiveness* (Syracuse, N.Y.: ERIC Clearinghouse of Information Resources, 1979).

[7]H. D. White and K. Calhoun, "Mapping a Curriculum by Computer," *Journal of the American Society for Information Science* 35 (March 1984): 82-89.

[8]*The Elementary Curriculum: An Overview* (Albany, N.Y.: New York State Education Department, 1977).

[9]F. W. English, "Curriculum Development within the School System," in Arthur W. Foshay, ed., *Considered Action for Curriculum Development* (Alexandria, Va.: Association for Supervision and Curriculum Development, 1980), 149.

[10]F. W. English, *Quality Control in Curriculum Development* (Alexandria, Va.: American Association of School Administrators, 1978), 15.

[11]F. W. English, "Re-tooling Curriculum with On-going School Systems," *Educational Technology* (May 1979): 8-9.

[12]File systems available for the microcomputers commonly available in public schools (Apple, TRS-80, IBM) include: DB Master, PFS: File, Profile III +, and Data Factory. For more information on file and data management systems available for microcomputers, refer to the numerous articles in computer journals reviewing these systems, e.g., D. Gabel, "How to Buy Data-Base Software," *Personal Computing* 8, no. 2 (February 1984): 116-22 +.

[13]*Elementary Library Media Skills Curriculum*, 27-41.

[14]English, *Quality Control in Curriculum Development*, 44.

DESIGNING THE
LIBRARY MEDIA PROGRAM
TO TEACH INQUIRY SKILLS*

M. Ellen Jay

INTRODUCTION

To inquire is defined by Webster as "to seek information, to ask a question or questions, to carry out an examination or an investigation." A strict interpretation of this definition assumes that inquiry stops with the locating of the desired information. A more appropriate interpretation would include the expectation that individuals would examine, analyze, organize, evaluate, and apply the information for a specific purpose. This broader concept makes inquiry one of the higher order thinking skills considered necessary for living in the information age.

Because it is impossible to prepare students for a successful lifetime merely by filling them full of facts, emphasis must shift to teaching students to become independent learners. Students must practice finding information, organizing it, analyzing and evaluating implications, and communicating conclusions. Independent learning further mandates access to a wide range of materials presenting multiple points of view related to curricular topics and personal interests. The logical source of these materials is the school library media center.

Materials alone, however, do not produce a quality library media program. There must be adequate space for large group instruction, small group activities, and individual use. There must also be professional and support library media personnel with the requisite expertise, personality, and philosophical outlook.

IMPLEMENTING AN INQUIRY APPROACH
TO LEARNING

A major obstacle to implementing an inquiry approach to learning is the amount of time it takes for students to develop the necessary skills to become effective information users. On the surface, it appears to be more efficient to have teachers present content which is then absorbed by students. However, this pattern for learning is effective only in a school setting which promotes the parroting of information on exams. In the real world, there is seldom a source to provide a preorganized, predigested set of facts sufficient to solve a given

*From M. Ellen Jay, "Designing the Library Media Program to Teach Inquiry Skills," in *School Library Media Annual 1987*, ed. Shirley L. Aaron and Pat R. Scales (Littleton, Colo.: Libraries Unlimited, 1987), 188-95. Reprinted by permission.

problem. To be successful, an individual needs to recognize and analyze a problem, search for suitable information, organize it, and communicate conclusions to colleagues. These skills need to be taught; students of all ages need to learn and practice them.

This creates a valid concern on the part of classroom teachers if they are evaluated primarily on their ability to cover a prescribed amount of subject content within a prescribed amount of time. Some classroom teachers avoid the library media program because they see it as usurping time needed to cover content with their students. Such teachers see the inclusion of thinking skills instruction as a problem. One of the most apparent obstacles observed in staff development sessions, which were intended to infuse thinking skills into the curriculum, is the emphasis by administrators on factual content when they evaluate teacher effectiveness. Until the classroom teacher is rewarded for developing inquiry skills in students rather than the regurgitation of facts, instructional emphasis will not change. Library media specialists can be a catalyst working to effect the integration of thinking skills, but they cannot effect this instructional change unilaterally. The total educational community must be convinced of the value of changing learning emphasis from content to process. Appropriate changes in teaching expectations and time frames must occur. While library media specialists cannot effect wholesale change immediately or completely, they can do some things to stimulate some elements of change.

It is a good idea to evaluate the library media program's ability to accommodate a shift in curriculum that fosters critical thinking before setting out to develop a demand for change. An evaluation of the reference collection and a reexamination of the criteria for differentiating reference and circulating materials should be considered. Factors influencing accessibility deserve a fresh look—hours, pass procedures, seating of classroom groups, and scheduling to permit simultaneous use by individuals and groups. Layout, furniture arrangement, traffic patterns, and the overall ease of use, as well as atmosphere, should also be examined to assure optimum productivity.

With increased emphasis on the inquiry process, beginning readers need better access to factual material. An easy-to-read collection should not be considered complete unless it includes nonfiction and biography as well as fiction. At the elementary level the library media specialist might consider dividing the nonfiction collection in the same way that picture books and fiction are divided. Place easy nonfiction in an area where primary students have access to these materials. Use Dewey classification order for these materials and do not interfile them with easy fiction. The use of this approach permits young learners to locate information on their level. As emphasis moves toward inquiry, especially in the primary grades, there is increased need for a larger easy-to-read nonfiction collection. Selection policies and ordering priorities may also need to be revamped.

Once a library media program is as prepared as possible, the focus changes to encouraging team planning and teaching. The initial step may be to change attitudes. Classroom teachers may need to be convinced that while there is additional content to be covered in teaching thinking processes, there is help available through teaming with the library media specialist. There are also long-term benefits when students are able to transfer process skills to new situations. Once students have developed a repertoire of learning strategies, the level of student involvement and motivation increases dramatically, and classroom teachers can begin to build their lesson plans to incorporate these skills. Classroom teachers no longer carry the full burden of imparting information. Students accept increased responsibility for their own learning through self and peer evaluation. Library media specialists may need to be convinced that library media program activities encouraging the application of thinking skills need not diminish the joy of books and reading. This is particularly true for elementary library media specialists who view their major responsibility as developing positive attitudes toward books. They need to realize that the active participation of students in library media sessions produces positive attitudes. Story hours can be improved through the incorporation of thinking skills activities.

A second step is to bring about the realization that library media specialists and teachers should work as a team to develop process skills. It is not a sign of weakness for a teacher to team with a library media specialist. Instead, each builds on the strengths of the other. For example, a classroom teacher asks, "My students have difficulty recognizing a character's goals in short narratives. How can we help the students develop this skill?" The library media specialist might suggest specific materials for students to read in which the character's goal is quite obvious. Together, both persons might brainstorm a cooperative activity. Another approach might be to divide the class according to mastery of the concept. While the teacher provides enrichment for those who understand, the library media specialist might work with those having difficulty. At times, the library media specialist might observe students having trouble with a concept and take the initiative in talking about the problem with the teacher.

Terminology and vocabulary can be significant obstacles to joint planning. For example, if a teacher accepts a page copied from an encyclopedia as "research," and the library media specialist considers only a synthesis of multiple sources as "research," then there is bound to be conflict. It is important to clarify terminology and perceptions during joint planning.

BRINGING ABOUT CHANGE

Given appropriate administrative backing, staff interest and enthusiasm, and the library media specialist's knowledge and skills, how should change begin? The library media specialist should select a grade level, a department, or an individual classroom teacher with whom he or she is most comfortable working. Decide on the content to be presented through an inquiry approach. In selecting a topic, attention must be given to the depth of the collection, the abilities of the students, and the specific thinking skills to be included. For example, a classroom teacher doing a unit on daily life in Colonial times might select occupations as a topic for inquiry.

During joint planning sessions, discussion would determine the background knowledge and the skill levels of students, would ascertain the quantity of materials available to support student inquiry, and would analyze the objectives of the lesson in terms of potential skill use. If the objective is that students will identify similarities between types of Colonial and contemporary occupations, then appropriate thinking skills might include brainstorming, categorizing, and comparing and contrasting.

For students who have limited background knowledge about Colonial occupations, little or no experience with brainstorming, and minimal reading skill, an alternative approach might be developed. Provide the students with a list of Colonial occupations in one column and a list of contemporary occupations in another. Students could be asked to select one occupation from each list and suggest a commonality or similarity such as "Colonial blacksmith" and "contemporary car mechanic." The similarity might be that both workers repair broken down transportation. If students are unable to produce at this level, the teacher would restructure the question to include a clue such as "what two occupations relate to transportation?" Summarizing the lesson, the teacher would insure that the students would have reached the desired objective either on their own or with help.

A format for students with both sufficient reading skills to locate information in references and experience with brainstorming, but who are lacking background knowledge on the topic, might be to provide them with selected materials on Colonial and contemporary occupations and a block of time to skim them for information. The purpose of doing this is to increase the students' background knowledge. Then students would be asked to create a list of Colonial occupations and a second list of contemporary occupations using the brainstorming technique. Students would also be asked to identify and give a rationale for similarities and differences they see among occupations.

For students with greater background knowledge and brainstorming and categorizing skills, the class might be divided into two groups with one brainstorming Colonial occupations and the other contemporary occupations. The lists could be evaluated and revised by total class review. Each group would then categorize and label subgroups of occupations on its list. These categories would be compared by the total class and similarities observed. Naturally, differences of opinion will arise when occupations can fit more than one category. Positions should be defended. Categories developed by both groups would probably include jobs which provide services, produce a product, or are governmental positions.

As these examples demonstrate, thinking skills can be infused into the curriculum once students have developed the ability to apply them. However, when introducing a thinking skill such as brainstorming, the students' attention needs to be focused on the process. Content becomes secondary. Once the brainstorming skill has been mastered, the content can become primary and the process secondary. In the literature there are thinking skills theorists who advocate teaching these skills in isolation and those who recommend teaching them through infusion in the total curriculum. In reality, both methods should be used in order to be successful.

Joint planning provides the opportunity to analyze content for appropriate places to infuse thinking skills. The classroom teacher is the content expert, and the library media specialist is the expert in the process of communicating content and in the knowledge of the collection. Both should be knowledgeable about thinking skills and their applications. It is the interaction of the joint planning that produces creative instructional opportunities.

After experiencing success with a few teachers, the next step is to widen the circle of interaction. This might be done through the interest of a department head, grade-level chairperson, or building administrator. The goal is to implement the inquiry approach universally throughout the school so that all students may benefit. Recognizing that there may be some classroom teachers and library media specialists who do not possess the skills or interest to carry out this type of programming, the need for staff development becomes apparent.

PLANNING AND IMPLEMENTING STAFF DEVELOPMENT ACTIVITIES

Staff development may take place in formal building- or system-wide sessions, and/or occur as workshops sponsored by state departments of education, professional associations, or local universities. Library media specialists should be knowledgeable about the procedures and personnel involved in planning these types of staff development sessions. They should make suggestions and encourage the inclusion of sessions that address the infusion of critical thinking into the curriculum and emphasize teaming between classroom teachers and library media specialists. They should expect to become involved in the planning and teaching of many of these sessions.

Whether the library media specialist is working in a formal staff development program or is working individually with colleagues, certain fundamentals need to be considered. Among these are the following:

Climate (also referred to as atmosphere or disposition)—Students need to be convinced that their ideas will be valued and respected by both the teacher and other students. Students will not be willing to risk a divergent answer if they are fearful of rejection or ridicule. Teachers need to be sensitive to students' reactions to their comments. They need to develop a repertoire of responses which are accepting and supportive of student effort, but remain neutral in terms of evaluation. When praise is used indiscriminately, it loses its credibility. Praise can be interpreted by students as an indication of correctness of a particular answer and thereby can reduce the willingness of other students to contribute divergent answers. Productive classroom discussions during which individual students offer and support conflicting points of view can only occur in a climate that values ideas.

Questioning—Questions are the key to encouraging critical thinking by students. Questions that ask students to compare and contrast, rank order, sequence, categorize, predict, and evaluate require a higher level of thinking than do questions which merely require students to identify, define, match, list, or describe. It is the verb that determines the thinking level required to answer the question. There are guidebooks and texts which suggest appropriate verbs for generating various types of thinking.

A related problem is wait time. Even when asking recall-level questions, teachers often find it difficult to provide sufficient wait time for a student to compose an answer. Often, a second student is called on almost immediately, or the teacher rephrases the question, rather than permitting an uncomfortable silence to exist. The importance of wait time is magnified when teachers ask questions which require higher order thought.

Another aspect of questioning is the need to help students learn to generate effective questions. Differing amounts of information result from different types of questions. For example, it would be more useful to inquire, "What color is ...?" rather than to ask, "Is it blue? Is it green?" The goal is to have students become aware of their questions and ways to improve them.

Metacognition (thinking about thinking)—Components of metacognition include teaching "for thinking," "of thinking," and "about thinking." Students need to be able to identify the requirements of a task, assess their own strengths and weaknesses in learning, and select appropriate strategies to complete the task at hand. These issues should be considered by teachers when developing assignments, and opportunities must be provided for students to monitor their own thinking processes.

Modeling—When introducing a process new to students, the teacher should model the process for the class. Having students observe someone applying the process helps them to grasp the concepts involved. For example, when introducing students to peer conferencing for revision of writing, the teacher would create a short passage incorporating the problems being studied. The teacher would model critiquing the passage, and verbalizing the kinds of statements the students would be expected to generate. The students could then critique a second passage with the teacher reacting to their comments. When the students understand the process, they would be put into small groups to react to each other's written passages. If the modeling steps are skipped, students will flounder and be unable to meet the teacher's expectations. They cannot apply a process they have not learned.

Transfer—The ultimate educational goal is for students to be able to transfer critical thinking to real life. In order for this to happen, students need to have experience in applying processes and skills learned in one situation to new situations. For example, the brainstorming technique introduced in social studies class can be applied in literature, science, or other content areas. The skills of note taking and organizing information by means of webbing, outlining, or flow-charting also have applications in other disciplines and in real life. Students need to be able independently to select appropriate strategies to fit the problem to be solved. Sufficient experiences with the transfer of thinking skills within the academic setting should facilitate their habitual use elsewhere.

DEVELOPING LESSONS THAT REQUIRE CRITICAL THINKING

When developing lessons that foster critical thinking, much of what classroom teachers and library media specialists already do when planning lessons can be retained. The greatest differences are in the implementation, the product or outcome, and the inclusion of thinking skills as part of the content to be learned. Lecture delivery is largely replaced by student interaction. Instead of requiring the questions to be answered at the end of the chapter or always demanding a paper-and-pencil product, teachers could ask for outcomes in a range of formats such as debates, role playing, small group interaction, visuals, and more. This does not mean that the student will not experience writing. On the contrary, more meaningful and more purposeful writing occurs because it becomes the foundation for presentations. Debates, role playing, TV scripts, journal entries, and newspapers all require a high level of communication skills. Information is being used to make a point and that point must be substantiated. Where factual content had been the primary focus of lessons, content is now broadened to include practice and development of thinking skills. The following example of a traditional lesson plan, revised to include thinking skills, may be instructive.

Traditional Lesson Plan

Objective: Students will be able to sequence events in a story.

Content: Choose a number of stories to use for daily practice. Select story to read. (*Jim and the Beanstalk* by Raymond Briggs. New York: Coward, McCann & Geoghegan, 1970).

Procedures: Teacher reads story to class.

Teacher asks who can remember something that happens in the story.

After general discussion of events, teacher gives students a worksheet that lists events and directs them to number the events in order of occurrence in the story.

Follow-up: Parallel activities for additional stories.

Lesson Plan Revised to
Incorporate Thinking Skills

Objective: Students will be able to identify similarities and differences between two versions of a traditional story.

Content: Select two versions of a familiar story such as *Jack and the Beanstalk* and *Jim and the Beanstalk*. Thinking skill to be incorporated: comparing and contrasting.

Procedures: Share the story of *Jack and the Beanstalk*. (Read it, listen to it on a phonodisc, or view a filmstrip.) Discuss sequence of events in the story with the class.

At a later date share the story of *Jim and the Beanstalk*. (Read the story to the class.) Put up a chart that says: "Ways *Jack and the Beanstalk* and *Jim and the Beanstalk* are similar." Ask for examples from the students and list them on the chart.

Put up a second chart labeled: "Differences between *Jack and the Beanstalk* and *Jim and the Beanstalk*." Again have students generate examples for the list.

Follow-up involving transfer: Ask students to identify other pairs of stories that have similarities or differences. (Two stories with dog characters, two stories using the same characters but using different events, two stories in which a lost object is found, etc. Differences might include settings—urban, rural, historical, contemporary; character traits—good, evil, real, make believe; problems faced and their resolutions.) When students identify additional relationships, their contributions will be added to an ongoing bulletin board.

Metacognition: The follow-up activity requires students to continue to think about the stories they read looking for similarities and differences with other things they have read.

While this example is designed to emphasize comparing and contrasting as a thinking skill, another thinking skill such as predicting and verifying one's predictions could form the basis for a lesson. Materials are rarely limited to developing a single thinking skill. These examples should indicate that thinking skills can and should be introduced in the elementary grades. Primary students can begin to compare and contrast, categorize, sequence, predict, and verify their predictions. The sophistication of the end product grows with the maturity and experience of the student. However, the process and the thinking skill strategy is essentially unchanged regardless of the grade level at which it is introduced. Therefore, the sooner these processes are introduced to students and the sooner they become working tools for them, the more use upper grade teachers can make of them, and the more beneficial they become for students in the conduct of their daily lives.

CONCLUSION

Library media specialists may face an image problem in their schools. Their expertise can be perceived as being limited to the stereotypical services related to circulation of materials, storytelling, housekeeping, and instruction in use of the card catalog. It comes as a surprise to many educators that library media specialists are indeed teachers capable of instructional design, curriculum improvement, and of using advanced technology including computers, interactive video, databases, and networking. When evaluating the effectiveness of the library media program, one must examine whether the range of instructional activities includes more than the teaching of location skills. The use made of the information found and its examination, analysis, and restructuring for specific needs are more important than mere location of information. As a result, the library media specialist should expect to be involved with the teaching of thinking skills, implementation of the writing curriculum, and computer instruction, as well as the support of the reading/literature program.

Indicators of progress in shifting toward schoolwide implementation of integrating thinking skills might include the development of an all-school objective that mentions improvement of thinking skills; a proliferation of individual teachers' goals statements that include use of the library media program in their teaching; increased requests for joint planning conferences; lively participation in schoolwide activities emanating from the library media center; increased budgets for reference materials and support staff; and community feedback during PTA meetings and parent conferences. More attention has been given to evaluation of personnel than of the program. Although related, the two are not identical, and it is more difficult to evaluate the effectiveness of a program than the fulfillment of a job description. The best program occurs in buildings where administrators, classroom teachers, and library media specialists share a common perception of what constitutes a quality library media program. If total support is not present, library media specialists should continue to work independently with receptive faculty and administrators.

ADDITIONAL READINGS

Gilliland, Mary J. "Can Libraries Make a Difference? Test Scores Say 'Yes'!" *School Library Media Quarterly* 14 (Winter 1986): 67-70.

Hughes, Carolyn S. "Teaching Strategies for Developing Student Thinking." *School Library Media Quarterly* 15 (Fall 1986): 33-36.

Kulleseid, Eleanor R. "Extending the Research Base: Schema Theory, Cognitive Styles, and Types of Intelligence." *School Library Media Quarterly* 15 (Fall 1986): 41-48.

Markuson, Carolyn. "Making It Happen: Taking Charge of the Information Curriculum." *School Library Media Quarterly* 15 (Fall 1986): 37-40.

Part 5
School Library Media Programs: Services Illustrated

Portrayals of real school libraries are provided in the articles in this section. Thea Holtan and Patricia Riggs describe their media programs through examples of actual student and teacher activities. Written for her school's PTA newsletter, Holtan's article describes a visit to an elementary school resource center. Student activities show how the goals of the program—self-reliance, accommodating learning styles, and transfer of skills—are accomplished. Riggs describes the media center as a happy place. Based on a philosophy of preparing students to be lifelong learners, she describes whole class, small group, and individual media activities. She attributes the success of her program to the support of the parents, community, and district program, as well as the efforts of a strong media specialist.

Technology provides the means for media specialists to teach lifelong information skills. Minnesota school media specialists describe how they use technology for student learning and to increase integration of information skills into the curriculum. Lee Vae Hakes and Wilma Wolner, media specialists in New Ulm elementary schools, illustrate how computer labs are used by students and teachers. Media specialist Dave Henschke describes electronic research by students in a Brainerd secondary school. Finally, media specialist Elsie Husom shows how Brainerd used a state-funded demonstration project to integrate technology and information skills throughout the curriculum in the school district. Another look at database searching as an information skill is provided by Elyse Evans Fiebert, who describes her experiences in a Pennsylvania high school.

Increased information use and database searching create resource needs beyond the scope of most media center collections. Resource sharing is the focus of Janice K. Doan's article in which she provides examples of school library participation in networking.

OUR RESOURCE CENTER
Visiting for a
Closer Look*

Thea Holtan

The door opens, and we are greeted by the music of children's voices, chatting, laughing, preparing for yet another day. The Resource Center finds some children returning books to find others. In their orderly ways they go about this task, confidently signing, stamping, filing, taking care of their business before the bell rings. Then, the bell; a sobering national song; the "Pledge of Allegiance", and the day of learning begins.

In the Center we watch adults prepare for the day's introductory activities. Second graders begin to enter; they head for their record-keeping forms, get their activity folders, and move straight to the carrels to set up their tapes, slides, transparencies, or other audio-visuals. They read and follow directions; they check their answers; they take their quizzes; and through the whole process are developing senses of self-reliance, under adult guidance. This week they are learning about maps and globes. They are learning through varieties of media and activities: viewing, listening, reading, manipulating, sketching, writing, and listing. These activities are beyond the paper-pencil style; they use media in styles for all learners.

On the other side of the Center we see that fifth and sixth graders have come with their teacher to continue research about a U.S. war. They are in the midst of arranging their notes into subtopics for their outlines. They have completed their introductory paragraphs, topic sentences, and are graduating to topic outlines ... a step up from the process which they used in third and fourth grades. Their reports will be filled not only with facts from their research, but also with their own thoughts about these facts ... thoughts like causes, results, likenesses, differences, and conclusions about their information. This thought-developing process causes them to develop their thinking skills as they deal with information from various sources.

We scan the Center and see some pairs of kindergarten students clad in earphones, carrying cassette players. They are on a tour; they listen to and follow the taped tour's directions. They will be taking eight of these tours throughout this second semester; each will focus on a different part of the Center. Students will become oriented to the area and its adults while developing their senses of confidence and security in the Center.

*From Thea Holtan, "Our Resource Center ... Visiting for a Closer Look," *PTA Newsletter*, March 1985, 6-7. (Oak Grove Elementary School, Bloomington, Minnesota). Reprinted with permission.

Moving through the Resource Center's office, we approach the Production Area. Here we see first graders taking slides on a copy stand, using macro-zoom lens. With adult help they are focusing on their photo images as they each prepare to shoot a pose of a different animal. They have been studying amphibians' survival methods, and they will need these slides next Friday when they will show and tell other classmates what they learned about amphibians. Their other classmates will come down during the following weeks to study mammals and reptiles. Later this spring they will reapply their skills by studying people's ways of surviving in various parts of the world.

Returning to the Center, we pass through the Video Studio. Here an adult is checking on a small group of students who are preparing a video-taped panel presentation from a research assignment which they have finished. Sometimes we might find students using the video camera to produce a creative advertisement, story, or poem. They use music effects, their own artwork, and animations.

Back in the Center again we see that the fifth-sixth grade class has left and third and fourth graders have been sent by their teacher to the Reference Area to follow directions typed on small cards. They are seeking specific information about contributors to America's history. They get their own sources, check their own answers, and put their sources away. When they have finished, they will have their answers recorded on computer cards; these cards are corrected in a "card reader". Then they can review and mend their errors.

Meanwhile one of the primary classes and its teacher have entered the Center to return and check out books for the week. Of course, if they finish reading the book before the week has passed, they can get another by returning the completed book. Two of them will manage the stamping and filing of cards. Before attending to this procedure, however, they congregate on the floor in a corner to hear a book being read to them. We hear the adult reader, often a volunteer parent, introduce the book to be read, show the drawer in the card catalog where students can find other books by this author, and tell information about this author.

Slipping past this cozy group we cross the hall and approach SkiDL, our *Ski*ll-*D*eveloping *L*ab. On the left side of this room we see all ages working on activities which teachers have planned and assigned. These activities focus on math, reading, and language skills. They are designed to give children practice with these skills. Children locate the assigned activities; the adult in the room helps them to follow the directions and gives feedback of results to teachers. Along the right wall we see several Apple computers. Teachers have assigned disks for practicing or applying skills. Often we will see the fourth graders learning keyboarding skills. Fifth and sixth graders learn programming skills. Soon we will see children using word processing programs to prepare their research reports. We predict that we can better help them to identify and correct their own errors once we get into this phase.

We are now out of time, so our brief visit to the Resource Center must end. Reflecting over what we have witnessed, we can see evidence of the three focuses of our Center's Program. 1. *Self-reliance* shows through the varieties of ways that students manage their own activities and progress; it even shows through the many signs which label the areas and sources in the Center. 2. *Styles of learning* present themselves through the varieties of media to give information and the varieties of activities to develop experiences with the knowledge and skills. 3. *Transfer of skills* shows through application and uses of skills like those in alphabetizing, reading, and map usage. Transfer is also evident in activities causing students to practice and use skills like those in math and computer operations.

As we leave the Center with its hum of busy workers, we cannot help feeling our fortune in having our team of teachers and support staff, our responsive students, and our supportive parents and principal. With this wonderful combination we have the magic of what is happening in our Resource Center.

THE LIBRARY MEDIA CENTER
A Vital Part of
Every School*

Patricia Riggs

"Put a Smile on Your Face, This is a Happy Place," is the cheerful greeting that immediately attracts the eye of anyone entering the Briar Glen Library Media Center. Visitors are initially struck by the size of the 4000 sq. ft. of open area located in the center of this K-5 elementary school in Wheaton, Illinois. The facility is certainly impressive, with colorful walls, pictures, posters, models and a visible abundance of books and audio-visual equipment and materials. However, it is the over-all program, diversity of activities, committed involvement of the staff and many parent volunteers that leave a more lasting impression!

Soon after the first bell rings, students of all ages flow into the Library Media Center (LMC) before school begins. Some check out books or magazines, while others may hold one of the resident guinea pigs, feed the parakeets, or reserve one of these pets for a weekend home visit. Some older students may be preparing for a weekly half hour tutoring position, depositing a goal sheet in their individual folder, collecting a certificate of congratulations or just interacting with one of the volunteer moms at the library desk. Professional, paraprofessional and volunteer staff work side by side as each endeavors to guide and assist students in exploring and using the wealth of resources available.

Direct service to students, staff and community is a prime ingredient of the program at Briar Glen. *Students* think of "LMC" as a part of their every day in school and look forward to spending time there. *Teachers* can depend on their students being regularly involved with materials and activities that are an extension and enrichment of the classroom curriculum. The *Principal* is knowledgeable of the services that are provided and views the LMC as an integral part of the total school. He not only provides administrative support, but takes a personal interest in the program. *Parents* want to volunteer because their talents are sought after and appropriately channeled in the Library Media Center as librarian-assistants, story readers, resource speakers or career day presenters.

The Briar Glen LMC is committed to a philosophy of preparing students to be life-long learners and does play a vital role in the total school program. While personnel, space, and resources are all important components, it is the unique manner in which each school utilizes them that makes the difference.

---

*From Patricia Riggs, "The Library Media Center: A Vital Part of Every School," *IAECT Journal* 21 (Winter 1987): 18-22. Reprinted by permission of Patricia L. Riggs, Media Specialist, Briar Glen Elementary School, 1800 Briarcliffe Blvd., Wheaton, Illinois.

AN OVERVIEW OF BRIAR GLEN'S LMC PROGRAM

Children are formally introduced to the LMC every year through a class orientation held by the media specialist during the first week of school. At that time students are familiarized with the many facets of the LMC program applicable to their particular age group. To ensure regular LMC participation for all 450 students the staff schedules weekly half hour sessions for each child: as a whole class, in a small reading or math group, and with the teacher accompanying the whole class.

WHOLE CLASS SESSIONS

Whole class activities are planned in trimesters. In order to implement the school goals of promoting recreational reading and introducing students to a variety of literary forms, the whole class remains together for two or three sessions of the trimester. During these sessions the media specialist or reading teachers use audio-visual presentations to stimulate student interest in reading.

First and second graders enjoy viewing and discussing public television's *Reading Rainbow* productions and enthusiastically clamor for the featured books. Third through fifth graders are introduced to Briar Glen's *Getting Hooked on Books (GHOB) Literature Program*. In GHOB each of the nine intermediate classrooms is introduced to a different category of literature and an author who writes books representing that particular category. After these audio-visual introductions, each class reads books in its designated literary field for approximately 10 weeks. Certificates and special "Getting Hooked on Books" badges are awarded to those reading designated amounts of books in the areas of folk tales, biography, animal fantasy, mystery, humorous fiction, fantasy, science fiction/adventure, historical fiction and realistic fiction. Students earning certificates and badges receive special recognition through award presentations at all-grade assemblies, posters in the school lobby where those students' names are listed, and articles in the monthly school and local newspapers. In this fourth year of the GHOB program's operation, book reading has increased in grades 3-5 from 500 books during the initial 10-week period of the program to over 2000 books during the most recent 10-week period!

After the large group literature presentations, each class is arranged into three smaller groups for approximately 10-12 weeks of work with a variety of instructional media presented by the LMC staff. One third of the class meets with the media specialist for a sequence of mini-courses in library/research skills and activities. First graders enjoy hearing and discussing Caldecott Medal winners or stories by a selected author or illustrator of the week. Second through fifth graders have hands-on experiences in the LMC with books, the card catalog and references, as they work through booklets covering parts of a book, alphabetical order, dictionary and encyclopedia usage, the Dewey Decimal System and application of research and reference skills.

Two LMC aides each work with the other sections of the class. Primary children are exposed to attribute and tangram puzzle activities, social studies and science activities with versatiles, a variety of language arts filmstrip/cassette presentations and computer assisted instruction (CAI) materials in thinking skills. Intermediate small groups use a research skills lab, view moviestrip versions of literature classics, discuss mystery stories that promote critical thinking, study major systems of the body using actual models along with audio/worksheet activities, or attend parent hobby presentations.

At the end of each semester the groups switch so that by the end of the year each child has attended all the activities planned by the media specialist for their grade level.

SMALL READING AND MATH GROUPS

All the students have the opportunity to come to the LMC in a small group for approximately ½ hour per week. Teachers assist the media specialist in the planning of specified LMC materials for primary children that support or extend the level of instruction for a particular group. Intermediate age students (grades 3-5) are encouraged to set goals and select multi-media materials available in the LMC to accomplish them. The LMC staff designs and distributes to teachers a bi-monthly goal sheet for students to use in planning their activities. The process of completing monthly goals on a calendar and the keeping of their own daily records of accomplishment, develops self-discipline in the students.

Students take pride in receiving a certificate of "Congratulations" of their choosing for completion of assigned or self-selected work completed in the LMC. The display of 14 or 15 choices designed to motivate a child to work on a task to its conclusion are revised often to include current popular themes, such as: Snoopy, Cabbage Patch Kids, Darth Vader, "No Lion, I've Been Trying," "One Success Leads to Another," or an Academy Award. A special reward for students working on goals for three consecutive weeks is the opportunity to select a game to play, free time at the computer or a chance to pet or hold one of the resident guinea pigs, "Mr. Hot Fudge Sundae" or "Ms. Peanut Butter," (appropriately named by the children for the resemblance to the animals' coloring!).

Another important school objective is enhancing self concept. One way the Library Media Center program implements this objective is by providing opportunities for third through fifth grade students to help younger children by participating in a weekly tutoring program. Tutors assist with primary students when they come to the LMC as a small group by supervising activities, clarifying directions, showing filmstrips or playing games. Teachers of those students wishing to be tutor-helpers monitor closely the tutor's own academic and social needs to ensure that the tutor does not over commit him/herself. Performing the tutorial duties designed by the media specialist and teachers has been instrumental in developing self confidence and leadership abilities of those participating in the program. The "tutees" (little children) enjoy working with the older students who sometimes coincidentally are their own brothers or sisters.

TEACHERS ACCOMPANYING THEIR WHOLE CLASS

As time in an already busy LMC schedule allows, teachers at Briar Glen may schedule a period when they can bring their whole class. This opportunity enables the teacher to work directly with LMC materials. The media specialist and teacher plan together the design of several learning stations for each of them and an LMC aide to supervise. One of the stations for intermediate students (grades 4-5) has been exposure to the computers. Literacy has been the focus in recent years; however, following the district computer committee recommendation, computer assisted instruction thinking skills programs are now being used. Activities at other stations include such things as: map and globe skills, science sound filmstrips, math manipulatives and additional research study skills.

UNSCHEDULED USE OF THE LMC

Students also have daily unscheduled access to the LMC to check out and return materials, use reference books, work on a weekly "Calendar Clue Research Contest" and spend a few moments of free time browsing or petting an animal. To confirm that the student has his teacher's permission to leave the classroom, he/she carries a wooden key. The keys, created by a parent in the community, are provided to every classroom and symbolize "keys to learning." Students are welcome and encouraged to explore the many resources available in their Library Media Center!

SERVICES TO STAFF

Some LMC services to students simultaneously provide a service to the teacher. For example, the whole class sessions are scheduled at a time when other classes of the same grade level have physical education or music, enabling a teacher team to have planning time together. Also, small group sessions are scheduled during reading or math times enabling the teacher to work with a smaller group in the classroom, which assists her in meeting individual needs.

Teachers at Briar Glen appreciate the many other services provided to them by the LMC staff, such as: ordering, listing and/or gathering of multi-media materials needed for classroom teaching units, coordination of community resource speakers, displaying of student projects and an interest in providing additional information regarding student needs, abilities and academic progress in the LMC.

COMMUNITY INVOLVEMENT

A unique aspect of the Briar Glen Library Media Center is a strong and effective parent volunteer program. Each week 25-30 ladies donate their time in the LMC to check out and shelve library books, send overdue notices, help students find available resources, conduct story hours, assist in creative dramatics activities and just eagerly and willingly give service to their children's school. The role of volunteers in the LMC has been the catalyst for parent participation throughout Briar Glen. Last year over 130 parents were cited for recognition by the staff as regular contributors. These parents, like the students, are always rewarded for their achievement and generosity. At an end-of-the-year party held in their honor, each "Lovely Lady in the Library Media Center," receives a special certificate of congratulations which highlights a current LMC theme.

A recurring theme displayed in the LMC is "Let Someone Discover You." Depicted by a turtle on its back viewing a reclining ladybug on its shell, the message conveys a feeling that anyone entering the Briar Glen LMC has something to give and share. One of the most impressive "discovery" programs is the exposure of parent knowledge and talent through periodic hobby presentations and an annual career day.

For the past five years an all-school career day has been coordinated by the media specialist and a parent volunteer. Last year twenty-two parents conducted two half-hour presentations about their roles in the world of work on a Friday afternoon during the final month of school. Students in grades 1-5 selected and attended two career presentations they found to be of interest. The parent participants included: a cake decorator, attorney, rabbi, physician, dentist, nurse, tole painter, minister, interior decorator, computer consultant, TV news reporter, medical transcriptionist, photographer, civil engineer, geologist, FBI agent, director of purchasing, drill team camp director, woodworking artist, accountant, police officer and stained glass designer. An informal social hour, following the program, yielded positive and enthusiastic comments from the many participants and an expressed desire to "try on this role again!"

One of the more creative and generous endeavors provided by a parent was the making of a 16mm movie feature of the Library Media Center. As a new parent in a new school with a new concept called "The Learning Center" fourteen years ago, this father wanted his community to experience the many facets of this growing concept of what most parents knew as "the library." He spent his own time, money, and most importantly, personal investment in his children's school, creating a half hour movie entitled "The Learning Center: What's it All About?" The Briar Glen children were excited to see themselves involved in actual day-to-day LMC activities. Parents were enlightened as the 1970's version of this Library Media Center took life, and before the popularity of videotapes, visitors were impressed with this format depicting the development of a then-called "Learning Center."

Communications and public relations have been significantly enhanced by the good fortune of having so many community volunteers share their talents in the Library Media Center. Briar Glen parents feel welcome in the school and they appreciate being involved. Children are proud that their parents are a part of their school. Teachers have discovered what a special asset they have with the many enthusiastic parent volunteers!

STRONG DISTRICT PROGRAM

To be effective, programs must be thoughtfully planned, periodically evaluated, and most importantly, supported philosophically and financially by staff, administration, community and school boards. Establishing continuity and commitment to common goals in the Library Media Center is a necessity in a district with several schools. The media specialists of Glen Ellyn District 89, of which Briar Glen School is a part, united efforts to put their program into print when state guidelines for library media centers emerged in Illinois. They approached their district administration and school board for support in developing an LMC Handbook for the junior high and four elementary schools. Three years and several revisions later, the finished product emerged and included: a district philosophy, student, staff and community goals, professional and paraprofessional job descriptions, selection and evaluation policies, standards for print & non-print materials and equipment and descriptions of the individual programs in each building. The handbook was cited by an Illinois State Board of Education evaluation team in a letter to the district administration "as a model for other school districts throughout the state to emulate."

While all District 89 Library Media Centers share common goals, each school may implement the goals for children and staff through the unique design of its own building program.

A CRUCIAL FACTOR: THE MEDIA SPECIALIST

Developing an interesting, coordinated, dynamic Library Media Center Program requires the supervision and management of a certified professional. Classroom experience and training in the use of library and media materials are crucial factors in creating, directing and organizing the LMC. Flexibility, resourcefulness and a sense of humor are helpful assets when working with students, teachers, aides, the principal, the custodian and a variety of spontaneous needs that arise daily. This is, indeed, a person who "wears many hats!"

At Briar Glen School the media specialist works closely with teachers to plan LMC activities and coordinate materials that will support, extend and enrich the classroom curriculum as well as be motivational to students. She develops the many schedules for individuals and large or small groups to provide maximum use of the LMC facility and resources. The media specialist directs the technical duties of an aide preparing and processing LMC materials. She coordinates the instructional responsibilities of the aide working with students under her supervision. She evaluates, selects and orders books, media and equipment, including requests from teachers and students. She manages the distribution and maintenance of audio-visual equipment in the LMC and all the classrooms. She plans and coordinates many special events and programs such as: the volunteer and cross-age tutoring programs, special interest/hobby resource presentations, the Getting Hooked on Books Literature Program, a birthday gift book program, the displays of student projects, the all-school career day and a writer-in-residence and artist-in residence program, co-funded by the Parent-Teacher Club and the Illinois Arts Council. Finally, she works with other media specialists in the district to share ideas, exchange materials and continually evaluate the district's LMC program in relation to building needs and national standards.

While the role of the media specialist requires a good deal of efficiency and organization, of equal importance is a warm, friendly, caring and positive attitude in operating an effective and meaningful program!

INVALUABLE SUPPORT STAFF

In a small district where direct service to students and staff is highly valued, instructional aides are essential to a Library Media Center Program. In a small district where central processing does not exist, library technical assistance is necessary for each building. Recognizing their commitment to a meaningful, multi-faceted LMC program, the District 89 school board provides aide time proportionate to the student population of each building. The list of services these unique paraprofessionals perform from the technical duties of ordering, typing, filing, dittoing, laminating and repairing to their personalized interacting, training, helping, smiling and soothing makes them remarkable and invaluable to an LMC program!

THE LIBRARY MEDIA CENTER CAN BE A VITAL PART OF EVERY SCHOOL

Computer technology is no longer a "wave of the future." It is rapidly taking its place in the present for any and all schools that can afford the investment. Hardware is becoming more "friendly" and software more "educationally sound." School boards and professionals are responding to the demands of the public for computers in education. Like computers, Library Media Centers are no longer a "wave of the future!" They are here to stay and can provide very vital services.

In the Briar Glen LMC, computers are being included as an important, but not exclusive, component in the wealth of resources available for learning. Still essential to the program is the printed page, which offers a wealth of exciting stories through books and magazines and a world of opportunity to research and explore topics in references. Of equal importance in serving a variety of learning styles are the many other audio-visual resources, such as, tapes, films and filmstrips. Finally, the human resource cannot be underestimated. The LMC provides many opportunities for interaction with other students, staff, and for those blessed in having them, parent volunteers.

While *finances* are critical to the support of any educational endeavor, *commitment* to the value of a program is paramount. Effective media professionals sell service, recruit community and staff support, involve parents, unite with other media professionals to "put the program on the curriculum map" in a district, work on committees that affect media services, become public relations experts, create interest activities, search for new avenues of growth for the expansion of the program and continue to be responsive to the needs of their students, staff and community. Those cast in the role of media professional can make the Library Media Center come alive and be a vital part of the school!

NEW ULM

Integration of
Technology into the Curriculum*

Wilma Wolner and
Lee Vae Hakes

Technology! The images that form in the minds of people when they hear the word 'technology' are as varied as the people and their occupations. To some, technology is a space shuttle mission, a weather satellite, or a computer controlled farm system. To others, it's a home computer, a microwave oven, a video cassette recorder, or a new stereo TV. Each person is correct in their images, but the image is only part of the whole picture. Technology touches every part of our daily lives, and will continue to affect us even more in the future.

To New Ulm Public School students, pre-school through senior high school, technology is as familiar as a black board and chalk. Students like using all forms of technology. They use computers, film projectors, video cameras, and various other educational devices to enhance the learning process.

When students use a computer, a videotape, a film or an overhead projector as an educational medium, the teacher is still the instructional leader. Technology should not add to the teaching load, but is another approach to helping the teacher enhance what is presently taught to make the lesson more exciting, interesting and enjoyable.

School District No. 88 has computer networking systems, or Corvus labs in four schools: Jefferson, Washington, Junior High and Senior High. A networking system allows the teacher the flexibility of having students work at their own rate. Each machine in the networking system has storage room for numerous disks containing programs which the teacher or students can access at a touch of the keyboard. Our satellite schools, Hanska and Lafayette, have computer rooms that operate on disk drives and floppy disks. Keyboarding labs are presently operating in Washington schools and one will be operating at the Junior high in the Fall of '87.

Integrating technology into the curriculum does not begin overnight. It requires a well constructed plan, an innovative school board, a dedicated staff, and an overall, well defined sense of purpose.

The teacher is the key person in a school technology program. Therefore, teacher training is essential in a well constructed plan. At the onset of the program, New Ulm teachers were given computer training as a workshop day. The rapid increase of new computer software and hardware created a need for frequent teacher inservice. After school classes were designed to teach staff

*From Wilma Wolner and Lee Vae Hakes, "New Ulm: Integration of Technology into the Curriculum," *Minnesota Media* 12 (Summer 1987): 16-17, 40-41. Reprinted by permission of *Minnesota Media*.

members more about word processing, grade management programs, graphics, beginning computer, spreadsheets, data bases, and other requested needs. Incentives are offered to teachers who were willing to make that extra effort. Teachers can earn renewal points for taking the after school classes.

The value of supportive staff for a computer program cannot be overlooked. Employees are more confident with the new technology if a good support staff is available as a resource. Our school district has the services of a full time computer coordinator to direct, maintain, and assure that a well rounded technology program is in place. In addition each location has a building coordinator. These coordinators act as resource people who are available to "trouble shoot," answer questions, and assist in the ordering of new materials. Computer aides are assigned to each computer room. These aides help students and teachers to assure the smooth operation of the room.

The New Ulm program starts in the elementary schools and builds as it progresses through the senior high. The primary students get an early start in the world of technology as they learn to run record players, overheads, filmstrip projectors and cassette recorders. Computers also play a large role in the total education of the elementary student.

The Jefferson School computer lab is a center for independent learning and discovery. The main thrust of this lab is computer assisted learning. This lab is open each day from 7:30 to 4:00.

All of the materials that are used in the computer lab have been selected by the classroom teachers. The classroom teachers order and evaluate all of the materials that are used in the lab. These materials are evaluated with regard to: the age of the user, the relevance of the subject matter, and the school curriculum. A formal evaluation sheet is kept on file for each program.

The majority of the programs that are used in the computer lab are stored on a Corvus hard disk. The hard disk allows the user quick easy access to programs. A Corvus system also eliminates the possibility of disk damage, which can occur from handling multiple copies of a program.

Jefferson teachers sign up for computer time on an erasable time schedule located on the wall in the computer lab. The computer aide is available to help schedule time and to accommodate any last minute changes. The children use this computer time to reinforce classroom lessons and to develop critical thinking skills. The teacher enters the computer room with a specific objective that has been developed for this "hands-on" teaching time.

The children who use the computer lab are between the ages of three and ten years old. The computer room is also used for summer school enrichment programs.

The Washington Computer program builds upon the Jefferson Computer program. The Corvus lab is scheduled on a weekly rotating schedule by grade levels. The Computer aide circulates an erasable sign out sheet to the assigned grade. Each teacher then fills in the times they would like to bring classes. The sheet is posted on the computer room door and open time slots can be filled in by any grade or designated area teacher. Objective sheets are filled out by the teacher, prior to using the lab, to insure that specific needs of students can be met. This also helps the computer aide be prepared for what will be taught during class usage of the Corvus room.

Students who attend Washington School are in the Fourth, Fifth and Sixth Grades. A new and enriching experience awaits them when they use the Keyboarding-Word Processing Room. Keyboarding, the skill of using the computer keyboard by touch typing, rather than a "hunt and peck method," is taught by a Business Education teacher. The Keyboarding Unit covers a six week span of time. Each class is scheduled for a 50 minute period each day. The Keyboarding instructor teaches touch typing and introduces a word processing program Magic Slate. Sixth Grade Language teachers expand upon the initial instruction of the 40 column version of Magic Slate. After students have become comfortable with using the 40 column version of this word processor, students are switched to the 80 column version. Most of the written homework assigned, at the sixth grade level, is expected to be completed using the keyboarding and word processing skills they have been taught.

Computer peripherals, such as Koala Pads, are used in the art curriculum, grade three on up, to help make art concepts easier to understand and enjoyable. An art unit has been developed using this device and different software programs to open up a new world of learning for them.

Computer graphics units are taught in some math classes. These units are only used as an awareness introduction as to what capabilities the computer has, besides running software programs.

Computers are only one of the areas of technology that students at Washington gain "hands-on" experience with. The Media person and classroom teachers have developed units that have students working with laminators, video cameras, opaque and overhead projectors and other forms of media to create an awareness of the ever expanding technology field.

We cannot discuss integrating technology into the curriculum without touching upon special areas, such as speech, special education, or the gifted programs. These areas use the computer lab to develop critical thinking skills. The use of Logo Writer and other special programs has created an environment where the student can formulate ideas and construct systems and create images. Problem solving computer usage has fostered risk taking. The students have learned that there is more than one way to solve a problem. Perfectionists have realized that if they don't get the "perfect right" answer the first time, it is all right to go back and try again. The ability to do creative problem solving will determine future success for students in special areas.

Technology in many forms is part of nearly every workplace. Students in District No. 88 enjoy and profit from our technology program. This ever expanding field generates excitement that can be felt in the air when kids are thinking and producing. Come and visit us in New Ulm. Join the FUN!!!

BRAINERD
Research in the
Information Age*

David Henschke

Technology has opened a whole new realm of research—not limited to the four walls of a library/media center. This type of research—electronic research—utilizes not only the information of the media center but expands outward, tapping the vast body of knowledge available. Electronic research needs to become an integral tool for student/teacher use. How is this achieved? At Brainerd Senior High School, this means media specialists working with teachers, combining online database information with standard research practices.

Initially, planning was done by the media specialists as to how electronic research could be implemented. Decisions were based on curriculum at the high school including particular areas of need. Methods of electronic research, including online databases, were chosen according to these needs. It was realized at this time that it was also necessary for the students to have a good base in search strategy in order to best utilize methods of electronic research. Finally, planning was done with staff on how to introduce electronic research to the students in their particular subject areas.

In dealing with the subject of search strategy, we first ask the students to define their problem, then break that problem down into key words or concepts. Working with the media specialists they then select the research tools that will best bring them their answer.

Since the biggest concern involving online database searching seems to be costs involved (long distance charges, database subscriptions, database access charges) the strategy that we developed for basic searches uses the free or inexpensive means first. The students must first check the available resources in the media center, including using the computerized card catalog. Once they feel they have exhausted those possibilities, they then turn to the next option; Grolier's Academic American Encyclopedia on CD-ROM.

The CD-ROM electronic encyclopedia provides an online type of experience without the costs associated with going online. The entire 20 volume encyclopedia is on a single compact disk (the entire encyclopedia actually takes up only about a fourth of the space on the disk). This disk is placed in a special compact disk player that is attached to an IBM type or modified Apple computer. With every word indexed, the encyclopedia can be efficiently and easily searched. Since this is basically a database of information the students employ their search strategy, hopefully find information, and also determine whether or not their strategy was effective.

*From David Henschke, "Brainerd: Research in the Information Age," *Minnesota Media* 12 (Summer 1987): 12-13, 40. Reprinted by permission of *Minnesota Media*.

If more information is needed, the search continues online; first by linking with the PALS online catalog. The PALS system is an online card catalog of state university and community college collections. In the case of Brainerd, we access this through St. Cloud State University. If we find information that we need, we can "order" it and have it sent to our school. This method of online searching costs only the price of the long distance phone call.

Finally, if the previous methods have not turned up the necessary information we will then access an online database such as *Dialog, CompuServe, DataTimes,* or *DataNet.* The online access is done by the media specialists working along with the students. This procedure is used for *basic* searches in our media center.

Telecommunications and online searching are also used in a variety of ways for curriculum projects. The CD-ROM encyclopedia for instance is used by science classes to find relationships between endangered species or developed food chains from information gathered. Social studies classes research American presidents to find information from which they write a fictional account of that president's administration, or students research broad topic areas from different aspects (social, political, economic, geographic, etc.), then draw conclusions from their findings. Language Arts classes find relationships between common factors within a chosen subject, which they use to write thesis statements, or find relationships and influences upon and of authors.

Social studies classes utilize information from the online databases in various ways. For example, economics classes use stock market information; current events classes rely on the ability to "electronically clip" articles on specific topics; and futurism classes evaluate and analyze demographic data to do trend extrapolation.

Science classes use information from Minnesota databases to evaluate and analyze wildlife and natural resources, obtain current meteorological information, and research very specific scientific topics.

English classes find that for major research papers, they now are not limited to information in the local media center. They can expand their research on chosen topics for which little information exists at the local level.

Although this is our first year utilizing electronic research, student and teacher response indicates continued and expanded use. Electronic research has definitely found a niche in the curriculum at Brainerd Senior High.

Note: For more information feel free to contact me:

David Henschke
Brainerd Senior High School
702 S. 5th Street
Brainerd, MN 56401
(218) 828-5284

ONLINE DATABASES USED AT BRAINERD SENIOR HIGH

Dialog—Over 250 databases covering most subjects. "Classmate" and "Classroom Instruction Program" offer reduced rates of $15.00 per hour for educational use.

> DIALOG Information Services, Inc.
> Marketing Dept.
> 3460 Hillview Avenue
> Palo Alto, CA 94304
> 800-3-DIALOG

CompuServe—Business and consumer information, current news information.

> CompuServe Information Service
> 5000 Arlington Centre Blvd.
> P.O. Box 20212
> Columbus, Ohio 43220
> 800-848-8199

DataNet—Thirteen databases of information specific to the state of Minnesota. Annual minimum subscription of $200.00.

> DataNet Subscription Service
> Minnesota State Planning Agency
> Planning Information Center
> LL 65, Metro Square Bldg.
> 7th and Robert Streets
> St. Paul, MN 55101

DataTimes—Database of several national and international newspapers including the Minneapolis Star and Tribune. Full text and searchable, toll free number included in subscription.

> DataTimes
> 818 N.W. 63rd Street
> Oklahoma City, OK 73116
> 800-642-2525

BRAINERD'S PROJECT TASK*

Elsie Husom

Project TASK (Brainerd's Courseware Integration Center) is nearing completion of its first term of funding from the State Legislature. When we wrote the grant application, Brainerd media specialists selected the TASK acronym for the idea Technology Advances Skills in Kids. Now it is time to evaluate our project by asking the questions, "Has TASK made a difference? What kind of impact has it had on Minnesota education?"

The following summary of Project TASK's activities is an attempt to address that issue. Evaluation is relatively easy if one just has to deal with numbers; however, in this case numbers won't tell the whole story. Thus, this evaluation of Brainerd's CIC will look at both quantitative and qualitative aspects.

In fulfilling one of the state requirements, four workshops in Brainerd schools have been offered focusing on the integration of various forms of technology as teaching/learning tools throughout the curriculum. Over 290 teachers, media specialists, computer coordinators and administrators from all areas of the state participated in these day-long workshops. Sessions on using technology in the subject areas of art, business, home economics, physical education, industrial arts, special education, social studies, careers and guidance, language arts, world language, and media were presented. Demonstrations and discussions were a part of all sessions, and, where possible, hands-on activities and observations of students were also a part. Did these workshops have any effect on the participants? Have they gleaned ideas that they now or will use in their own schools? Most of the evaluative comments we received indicated that the answer is yes. I'd like to share with you one written comment: "I have attended several workshops in the past, and in no way did they compare with this one where classroom teachers and media personnel—the front line people—did the presentations. Wonderful!!" One oral comment from a computer coordinator in a smaller school district is also noteworthy: "Project TASK workshops have been the biggest influence in getting technology integrated into our secondary curriculum. Teachers have really gained much."

*From Elsie Husom, "Brainerd's Project Task," *Minnesota Media* 12 (Summer 1987): 22-23, 43-44. Reprinted by permission of *Minnesota Media*.

Many other activities besides the workshops kept us busy all year. Brainerd media professionals and/or teachers presented sessions on integrating technology into the curriculum at many conferences and conventions: seven regional, four state, three national and two international. We have planned and conducted many inservice sessions for Brainerd teachers and for three other Minnesota school districts. Representatives from nine other school districts have come to Brainerd for consultation on various aspects of our program, and we have sponsored mentorship programs for four Minnesota teachers. A Technology Fair for Brainerd and other communities within 50 miles of Brainerd was another activity hosted by Project TASK. Two consultations with out of state educators have been scheduled for this summer.

Project TASK exhibits were set up at various conferences and meetings. The largest of these was the three day Commerce and Industry Show (with visitors numbering in the thousands) where we had students and teachers demonstrating the use of technology in education. We also had a display and met with our legislators at Library Legislative Day in the State Capitol in 1986.

More than 750 packets on Brainerd District's media program and on integrating media/technology into the curriculum have been distributed to Minnesota schools and to others throughout the United States. We have answered more than 60 requests for information on such topics as our copyright policy, flexible scheduling, courseware evaluations, our district technology inservice plan, designing a media program, and our information literacy scope and sequence. Eight professional journals, newsletters and newspapers have carried articles about our project, and we have participated in one radio and one television broadcast. Media specialists produced a Project TASK video tape which has been shown at many organizational meetings.

Now you have the numbers or quantitative evaluation of Project TASK. But, what about the qualitative measurement? What have we learned and what impact can that have on media programs in Minnesota schools? Brainerd doesn't pretend to have all the answers. What we do have to offer other school districts is the benefit of our experiences; we can tell what worked for us and also what didn't work. Others can learn from our mistakes as well as our successes.

One of the most important things we learned is that technology is just technology. It is not a panacea; it cannot work miracles. But, if technology is put into the hands of a person who knows how to use it appropriately, it becomes a tool that facilitates teaching and learning. Project TASK attempted to show how Brainerd is integrating the various technological tools into all areas of the curriculum.

It becomes obvious to us that cooperation is the key to successful integration of media/technology. From early planning stages on through implementation, evaluation and revision, teachers, administrators, media specialists and parents need to be involved so that all feel a responsibility for using technology to benefit student achievement.

The need for cooperation perhaps is felt most directly in our writing and implementing the Information Literacy Scope and Sequence on a district-wide basis. Our district has had a Computer Curriculum and a Media Skills Curriculum in place for several years. However, with the recognition that the various forms of technology are merely means to an end, not the goal itself, Brainerd staff worked toward integrating both of these separate curriculums into the existing subject areas. After completing a list of learner outcomes, media specialists and teachers have been collaborating on developing a list of activities for different subject areas. These activities are meant to meet individual learning styles, varying interests, and varying ability levels. Students will not just learn facts but will be learning how to learn — how to find information, how to gather meaning from the information found, how to use or apply that information, and how to communicate what they have learned.

Cooperation again is needed when this Scope and Sequence is put into place. The district has decided that a flexible schedule for elementary media program is the best way to insure that the skills are integrated, so Baxter Elementary piloted this type of schedule this year. Media specialists and teachers worked together in planning the media/technology skills activities for classroom and/or media center. The success of this program precipitated the move to extend the flexible plan to all of the elementary building programs in 1987-88.

How do we bring teachers to a point of feeling comfortable in using technology? Inservice seems to be the answer. However, I have read that less than five percent of what is covered in inservice sessions ever gets used in a classroom situation. Brainerd has established a technology inservice plan in the hopes of raising that percentage. The plan is divided into three types of inservice: 1) Awareness, 2) Skills building, and 3) Integration. The goals are 1) to provide in-depth, on-going and meaningful training for all staff, 2) to provide follow up activities, refresher sessions, and in-school support, 3) to incorporate effective instructional techniques and organizational skills development as part of the training, and 4) to cooperate with users to experiment and adapt the technology to their instructional needs. It is not our goal to purchase every new technological toy and then have it sit collecting dust. Along with each major purchase, there needs to be a plan for its utilization.

Questions may now arise as to just how technology is used in Brainerd schools. What technology works in what subject area? Is there any subject area that doesn't need the use of technology tools? In this article I will not attempt to answer in great detail. However, an overview of activities will give some idea of the extent of technology usage. Art students use computers in designing, drawing, painting and creating; they also use video cameras linked to computers for high tech images. Home economics classes study nutrition, child care, and wardrobe planning through the use of computers. They also match pattern type to figure type, make consumer decisions, and do home budgeting via computer. Computers are also used in drivers' education, office practices and other business classes, SAT and ACT preparation, reprographics, drafting, athletic analysis and measurement, and farm management. Word processing, with emphasis on writing as a process of thinking, writing, evaluating and revising, is a part of the language arts curriculum from 6th grade through 12th. Also included in language arts classes are vocabulary building, reading comprehension and speed, improving communication skills with video and computer, and electronic research (see chapter by David Henschke also in this book).

Social studies classes also utilize computers, videotape/disc and video production to make their studies more meaningful. Students learn from historical simulations, study economic systems by being a part of decision-making, simulate the legislative process, and study the geography of other countries via computer courseware. An oral history project and other historical activities involve use of computers, electronic research, video cameras and videodisc in meeting learner outcomes. Career guidance is more individualized and more extensive with use of databases, self-analysis, on-the-job simulations, and resume writing on computer.

Science and health are other areas in which computers are used to learn. Laboratory simulations, solar explorations, astronomy study, study of the human body, simulations of the effects of alcohol and drug use, physical health measurements, and many other activities are more feasible through the use of computers. Outdoor Science classes conduct a student-produced videotape exchange with classes in other parts of the country sharing ideas about our natural world.

Numerous other activities in all subject areas are aided by the use of computers and other technology tools from drill and practice for remedial work to simulations and database manipulations for higher order thinking skills.

The two-way television link between St. Cloud State University, Brainerd Senior and Junior High buildings and the Mid State Cooperative has been delayed, but we are looking forward to implementing many of the plans for its utilization next fall. This certainly will open up new avenues of learning and new lanes of cooperation for both the university and public schools.

Brainerd has nearly completed a district packet including its Information Literacy Scope and Sequence, technology inservice plan, flexible schedule guidelines, copyright policy, and many other aids for integrating technology into the curriculum. This will be available upon request next fall.

Project TASK has been a welcome challenge to Brainerd schools. Although we wrote nothing in our original proposal that wasn't already in our long term plans, funding from the state has allowed us to implement these at a more rapid pace. Brainerd greatly appreciates the opportunities Project TASK has given. We definitely feel that technology makes available tools that can benefit the education process and wish to share our experience and the knowledge we've gained. In our next biennium of funding, we plan to expand our offerings, work even more on mentorships and inservice to other school districts, and try to fill as many requests from Minnesota schools as possible.

At this time, Brainerd and Minneapolis Courseware Integration Centers wish to thank MEMO [Minnesota Educational Media Organization] for the foresight it showed in writing the original concept and for its continued support of what we feel is a very worthwhile program.

THE INTEGRATION OF ONLINE BIBLIOGRAPHIC INSTRUCTION INTO THE HIGH SCHOOL LIBRARY CURRICULUM*

Elyse Evans Fiebert

In a little over a decade, Radnor High School Library (Radnor, Pa.) has evolved from a browsing and study room to a teaching center. This significant shift in library philosophy, some of which was planned and some of which "just grew," came together with clarity with the introduction of online bibliographic searching in March, 1980. To the best of my knowledge, Radnor was the first high school to teach online bibliographic searching techniques to secondary school students. As of the 1982-83 academic year, online bibliographic instruction was included in the library skills unit for all incoming ninth grade students. Now, with three year's experience behind us, it is timely to look at where we have been, where we are going, and to attempt to assess the impact of this new philosophy and technology on students and future library curricula.

When the new library facility was opened in the fall of 1971, the architecture, program, collection and staff clearly reflected the times. Bright colors, conversation pit, wired AV carrels, and lounge chairs were intended to lure the reluctant student. Browsing collections of paperbacks and large holdings of tapes, filmstrips, and filmloops augmented the prevailing educational philosophy of experiencing that which was "relevant". Because Radnor High School is a highly academic school in a suburban, professional community, the book and reference collections and the periodical holdings were also strong. But library curriculum and library instruction were absent. Our raison d'être was purely supportive and supplemental. The library (and we were trying to remember to call it the "Media Center" back then) had no academic responsibilities of its own. In truth, a visitor to the library in that era might understandably have thought that he was in the student lounge. The "conversation pit" aura clearly dominated.

Although library skills were being taught in the elementary and middle schools, high school teachers began to see that without some reinforcement these skills did not carry over and many students were unable to locate needed information to complete assignments. This was especially acute at a time when independent study projects were proliferating. The high school librarians and some subject area teachers began to develop library units focusing on specific reference materials and research skills within the context of the teachers' goals for individual study units. By the mid-'70's, the librarians were teaching tailor-made

*From Elyse Evans Fiebert, "The Integration of Online Bibliographic Instruction into the High School Curriculum," *School Library Media Quarterly* 13 (Spring 1985): 96-99. Reprinted by permission.

skills units in all subject areas as well as designing teaching materials. The "conversation pit" became the reference area and the emphasis on skills and research was established.

Concurrently, at the administrative level, district-wide curricula design in all subject disciplines was underway. The K-12 library curriculum,[1] three years in the making, was adopted by the School Board in 1980. Section IV, *A Sequential Program of Library Instruction*, details a progression of skill development from kindergarten through high school, i.e., from simple to complex. Identifiable skills and concepts are coded by grade level as I (introduced), T (taught), or R (review or expansion of concepts). Therefore, at the high school level, we have a clear understanding of the skills and concepts taught K-8.

To meet the informational needs in the high school, the librarians and English teachers have devised a two-part library unit for all incoming 9th grade students. This unit has several goals: a) to assist students in becoming familiar with the location of materials in the library as well as the wide variety of services offered; b) a review in the use of the *Readers' Guide to Periodical Literature*, and the use of general encyclopedia indices; c) the introduction of specialized reference materials in the areas of literature and the social sciences. Both the review unit and the second unit in which new reference materials are introduced are accompanied by work sheets which provide a basis for evaluation by the English teachers.

At the same time, the ninth grade English teachers introduce and distribute copies of the *Library Handbook*,[2] co-authored by an English teacher, a social studies teacher, and myself. The *Library Handbook* includes an extensive section on the library holdings in the reference collection, and large segment on the research paper including samples of a bibliography and footnotes. English teachers assume the responsibility for instruction in research methodology, and teachers in other subject disciplines refer to the *Library Handbook* when instructing their students in term paper assignments.

In effect, the two-part ninth grade unit became three parts with the introduction of online bibliographic instruction to all ninth graders in the 1982-83 academic year. This was accomplished by adding one more English class period to the library unit. Within this additional forty-four minute class period we were able to provide a brief lecture on online searching (what it is, what it will and will not do, vendors, selection of databases, etc.) and to design a search strategy. We then went from the library classroom to the adjacent computer room and completed one or more searches with students at the terminal. Often there was time for questions and answers.

Our goals in adding the online demonstration to the ninth grade units were several: a) to make students aware that such a facility exists; b) to introduce the process of search strategy so that they could begin to think in those terms; c) to eliminate any of the elements of the "spectacular" or "magical" that might accompany it, and, d) to incorporate the unit into the whole range of available informational resources.

The decision to incorporate online bibliographic searching instruction in the established ninth grade library instruction unit is the logical culmination of three years of experience with this form of information retrieval. In the late '70's, the librarians and a teacher of ninth grade honors physical science were wrestling with a mutual and not uncommon problem—how to help students define more specifically their term paper topics. All school librarians have had the frustrating experience of working with students whose initial topic choices are too large and lack focus. We were struggling to understand intellectually the process that each researcher goes through to get a topic from, for example, "Ecology" as a starting topic to the final one of "the effects of acid rain on lakes." (My example is, in fact, a real one that a ninth grader and I worked on together.) Becoming aware of this process was an important first step. The development of search strategy design for computer retrieval appears to be at the core of the process for it incorporates the necessary specificity.

At about the same time, Lockheed/Dialog, Palo Alto, California, one of the earliest and largest online vendors, was approached to make their services available to Radnor High School students at the classroom teaching rate. Lockheed, already well established at the university level, was interested in our teaching philosophy as well as our intellectual musings and about processes in research. Thus, Radnor became the first high school in the country to introduce the technology to its students, and equally important at that point, to its faculty.

With all equipment (printer, modem, and telephone) and arrangements in place by March 1980, we spent the rest of that year learning for ourselves what Dialog was all about. The librarians and a ninth grade physical science teacher took the Dialog training. (Subsequently, the library secretary, always eager to try new things, took the training, and we gave intensive training to three eager and responsible students. They then worked independently at the terminal with their peers.) The formal instruction and the availability of a mentor at a nearby university were invaluable.

The faculty was introduced to the new service and concept by means of mini-workshops on in-service half days. Coffee, donuts and natural curiosity resulted in an overflow and we had to schedule additional workshops to meet the demands. Included in the workshops were librarians and administrators from other institutions in the community as well.

Out of this experience came requests from teachers for online instruction for their classes. So, in addition to the ninth grade honors physical science classes, we began to teach the strategy and process to classes in expository writing, speech and debate, literature (both English and American), American studies, and Sociology.

Originally, the initial instruction with a class, using materials designed by the librarian, was in considerable depth and took three days in the classroom before going to the terminal. It is some measure of our expertise that we now do all of the introductory teaching in a single class period and we feel that this is equally effective.

As the demand for the instruction and service grew, it seemed a logical decision to add it to the ninth grade English classes library unit. With that as a base, students are encouraged to use it whenever appropriate for further research needs. Also, subject teachers are encouraged to arrange for further online instruction in their specialized disciplines.

A word about library instruction in grades 10, 11, and 12 seems appropriate at this point to complete the picture of our library curriculum program. We hold conferences individually with all teachers desiring library services and together we design teaching units to meet their goals. It is at this point that we will include online bibliographic instruction as needed. The extent to which we are involved in instruction can best be conveyed by some of the data. Radnor High School had a student population of about 1250 students in four grades during the 1982-83 year.

During that time we taught 128 classes, assisted with another 457 classes, and accounted for 547 online bibliographic searches—some whole class, some small group, and many individual searches. Quarterly statistics show the developmental nature of the online bibliographic searching instruction. The number of searches first through fourth quarter are 26, 122, 63, and 336 for a total of 547. (Almost all of our English courses are one semester in length.)

Because our focus is always on teaching the process and concept, and the resulting bibliography is the exciting byproduct, we select files for demonstration purposes that best meet that need. A study of file use shows this quite clearly. Of the 547 searches in the past year, *Magazine Index* was used 329 times. Other file usage includes: *Biography Master Index* (38), *America: History and Life* (28), *National Newspaper Index* (25), *MLA Bibliography* (17), *ERIC* (16), *Energyline* (10). In all, thirty files were used at least once during the year.

A random sample of topics searched shows the wide diversity. Each student logs his/her name, the date, file used, topic, and connect charges. Some of the topics logged include life on Mars, John Updike, OPEC, nuclear waste, Woodstock, foster home care, Chrysler Corporation, listening comprehension, child abuse, the relation between fashion and national economics, Harriet Tubman, and racism in South Africa.

Consideration of online bibliographic instruction must, of necessity, include the cost factors. Start-up costs include equipment, training, manuals, and supplies. We are currently upgrading our equipment and taking advantage of the general reduction in prices as a result of competition. We have budgeted $1,800.00 for a terminal with a CRT, a printer, a modem, and the necessary connecting cables. Initial supplies for the printer will be about $150.00. A telephone line, direct, (i.e., not through a switchboard) and at the prevailing business rate, completes the equipment. Vendors offer training sessions at convenient times and locations and $150.00 per staff person should be adequate to cover these costs. One might budget $75.00 or so for manuals for the start-up year.

Vendors vary somewhat in their online fee arrangements. Dialog has no subscription fees and one is billed only for the amount of time connected at the classroom teaching rate of $15.00 per hour (including the tele-communication company's fees). Our per search costs have gone down as we have become more proficient and at this point we average about $2.50 per search. Our total operating budget for 1982-83 was $2000.00.

Some effects of online bibliographic searching instruction are fairly immediate and apparent while others are, at most, only distantly sensed. The impact on staffing is immediate. Library personnel must be available, well trained, and comfortable with the new technology. Online bibliographic searching, by its very nature (equipment, cost, password security, search strategy design, etc.) results in much more small group or individual instruction and supervision than do other aspects of library instruction.

We are beginning to add new periodical titles to the library holdings in response to the frequency of citations by the computer. And our community libraries (both public and university) are feeling the impact as well. Our students have a new and meaningful awareness of the wide range and types of materials available at both the general and the technical levels, and there has been a significant increase in the use of interlibrary loan services. We have always taught with community services in mind, and they are becoming increasingly important.

An interesting component is the identification of needed and desirable new skills that are a direct outgrowth of online searching. Two have emerged so far, the first being the necessity to be able to read the printouts. We plan to teach this with the same attention to detail that we give to the citations in *Readers' Guide* and the *New York Times Index*. We are in the process of designing a handout that will identify each item on the printout.

The other newly identified skill is that of abstract writing. This year, for the first time, the librarian taught this skill to students in three biology classes. The abstracts were incorporated into the ongoing assignment of producing a scientific journal which included student's lab reports. In this case, the biology teacher found an unexpected benefit in that the process of writing the abstract helped students to clarify and to synthesize their lab results.

Other aspects are sensed but are less directly measurable. We are teaching online bibliographic searching in terms of process and specificity and language is crucial. Students love to wrestle with key words and synonyms, the concept of hierarchy, variants of spelling and truncation. In the process of dealing with the language they, themselves, are defining and re-defining their topics. They must do a good bit of background reading in their subject area before they can develop a successful search strategy design. It is exciting to see a student begin to master a topic of his/her own choosing, work with the librarian in the specific area where more information is needed, and find his topic coming up on the computer. This is the process in action. The student feels in charge and there is no substitute for this feeling of mastery.

One anticipated result of online bibliographic searching is the awareness of out-of-date and current materials. One would logically expect students who use the computer for locating information to have more current sources in their bibliographies than students who are relying on the traditional card catalog and printed indices. One might also anticipate a wider range of types of materials used by students who had access to a diversity of online databases. Lucy Wozny studied term papers of ninth grade honors science students[3] and Dr. Jacqueline Mancall is currently studying the bibliographies produced by students in expository writing classes. The results will be compared with an earlier study that predates the online bibliographic searching instruction.[4] The results are eagerly awaited, since at one level, they represent a measurement of the impact of this new technology and the effectiveness of our instruction.

At a less concrete level, we know that the library and the librarians are being perceived in a new and very positive way. We are at the forefront of information access with the user clearly in mind. And that user, regardless of his/her academic level, knows what she/he needs. She/he has not always been able to express that need adequately when encountering the traditional, printed, indexed sources. Now, she/he has another way of expressing him/herself and of approaching the topic with a method that is much more specific, much more current, and much faster. We cannot foresee the total impact of this new technology and approach on the school library curriculum. But we do see the impact on an individual student. It's exciting to see the student's face light up as the printer produces his/her custom designed bibliography citing sources and his/her level of accomplishment and available close at hand. The student has learned several new skills and has something to show for it.

NOTES

[1]"1980-81 Library Curriculum Study," Wayne, Pa., Radnor Township School District, 1980.

[2]Mary Anne Dewsnap, et al., "Radnor High School Library Handbook," Radnor, Pa., Radnor High School, 1980.

[3]Lucy Anne Wozny, "Online Bibliographic Searching and Students Use of Information: An Innovative Teaching Approach," *School Library Media Quarterly* 11 (Fall 1982): 35-42.

[4]Carl M. Drott and Jacqueline C. Mancall, *Materials Students Use: A Direct Measurement Approach* (Arlington, Va.: ERIC Document Reproduction Service, 1980), ERIC Document 195 287.

SCHOOL LIBRARY MEDIA CENTERS IN NETWORKS*

Janice K. Doan

When one talks of networks, different images come to mind depending upon one's previous experiences. In many instances, any type of library cooperation is thought of in this respect. Markuson defines library cooperation as any activity between two or more libraries to facilitate, promote, and enhance library operations, services to users, or use of resources.[1] Library networks are a subset of library cooperation of the most formal type. They are set apart by legal bases for organization, central staff, and contracts for services. In Swank's definition, a network has the following six characteristics: (1) information resources; (2) readers or users; (3) schemes for intellectual organization of documents or data; (4) methods of delivery of resources; (5) formal organization; and (6) bidirectional communication networks.

Martin stated that a network is any group of interconnected individuals or organizations in which linking includes communication channels; many networks exist for the express purpose of fostering a certain type of communication among their members. Library institutions form networks primarily to achieve better sharing of resources and better service to patrons.[2] In 1976, Allen Kent, from the University of Pittsburgh, shared some ideas on resource sharing. He stated that resource sharing was a method of operation whereby functions are shared in common by a number of libraries. A network, a consortium, or a cooperative are all terms used to label the organizational structure for achieving various resource sharing goals. Resource sharing goes far beyond the idea of two libraries exchanging documents containing printed words, and networking goes beyond the idea of two or more libraries engaged in the exchange. Materials in library collections are one resource to be shared in network arrangements, but certainly not the only one.[3]

Buchinski, reporting in 1978 on the Network Development Office of the Library of Congress, states that those included in a national library network would be a network coordinating agency, bibliographic utilities, service centers, and libraries. Many kinds of libraries such as academic, public, medical, law, and research were named, but school library media centers were excluded.[4]

The inclusion of school library media centers in a national library network rests on the assumption that students — children, and young people — are citizens who have a right to equality under the law. This equal access for every individual was one of the major goals addressed by National Commission on Libraries and

*From Janice K. Doan, "School Library Media Centers in Networks," *School Library Media Quarterly* 13 (Summer 1985): 191-99. Reprinted by permission.

Information Science (NCLIS) in 1975. To achieve this goal, therefore, requires school library media centers to be included in the national network.[5] In 1977, NCLIS, with the assistance of AASL, appointed a Task Force on the Role of the School Library Media Program in the National Network. This group felt that it was essential that school libraries become a part of a nationwide resource sharing network.

As a result of this task force, a lengthy report on *The Role of the School Library Media Program in Networking* was published in 1978. "In this report *library network* means a full-service network; that is, in the words of the Commission, one that: consists of a formal arrangement whereby materials, information, and services provided by a variety of types of libraries and/or other organizations are made available to all potential users. (Libraries may be in different jurisdictions but agree to serve one another on the same basis as each serves its own constituents. Computers and telecommunications may be among the tools used for facilitating communication among them.)"[6]

Some may wonder why school library media centers should be included in a national network. There are a number of good reasons for such inclusion. Other than the very important idea that a great segment of our population would be discriminated against if schools were not participants in a network, there are other legitimate reasons for their inclusion. "The school library gives the child the first exposure to information resources and molds the child's information behavior for the future." Thus the school library plays an essential part in readying the child for an adult role in society. *Media Programs: District and School,* published in 1975, very briefly described the functions of networks and suggested that schools participate in them.

Many strong school library media programs have excellent resources, particularly in those areas that support the curriculum, which could be shared with others. School librarians bring unique qualifications; they are trained as teachers as well as professional librarians and are responsible for the teaching of library and information skills. In this dual role, they do an expert job in selection and organization of materials, particularly audiovisuals to support school curriculum. Many of these audiovisual holdings are titles that in many instances are not held by a public library although there could be use for such. Other assets include professional libraries; specialized ethnic collections; career education collections; high interest/low reading level collections; collections of children's and young adult literature; collections for special students such as learning disabled, gifted, etc.; instructional equipment; and computer-assisted instruction materials.

Professional knowledge of individual faculties is not to be overlooked. Some large school systems already have ordering, processing, and cataloging services, repair services, local production of materials, material examination centers, and computer terminals. Some have a delivery system in place in their districts. These school library media specialists share some of the same problems as other librarians, particularly inadequate budgets and staff. Participation in a national network would greatly facilitate better professional relationships among librarians from all types of libraries as they shared not only materials and services but common concerns and expertise as well.[7]

If school library media centers indeed have so much to offer, why should they need a network? Obviously what has just been stated was the ideal, and even if it were not, there are information needs beyond even the excellent school library media center. These needs could be met by journals held by a university, a newspaper file at a local public library, a demographic database of a municipal or state information agency or materials from other special libraries. "Participation in a library network will bring within reach of the student those materials that are just outside the curriculum orientation of the school's collection but well within the range of a serious student's quest for information."[8] A well-coordinated library network enables the student to know the holdings of the public library, how to request it, and how to receive it through the school library media center.

This network would be of value to teachers also as they often need additional instructional materials to use in the classroom. Administrators who need specific information about tax base changes, funding programs, etc., could receive it via a network. School specialists such as counselors, nurses, and psychologists could also benefit. The parents, who many times are in the schools for other purposes, might desire information to help them understand their child's intellectual growth. Much of the time this type of material would be more likely to be found at an academic library than at an elementary or secondary school. A very important service could be to the school library media specialists themselves. Some useful shared services through a network might be bibliographic searches, high quality cataloging and processing, union lists, cooperative examination centers, and, obviously, interlibrary loan, which could help the school library media specialist in collection development.[9]

There are five basic factors that contribute to the exclusion of school library media centers from library networks. They are psychological, political and legal, funding, communication, and planning factors. First, the psychological factor deals with attitudes of librarians. Some other types of libraries fear that there will be so many requests from school library media centers that it will seriously drain their resources. Another fear is that membership in a network will erase an individual library's control over its loan policies. Librarians have to learn to share and not jealously guard their collections. One of the most valid problems is the one of lack of time and effort. School librarians are not eager to take on added responsibilities. Another equally real problem is the fact that many librarians, particularly those who have not kept abreast professionally, are unwilling to try something new. School librarians tend to identify with the school community and thus isolate themselves from other professional librarians. As a result of this, librarians in one type of library fail to understand the problems of others. School librarians need to become more knowledgeable of the needs of young people as they relate to other libraries.

Rogers stated that their lack of information about such networks is a result of the type of library education that has traditionally been espoused for those training for school library media center positions. Even at the graduate level, these people do not often take courses that pertain to a more general area of library science. School library media specialists have been and continue to be separated from the rest of the library profession. She stated that it will be only the exceptional person or group within school library media centers who will be able to participate as equal members in multitype library networks.[10] Inservice education and public relations activities on the part of other groups can help to bring about a long-range positive attitude toward library networks. The administrative fear of loss of autonomy, personal status, and institutional pride can also be a real problem. An administrator may think that the library is inadequate if a student has to go to another source.[11]

While the psychological factors may not seem like real obstacles, the political and legal factors certainly present some serious problems. In school library media centers, the librarian has little decision-making power. He/she is accountable to the principal, who is accountable to the superintendent, who is accountable to the school board. In some states, such as Kentucky, the responsibility for coordinating the development of networks is not fully defined. Public libraries are under the authority of the state library, while school library media centers are under the authority of the Department of Education. In some instances, state and federal funding programs have created barriers to cooperation as some purchased materials were only to be used with specific targeted groups. The interpretation of the copyright law can even create barriers to resource sharing.[12]

While networks sound like a good idea, they do cost money. Most school boards are not willing to expend dwindling school finances for a program without knowing if it is cost effective and the extent of its benefits. What librarians must convince the funding authorities of is that school library media centers cannot meet all the information needs of the students and thus they should be in a network, even though it will cost more money. "The only secure money comes from funding formulas written into law or from membership assessments."[13]

Another essential factor is communications. "Active cooperation requires extensive communication, and it should be based on active participation in decision-making on the part of librarians from various kinds of libraries."[14] Effective library resource sharing depends upon a good communication system that links libraries. The communication tools used by various libraries must be compatible. The speed of the communication is very important. Knowledge of other libraries' resources, rapid transmission of information requests, and prompt delivery of materials are of particular importance to users of school media programs for whom a week's delay can render the materials useless.[15]

To develop an effective library network in which school participation is encouraged, much planning on the part of all participants is required. One of the basic principles is that the same people who are to implement the program should be the ones involved in the planning and policy making stages. Geographic distances sometimes prohibit planning also. All participants in the network should come together as equals, each having its own strengths to share from its particular type of library. Each library must realize the responsibilities and costs involved in the network.[16]

After the task force analyzed the various factors that have been barriers to school library media center participation in networks, they made a number of recommendations to remedy the situation. Some of the more pertinent are included here:

1. Establishment of a clearinghouse for information about school library media programs in networking.

2. Developing a public relations program promoting schools in networks.

3. Producing materials that provide information to groups and individuals.

4. Securing funding for workshops for state education and state agencies.

5. Providing communication opportunities for school media specialists and professionals in other types of libraries.

6. Identifying materials and services in schools appropriate for sharing.

7. Studying the feasibility of network activity.

8. Developing preservice and continuing education curriculum units on schools in networking.

9. Providing materials for use with the education effort.

10. Holding area-level workshops for school-related personnel outside the library profession.

11. Securing funding for research.

The American Association of School Librarians, the Association for Educational Communications and Technology, and the Council of Chief State School Officers were the agencies identified to implement research recommendations, and, unfortunately, members of these groups are not any more knowledgeable about what should be done than individual school librarians. The long-range recommendation of the task force that stated that school library media centers should be equal participants in networks in every region and state in the nation may well be the most important one. This may seem impossible at the present time, but there are some states that have pilot projects that might be used as a model for others.[17]

Colorado can serve as an example of the way to reduce barriers to school participation in library networks. The Colorado Regional Library Service System (RLSS) has been in operation since the 1976-77 school year. Immroth identified the leadership of the Colorado Department of Education as having played an important role in RLSS success. Annemarie Falsone, deputy state librarian and assistant commissioner of State Department of Education has a background as a school librarian. Her inclusion of school library media personnel as equal partners in the network was instrumental in its success. The RLSS has provided inservice education that has given the school library media specialist more understanding of the system and thus reduced barriers.

Legal and political barriers were reduced by passage of enabling legislation for networks, which included schools and made them equal to all other types of library members. There has been a concentrated effort to secure state funds so that smaller, poorer school districts could be a part of the network. "Communication barriers have been reduced by the provision of links for location and referral of ILL requests, reference computer searches, and telephone communication from RLSS." The system newsletter has been an effective communication tool. Document delivery is by courier or mail, and distances have not proved any great problem. In some rural isolated areas, the school library media center is the main source of information for many adults as well as young people.[18]

Illinois has a multitype, multipurpose Regional Library Council. This coordinates the activities of all kinds of libraries in sixteen counties in northern Illinois and metropolitan Chicago. There are many services available, such as Datapass, which allows members to have access to online searching services. It provides daily delivery of interlibrary-loan materials. Shared cataloging is also available to members. Schools are recommended on its governing board.[19]

A 1981 evaluation of the multitype network revealed some problems for school library participation. Only 17 percent of eligible school library media centers have joined the network. Some data revealed that many thought that schools should develop separate networks from other types of libraries. Other problems indicated a lack of information on the part of school librarians about resource sharing, and their inability to change district policies and funding in order to participate. Also some public libraries feared that schools would try to take over the system because of their numbers. Public librarians were also reluctant to share funds that have in the past been "earmarked" for public libraries; they also felt that school libraries had little to share. Following this evaluation, some steps were initiated by the Illinois secretary of state, the state librarian, and the state superintendent of education to address some of these problems.[20]

Indiana has had some cooperative efforts for a number of years through the Indiana Library and Historical Board, Area Library Services Authorities, which is open to all types of libraries. A more recent project is Indiana Cooperative Library Services Authority (INCOLSA). A committee of school representatives in INCOLSA identified the problems of bibliographic control of audiovisual materials as a network service priority. The project was funded and developed through several agencies.

The hypothesis for their project was that the cost of bibliographic control of audiovisual materials could be reduced through sharing of human, machine, and network database resources. "Eleven school districts agreed to participate in the project and to meet the requirements for participation: (1) a commitment to cataloging to a national standard; (2) professional staff capable of doing high quality cataloging; (3) commitment to permit staff to attend three days of training; (4) an agreement to pay the cost of catalog cards produced by OCLC." For each audiovisual item to be processed, they search the OCLC database. If its record is in OCLC, then cards are purchased. If no data are found, that school must produce original cataloging, which is placed into OCLC by INCOLSA. These eleven school districts are contributing high quality bibliographic records and receiving such from others as they are creating an audiovisual database that will be shared with others.[21]

New York has been a leader in school library networking. "Authorization and funding for the development of school library systems and regional networks as pilot projects has made it possible for the schools to participate in cooperation with public library systems and reference and research library resources systems, as a step toward full network participation." Two pilot regional networks are RARE (Rochester Area Resources Exchange) and INTERSHARE, which covers metropolitan New York City. "There are five unaffiliated school library systems, four of which are based on Boards of Cooperative Educational Services (BOCES) and one city school system." There have been many positive results from this resource sharing in New York. Resource sharing has increased greatly. More people are aware of and have access to more service. Students are benefiting as teachers and librarians are working together more closely. Improved delivery systems, development of union catalogs and locator tools have all resulted. Media and online searches have also been shared. Attitudes of public, academic and special libraries changed when they realized that 93 percent of all school requests would be filled by other schools. They had feared that they would spend too much time in filling their requests and get nothing in return. four schools in a RARE project loaned books to public libraries for the summer. School library systems made more than 300,000 entries into union catalog of books in one year and there are six thousand periodical listings from school libraries. Some of the factors that have encouraged this school participation in multitype networks are the following:

1. Support from the State Department of Education.

2. State legislation fostering and funding the network; $600,000 per year for regional system pilot projects and $50,000 maximum for each school library system.

3. Inclusion of two school library representatives on the council of seven.[22]

Turock studied RARE and her data indicated little increased activity after the inclusion of schools. She also stated that schools did not contribute materials in this system and that schools borrowed from public libraries more than from each other. Weeks' dissertation on school library networking in New York State reported that school library media specialists were positive in their attitudes about networks. Four services were considered the most important for school library media centers: interlibrary loan, delivery systems, reference services, and development of union catalogs.[23]

Morrison describes the Putnam/Northern Westchester BOCES School Library Pilot Project. This group became a member of INTERSHARE, which also consisted of public libraries in New York City, public schools in New York City and Yonkers, and New York Metropolitan Reference and Research Library. This represents 48 percent of the population of New York State. They had both state and federal support. They used OCLC through SUNY for bibliographic database because it offered free retrospective conversion in exchange for inputting current cataloging, and because the hit rate was fairly high and the service was offered at a modest cost.

Unfortunately, in 1980 OCLC decided to charge for retrospective conversion so the budget was soon exhausted. A higher level of funding is being sought to continue that effort. One of the achievements of the project was the attitudinal change that has been noted by the librarians in regards to cooperation. A formal interlibrary loan policy was developed linking schools and public libraries in Westchester County. Newsletters, workshops, and training programs have all been implemented to further this cooperation.[24]

Maryland has been a leader in interlibrary loan through MILO (Maryland Interlibrary Organization). Prior to 1980, MILO and SLRC (State Library Resource Center) had paid little attention to the needs of public school library media centers and their students for direct access to network services. MILO did receive some funding from the State Department of Education. Students did sometimes gain access through public libraries, but school library media centers had no direct access nor did they have copies of the microfiche union catalog (MICROCAT). Negotiations between the public library and SLRC-MILO resulted in pilot projects in school library media centers in four Maryland counties, one of which was Howard County. Copies of MICROCAT were placed in all forty-seven schools in the Howard County School system. The schools agreed to process interlibrary-loan requests from both students and faculty, to distribute ILL materials, and to provide detailed statistical data regarding the interlibrary loan uses of students and staff. These data were based on 1981-82 school year. The following are some of the more pertinent results reported by Walker:

1. 703 ILL requests were placed by the Howard County Public School System with MILO during the first semester of 1981-82 year.

2. High school students were the heaviest users, with elementary students the lightest.

3. Others using the service were teachers at all levels, administrators, and clerical staff.

4. School library media specialists at all grade levels ranked usefulness to be high in the survey; however, Walker felt that some of these overrated the perceived usefulness of MILO to students and teachers and the degree to which they have encouraged student use.

5. Students in high school reported use for classroom assignments and elementary schools for personal interests. Teachers' reasons for use were college courses, personal interest, and preparation of instructional units. Central office personnel reasons for using MILO was for detailed research information that was used in making administrative decisions.

6. 74.25 percent of the total requests were author/title requests for monographic materials. 24.89 percent of the total were serial/ periodical with teachers using more of these.

7. High school requests were most often for classroom assignments in English, science, and social studies in that order. Middle school students' requests were in reading, science, and social studies.

8. Materials requested by teachers were more current than those requested by students, due to the fact that many of the teachers' materials were for college course work, and many of the students' were for English literature, which is timeless.

9. The "fill" rate for requests was 78.24 percent with an average "turnover time" of twelve days.

10. Some felt that maybe the students would have made trivial requests, but this was not the case. A large majority of the students indicated that they would have gone elsewhere for their information if MILO had not been available to them.

11. In a random sample check of requests, a check was made of holdings of the Howard County Media Center and this provided an indication that the materials desired were not normally found in a school library media collection.

12. The volume of requests was surprisingly small given the total number of students and staff, and surprisingly large going on the assumption by SLRC/MILO that their services wouldn't be useful to schools. Initially interlibrary-loan borrowing represents a small proportion of any library's circulation. The small number of requests might reflect on the adequacy of their School Library Media collections. This service by MILO was not intended to replace the school library media services, but was intended to supply the unusual and rare requests for information that would not normally be found in school collections.

It has been noted by Mary Kahler that, "Service to library users should be measured not in terms of ordinary needs, but in terms of the extraordinary requirements of certain users." If one looks at the pilot project in this way, it was certainly a success. Another question raised was the cost-effectiveness of MILO. In this case, it was $18,000 or $15 a request. It was felt that this money would not significantly improve the collections of the forty-seven schools, but that these students and teachers had been given access to an enormous collection of information, much beyond the scope of the local school library media center.[25]

In Montgomery County, Maryland, secondary students have had access to large bibliographic databases since 1976. In this school system, the professional library handles interlibrary loan requests. Before sending their requests to the professional library, students have identified the material desired through using a Union List of Periodicals in Maryland and MICROCAT. The materials are picked up by courier and delivered to the professional library, which disseminates the materials to the requesting schools. The items may come from the Enoch Pratt Library, which has been designated as the State Library Resource Center, University of Maryland libraries, public libraries throughout the state, community college libraries or special libraries. In Montgomery County, computer terminals were located in the library media centers for a specific period of time for the students to learn how to search. As a part of their training, library media specialists had learned the techniques necessary to conduct a computer search. This was all part of the service they received through MILO.[26]

Unfortunately, the same opportunities for access are not uniform throughout the state of Maryland. In Prince George County, the schools and public library have cordial relations, but little planned cooperation exists. There is no sharing of resources between the school and public libraries; the hours of the libraries do not coincide. ILL services are not used by school library staff for their students. Access to MILO is for faculty only. There is informal exchange of orders, so that each knows what the other is ordering, but there is no union catalog in the making. The public library staff makes regularly scheduled visits to the classrooms. Gerhardt feels that a positive statement concerning full equal access to libraries by minors is long overdue.[27]

MAISLIC (Memphis Association of Independent Schools Library Center) is a single-type network worth mentioning. In 1978, the chief of technical services at Memphis/Shelby County Public Library and Information Center talked about online cataloging, OCLC, and SOLINET at a regular meeting of the librarians of the Memphis Association of Independent Schools. They became very interested in the possibilities for shared cataloging and within twenty-two months they were accepted for membership in SOLINET. There are seventeen private schools in Memphis that belong to this association, but only seven decided to join at that time. One of these was an elementary school. MAISLIC has pioneered the entry of libraries below the college level into SOLINET; it is also the only independent school network in OCLC. They have one computer terminal located at Memphis University School with plans for another. They recognize that in order to share resources they must have a union catalog, and they are presently working on this. Initially, this project began with a $20,000 grant from a local foundation in Memphis. They have sought other grants to continue it as funds are limited from individual schools since they are all private.[28]

In 1982, in Ohio, Cleveland Heights-University Heights Public Library went online for circulation, cataloging, and acquisition. The Fairfax Elementary School is part of a pilot project to determine if schools should be a part of this regional network. In some of the public libraries in this network, patrons have immediate access to short entries and full bibliographic records can also be called up by means of the browsing mode. At this time, there are no data regarding the extent of the school's usage of and involvement in this computer network.[29]

The GCLC (Greater Cincinnati Library Consortium) is a cooperative of twenty-seven academic, school, and special libraries located within the metropolitan Cincinnati area. It has more than 2.9 million books and over 28,000 periodicals. The following are the services offered by the GCLC: direct lending, reciprocal returns, interlibrary loans, film delivery service, and cooperative film library. All members of the GCLC do not receive all of these services; it depends upon the financial participation of the member library. Seven high school libraries, two public libraries, and one university library were contacted to try to get a realistic view of the value of this consortium to the participating libraries. Some of my findings are as follows:

1. Extremely positive attitude toward GCLC.

2. Beneficial to both faculty and students.

3. Student usage was mostly juniors and seniors.

4. Most of the usage was by direct loan—schools validated student ID so they could use university libraries.

5. Some interlibrary loan usage, more for faculty than students.

6. One librarian reported sixty to one hundred validation forms for ID filled out in a year.

7. Most of usage was to universities; a few were to other high schools through ILL.

8. Some of them used the cooperative film service.

9. One librarian reported that she sometimes called the host library for an OCLC search.

Other benefits cited by the librarians were the workshops and other planned activities to keep librarians abreast of current happenings and bibliographic instruction for students at some of the colleges and universities. One parochial school reported that they received a number of books each year when one university library weeded its collection. Most of the librarians surveyed felt that this was just the beginning, that much more use would be made in the future, especially when the universities had their holdings online.

Single-type cooperatives within or among school districts have been in operation for a number of years. They have been involved in film cooperatives, centralized cataloging and processing, centralized purchase, and circulation of professional materials. Some schools have joined a bibliographic network such as OCLC. Access to information dissemination networks through the school media center would seem to be the most obvious way to expand the school library media program, and yet this seems to be a relatively innovative idea for many school media specialists. Many media centers only assume the responsibility of providing access to the items physically located on that shelf. Thus they fail to realize the full potential that can be offered to students and faculty.

Some that could be made available to schools are ERIC (Educational Resources Information Center), NICSEM (National Information Center for Special Education Materials), National Career Guidance Communication Network for Rural and Small Schools, and NICEM (National Information Center for Educational Media), which indexes nonprint material and is now available as an online database through Lockheed's DIALOG. NICEM provides bibliographic information for videotapes, films, audiotapes, disks, etc., which can be used for selection, acquisition, and cataloging. There are still differences between the audiovisual and library community. If the school library media center is going to house these audiovisual materials, then it needs to provide access, which thus leads to standards of bibliographic control. Before nonprint materials can be included in network databases this must be done, and school library media centers must take the lead as much of the nonprint material is located there. The adoption of AACR2 has been very important in furthering the goal of print and nonprint materials integrated into a network.[30]

Cooperative programming may either be direct or indirect. Some direct methods of cooperation are interlibrary loan and cooperative film centers. There may be some indirect cooperation already in place, such as inservice education and cooperative purchasing, of which the public is unaware. For those of us who see our situations as such small cogs in a large wheel, perhaps we need to start at the local level. We might decide to forego summer reading programs in the schools and encourage our students to participate in public library summer reading programs. Schools might also make available films to public libraries for their programming. We might cooperatively plan for author visits or book talks, and we might borrow materials for student use for special projects. These are just starting points. If we haven't effectively learned to cooperate within school systems or within public library districts, how can we expect to achieve practical networking across systems and types of libraries?

At the state level, the Kentucky Library Association (KLA), for example, has workshops for its members throughout the year. In some instances, two different library groups within KLA will offer these workshops at the same time, thus creating difficult decisions for persons who have a need for both, but who normally go to the one with which he/she is affiliated. It is not the fault of superintendents of schools or public library boards, but of the librarians themselves.[31]

Some have felt that school and public libraries have very similar collections. Doll did a study on the overlap of collections in school and public libraries and the implications for networking. This study was done in Illinois in 1981-82. It was found that networking was not a top priority for libraries. Rather, the building of collections was given top priority. There was little active opposition to networking, and a high percentage of school administrators revealed that they were in favor of cooperative resources sharing, but other answers revealed that they were not likely to take the initiative in establishing networks in which schools participate. Doll found that the average overlap in school collections is 30 percent and the average overlap in school and public library collections is 50 percent. When public library titles are compared with school library collections, the overlap is lower, averaging 30 percent. About one-third of the titles in public library collections will be in school library collections. There is little overlap in periodicals, and schools generally had little to share of this resource.[32]

There are two categories of cooperation according to Aaron—first, those devices that serve to locate and mobilize for use existing library resources and second, those that seek to develop or add to existing resources. The first is the most common form of cooperation between school and public libraries and may take the form of union catalogs and interlibrary loan. The second category of cooperation, cooperatively adding additional resources, is rarely done because of institutional restraints as there are differing funding bases and governing bodies. Broderick says that the "higher in the organizational structure the decision to cooperate is made, the more likely the chance of achieving success." James Nelson, Kentucky state librarian, states that if cooperation is to be successful the following advice should be followed:

1. It needs to benefit institutions individually.

2. It needs to be a voluntary act.

3. Benefits cannot always be seen in advance.

4. Some competition is inevitable.

5. Must recognize present status and legitimate ambitions.

6. Must not impose uniformities that tend to destroy special character of individual cooperating institutions.

7. When economics or other benefits can be achieved through uniform practices, it should not be feared.

8. No institution is so rich in resources that it can be assumed that it has nothing to gain by cooperation.

9. Cash transactions can be an appropriate element in cooperative efforts.

10. The cooperative effort must be professionally staffed if permanent and significant results are to be achieved.

The gains from this type of cooperation must be worth the effort in improved service to young people. Librarians and administrators must think more of collection utility than size. Unfortunately, quantitative standards for the school library are the primary measuring tool.[33]

The motivation for cooperation is within the power of legislative units since they control government funds. This has been set in motion in some states. Federal legislation has required cooperative networks to be implemented in states also. However, Gerhardt does not see a great amount of progress being made. In her study of patterns of access, she found that access to materials for children was still inadequate. She noted that while outwardly cooperation between school and public libraries was in place, it was not fully used. She noted that ILL was not publicized to children and that children's literature was not in the database that was used in Maryland.[34]

From all that has been mentioned in this paper, one can see that the integration of school library media centers into library networks has only just begun and that it will be a slow process. However, we must not continue to dwell on the past but look forward to the future. We must realize that "networking and resource sharing are no longer supplementary to basic local library operation. Instead networking and resource sharing have become an intrinsic, integral, basic, high priority element in daily library operations." School library media specialists have a public to serve—students, teachers, administrators, and parents—and in order to provide them with high quality service, the craft of networking must be learned and practiced.[35]

NOTES

[1]S. L. Aaron, *School/Public Library Cooperation: A State of the Art Review* (Syracuse, N.Y.: ERIC Clearinghouse on Information Resources, 1980), ERIC Document 192 810, 2.

[2]B. Immroth, "Networking and the School Library Media Program," in *School Library Media Annual 1983*, v. 1 (Littleton, Colo.: Libraries Unlimited, 1983), 410.

[3]J. V. Rogers, "Networking and School Library Media Centers," in *Advances in Librarianship*, v. 2, ed. Michael Harris (New York: Academic Press, 1981), 82.

[4]Ibid., 81.

[5]Ibid., 78.

[6]Task Force on the Role of the School Library Media Program in the National Program, National Commission on Libraries and Information Science, *The Role of the School Library Media Program in Networking* (Washington, D.C.: U.S. Government Printing Office, 1978), 5.

[7]Ibid., 9.

[8]Ibid., 25-26.

[9]Ibid., 30.

[10]P. A. Sullivan, "Library Cooperation to Serve Youths," in *Libraries and Young Adults*, ed. JoAnn V. Rogers (Littleton, Colo.: Libraries Unlimited, 1979), 114.

[11]Aaron, 16.

[12]Task Force, 36-37.

[13]Ibid., 49-50.

[14]Ibid., 53.

[15]Ibid., 53-54.

[16]Ibid., 58-59.

[17]Rogers, 102-3.

[18]Immroth, 419.

[19]Task Force, 75.

[20]Immroth, 420.

[21]Ibid., 421.

[22]Ibid., 422-23.

[23]J. Mancall, ed., "Current Research," *School Library Media Quarterly* 12 (Winter 1984): 159.

[24]G. Morrison, "Networking is Working, a School Library Pilot Project Report," *Education Libraries* 7 (Spring-Summer 1982): 21-23.

[25]H. T. Walker, "Networks and School Library Media Centers: A Report of a Pilot Project of the Howard County (Maryland) Public School System and the Maryland Interlibrary Organization," *School Library Media Quarterly* 12 (Fall 1983): 20-26.

[26]K. Dowling, "The School Media Center Goes Online," *Catholic Library World* 53 (October 1981): 120-21.

[27]L. N. Gerhardt, "Children's Access to Public Library Services: Prince George's County Memorial Public Library, Maryland, 1980" in *Children in Libraries: Patterns of Access to Materials in Schools and Public Libraries*, ed. Zena Sutherland (Chicago: University of Chicago Press, 1981), 35-36.

[28]P. Hamilton, "United We Catalog: Networking in Memphis," *Tennessee Librarian* 34 (Fall 1982): 27-33.

[29]"Cleveland Heights Goes Online; Networks with a School Library," *Library Journal* 108 (January 1, 1983): 10-11.

[30]J. V. Rogers, "Progress in Access to Nonprint Materials," *School Library Media Quarterly* 12 (Winter 1984): 127-35.

[31]Sullivan, 115.

[32]C. Doll, "School and Public Library Collection Overlap and the Implications for Networking," *School Library Media Quarterly* 11 (Spring 1983): 193-99.

[33]Aaron, 15-16.

[34]Gerhardt, 22-25.

[35]Immroth, 424.

ADDITIONAL READINGS

Craver, Kathleen W. "Teaching Online Bibliographic Searching to High School Students." *Top of the News* 41 (Winter 1985): 131-38.

Dresang, Eliza T. "School Library Media Services for Gifted Young People." *School Library Media Annual* v. 3. Shirley Aaron and Pat Scales, eds. Littleton, Colo.: Libraries Unlimited, 1985.

Hutchinson, Barbara. "School Library Scheduling: Problems and Solutions." *School Library Journal* 33 (December 1986): 30-33.

Roberts, Beverly J., and Isabel Schon. "Student Aides in Arizona School Libraries: A Descriptive Study." *School Library Journal* 31 (May 1985): 32-35.

Schuman, Patricia Glass. "Library Networks: A Means, Not an End." *Library Journal* 112 (February 1, 1987): 33-37.

Shaw, Ruth Jean. "Alaska's Multilibrary Network: The Best of All Possible Worlds for the Anchorage School District." *School Library Media Quarterly* 12 (Summer 1984): 297-300.

Walker, H. Thomas. "Networking and School Library Media Centers: A Report of a Pilot Project of the Howard County (Maryland) Public School System and the Maryland Interlibrary Organization." *School Library Media Quarterly* 12 (Fall 1983): 20-28.

Wozny, Lucy Anne. "Online Bibliographic Searching and Student use of Information: An Innovative Teaching Approach." *School Library Media Quarterly* 11 (Fall 1982): 35-42.

Part 6

School Library Media Professionals: Leaders and Change Agents

The following two articles describe the implications of an expanded role for the school library media professional. Both stem from a more active involvement in the instructional process. Both address different ways for media professionals to look at their roles. Rosalind Miller and Allan Spanjer suggest that media specialists hoping to implement instructional improvement in the school must focus on staff development with teachers to succeed. Relying on training research, they describe factors that influence successful staff development and in-service efforts. Their focus is on the school library media specialist as change agent.

Eleanor R. Kulleseid addresses the leadership role of the school library media professional in the process of innovation and change. She explores areas of leadership, including informal patterns of influence. Using a person-based model and a humanistic approach, Kulleseid encourages school library media specialists to consider their role as instructional leader.

THE LIBRARY MEDIA SPECIALIST AS CHANGE MAKER

Implications from Research*

Rosalind Miller and Allan Spanjer

Over twenty years ago the United States, jolted from the complacency of the 1950s by Sputnik, entered a "decade of educational reform." This was a period characterized by sweeping curriculum revisions and experimental projects backed by large-scale federal and private funding. Today, various reports, including those from the National Commission on Excellence in Education and the Carnegie Foundation for the Advancement of Teaching, have again prompted demands for educational reform—however, not accompanied this time by increases in funding from either the public or the private sector. Meanwhile, the lessons that could be learned from the last large-scale attempts at educational innovation have been largely overlooked or ignored. Research that answers such questions as "Why do innovations work?" and "When do they work?" remains elusive.

There is, however, a body of research that examines the programs of the 1970s that were designed to introduce innovative practices in public schools. This research identifies strategies and conditions that promote changes and those that prevent innovation from succeeding. It is our purpose in this chapter to identify and outline these findings and then to summarize their implications for today's media specialists who wish to successfully initiate and support instructional improvement within their schools.

THE CHANGE PROCESS IN EDUCATION

The huge sums of money provided by the National Defense Education Act (NDEA) and the Elementary and Secondary Education Act (ESEA) and the millions for innovation from the Ford Foundation are today a rapidly fading memory for most educators. Likewise, the impetus received during this period for school library development through purchase of books and equipment by the NDEA, the millions funneled by Title II of ESEA into school library growth,

*From Rosalind Miller and Allan Spanjer, "The Library Media Specialist as Change Maker: Implications from Research," *School Library Media Annual 1985*, ed. Shirley L. Aaron and Pat R. Scales (Littleton: Colo.: Libraries Unlimited, 1985), 323-35. Reprinted by permission.

297

and the massive efforts promoted by grants from the Knapp Foundation seem to have ended in the 1980s with declining financial support, erosion of staff, increased work load, increased competition for existing funds, and rising costs for educational materials. Knapp's dream of demonstrating the value of school library programs, services, and resources and promoting improved understanding and use of library resources on the part of teachers and administrators still seems an elusive goal, while the effectiveness of the "decade of reform" in improving local educational practice is open to question. For example, after visiting seventy schools, Silverman reported the efforts of the new curricula in *Crisis in the Classroom* and found that "things are much the same as they were forty years ago."[1] Goodlad et al., reported in *Looking Behind the Classroom Door* that there was little indication that innovations, individualized instruction, team teaching, and inquiry learning were being used or that changes were getting into the classroom.[2] Brandwein concluded from such observations as these that (1) new curriculum is relatively easy to introduce but (2) instructional modes are difficult to alter.[3]

Such observations concerning the inconsistent and generally disappointing results of reform led the U.S. Office of Education to contract with the Rand Corporation for an in-depth study of educational innovation funded by federal monies. Rand conducted a four-year study, from 1973 to 1977, first focusing on how projects were initiated and implemented and then, in the second phase, examining factors in both the institutions and the projects themselves that promoted or deterred success in innovation. The results of this study appeared in an eight-volume publication entitled *Federal Programs Supporting Educational Change*. Volume 7, *Factors Affecting Implementation and Continuation*, written by Paul Berman and Milbrey Wallin McLaughlin, specifically deals with questions of sustaining innovation. Overall, Rand found that an outside agency introducing new technologies into a school and providing incentives for its adaptation does not improve educational practice. Instead, local schools and school districts must assume responsibility for improving their own performance and will be successful insofar as they identify and work through stages of the change process. The Rand study identified the factors that determine the success of innovation within a school and a district.[4]

Rand defined a project as successful when it resulted in teacher change, either in classroom organization or in classroom behavior, or in delivery of a service. They then explored characteristics of both successful projects and institutional settings that promoted implementation. Projects that originated within a school had a better chance of success than those imposed from without. Projects generated enthusiasm only when teachers and administrators were convinced of their scope and promise and jointly participated in their planning. The more effort required of teachers, the higher the level of commitment. Projects that required an overall change in teaching styles elicited the most teacher support. When teachers were convinced that an innovation had educational promise and would benefit their students, they were willing to undertake extra work. In contrast to such "intrinsic" motivations, external rewards such as extra pay were not successful in changing teaching habits. If teachers did not have professional motivation, extra pay did not induce them to work harder.

Successful projects had clear and specific goals. When teachers were unsure of what was expected of them, projects dwindled and died. Goals, however, could not be successfully "given" either by lectures or from packaged materials. Teachers seemed unable to conceptualize clearly about goals unless they were engaged in practical concrete training activities they could apply in their own classes. Goals were then achieved in the course of implementation. The more teachers perceived a project's outcome as specific, the more committed they became, the more materials they prepared, and the more their students achieved.

Skill-specific training improved student outcomes and promoted project implementation; however, alone it did not produce long-term teacher change. The most valuable factor in promoting teacher change and increasing the use of materials, more than all other factors combined, was well-conducted staff training development and support activities. In order to actually change their behavior teachers needed activities that helped them adapt procedures to the day-by-day realities of the classroom and activities that provided feedback, individualized training, and moral support. Classroom support, from resource people, consultants, district staff, and so on, proved extremely important. General workshop activities could not anticipate teachers' needs, especially in relation to their individual classrooms. Teachers wanted "hands-on" activities that showed them how to adapt methods or materials to their own situation. They preferred learning how to solve problems for themselves to receiving abstracts on how to solve problems. The amount of assistance was not as important as how helpful the assistance was perceived to be; a little high-quality support was better than a great deal of low-quality support.

The institutional setting also affected the successfulness of innovation. Leadership of the administration, organizational climate of the school, and quality of the staff had a powerful effect on the success of innovation. Referring to the principal as the "gatekeeper of change," Rand discovered that supportive principals were practically a necessity if innovations were to be initiated, especially in projects involving classroom organization.[5] Projects that required teachers to master specific techniques and procedures required a principal to be supportive, but less involved. Working relationships among the teachers were also important. Not only did good working relations enhance morale, they allowed open sharing of problems and solutions. Good working relations resulted from projects that required teacher participation and frequent interaction. As far as the setting of the school was concerned, neither the size nor the makeup of the student body affected the success of innovation. Only one important organizational characteristic was apparent: whether the school was secondary or elementary. Elementary school projects were much more likely to achieve goals and produce teacher change than projects in the secondary school.

As for teacher characteristics, three teacher attributes significantly affected outcomes: years of experience, sense of efficacy, and verbal ability.[6] Number of years of teacher experience was negatively related to achievement of a project's goals. The more experienced a teacher, the less likely was the project to improve student performance or change classroom practice. However, when teachers believed that it was possible to help even the most difficult and unmotivated student, more goals were achieved, student performance improved, and teaching behavior changed. Teachers' attitudes about their own professional competence appeared to have a major effect on how effective the projects were.

In summary, Rand found that a project's methods had a limited effect on its outcome, as did project resources. Expensive projects were no more likely to elicit teacher change or to improve student performance than less expensive ones.

Ambitious and demanding innovations were more successful with teachers when they understood the project's goals and their relation to their classroom, but success depended almost totally on the implementation strategies. Further, outside consultants, packaged management approaches, one-shot training, and formal evaluation were ineffective. Effective strategies included concrete, teacher-specific training followed up with classroom assistance, meetings that focused on practical problems, teacher participation in discussions, and principal participation. In fact, the role of principals could not be overstated. Without their moral support to the staff, teachers were unlikely to adopt new methods. Even then, teachers with many years on the job were unlikely to change, especially at the secondary level.

Rand thus identified in its massive study a number of elements which have strong implications for staff development and for successful planning for innovation.

In 1978, taking a cue from the less than favorable reports on school reform and educational innovation, and analyzing studies, such as the Rand study, which investigated the effectiveness of various methods of teacher training, Bruce Joyce and Beverly Showers collaborated on a two-year study to examine research on the in-service training of teachers and their ability to acquire new teaching skills and strategies.[7] They found, as had the Rand study, that in order for teachers to change their behaviors certain conditions had to be present, and it was difficult to master or implement new skills. They first classified the outcomes of in-service training according to the level of impact on students' classroom learning. These levels were described as awareness, acquisition of concepts or organized knowledge, skill development, and application of concepts and skills in problem-solving situations.

> *Awareness.* The awareness level occurs when training brings about realization of the importance of an area of knowledge. For example, introduction of microcomputers into the classroom begins with the teacher's awareness of the possible educational role of computers.

> *Concepts or organized knowledge.* The participant gains intellectual control over relevant content. At this level the teacher will understand how a computer works and will recognize and be familiar with computer-assisted instruction and management software.

> *Skill development.* The teacher then needs to learn the skills necessary to act. For example, programming skills might be acquired, as well as mastery over word processors and other basic programs.

> *Application and problem solving.* Finally, the teacher learns to apply the concepts, principles, and skills to improve classroom learning. In this case the teacher might introduce students to a variety of computer-assisted instructional programs that individualize and instruct, teach programming to students to develop their logical skills, or utilize management programs in improving record keeping.

Only when this fourth level of impact is reached will the majority of teachers influence their students' learning.

Next, Joyce and Showers identified the levels of impact of various training strategies.[8] According to their findings, successful classroom implementation of a new approach is virtually dependent on using training procedures that include all of the following:

Study of the rationale or theoretical basis for the skill or instructional technique being learned. Presentation of theory, usually provided by readings, lectures, film, or discussion, can raise awareness, but few teachers (perhaps 10 percent) will be able to acquire or transfer these skills to the classroom, and impact on learning is limited to the students of these few teachers.

Observation of demonstrations by persons who are competent in the use of the skill or instructional technique. Understanding can be accomplished through live demonstrations, television, films, or other media and has a considerable effect on awareness and conceptual control; however, fewer than 15 percent of teachers will be able to imitate the skill or technique and transfer it to classroom practice.

Practice and feedback in protected conditions. Once awareness and knowledge are gained, teachers acquire skills by trying out the techniques on each other and then on small groups of students. Practice increases the potential level of impact, but probably fewer than 25 percent of teachers will actually be able to transfer the skill into their instructional situations. The more complex and unfamiliar the skill or strategy, the lower will be the level of transfer.

Coaching for application. In order to help teachers adapt new instructional practices, observation, encouragement, and feedback are needed. These may be provided by peers, supervisors, consultants, or others and, when used in combination with the aforementioned components of training, result in the highest level of impact on students' learning. With effective coaching nearly all teachers can transfer newly learned skills into their active repertoire.

Teachers need help in adapting skills to fit their individual classroom conditions. Rand found that well-conducted staff support strategies were the key to successful innovations, and Joyce and Showers identified coaching as the key ingredient that increases the possibility that skills learned in the study of theory and observation of demonstration will eventually translate into practice.

Joyce and Showers also identified components of coaching that seem essential to the successful training program. These include companionship, feedback, analysis of application, adaptation to the students, and personal facilitation.

Companionship makes the training process become more pleasant and reassuring.

Feedback helps keep the teacher's mind on perfecting and polishing skills. Feedback is also beneficial to the person providing it because observations of live demonstrations facilitate intellectual control of a skill.

Analysis of application refers to determining when a new model can be used appropriately and what will be achieved as a consequence. Nearly everyone needs help in learning to pick the right spots for exercising a new skill and in determining the outcome of using the skill.

Adaptation to the students is helping teachers to become acquainted with what behavior is needed to fulfill the demands of the new method and to gauge their own progress. One of the main functions of the coach is to help teachers read the responses of the students, since the teachers tend to be preoccupied with their own behavior.

Personal facilitation is intended to help teachers feel good about themselves during the early and numerous practice trials, to reduce isolation, and to increase interpersonal support.

According to Joyce and Showers, at the root of coaching is developing an environment in which members feel free to give and receive feedback. Feedback facilitates improvement through classroom practice by helping the teacher attend to perfecting skills and working through problems. Essential to coaching is helping teachers decide when it is appropriate to use a new technique and what might be the outcome of using it. A side function of coaching is helping teachers be sensitive to the responses of the students as they adapt to the new approach.

In an earlier article, Kenneth Howey and Joyce[9] found that while educators were quick to criticize in-service education as a means of improving instruction, they were less able to define exactly what in-service education was. For some it could be any activity from personal projects to formal graduate studies. For others it meant only those activities sponsored by local schools or districts. Feeling that a conceptualization was needed, they developed a more precise delineation of the varieties of in-service education:

1. *Job-embedded:* dealing with actual performance in the classroom, such as analysis of videotapes of one's teaching

2. *Job-related:* related to the job, but not taken while teaching is going on; includes after-school workshops and demonstrations

3. *General professional:* designed to improve competence but not tailored to any specific identified needs

4. *Career and credential:* organized to help teachers obtain the proper credentials

5. *Personal experience:* designed for personal enrichment.

When teachers were asked who would be the best persons to conduct these various types of in-service education, professors were identified as the most desirable for the last three types, but either fellow teachers or other related school personnel were selected as the most desirable for job-embedded and job-related endeavors. Although apparently no effort was made to identify "other related school personnel," it must certainly be assumed that the school library media specialist is in some way an appropriate partner in this process of improving instruction through in-service education.

IMPLICATIONS FOR LIBRARY MEDIA SPECIALISTS

Many educators have seen the school library as a force in improving instruction. Early in 1963, the Knapp project distributed a brochure stating an interest in school libraries where librarians were working with new patterns of curriculum organization, team teaching, flexible scheduling, and the like.[10] In 1969, Ruth Ann Davies described the schools as moving from traditional ineffectiveness to innovative excellence, with the librarian being a contributing member of a teaching team working to individualize instruction, introduce the multimedia approach, restructure curriculum, and promote creative inventiveness in learning;[11] and in 1979 she identified the library media specialist as directly "involved in the total teaching-learning process," planning with individual teachers and committees of teachers for the integration of the resources and services of the library media center with the day-to-day, ongoing teaching and learning progress.[12] David Loertscher, in 1980, placed the library media specialist as an equal partner with the teacher, creating objectives, assembling materials, and participating in instruction.[13] Yet an honest appraisal would reveal that such an instructional role for library media specialists has never been fully realized. Instead, in most situations they are expected to play a supporting role by reading stories, teaching library skills, and managing equipment.

Indeed, there seems to be a general skepticism and lack of theory about teaching and the process of change that is partly responsible for the recent return to emphasis on the more traditional processes of education and the resort to such unlikely instruments of improvement as "merit pay." Media specialists, armed with an understanding, based on research, of the factors that promote innovation, would have a realistic basis on which to work for improvement of instruction within their individual school, reduce their frustration level, and make more meaningful decisions about their priorities.

The school principal's moral support is the key to implementation and continuation of innovation at the classroom level, but principals as a rule are not expected to assume personal responsibility for training and in-service education.[14] Since teachers have indicated that they prefer fellow teachers and/or related school personnel in this role, and since the utilization of library media resources will normally require changes in teachers' behavior, library media specialists seem ideally placed to assume a role in job-embedded or job-related in-service activities. In reality, because of their myriad other responsibilities and because of a lack of assurance that such efforts will make any substantial changes in instruction, many library media specialists are reluctant to view themselves in this role. It is true that taking an active role in a school's instructional program and positively influencing the quality of teaching and learning cannot be left to happenstance. To be successful, one must approach this role with a purpose and a set of strategies for making change. However, strategies that are consistent with the messages of research are certainly more assured of success than those based on assumptions.

The research reviewed above carries a message for those library media specialists who wish to be involved in creating change. They need to evaluate their efforts to influence change in light of the impact they seek. Making teachers aware of resources pertinent to a given unit of study can be accomplished by circulating a bibliography, but having an impact on students' learning regarding these resources will necessitate much greater involvement. Teachers will need sufficient training to gain control over the content of resources and to acquire skills necessary for utilizing them and applying them effectively in their own classrooms. Furthermore, teachers cannot simply move directly from a training session into the classroom with a concept or skill ready, but need assistance in fitting the training into their own particular classroom conditions. Coaching is the key to this transfer process, but coaching itself will be ineffective without study, observation, and opportunities for practice with feedback.

Early and lasting support from the principal is the most important factor in the success of any project. Rand found that principals gave subtle but nonetheless strong messages concerning the types of activities in their school, and teachers received and interpreted those messages in terms of their professional self-interest.[15] A library media specialist who wishes to have an impact on instruction should support projects identified by the principal as important for the school, rather than projects that happen to be close to the media specialist's heart. For example, in many schools, principals, perhaps with teacher or district input, select a thrust or theme for the year, and each teacher is expected to work for student improvement in that area. At other times standard tests will reveal weaknesses in areas of instruction that require a strong school emphasis to correct. By identifying a central role in such projects, the media specialist will have a good chance of obtaining strong encouragement and support from the principal.

A SCENARIO FOR IMPLEMENTING CHANGE STRATEGIES

A possible application of the above research in a school setting is presented in the following scenario. Students enrolled in grades three to six are scoring low in comprehensive skills on standardized tests. The principal is forming task groups of teachers to work on improving these skills. In this situation, the media specialist might be content to seek out and purchase materials recommended to help students improve comprehension and then to prepare and distribute a bibliography. This would increase the awareness level of teachers, who at least would realize that there were materials in the media center that, if properly utilized, could increase reading comprehension. According to research, however, it is unlikely that this effort would produce any changes in the teaching of even one teacher, and thus it would have little impact on student learning.

Suppose the library media specialist wishes, however, to make an effort to achieve maximum utilization by teachers of materials that promote learning. This might require that the teachers gain conceptual control of the material and develop new teaching or audiovisual techniques. It is an ambitious project that will require a large commitment of time, plus an awareness of the demands for successful in-service education. By utilizing the messages of research that define levels of impact and in-service strategies, the library media specialist will be able to define for the principal the amount of support that must be committed if the project is to succeed.

According to the Rand study,[16] teachers prefer projects that require them to make significant changes in their overall teaching style, that require them to make an extra effort, and that, above all, are skill-specific. Projects do not fail because they are too ambitious, but rather because teachers do not understand their goals or consider them relevant to the classroom. The library media specialist must first define exactly what skills the teachers could learn and how they would need to change their classroom behavior in order to utilize these learning materials. If these recommendations are specific enough and have the principal's support, research indicates that teachers who view themselves as professionals and their roles as important should be more willing to cooperate with this project.

Level One—Awareness

Each teacher will become aware of those materials available in the library media center that can be used in the classroom to increase reading comprehension (see figure 1, page 306). At this level, the library media specialist must identify and purchase necessary materials, carefully examine each item to prepare the bibliography, and search the literature for appropriate readings.

Level Two—Concepts or Organized Knowledge

The teacher will gain an intellectual understanding of the content of the materials and how they can be used in the classroom. Joyce and Showers found that this required twenty to thirty hours of study coupled with observation of at least fifteen to twenty demonstrations (see figure 2, page 306).[17] At level two the library media specialist must identify teachers who are familiar with the materials and who are willing to demonstrate at workshops or in the classroom.

Level Three—Skill Development

By practicing in protected to simulated conditions, teachers begin to acquire the skills needed to use the materials. Joyce and Showers found that teachers need to practice a skill ten to fifteen times to master it (see figure 3, page 307).[18]

Level Four—Application and Problem Solving

The teachers are ready to transfer their newly acquired skills to a particular classroom. In this case, they start by using the materials from the media center and applying new skills with their students to improve comprehension (see figure 4, page 307). Coaching appears critical to this process. Joyce and Showers found that coaching was a mutually beneficial activity. The Rand study discovered that relationships among teachers significantly affected a project's outcome. When teachers could work closely together, an innovation was more likely to succeed; in addition, the development of a "critical mass" of teachers allowed them to openly share their problems and solutions and to learn from each other. Morale was also enhanced. The more teachers coached one another, the more they indicated that their school was a good one to work in.[19]

Type of in-service education	Strategies	Time required from teachers	Level of impact
Job-related	Present theory, rationale, or description. Library media specialist prepares and distributes annotated bibliography and selected readings to teachers.	20-45 minutes to read bibliography and selected readings.	Fewer than 10% of the teachers will use the materials. There will be little impact on student learning.

Fig. 1. Level one—awareness.

Type of in-service education	Strategies	Time required from teachers	Level of impact
Job-related, possibly job-embedded	Observation of demonstrations by teachers, consultants, or others familiar with the material in workshops or classrooms.	Combined with awareness level, 20-30 hours. Should include 15-20 demonstrations in varied teaching environments.	About 10% of the teachers may be able to transfer this to the classroom. There will be some impact on student learning.

Fig. 2. Level two—concepts or organized knowledge.

Type of in-service education	Strategies	Time required from teachers	Level of impact
Job-related and job-embedded	Practice and feed-back. Workshops where teachers work together in simulated conditions, giving and receiving feedback, or where one teacher observes and gives feedback to another working with a small group in the classroom.	5-10 hours.	Up to 25% of the teachers may be able at this point to transfer their skills. Student learning will be affected in those classrooms.

Fig. 3. Level three—skill development.

Type of in-service education	Strategies	Time required from teachers	Level of impact
Job-embedded	Coaching. Teachers, with library media specialist, form coaching teams to observe one another's technique, to provide feedback and companionship, and to help in analyzing applications.	Depends on quality of teams. As Rand reported, a small amount of high-level assistance is more valuable than a great deal of low-level help.	90-100% of teachers will utilize the materials. There will be a maximum impact on student learning.

Fig. 4. Level four—application and problem solving.

Assuming a role as change maker, as suggested in this paper, will seem to many library media specialists as one more task in a sea of expectations, and not a task of highest priority. In many schools the library media specialists are expected to spend their time working directly with students—teaching library skills, reading stories, giving book talks, and providing reference services—with their main service to teachers being the maintenance and distribution of audiovisual equipment. Indeed, when asked to identify their role, many are quick to respond, "I'm mainly a teacher."[20] However, important as these activities may be, they can also be achieved through careful management with teachers, parent volunteers, and student aides.

A basic assumption in the Rand report[21] was that improvement of student performance depends on changing teachers' styles either in their classroom behavior or in their use of materials. If this assumption is true, and classroom teachers are the decisive element in promoting student learning, then providing them with resources and materials, the skills to effectively utilize them, and the support and encouragement to sustain these changes is a key role in education. The one person in the school who is potentially equipped to meet these needs is the library media specialist. Thus, by choosing to work directly with teachers, helping them to help students, a library media specialist can better use the resources of the media center to influence student learning. Library media specialists who spend most of their time working one-on-one with students or on clerical tasks can seriously diminish and curtail a school's potential to have an impact on learning.

Library media specialists who accept the role of change makers must carefully rethink their priorities and establish modes of in-service education that promote effective utilization of resources. Too often, in a flush of enthusiasm a library media specialist will start an ambitious program, only to have it flounder. This may mean a retreat to the media center and a return to traditional service. Messages from research provide guidelines that can be used to design projects that have a chance to succeed in improving student learning.

NOTES

[1]C. E. Silverman, *Crisis in the Classroom: The Making of American Education* (New York: Random House, 1970), 154.

[2]J. Goodlad et al., *Looking Behind the Classroom Door* (Worthington, Ohio: Charles H. Jones, 1974), 33.

[3]P. F. Brandwein, *Memorandum: On Renewing Schooling and Education* (New York: Harcourt Brace Jovanovich, 1981), 135.

[4]P. Berman and Milbrey Wallin McLoughlin, *Factors Affecting Implementation and Continuation*, v. VII of *Federal Programs Supporting Educational Change* (Santa Monica, Calif.: Rand Corp., 1978), vii-xiii.

[5]Ibid., 123.

[6]Ibid., 136.

[7]B. Joyce and B. Showers, "Improving Inservice Training: The Message of Research," *Educational Research* (February 1980), 380.

[8]B. Joyce and B. Showers, "The Coaching of Teaching," *Educational Leadership* (October 1982), 5-7.

[9]K. Howey and B. Joyce, "A Data Base for Future Directions in Inservice Education," *Theory into Practice* 17, no. 3 (1978): 208-10.

[10]P. Sullivan, ed., *Realization: The Final Report of the Knapp School Libraries Project* (Chicago: American Library Association, 1968).

[11]R. A. Davies, *The School Library: A Force for Educational Excellence* (New York: R. R. Bowker, 1969), 18.

[12]R. A. Davies, *The School Library Media Program: Instructional Force for Excellence*, 3d ed. (New York: R. R. Bowker, 1979).

[13]D. Loertscher, "The School Library Media Center: A New Force in American Education," *Arkansas Librarian* 37, no. 24 (September 1982): 12.

[14]"Practical Applications of Research," *Newsletter* (Phi Delta Kappa Center on Evaluation, Development, and Research) 5, no. 3 (March 1983): 2.

[15]Berman and McLoughlin, 127.

[16]Ibid., 71.

[17]Joyce and Showers, "Coaching," 4.

[18]Ibid.

[19]Berman and McLoughlin, 19.

[20]V. Moore, "Quality Education," *Today's Education* (1984-1985 annual ed.): 57.

[21]Berman and McLoughlin, 46.

THE LEADERSHIP ROLE OF THE
LIBRARY MEDIA SPECIALIST

Some Humanistic
Models of Cooperation*

Eleanor R. Kulleseid

Human beings are obsessed with leadership; no concept has been subjected to more study, debate, or written commentary by scholars and practitioners from Socrates to Lee Iacocca. Whatever the setting—a remote rural culture, a fast food organization, or a public high school—the examination of leadership is invariably linked to an effort to change from the status quo to some new order of being. Leadership is inextricably related to the exercise of some form of power, social status, for example, or expertise, or control of resources (money, jobs, etc.). Leadership is also connected to the idea of ultimate moral purpose or utility, to long-range objectives meant to achieve a shared vision. "Whatever the separate interests persons might hold, they are presently or potentially united in the pursuit of 'higher' goals, the realization of which is tested by the achievement of significant change that represents the collective or pooled interests of leaders and followers."[1]

One looks in vain for the term "leadership" in recent volumes of *Library Literature*.[2] Anyone who has taken a library administration course knows that librarians tend to be trained as managers and administrators, not leaders.[3] Some practitioners would agree with the school library media supervisor who, while dutifully filling out a survey of professional development interests, scribbled next to a topic on leadership, "Who are we kidding?"[4]

It is true that most school library media professionals do not have much formal authority attached to their natural power bases in three critical policy areas: curriculum, personnel, and budget.[5] It is also true that many feel excluded and would welcome an opportunity to take a participative role, especially in the curriculum development process. While formal authority in these areas may be limited or nonexistent, informal influence may be exercised in many powerful ways suggested by documented successful experience. These approaches are strengthened by a growing interdisciplinary literature which offers interesting models for the development and exercise of informal leadership in the school setting, leadership based on cooperation rather than competition with peers and supervisors.

*From Eleanor R. Kulleseid, "The Leadership Role of the Library Media Specialist: Some Humanistic Models of Cooperation," *School Library Media Annual 1987*, ed. Shirley L. Aaron and Pat R. Scales (Littleton, Colo.: Libraries Unlimited, 1987), 155-66. Reprinted by permission.

The following discussion, informed by theory and practice in business management, educational administration, and psychology, is based on an underlying premise expressed by a distinguished political scientist who argues that "a person, whether leader or follower, girded with moral purpose, is a tiny principality of power."[6]

Leadership sometimes arises out of discomfort. An individual must want to change something specific about himself or herself or the environment, must take responsibility for examining current professional activities and attitudes, for making decisions and taking actions which lead to a change of behavior resulting in a change of role, function, visibility, and expertise. This experience, characterized by high personal motivation, must occur before the individual can motivate others to achieve a desired change.

Change for what? And from what? From whole-group to individualized programming? From no involvement in curriculum development to membership, maybe even leadership on a committee? From zero dollars in the budget to some dollars for the purchase of new titles? From the clerical role demanded by a hand-sorted circulation system to the more professional role allowed by the liberating influence of a microcomputer program? The possibilities are as varied as the settings in which we work, but the changes we seek must always rise from a vision of improving the educational process for young people in some specific and concrete way.

There is much to learn from the evidence offered in oft-cited critiques of educational innovation and change, as well as numerous studies of effective schools and school failure.[7] They suggest that conscientious library media specialists who carry out mandates prescribed in the professional standards could, in many settings, regard themselves as the loyal opposition to, if not downright subversive of, the status quo. This "change agent" role[8] must carry with it some form of power if the good practitioner is to survive and flourish in schools which are characterized by a traditional hierarchical organization borrowed from industries, corporations, and centralized government agencies. Leadership in the traditional school organization is based on rational, formal authority and centralized control of resources; the focus is on task management, top-down communication, and quantitative measurement of achievement. The library media specialist is one of a peer group of teaching or district-level staff members who see themselves ideally as equals and cooperative coworkers, but in reality are often pitted against one another in the scramble for limited resources.

The vast majority of library media specialists are working within what Schon has described as "adversarial contexts."[9] Their roles are ambiguous, their functions and goals misunderstood, and their status unclear. They are different from their colleagues in the classroom, and feel isolated. Yet they are included in collective bargaining agreements which define working conditions for classroom teachers. Their educational philosophy—individualized and small group interaction using a wide range of resources in many formats—is often antithetical to the instructional biases of most schools. Such biases are based more on the need to make efficient use of limited resources than on an educational philosophy. These problems can inhibit leadership, or they can stimulate actions which lead to empowerment not only for the library media specialist, but for teachers, students, and administrators as well.

Those who take positive action usually become informal leaders by conducting "cooperative inquiry within adversarial contexts."[10] They converse with students, teachers, administrators, and parents on matters of concern to them. They often take on responsibility for activities which are not in their job description, but which put them in touch with the rest of the school community in ways which increase communication, build trust, and draw clients into their program frame of reference. They identify projects which will allow them to initiate, adapt to, or resist changes in their working environments, and to preserve or expand programs already in place. "The best managed library media programs have a clear focus of leadership, a visible leader willing to accept responsibilities and a 'presence' throughout the school—not just in the library media center."[11]

The savvy library media specialist comes to realize that everybody in the school, regardless of formal role, feels isolated and powerless at one time or another. It behooves us all to scan the recent literature in educational administration to verify this fact. The editors of a recent issue of *Teachers College Record* devoted to the topic of authority in education put it succinctly: "These days, due to a multiplicity of influences, the bearers of educational authority receive very little respect from anyone; therefore, their claims to authority are weak, and they often feel ineffective."[12] Although current reform efforts for the improvement of teaching and learning place every school professional under public scrutiny, formal power-holders (notably principals and superintendents) are often alone on the front lines with parents, school, state and regional boards, and teachers' unions. The solo performances required of those vested with authority have, in this day and age, many of the characteristics of those performed by library media and other educational specialists who operate from the only power base available to them—informal influence and expertise.

Much of the literature on leadership in administration and supervision is focused on getting the person in authority to change behaviors within the organization by adopting models based on participatory management, organizational development, and leadership by consensus (LBC).[13] *Team Management*, which typifies the application of LBC to the school settings, includes a step-by-step manual for introducing and implementing this model in a school district.[14] In most versions of participative management, power is shared by those holding formal authority with those exercising leadership in particular areas, functions, or situations. It involves some blend of formal authority with informal influence usually based on expertise. This approach has been stimulated, in part, by the decline in American economic productivity, and awareness of apparently successful organizational innovations by foreign competitors, for example, "quality circles" in Japanese industry which inspired William Ouchi's Theory Z.[15] Increased communication is an essential component in improving organizational climate and decision-making. Studies of communication patterns emphasize the value of reciprocal networks in which information is exchanged, rather than passed down from the top in a one-way flow.[16] Although these models are oriented toward those already in the driver's seat, there is much of value for those in the ranks who wish to improve the educational process and climate within their schools.

Role ambiguity can be a liability or an asset. Library media specialists teach people and manage resources. They have much in common with both classroom teachers and administrative staff. Yet they belong, in most cases, to neither group. Is this a negative? Not necessarily, if library media specialists recognize the possibilities of being in a "neutral" position and become magnets for communication, drawing fragmented people and programs together. This is a highly valued function in many schools which, even at the elementary level, are divided into a checkerboard of grade levels, tracks, subject departments, and programs for special pupil populations. Opportunities for interaction are extremely limited, and time is at a premium for most professionals with heavy teaching schedules.

Patterns of communication between teachers are invariably described as "far from open. Teachers choose to talk about nonschool themes with other teachers. They prefer to keep their distance as a way of preserving their autonomy in the classroom. They do not work collectively, even when there are strong unions...."[17] Most of their informal communication is confined to complaining or joking about the workplace, usually at lunch or in the faculty room; little talk or time is devoted to professional interaction about curricula or students.

If library media specialists recognize this and want to open up discussion about professional matters, they must adapt their own schedules in some way to make time for more informal contact with individual teachers and administrators, and they must be ready to offer concrete suggestions or assistance. The time should be used to plan or implement direct service to students, meeting needs as perceived by teachers and administrators. This means, sometimes, sacrificing one's own personal professional goals to establish a good working relationship with others. You may believe that daily story-reading aloud is essential for literacy, while the principal insists that classroom teachers spend that precious fifteen minutes on phonics exercises. "Consensus, accommodation, cooperative working relationships, and a balance among conflicting forces are what the sensitive politician seeks to achieve.... Failure to understand the nature of compromise and the need for accommodation has blighted the leadership of more than one library media specialist."[18] And from a summary and interpretation of the Rand studies quoted above: "A library media specialist who wishes to have an impact on instruction should support projects identified by the principal as important for the school, rather than projects that happen to be close to the media specialist's heart."[19] Compromise and consensus — not perfect, but realistic. Innovation and change — we still have our own long-range agendas to pursue — are a slow and, sometimes, tedious process.

Knowing where we want to go, so we don't get lost on the way, is important. And if we want to take others with us on an educational journey which improves school climate, professional performances, and the teaching-learning process, we are more likely to stay on course if we exercise that special kind of leadership based on expertise and knowledge, on informal influence which involves open, shared, consensual decision making. The journey begins with self-assessment, a core function of the "reflective practitioner" whose intuitive decision making based on expertise offers a promising model for the library media specialist.[20] In this model the traditional interaction, based on student submission to teacher authority (or teacher submission to administrative authority), is abandoned. The teacher or administrator acts as a coach, inviting students or peers to "step into a situation" and make explicit what it is they want to do; he or she suggests an approach to learning and problem solving that is collegial and experimental. Stressing the importance of the library media specialist's work with teachers in adapting new instructional materials and strategies to classroom settings, Miller and Spanier outline a specific situation in which the coaching role is used.[21]

The coaching function is suggested in a growing literature which emphasizes the teaching and facilitative dimensions of leadership, and offers positive alternatives to professionals whose practice is rooted in ideals of collaboration and support. Most library media specialists who are motivated or thrust into a leadership role try to achieve their goals without getting ahead of the pack. They are, like their colleagues in the classroom, oriented toward helping rather than competing. The idea of holding and exercising power does not feel consonant with their roles; yet they cannot perform effectively unless they are powerful advocates and communicators. They must take risks, step out of the crowd into the spotlight, and become highly visible members of the school community.

The literature of clinical supervision and staff development presents concepts of leadership as empowerment, which should be congenial to school specialists in helping roles. Goldhammer's clinical supervision model[22] stresses such elements as team teaching, peer review, and participant observation. As Bingham points out in her summary for district library media supervisors,[23] this model is focused on instructional improvement, not on crucifying a coworker. Coaching or mentoring, like clinical supervision, presumes a one-to-one sharing and negotiation which many library media specialists already enact in their contacts with individual clients. Those who hold formal responsibilities for such efforts at instructional improvement (principals and assistant principals) often are not trained as mentors or coaches, and have little time or inclination for such things. Thus, instructional development and improvement are often a workplace vacuum, waiting to be filled informally by some intrepid, motivated expert, whose most recent incarnation seems to be that of the "master" teacher.

The Carnegie report, *A Nation Prepared: Teachers for the 21st Century*, identifies the building-level teacher as the ultimate source of excellence in education, and calls for teacher control, collegiality, and professionalism as touchstones for educational reform. One of their recommendations is to "restructure the teaching force, and introduce a new category of Lead Teachers with the proven ability to provide active leadership in the redesign of the schools and in helping their colleagues to uphold high standards of learning and teaching."[24] The report not only places control of instructional improvement just where it has always resided, behind the classroom door, but it also stresses direct teacher responsibility for outcomes, evaluation, and change strategies.

The ongoing debate on how mastery and, therefore, teacher leadership is defined and recognized has a familiar ring. There are two prevailing conceptions of the master teacher. One is competitive, based on the notion that "one teacher engages in essentially the same activities as another but is judged to be better at accomplishing these activities than the other."[25] The other is based on the notion that "the master teacher is one who may or may not engage in conventional teaching activity but who also performs specialized functions in schools and classrooms ... [such as] plan curricula for a group of other teachers, monitor student progress, formulate and administer evaluation schemes, or serve as mentor to new or experienced teachers who need special assistance in order to become more effective."[26] Griffin and others argue that the latter, based on a differentiated role structure, is more congruent with the mores of collegiality in school culture.

Criticism has been leveled at plans which connect recognition of mastery to merit pay. "The values central to the teaching profession are collegial and cooperative, nurturing and sustaining, not competitive and entrepreneurial."[27] Rauh[28] and Klein[29] describe forms of master teaching which are highly congruent with the ideal professional role of the library media specialist as internal agent of change and curriculum leader. Library media professionals should make themselves aware of this trend in their school districts as a model to test against their own performances and as a potential source of recognition and/or role expansion.

If the idea of the library media specialist acting as staff developer or master teacher to teacher colleagues is daunting, those old mores of collegiality which prevent teachers and specialists from assuming leadership roles[30] may be invoked in the name of "cooperative learning," the latest buzz phrase in curriculum and staff development. The training model developed by the Johnson brothers,[31] disseminated through publications and introduced to many school districts around the country, is reminiscent of John Dewey's child-centered progressive curriculum, in which "every method is used to have the children do all the work, not to keep the responsibility and initiative in the hands of the teacher."[32] Students of varying capacities learn how to work together on a problem in the classroom and, in doing so, teach and learn from each other. The teacher functions as a facilitator or resource person, and students come to rely upon one another as sources of information and accountability.

This paradigmatic shift in authority and leadership is of sufficient impact to stimulate teachers to work together in new ways which, according to one report, involve voluntary peer observation and feedback.[33] An increase in professional collegiality and communication has been noted as an additional benefit in other studies which describe the introduction of cooperative learning methods in the classroom.[34] Leadership in these settings is comparable to that which emerges in curriculum lessons structured for students learning in peer groups. It is fluid, situational, shared. No one person is responsible for it all; yet all are responsible for some, depending on the level of commitment, prior knowledge, and courage. And all are responsible for one another: the group succeeds or fails on the performance of its weakest member. There is something in this old-fashioned "team spirit" which has an ethical dimension for teachers. If the teaching team plays well, the students win.

The desire to foster cooperation between potentially competitive groups and individuals in all sorts of endeavors, from world peace to worker productivity, places emphasis on the dynamics between formal authority and informal influence exercised within and between various groups. This has a counterpart in current efforts to develop trusting and stable relationships between different types of libraries and information providers through strong regional service networks.

There is plenty of room in these models for a proactive, energetic library media specialist to function as an instructional leader without feeling that he or she must have the initiative and ambition of Attila the Hun. The important thing seems to be a level of trust which permits discussion about professional teaching-learning issues. Research tells us that, while circumstances differ among individual cases, more effective schools are always characterized by a professional staff which operates through "collective action, agreed-upon purpose, and belief in attainment."[35] Characterizing teacher interactions in effective school settings, Little calls attention to cooperative communication behaviors which are easily applicable to the library media specialist's domain. They include such familiar activities as reviewing, lending, borrowing, designing, and preparing materials; teaching others informally or formally, and designing inservice; asking informally about curriculum at various grade levels and talking about what one is learning or wants to learn; making suggestions and helping new teachers; and planning, discussing, and defending classroom practices or curriculum, etc.[36] A high frequency of professional interaction among colleagues and between teachers and administrators is one of the salient factors for improving instruction and morale.

All of these humanistic—person-based rather than systems-based—models and practices call for a type of professional leadership which is congruent with the professional role and values of library media specialists. The picture is complicated by research findings which deal with the continuing efforts of minority groups—particularly women, Blacks, and Hispanics—to obtain access to positions of authority and power in our society. Fueled by the civil rights and feminist movements, this struggle has important implications for school library media professionals, who all are members of a minority group politely referred to as "semi-professional"[37]; most are female, and many are also members of racial/ethnic minorities. The increased attention given to minority group leadership as a topic of investigation is demonstrated by new chapters on women and Blacks in Bass's revised edition of *Stogdill's Handbook of Leadership.*[38]

Many recent studies offer both good and bad news. On the one hand, women who occupy administrative roles in educational settings seem to have leadership styles which are consonant with the school culture.[39] On the other, in spite of "their propensity toward democratic leadership, thoroughness of approach to problem solving, and bent toward instructional leadership, as well as the general effectiveness of their performance as rated by both teachers and superiors—we puzzle over the small number of women administrators employed by school districts."[40] Access to formal leadership roles will continue to be a problem for women professionals in every field of endeavor.

Another well-documented problem is women's apparent ambivalence about holding and using power. For example, a workshop conducted by the Center for Women in Educational Leadership at the University of North Carolina, Chapel Hill, confirmed studies which "found that the women felt very uncomfortable when they were *vying* for power—and even more uncomfortable when they had *achieved* power. Many women found psychological separation and alienation from the rest of the group too much to bear."[41] This attitude is reinforced by the traditional values of collegiality associated with school culture.

This analysis can be modified by some recent research in developmental psychology conducted by Carol Gilligan, who worked with Lawrence Kohlberg on studies tracing the development of moral judgment and logical decision making in children.[42] She was puzzled by the fact that girls consistently scored lower than boys in testing situations where Kohlberg's and Piaget's yardsticks were used for measuring the level of development. Drawing on her own research, as well as the work of other psychologists, Gilligan has created a female developmental model which may serve as a reference point for women educators, including library media specialists, in search of leadership roles which are personally comfortable and institutionally consonant with their current roles.[43]

Gilligan suggests that women's ethical development proceeds from right behavior based on physical or emotional survival, through consideration of right behavior defined as not hurting others, to a mature ethic of care and responsibility within a network of social relationships. Cooperative behaviors which arise from this ethical core are contrasted with competitive behaviors which arise from the male developmental model as conceptualized in figure 1.

Model Components	Kohlberg (Male)	Gilligan (Female)
Metaphor for Judgment	Pyramid	Circle
Order of Relationship	Hierarchical	Network
Basic Developmental Task at Adolescence	Separation & Individuation	Connection & Intimacy
Later Developmental Issue at Mid-Life	Connection & Intimacy	Separation & Individuation
Conception of Moral Problem	Conflicting Rights	Conflicting Responsibilities
Conception of Moral Judgment	Ethic of Rights	Ethic of Care & Responsibility
Basis of Conflict Resolution	Rules of Equality & Reciprocity	Rules of Negotiation & Relationships
Basic Life Perspective	Objective	Contextual

Fig. 1. Two developmental models of moral judgment.

These hypothetical models are, admittedly, abstractions which are far removed from school life or issues of leadership as we ordinarily think of them. Nevertheless, they offer useful analogies to the two styles of leadership described in many studies of schools and other organizations. The Kohlberg model can be associated with hierarchical, vested, formal authority, rational decision making, and top-down communication. The Gilligan model can be associated with informal power, situational leadership rooted in expertise and collaboration which involves shared decision making. It also furnishes a valid psychological rationale for the informal entrepreneurship which has been displayed by many library media specialists in their quests for program survival and continuation, as well as professional renewal. Finally, it springs from the study of ethical judgment which is essential for true leadership, as Warren Bennis's well-known definition suggests: "Leaders are people who do the right thing; managers are people who do things right."[44]

What are the implications for the library media specialists who aspire to or already hold leadership roles in the school organization? These professionals should:

- take responsibility for the professional vision and convictions which motivate them to change the status quo in some significant way.

- give themselves permission to be active, inquiring, and self-enabling, assuming the role of agents of change even if the role is not formally acknowledged.

- become comfortable with the idea of holding and using power based on persuasion and expertise.

- identify those aspects of their behaviors which are potentially subversive of school culture and mores.

- become comfortable about being highly visible and highly communicative staff members.

- feel at ease with conducting proactive, cooperative inquiry within adversarial contexts of isolation, competition, restricted choices, and lack of professional dialogue.

- trust in their ability to maintain positive relations with peers and administrators while exercising leadership.

- trust in their ability to resolve conflicts in confrontational situations by using skills of compromise and negotiation within a contextual network of relationships.

- conceptualize their roles as empowering, rather than having power over, others and to think of themselves (using a familiar baseball analogy) as part-time coaches rather than owners or full-time team members.

The traditional language of educational leadership has been couched in business jargon borrowed from production-oriented corporate models of quantitative, mechanistic, systems analysis. The models are useful, but they have not fulfilled their promise. Schools and people are not inherently efficient, even when they are pursuing management by objectives. We in the school library media field have, in the past, adopted these metaphors to express our vision, and AASL's Certification Model reflects this orientation: "Leadership and professionalism are the ability to conceive, synthesize, promote, and direct media programs reflecting a commitment to professional ethics."[45] This definition and the competencies which follow are clear and appropriate, but hard to translate into or connect with complex social behaviors required in the school setting.

There is an alternative. The research and practice summarized in this article offer promising conceptions, definitions, and metaphors for leadership, borrowed from the soft sciences. These humanistic developmental models are based on process rather than product, on qualitative as well as quantitative analysis, and on the assumption that cooperation yields more benefits than competition in organizational as well as personal relationships. At a time when decision-making systems in our schools are changing very slowly, these models offer us alternative paths to proactive leadership and empowerment. They represent a philosophical and psychological outlook which reflects the "feminine" ethic of care and responsibility for self and others, and also the exercise of responsible leadership and power through negotiation within a network of collegial relationships. The need for this type of leadership in the school library media field has never been more urgent.

NOTES

[1] J. M. Burns, *Leadership* (New York: Harper & Row, 1978), 425-26.

[2] *Library Literature* (New York: H. W. Wilson, 1983-June 1986).

[3] A sign of healthy change is the new chapter on "Leadership in Management," in G. E. Evans's standard text on library administration, *Management Techniques for Librarians*, 2d ed. (New York: Academic Press, 1983). Some interesting conceptions of informal leadership come from public library people like Patrick R. Penland whose *Leadership Development for Librarians* (Pittsburgh, Pa.: University of Pittsburgh Press, 1971), focuses on interpersonal communications with citizen liaison leaders.

[4] A "Survey of Professional Development Interests" was sent by the author in April 1986 to 1,200 members of the Supervisors Section of AASL.

[5] E. R. Kulleseid, *Beyond Survival to Power for School Library Media Professionals* (Hamden, Conn.: Library Professional Publications, 1985), 47ff and 122ff. See also J. Lindelow, "School-Based Management," in *School Leadership: Handbook for Survival*, ed. S. C. Smith, J. A. Mazzarella, and P. K. Piele (Eugene, Oreg.: ERIC Clearinghouse on Educational Management, 1981), 121ff.

[6] Burns, 457.

[7] Among the best known are P. Berman and M. W. McLoughlin, *Factors Affecting Implementation and Continuation*, v. VII of *Federal Programs Supporting Educational Change* (Santa Monica, Calif.: Rand Corp., 1978); *Implementing and Sustaining Innovations*, v. VIII of *Federal Programs Supporting Educational Change* (Santa Monica, Calif.: Rand Corp., 1980); S. B. Sarason, *The Culture of the School and the Problem of Change*, 2d ed. (Boston: Allyn and Bacon, 1982); and J. I. Goodlad, *A Place Called School: Prospects for the Future* (New York: McGraw-Hill, 1984).

[8] R. Miller and A. Spanjer, "The Library Media Specialist as Change Maker: Implications from Research," in *School Library Media Annual 1985*, v. 3, ed. S. L. Aaron and P. R. Scales (Littleton, Colo.: Libraries Unlimited, 1985), 323-35.

[9] D. A. Schon, *The Reflective Practitioner: How Professionals Think in Action* (New York: Basic Books, 1983), 353.

[10] Ibid.

[11]D. P. Baker, *The Library Media Program and the School* (Littleton, Colo.: Libraries Unlimited, 1984), 67.

[12]D. Nyberg and P. Farber, "For the Record," *Teachers College Record* 88 (Fall 1986): 1. See also S. C. Smith, J. A. Mazzarella, and P. K. Piele, "Introduction: Leadership for Survival," in *School Leadership: Handbook for Survival*, 1-11.

[13]J. Lindelow, D. Coursen, and J. A. Mazzarella, "Participative Decision-Making," in *School Leadership: Handbook for Survival*, 150-68.

[14]R. Wynn and C. W. Guditus, *Team Management: Leadership by Consensus* (Columbus, Ohio: Charles E. Merrill, 1984).

[15]W. C. Miller and D. Sparks, "Theory Z: The Promise for U.S. Schools," *The Educational Forum* 49 (Fall 1984): 48-54.

[16]Wynn and Guditus, 71-91.

[17]A. Lieberman and L. Miller, "The Social Realities of Teaching," in *Staff Development: New Demands, New Realities, New Perspectives*, ed. Ann Lieberman and Lynne Miller (New York: Teachers College Press, 1979), 61. See also Carl D. Glickman, "The Supervisor's Challenge: Changing the Teacher's Work Environment," *Educational Leadership* 42 (December 1984-January 1985): 38-40.

[18]Baker, 39.

[19]Miller and Spanjer, 330.

[20]Schon.

[21]Miller and Spanjer.

[22]R. Goldhammer, R. H. Anderson, and R. J. Krajewski, *Clinical Supervision: Special Methods for the Supervision of Teachers*, 2d ed. (New York: Holt, Rinehart & Winston, 1980).

[23]R. T. Bingham, "The Role of the District Library Media Supervisor in Today's Educational Setting," in *School Library Media Annual 1983*, v. 1, ed. Shirley L. Aaron and Pat R. Scales (Littleton, Colo.: Libraries Unlimited, 1983), 172-84.

[24]The Carnegie Task Force on Teaching as a Profession, *A Nation Prepared: Teachers for the 21st Century* (New York: Carnegie Corp., 1986), 3.

[25]G. A. Griffin, "The School as a Workplace and the Master Teacher Concept," *The Elementary School Journal* 86 (September 1985): 2.

[26]Ibid., 3.

[27]D. P. Doyle and T. W. Hartle, "Leadership in Education: Governors, Legislators, and Teachers," *Phi Delta Kappan* 67 (September 1985): 26.

[28]P. S. Rauh, "Helping Teacher: A Model for Staff Development," in *Staff Development: New Demands, New Realities, New Perspectives*, 174-88.

[29]M. F. Klein, "The Master Teacher as Curriculum Leader," *The Elementary School Journal* 86 (September 1985): 35-43.

[30]Doyle and Hartle.

[31]D. W. Johnson, et al., *Circles of Learning: Cooperation in the Classroom* (Alexandria, Va.: Association for Supervision and Curriculum Development, 1984). A list of additional publications on cooperative learning is available from the Cooperative Learning Center, University of Minnesota, Minneapolis, MN 55455.

[32]J. Dewey and E. Dewey, *Schools of Tomorrow* (New York: E. P. Dutton, 1915), 78.

[33]P. A. Roy, Shirley Denton Laurie, and Diane Browne, "Cooperative Learning: Training and Follow-Up in Two School Districts," *Journal of Staff Development* 6 (October 1985): 41-51.

[34]S. Ellis, "Introducing Cooperative Learning Groups: A District-Wide Effort," *Journal of Staff Development* 6 (October 1985): 52-59.

[35]Glickman, 38.

[36]J. W. Little, "Norms of Collegiality and Experimentation: Workplace Conditions of School Success," *American Educational Research Journal* 19 (Fall 1982): 330.

[37]D. C. Lortie, *Schoolteacher: A Sociological Study* (Chicago: University of Chicago Press, 1975).

[38]B. M. Bass, *Stogdill's Handbook of Leadership: A Survey of Theory and Research*, rev. and expanded ed. (New York: Free Press, 1981).

[39]J. C. Conoley, "The Psychology of Leadership: Implications for Women," in *Women and Educational Leadership*, ed. S. K. Biklen and M. B. Brannigan (Lexington, Mass.: D.C. Heath, 1980), 44.

[40]J. D. Meskin, "The Performance of Women School Administrators—A Review of the Literature," *Administrator's Notebook* 23 (1974), cited in D. Coursen and J. A. Mazzarella's "Two Special Cases: Women and Blacks," in *School Leadership: Handbook for Survival*, 44. See also G. C. Fauth's "Women in Educational Administration: A Research Profile," *The Educational Forum* 49 (Fall 1984): 65-79.

[41]L. C. Woo, "Women Administrators: Profiles of Success," *Phi Delta Kappan* 67 (December 1985): 287.

[42]L. Kohlberg and C. Gilligan, "The Adolescent as a Philosopher: The Discovery of the Self in a Postconventional World," *Daedalus* 100 (Fall 1971): 1051-86.

[43]C. Gilligan, *In a Different Voice: Psychological Theory and Women's Development* (Cambridge, Mass.: Harvard University Press, 1982).

[44]W. Bennis, "The 4 Competencies of Leadership," *Training and Development Journal* 38 (August 1984): 16.

[45]American Association of School Librarians, *Certification Model for Professional School Media Personnel* (Chicago: American Library Association, 1976), 17.

ADDITIONAL READINGS

Edwards, Karlene K., and Isabel Schon. "Professional Development Activities as Viewed by School Library Media Specialists." *School Library Media Quarterly* 14 (Spring 1986): 138-41.

Kulleseid, Eleanor R., and Carolyn A. Markuson. "Empowering the Professional: Alternative Visions of Leadership." *School Library Media Quarterly* 15 (Summer 1987): 195.

Robbins, Kikanza Nuri, and Raymond D. Terrell. "Women, Power, and the 'Old Boys Club': Ascending to Leadership in Male-Dominated Organizations." *School Library Media Quarterly* 15 (Summer 1987): 205-10.

Wehmeyer, Lillian Biermann. "Indirect Leadership: The Library Media Specialist as *Consigliere.*" *School Library Media Quarterly* 15 (Summer 1987): 200-204.

INDEX